THE ROYAL AIR FORCE: AN ILLUSTRATED HISTORY

This book belongs to:

Robert Wallace

During the Gulf War of 1991, Jaguars were modified to carry
AIM-9L missiles on overwing rails for self-defence. The
device under the port wing is a Westinghouse ECM pod, and
a centreline fuel tank is fitted. Just visible under the starboard
wing is a Phimat chaff dispenser. (BAe)

THE ROYAL AIR FORCE

An Illustrated History

MICHAEL ARMITAGE

ARMS AND
ARMOUR

For Gretl, co-pilot

Arms and Armour Press
An Imprint of the Cassell Group
Wellington House, 125 Strand, London WC2R 0BB

Distributed in the USA by Sterling Publishing Co. Inc.,
387 Park Avenue South, New York, NY 10016-8810.

Distributed in Australia by Capricorn Link (Australia) Pty. Ltd, 2/13 Car-
rington Road, Castle Hill, NSW 2154.

First published 1993
Revised edition 1995

British Library Cataloguing-in-Publication Data: a catalogue record for
this book is available from the British Library

ISBN 1-85409-279-0

Designed and edited by DAG Publications Ltd.
Designed by David Gibbons; layout by Roger Chesneau; edited
by Roger Chesneau; printed and bound in Great Britain.

CONTENTS

LIST OF MAPS

A fitting symbol of RAF history: three familiar aircraft
of the Battle of Britain Memorial Fiight (DPR[RAF])

BIBLIOGRAPHY

Armitage, M. *Unmanned Aircraft*. Brassey's, 1988

Bowyer, Chaz. *RAF Operations 1918–1938*. Kimber, 1988

Boyle, Andrew. *Trenchard*. Collins, 1962

Brookes, Andrew. *V-Force*. Janes, 1982

Burns. *The Queen's Flight*. Blandford Press, 1986

Dean, Sir Maurice. *The Royal Air Force and Two World Wars*. Cassell, 1979

Dowling, J.R. *Helicopters in the Royal Air Force 1950–71*. Air Historical Branch (RAF), 1989

Flintham, Victor. *Air Wars and Aircraft*. Arms & Armour, 1990

Haslam. E.B. *The History of Royal Air Force Cranwell*. HMSO, 1982

Hough and Richards. *The Battle of Britain*. Hodder and Stoughton, 1990

Hunt, Leslie *Twenty-One Squadrons. The RAuxAF 1925–1957*. Garstone Press, 1972

Jones, H.A. *The War in the Air* (First World War). Oxford, 1934

K.M.O. *A Short History of the Royal Air Force Regiment*. RAF Regt Fund, 1974

Kennett, Lee. *The First Air War*. Free Press, 1991

Lee, Sir David. *And They Told Us the War Was Over*. HMSO, 1991

Eastward (The RAF in the Far East 1945–1972). HMSO, 1984

Royal Air Force in Germany 1945–78. Air Historical Branch (RAF), HMSO, 1979

Wings in the Sun (The RAF in the Mediterranean 1945–1986). HMSO, 1989

Flight from the Middle East (The RAF in the ME 1945–1972). HMSO, 1978

Mason, R.A. *The Royal Air Force Staff College*

Middlebrook & Everitt. *The Bomber Command War Diaries*. Viking, 1985

Musgrave, Gordon. *Pathfinder Force*. Macdonald and Janes, 1976

Militaergeschichtlichen Forschungsamt. *Das Deutsche Reich und Der Zweite Weltkrieg*. Deutsche Verlags-anstalt, 1979–92

Omissi, David. *Air Power & Colonial Control*. MUP, 1990

Probert, Henry. *High Commanders of the Royal Air Force*. HMSO, 1991

Richards and Saunders. *Royal Air Force 1939–1945*. HMSO, 1954

Taylor, J.W.R. *CFS – Birthplace of Air Power*.

Terraine, John. *The Right of the Line*. Hodder and Stoughton, 1985

Thetford, Owen. *Aircraft of the Royal Air Force since 1918*. Putnam, 1979

Webster and Frankland. *The Strategic Air Offensive Against Germany*. HMSO, 1961

Wood, Derek. *Project Cancelled*. Tri-Service Press, 1990

Journals:

RUSI Journal

Royal Air Force Historical Society: Proceedings

INTRODUCTION

Forty-three years spent in a Service that has existed for only seventy-five seemed a not unreasonable qualification for writing this book when I began it. But that was no help with what became the main problem — compressing the story within the covers of a modest volume. The result is a book that has had to ignore countless episodes of Royal Air Force history. It has had to skirt round much more detail than I would have wished; it could cover only a sample of the many distinguished units that have fought under the RAF ensign; many famous leaders are given no mention; and the praises of numerous heroes are left unsung. I accept all these criticisms.

What I have tried to do is to say something useful about how the Service as a whole evolved, to plot the formative influences over the years and to explain why the Royal Air Force took the paths that it did. The book tries, for example, to show why certain aircraft were procured, why some of them were world-beaters and why others were disasters. What I therefore hope will distinguish this book from the many others that deal with the Royal Air Force is that it offers some analysis of the whole seventy-five years of the RAF's history, rather than merely trying to give an account of them.

Nor, I hope, does it shrink from criticism. In a field of warfare that was totally new at the start of this story, and which developed at times with bewildering rapidity in the years that followed, the Service was bound to make mistakes; some of the more relevant ones are included here. I have sometimes had to weigh conflicting facts and varying accounts as I have gone along, and I have come down on the side of what seems to be the most reasonable version in each case. Nevertheless, as far as the judgements in the book are concerned — and there are many of them — I plead guilty to making my own.

ACKNOWLEDGEMENTS

Wherever possible I have drawn on the Official Histories of the Royal Air Force, notably when discussing the two World Wars, though there are also the invaluable accounts by Air Chief Marshal Sir David Lee, which cover important years after 1945. I list all these official accounts in the Bibliography, together with most of the other and mainly secondary sources on which I have drawn. There has not been space to mention the numerous other sources to which I have referred; nor would it be reasonable to try to list the articles from the many professional and other journals to which I turned to fill certain gaps, journals such as *Cross & Cockade*, that of the Royal United Services Institute, the long-defunct *RAF Quarterly*, and several others. For many details, and particularly where facts seemed to be in dispute or were altogether missing in the literature, I have used primary sources. These have included Minutes of Air Force Board meetings, Defence White Papers, Air Estimates, official RAF Air Publications and individual Papers of particular interest such as Trenchard's 'Permanent Organization of the Royal Air Force'.

For the photographic illustrations, I am greatly indebted to the Air Historical Branch of the Ministry of Defence, to the Royal Air Force Museum, to the Imperial War Museum, to the Royal Air Force Staff College at Bracknell, to the Joint Air Reconnaissance Intelligence Centre, to the Royal Air Force College, Cranwell, and to British Aerospace, as well as to Wing Commander John Broadbent, DSO, RAF, Mr. R. C. Sturtivant and Mrs. Faid. An acknowledgement is also given with each photograph. The illustrations follow no particular theme: I have merely made a selection that I hope shows something of the variety and the spread of RAF experience over the years.

Many colleagues and other contacts have given help and advice throughout. Air Commodore Henry Probert, formerly head of the Air Historical Branch, very kindly read through all the early chapters and offered invaluable suggestions. The present head of the Branch, Group Captain Ian Madelin, has also been very supportive, while two of his staff, Squadron Leader Peter Singleton and Mr. Graham Day, devoted more time to research and to devilling than I had any right to expect. The former Head Librarian, Ministry of Defence, Mr. John Andrews, showed exemplary patience over the late return of his library books during the past twenty years, and I am glad of this opportunity to thank him for all his support in this book and in other writings. Group Captain Bill Burnett, a pilot with long experience in the V-Force, generously checked through Chapter 10 and offered some very helpful insights. Mr. C. M. Hobson and Corin Broadley at the RAF Staff College were very prompt in offering assistance; and, finally, Andrew Kemp and Jack Bruce of Cross & Cockade International, generously helped by giving very useful information about early RFC and RNAS aircraft markings.

The author and publishers are grateful for the permission granted by the Controller of Her Britannic Majesty's Stationery Office to reproduce the photographs that appear on the following pages of this book: 144 (top), 144 (bottom), 158, 161 (top), 162 (bottom), 169, 177 (right), 182 (top), 184 (top), 185 (bottom), 192, 194, 198 (top), 199, 205, 218, 219, 220, 223, 229, 230, 233 (top), 233 (bottom), 235, 244, 254, 255, 259 (top), 259 (bottom), 276, They are grateful also for the permission granted by the Air Historical Branch to reproduce the photographs that appear on the following pages: 13, 15, 16, 18, 20, 22, 25, 27, 30, 34, 36, 38 (bottom), 40, 43, 46, 50 (top), 50 (bottom), 51 (top), 51 (bottom), 54 (bottom), 56, 59, 60, 61 (top), 61 (bottom), 62, 63, 65 (bottom), 66, 67, 69, 71, 72, 73, 74, 75, 81, 82, 83, 89, 91, 94, 98, 102, 104–5, 108, 115 (top), 115 (bottom), 116, 119, 135, 137, 141, 148, 149, 150, 152 (top), 152 (bottom), 157, 159, 161 (bottom), 162 (top), 163, 165 (top), 166, 167, 170, 175 (top), 175 (bottom), 177 (left), 178, 179 (top), 179 (bottom), 180, 182 (bottom), 183, 184 (bottom), 188, 193, 198 (bottom), 200, 201, 203, 204, 208, 210, 211, 221 (tip), 222, 226, 227.

CHAPTER 1

IN THE BEGINNING

Great military endeavours often have quite modest beginnings, and so it was with the Royal Air Force. To be sure, when this newly formed military arm took on its present title on 1 April 1918, it was already a huge organization. Its strength was over a quarter of a million officers and other ranks, and it held an inventory of something over 23,000 aircraft. But all this was the inheritance from the Royal Naval Air Service and from the Royal Flying Corps, and it is particularly to the latter that we must turn to see the real beginnings of the RAF. It was an inheritance that not only included a very powerful fighting force in the air but also held the origins of many of the Service traditions that still colour the Royal Air Force today, and it was also a legacy that brought with it the seeds of later roles and tasks, tactics and patterns of aircraft procurement.

If we ignore the early balloonists and the very modest part they played in wars of the eighteenth and nineteenth centuries, there are still many milestones that mark the road to the foundation of the new Service. The story has its real beginning when the first viable manned aircraft, the Wright Flyer, flew at Kittyhawk on 7 December 1903. During the next few years there was great enthusiasm for what was widely seen as an exciting new sport. Many air races and aviation gatherings were held, one of the more notable being the International Air Meet at Rheims in France in August 1909 at which twenty-three participants and an estimated one million spectators appeared. In virtually every advanced country in the world, balloons, airships and primitive aeroplanes were being built and flown with a fervour that even the faded photographs of the time fail to convey.

But the potential of these new machines for war was also clear, and aeronautical units were set up in the armies and navies of almost a dozen countries by 1911, including the United States, Germany, Russia, France and even Japan. In Britain the first military flight by a heavier-than-air machine was made on 16 October 1908 by Samuel Cody in British Army Aeroplane No 1 at Farnborough. The following three years saw many military trials and experiments, culminating on 28 February 1911 in the formation of the Air Battalion of the Royal Engineers. This unit was made up of two companies, No 1 (Airship) Company, based at South Farnborough, and No 2 (Aeroplane) Company, based at Larkhill. In that same year the Royal Navy set up a school of flying at Eastchurch, a small affair but one that was to become the foundation of British naval aviation; and already by early 1913 there had been such an expansion of effort that the Admiralty was able to set up a chain of six airship sites along the east coast of England and Scotland.

These early steps by the two Services, and the general climate of intense interest in aviation, made it clear that the whole topic of flying and its place in the military context needed to be reviewed, with the result that a technical sub-committee of the Imperial Defence Committee was set up under Lord Haldane to consider the wider question of a future national air service. The committee eventually recommended the formation of a British military aeronautical service, to be called 'The Flying Corps', which was to be made up of a Military Wing, a Naval Wing, a Central Flying School to train pilots for both Wings and what was to be called the Royal Aircraft Factory at Farnborough, where research and experiments would be carried out. By Royal Warrant dated 13 April 1912, the corps was embodied as 'The Royal Flying Corps', on 15 April a special Army Order laid down regulations for the new arm and on 13 May the corps absorbed the Air Battalion of the Royal Engineers. The establishment of the Royal Flying Corps was planned to reach a strength of seven squadrons, each of twelve aircraft with 24 pilots plus a small reserve. The Central Flying School was to be made up of twelve officers and 66 NCOs, who were expected to train 180 pilots each year.

The first commander of the Royal Flying Corps was Captain (temporary Major) Frederick H. Sykes of the 15th (The King's) Hussars, whose small force was in fact at this time made up of only four serviceable machines. But there was no lack of enthusiasm among the pioneers in the venture as they worked to construct something lasting from the handful of aircraft at their disposal. One of the abiding features that they devised was that of a motto for the new Corps. Major Sykes asked for ideas on the subject, and J. S. Yule, a young officer of the Royal Engineers, recalled the motto of the Irish Mulvany family, 'Per Ardua ad Astra', that he had seen quoted in H. Rider Haggard's book *The People of the Mist*, and proposed its use by the RFC. His suggestion was taken up, Royal Assent was soon forthcoming, and a motto was adopted that survives to the present day.

WAR FOOTING

So it was that in just over a year, military aviation had been introduced into the British armed services, and consolidated into a single formation. But this unity was not all it seemed. The RFC was formed to deal with questions of supply and training rather than to produce a single air service with common operating methods and joint doctrines. The Naval and Army Wings were administered by the Admiralty and the War Office respectively. The only inter-service authority was a permanent consultative committee under the Committee for Imperial Defence; but there was a serious weakness in the fact that the committee had no executive authority. The only real link was the Central Flying School, but even this was to some extent duplicated by the Naval flying school at Eastchurch. And then after only two years, in June 1914, the Admiralty took the Naval Wing away from the RFC, giving it the independent title of the Royal Naval Air Service from 1 July of that year. By August 1914 the RNAS had grown to a strength of 128 officers and about 700 ratings, operating seven airships and some seventy aircraft (though many of these were of dubious quality).

Rapid progress was meanwhile being made by the Military Wing of the RFC. In May 1912 the old No 1 (Airship) Company, Air Battalion, RE, first became No 1 Airship and Kite Squadron, RFC, holding a mixture of dirigible airships, spherical balloons and man-lifting kites; but then this equipment was transferred to the Naval Wing on 1 January 1914, leaving No 1 Squadron to re-equip as a heavier-than-air unit. No 2 Company of the old Air Battalion meanwhile became No 3 Squadron, RFC, and it expanded on the basis of its original five aircraft until by September 1912 it held a total of eighteen machines, fourteen of them monoplanes and the other four biplanes. No 3 Squadron is thus the oldest British aeroplane squadron (hence its motto, 'The Third shall be First'), though No 1 is the oldest squadron in the Services. A third squadron, No 2, was formed in May 1912, and it was from this unit that the nucleus was then drawn in turn to form No 4 Squadron in September 1912. No 5 Squadron followed, formed on a flight from No 3 Squadron in July 1913, and No 6 Squadron was made up from men drawn from all the first four squadrons.

Most of the aircraft of the infant Corps in 1914 were produced by the Royal Aircraft Factory, which was designing two basic types of machine, REs (Reconnaissance Experimental) and FEs (Farman Experimental). It was also building, though not designing, BEs (Blériot Experimental). The BE2c was eventually adopted as the main RFC aircraft for reconnaissance and army co-operation work.

In June 1914 the six squadrons of the RFC, together with the HQ Flight, the Aircraft Park and a detachment of the Kite Section, were brought together at Netheravon for a month's training at what was called a 'Camp of Concentration'. Lectures, discussions, trials and experiments were conducted so that the military potential of the various flying machines could be explored, after which the units all returned to their home bases on 2 July to prepare for the Army's annual summer manoeuvres. But the international crisis of 1914 was already erupting, and within only four weeks the whole of the Royal Flying Corps was put on a war footing. With virtually all the protagonists believing that the conflict would be a short and decisive one, the 'Great War' broke out on 4 August, and preparations for the move of the British Expeditionary Force to France were hastily completed. At this stage it was decided that Sykes, who

Royal Aircraft Factory BE2c

Although designated BE (for Blériot Experimental), this referred only to the type of design, that of a two-seat biplane powered by a tractor engine. The principal designer was Geoffrey de Havilland, who in 1911 derived this aircraft from his earlier BE1 while working at the Army Aircraft Factory. The BE2 was the first British machine specifically intended for a military role. In the years just before the First World War, the only war role for aircraft seemed to be that of reconnaissance and spotting for the artillery. The BE2 was therefore designed to have high stability in flight. Unlike the earlier models of the same aircraft, the BE2c version relied for lateral control on ailerons rather than on wing warping, a decisive step forward in design. Its 70hp Renault V8 water-cooled engine gave the aircraft a top speed of 82mph, and it had an endurance of 3 1/2 hours. The BE2c proved so successful that in various forms it remained in service with the RFC throughout the First World War.

Above: The Royal Flying Corps 'Camp of Concentration' at Netheravon, 29 June 1914. (AHB)

was still only 36 years old, was too junior to command the new Corps and General Sir David Henderson was given the appointment, Sykes agreeing to serve as his deputy.

On 13 August Nos 2 and 3 Squadrons flew to Amiens in France to join the BEF, which had begun to embark for France four days earlier. Nos 4 and 5 Squadrons followed during the next few days. All four squadrons were originally intended for the only clear role open to them, that of reconnaissance. These reconnaissance missions, together with all the important additional roles that later developed, were carried out by the RFC almost entirely on the British Front — there was little attempt to transfer the weight of the Allied air effort from one sector of the long front line to another.

The foundation and then the growth of the Royal Flying Corps was paralleled by similar developments in the French Army, and later in the American; but this narrative has space to deal only with some of the main features of the British efforts, and the reader must be left to consult other sources if he is to gain any idea of the vast efforts that were made in each of the warring countries to build up their air arms.

When it moved across to France, the RFC left behind in Britain only 41 officers, a small number of other ranks and 116 aircraft, most of which were scarcely airworthy and many of which were actually ready for the scrap-heap. This deployment of practically the whole strength of the RFC at a stroke was, in the circumstances, not entirely surprising, but it meant that once the need for reinforcements and replacements became clear (which it soon did) there were no cadres at home on which to build. Nor was anything left at home for defence against raids by Zeppelins, attacks that had been widely feared as soon as the successful pre-war experiments with these airships had become known. It had earlier been decided that home defence should be left to the Royal Naval Air Service, but once the needs of coastal patrols had been at least partly met there was only a single Caudron aircraft actually allocated to air defence. It was as well that the Zeppelin force was not at a stage of operational readiness to launch raids on Britain in these early days of the war.

ROLE OF AIRCRAFT

Thus it was that the Royal Flying Corps went to war with the maximum strength that could be put into the field — 105 officers, 755 men, 95 transport vehicles and 63 aeroplanes in the fighting units, with another twenty machines in the Aircraft Park. The aircraft themselves were of course at this time very primitive affairs. Although some remarkable steps forward had been made in manned flight during the preceding eleven years with, for example, innovations such as the Gnome rotary engine of 1909, which delivered 50 horsepower for a weight of only 165lb, the craft were very flimsy and often distressingly unreliable. Indeed, after a number of aeronautical disasters in the years up until 1912, monoplanes were held to be so prone to disintegration in the air that there was a War Office ban on the use of this type of aircraft by the RFC. Although the ban was lifted a few months later, a prejudice against monoplanes remained — which helps to explain both the preponderance of biplanes in the RFC during the war and afterwards, as well as the somewhat sporadic progress in British military aviation that was made during the two following decades.

When the RFC arrived in northern France, No 2 Squadron was equipped with BE2s, No 3 held Blériot monoplanes and Henry Farman biplanes and No 4 had BE2s, while No 5 Squadron held a mixture of Farmans, Avros and BE8s. None of these machines was powered by an engine that developed more than about 100hp, which meant that no aircraft had a top speed of more than perhaps 100mph. It may, incidentally, seem odd that there was such a mix within squadrons of aircraft types with their varying capabilities, particularly in maximum speed, but in fact it was of little consequence at a time when neither formation flying nor co-ordinated air tactics had yet been developed. Aircraft were nevertheless seen as very useful items of equipment for the armies as they deployed in the field. To begin with, they had clear advantages over balloons, primitive types of which had for some time been used as observation platforms in war, though in only very limited numbers. One of the main disadvantages of balloons was the difficulty of moving them rapidly to the scene of operations. Aircraft suffered no such drawback, and in the relatively fluid manoeuvrings that characterized the first weeks of the First World War, the aircraft of the RFC proved to be invaluable sources of intelligence from as early as 19 August, when the first missions were flown.

These very early reconnaissance efforts by the RFC became of crucial importance to the British Expeditionary Force, which was deployed on the left flank of the main Allied position in north-eastern France and Belgium. When the advancing German Army under General von Kluck sought to envelop the British troops by an outflanking manoeuvre, his columns were detected from the air, which made it possible for the commander of the BEF, General Sir John French, to escape the trap. As General French was to say in his initial dispatch on 7 September, 'they [i.e. the aircraft of the RFC] have furnished me with the most complete and accurate information which has been of incalculable value in the conduct of operations.'

As the momentum of the German invasion ran down, the phase of manoeuvre was replaced by positional warfare that was to dominate the conflict until its final stages some four years later. With this change in style on the ground, the very significant role of artillery spotting was added to that of simple aerial reconnaissance, and it was an innovation that helped to make artillery the most effective battlefield weapon in the armouries of both sides. Elementary systems of air-to-ground communication were improvised for this new role, often using wing-waggling or simply dropping messages from the air, while, from the ground, coloured panels and other visual devices were sometimes employed. Although the first successful experiments with airborne wirelesses had been made in the United States in 1910, the available equipment was both unwieldy and unreliable. A very few wirelesses were in use with the RFC by late September 1914, but it was some time before receivers as well as transmitters could be carried aloft. Aerial photography had also been the subject of experiment before the war, and the value of this kind of intelligence to supplement the observations of the air crew was obvious. The first photographs of German troop dispositions from the air were taken on 15 September 1914, and in the months that followed techniques were refined to the point where photographs, and very accurate maps prepared from

photographs, played a routine but vital part in the campaigns of the war.

Other innovations quickly followed the early use of airborne cameras. In the very first weeks of the war, air crews had flown carrying side-arms and occasionally rifles. It was true that the value of more effective airborne weapons had been foreseen for some time, resulting among other measures in a Lewis gun being fitted in the nose of a few Maurice Farmans of No 4 Squadron in that same September; but the aircraft itself was far too slow and cumbersome for such a weapon to have had any real military utility. Instead, weapons such as hand-grenades and improvised bombs slung or tied about the person of the crewman were more commonly seen in these early days. But the absence of bomb-dropping gear and even the crudest of bomb sights meant that success with these missives was very much a matter of luck.

Interestingly enough, these very rudimentary features of the first British warplanes were accompanied by one innovation that was to remain unchanged throughout the rest of the history of the RFC, and later of the Royal Air Force. Before the outbreak of war, British military aircraft had carried only a serial number, painted on the fin. Under an order issued to the RFC on 30 October 1914, a large Union Flag was painted on the undersides of the wings as an aid to recognition, and in the often vain hope that this would save them from the rifle-fire of friendly troops on the ground. But when it was realized that the prominent red cross of St George could at a distance be mistaken for the cross that was being used to distinguish German aeroplanes, the Royal Flying Corps on 14 December 1914, issued an order that the French roundel be adopted, but with the difference that the arrangement of the red, white and blue colours of that design was reversed. On a few aircraft, the Union

Right: A Vickers FB5 (Fighter Biplane No 5) Gunbus of 1914 – one of the earliest air combat aircraft in the world. (AHB)

Below left: A Bristol Scout of No 2 Squadron Royal Naval Air Service in 1915, showing the then current Union Flag fuselage marking. The pilot is Flt Sub-Lt G. G. Dawson, who features in Chapter 8 of this book as one of the architects of victory in North Africa during the Second World War. (Mrs Faid).

Jack was retained in miniature on each side of the roundel, but very soon these were removed, and on 16 May 1915 the familiar red, white and blue bars were added to the fins of aircraft instead. Although the Union Flag thus disappeared from all aircraft of the RFC, it was retained by the RNAS as a fuselage and tail marking. As a naval wing marking, a 5ft red circle with a white centre was introduced.

Together with the RFC, the RNAS had also responded quickly to the continental deployment of the British Expeditionary Force. The Eastchurch squadron, with seventeen officers together with an airship and ten aircraft of various types, crossed to the Dunkirk area on 26 August, and formed No 2 Wing, RNAS. It was from this small RNAS unit under the command of Commander C. R. Samson that the first long-range bombing attack was launched on 8 October 1914, in the course of which two machines dropped 20lb bombs on Zeppelin sheds at Düsseldorf, destroying one of the airships inside. A further and very remarkable raid by the RNAS followed on 21 November, this time against the Zeppelin works at Friedrichshaven on Lake Constance and involving a round flight of some 800 miles. This raid, carried out by three Avros, succeeded in damaging one airship as well as the huge Zeppelin sheds, and the gas generating plant was set on fire. Modest in scale though

this and other attacks were, they were highly effective in causing the enemy to divert hugely disproportionate resources to the defence of his vulnerable targets — a feature of air warfare that was to be seen time and again in this and in later conflicts.

Other bombing missions on the Western Front followed, but by now most of them, like those made during the Battle of Neuve Chapelle in March 1915, were directed against pre-selected targets such as railway stations through which enemy reinforcements were arriving, rather than flown against targets of opportunity identified during reconnaissance missions. Weapons were changing, too. The crude early bombs, usually nothing more than artillery shells fitted with fins, were replaced by three basic types of purpose-made bombs, fragmentation (for use against troops on the ground), high-explosive and incendiary.

So as to be able to destroy the often lumbering and overloaded enemy reconnaissance machines, other aircraft were soon armed with machine guns, carried in the nose of those aircraft fitted with rear-mounted engines or above the top wing of aircraft with tractor engines. Then, in late July 1915, the German Fokker Monoplane appeared. This machine was a single-seat tractor fighter carrying a machine gun that employed an interrupter gear to fire forward through the arc of the propeller. The advantages of such an arrangement were both obvious and deadly. Until this time the German squadrons, like those of the RFC, had all held a mixture of aircraft types with which they were expected to carry out virtually any type of mission that was assigned to them. But now the Germans introduced single-role squadrons, and from September onwards Leutnant Oswald Boelke was leading one of seven dedicated fighter units into aerial battle as part of a determined attempt to establish air superiority over the Western Front.

But it was not merely the new aircraft nor only the new style of fighting unit that accounted for the advantage that the German Air Force began to enjoy. There was also the fact that large orders for military aircraft had led to standardized production lines in the many factories turning them out. Skilful commanders such as Boelke, Richthofen and Max Immelman took advantage of this new standardization of aircraft types to develop air tactics that involved the closely co-ordinated efforts of pairs of aircraft, and later the use of larger formations based on mutually supporting pairs. It was the start of aerial tactics that are still familiar to fighter pilots today. On the British side, the picture changed more gradually, beginning in that same summer of 1915 with the arrival of No 11 Squadron equipped entirely with Vickers FB5 Gunbus two-seat machines for what were described as

'Fighting Duties' — in other words it was a fighter squadron.

As for bomber aircraft, the rapid spread of aerial combat soon made it essential to provide a good degree of self-protection for these machines to augment the efforts of escorting fighters. By December 1916 the general practice was for bomber aircraft to carry a machine gun in addition to the usual weapon-load of two 112lb bombs, and to be escorted by a BE2c armed with two machine guns. The same was true of reconnaissance missions, and we see this change in tactics being formalized in the RFC by an order of 14 January 1916, laying down that 'a machine proceeding on reconnaissance must be accompanied by at least three other fighting machines. These machines must fly in close formation...'.

In another development, the scout or fighter aircraft of the RFC were taken away from their squadrons of mixed aircraft types allocated to Army Corps and instead concentrated in Wings attached to Armies. The efforts of the fighters could thus be focused where they were most needed instead of being scattered along the whole front, a move that left other squadrons to devote their efforts to the direct support of ground forces. The advent of single-seat scouts in the air arms of the combatants, and the tactics which then emerged, led to more intensive air-to-air fighting as each side tried to

Right: The last fight of Captain Ball, VC, DSO, MC, on 17 May 1917: a painting by Norman Arnold. (IWM)

Below left: The FE8 (Farman Experimental No 8) of 1915, a product of the Royal Aircraft Factory. This early single-seat fighter was already outdated by the time it reached squadrons in France. (AHB)

gain superiority in the skies over the battlefields. That in turn drew a focus of public attention on to the pilots involved, and thus was born the air ace. It was perhaps not surprising in a war being fought on such a vast and impersonal scale that solitary pilots should attract the kind of fame reserved for legendary heroes in earlier conflicts. These men were the heroes of a new kind of war, and from 1916 onwards the names of figures such as Albert Ball and James McCudden were as well known in Britain as were those of Oswald Boelke and Max Immelman in Germany.

De Havilland DH2

There had been a handful of earlier scout (i.e. fighter) aircraft types in the Royal Flying Corps such as the two-seat FE2b, but, the first single-seat fighter squadron was No 24, which was equipped with DH2s in February 1916. Its pusher design overcame the problem of fitting a forward-firing machine gun, since at this time no effective British interrupter gear had been developed. The DH2 was powered by a 100hp Gnome Monosoupape (i.e. single-valve) rotary engine, giving the aircraft a top speed of 93mph. Once in service, this aircraft brought to an end a phase of the air war during 1916 in which German Fokkers had been wresting air superiority from the Allied squadrons.

The war produced very many other aces and distinguished fliers, and indeed all of the airmen were remarkable for their acceptance of the high chances of becoming casualties. Parachutes were never issued to the crews of RFC aircraft, and there was little hope of escape from a badly damaged machine, and no hope at all of escape from one that caught fire well above the ground, something that was a frequent occurrence in air-to-air combat. Statistics from 1917 give some idea of the odds facing these men. On average, the war service of a pilot with an observation unit was about four months and for one with a day bomber unit it was three and a half months, while the pilot of a single-seat fighter could expect his war to last an average of only two and a half months. The fact that these figures include all casualties, wounded as well as fatalities, and those suffering from sickness or mental breakdown, does nothing to diminish their sobering impact.

NEW AIRCRAFT TYPES

Another, and crucial, change in air warfare came in early 1916 with the arrival of new arcraft types such as the DH2. This was a machine designed specifically for air fighting, with the pilot and his machine gun mounted in the nose ahead of the 100hp pusher engine. The aircraft entered service in February 1916 with No 24 Squadron,

Above: A Sopwith Camel of 1917, carrying the standard armament of two Vickers .303 machine guns. (AHB)

the first single-seat fighter squadron with the RFC in France. Nos 29 and 32 Squadrons soon followed with the same type of aircraft and in the same fighter role. Although the performance of the new aircraft in terms of speed and endurance was often no better than that of existing machines, they were far more reliable and, of great importance for their role, they were much more manoeuvrable. Another significant improvement in the equipment of the RFC was seen with the arrival in No 70 Squadron during May 1916 of the first Sopwith Two-Seater, soon better known as the 1½-strutter because of its unusual arrangement of long and short centre-section struts, set in pairs. This was a tractor biplane equipped with a Vickers gun synchronized to fire through the propeller arc (the first British aircraft with such an arrangement), and it also carried a Lewis gun in the rear cockpit. With a 110hp Clerget engine, giving a top speed of 106mph, this fighter was a classic type whose basic layout was to form the pattern for many aircraft of the RFC and later of the RAF. Not the least important among the many types that were by now emerging was the single-seat Sopwith Scout (more commonly known as the 'Pup' because of its smaller size), an aircraft that entered the front line in late 1916. From early 1917 another very successful aircraft arrived from the same

stable and with the same basic layout, the Sopwith F1 'Camel', so named by the RFC because of the raised fairing behind the cockpit. It is a measure of the extent to which military aviation was expanding at this time that over 5,000 Sopwith Pups were eventually produced.

Other improvements in aircraft design now began to follow as the science of aeronautics flourished under the pressures of war. The main concern of designers was, naturally enough, to gain improved performance in terms not only of speed (though that was important) but also of operational ceiling and of the payload that could be carried. There were three possible approaches in the search for better performance. The first was to try to improve the aerodynamic efficiency of the machine. However, this presented many practical difficulties. For one thing, a high coefficient of drag inevitably followed from the design features of the time. For example, all contemporary aircraft had a fixed undercarriage; the preponderance of biplanes meant a structure that depended on a braced frame of struts and wires for such strength as it possessed, with all the drag that such an arrangement meant; weapons were almost always stowed externally, so that they too added to the air resistance; and finally, cockpits were not yet enclosed, resulting in a further drag penalty. Little, therefore, could be done to improve aerodynamics.

A second route towards improved performance might have been to make the whole aircraft lighter. Yet already the machines were of such flimsy construction that saving weight could only mean reducing strength, and there was thus no room here for manoeuvre. The only remaining option was to increase the power available, and this is what was now done. Engines at this time were of two types, rotary and stationary. The most widely used rotary was the Gnome engine of 1909, later called the Gnome-Rhône rotary. In 1914, about 80 per cent of all aircraft in the West were powered by the Gnome. It was a remarkably light engine giving a high power-to-weight ratio, and, because the radial pistons rotated around the fixed crankshaft, it was exposed to very efficient air cooling. Its disadvantages were that the revolving mass of the engine acted as a gyroscope, producing precessional forces that complicated aircraft manoeuvre. It also had a higher fuel consumption than stationary engines, and it could use only castor oil as a lubricant since that oil retains its lubricating properties when associated with gasoline (which was another feature of that particular type of engine). A final difficulty with rotaries was that large powerplants were not technically feasible. A large rotary absorbs a great deal of useful power in simply overcoming air resistance as it whirls around, the torque also becomes a serious problem, and finally it was found that the centrifugal force generated by the high speed of rotation tended to throw off rocker arms, valve rods and even complete cylinder assemblies.

Stationary engines suffered from none of these limitations. There were three basic types of stationaries: radial, in-line and V-banked cylinder layouts. In the first, the cylinders are arranged in a star shape around the crankshaft. An in-line engine has all the cylinders fore and aft, while the 'V' layout has two rows of cylinders at an angle of about 90 degrees to each other. During the war all three types grew larger, and were made more powerful by increasing the compression ratio, but the possibilities here were limited by the relatively low quality gasoline that was available, usually between 45 and 70 octane. Another difficulty arose once stationary engines developed speeds of more than about 1,500rpm, because this meant that the propeller was rotating at a speed above its optimum efficiency. This made necessary reduction gears, with the associated weight penalty; but without variable-pitch propellers, which were a much later invention, there was no other option.

Nevertheless, and despite all these limitations, by the end of the war both the speed and the operational ceiling of the latest aircraft were about double what had been possible only four years earlier. Available horsepower had quadrupled, and payload capacity had increased several times over. During those same years,

more and more aircraft types had also become available. Partly this was because of the relative ease with which a new design could be drawn up and then constructed. This was true both of airframes and of engines. A new aircraft could be designed and built within about three months, and one notable powerplant, the American Liberty engine, was designed in six days and nights at the end of June 1917, with the first model being produced only a few days later. Versions of this same remarkable engine were still in use with the US Services two decades later.

A fourth and very significant change in the use of the air arm as the war progressed was in the sheer numbers of aircraft available. By the start of the Battle of the Somme on 1 July 1916, for example, the RFC in France had grown from the original four squadrons with 64 aeroplanes to 31 squadrons with 410 aircraft fit to fly, and 426 pilots to fly them. At the same time, the growing intensity of the air war is shown by the casualty figures. The average replacement rate was ten aircraft per squadron each month, and during the Somme battle from July to mid-November, the RFC in France lost 308 airmen killed, wounded or missing. War on this scale demanded even more reinforcements, and in June 1916 General Haig asked that the number of squadrons in France be raised to 56, followed by a request in November for a further 20 fighting squadrons. By December 1916 the RFC was authorized for no fewer than 106 service squadrons and 95 reserve squadrons.

Expansion at this extraordinary rate clearly called for new thinking, not only to train the necessary air and ground crews but also to produce even more aircraft. In August 1914 there had been only twelve small aeroplane manufacturing companies in Britain, and three of those were specializing in seaplanes. In the early stages of the war, most military aircraft designs came from the Royal Aircraft Factory, which held a virtual monopoly, merely passing production orders for its own designs out to the private firms. Now new companies sprang up and old ones rapidly expanded, with the result that deliveries of aeroplanes to the RFC in France rose dramatically. Only 84 aeroplanes had been made available during 1914, and 399 in 1915. In 1916 the figure rose to 1,782, and after it was decided to increase the number of squadrons from 108 to 200, the number of deliveries rose to 7,320 between January and October 1918.

Training for pilots was expanded by opening two new flying schools in Britain, and by forming twenty Reserve (i.e. training) squadrons in Canada. Soon pilots were being trained at the rate of 1,300 a month, though it has to be remembered that their flying course amounted to a mere 17 to 18 hours. This total had to include two night landings and a cross-country flight of 60 miles, the whole training being by any standards an extraordinarily brief preparation for war. But oddly enough the main problem was not a shortage of pilots; the limiting factor on the expansion of the Corps turned out to be a lack of skilled tradesmen on the ground, some 47 of whom were needed in order to support each front-line aircraft. The ranks of the Army were therefore combed to find as many skilled mechanics as possible from among those who had volunteered for other branches of the Service, and the very large number of servicemen being inducted once conscription was introduced in January 1916 were screened with the same purpose.

None of these measures, however, produced the required numbers, and the RFC now realized that it would need to train its own skilled men, ranging from sailmakers and acetylene welders to boatwrights and magneto repairers. Several small and unco-ordinated training schools were set up to try to meet the demand for skilled men, but these efforts also proved to be inadequate. In June 1917 it was therefore decided to consolidate the training of mechanics for the RFC at one large school, and the choice fell on Halton Park. At about the same time, the idea arose of recruiting boys into the Service as mechanics, and in April 1917 a scheme was set up with an initial intake of 500 boys between the ages of

15½ and 17½. As Chapter 3 will describe, this was the origin of the Halton Apprentice scheme.

Another innovation as the pressure on human resources intensified was the employment of women, both in factories and in the Services. By 1917 the women's Services included Women's Companies in the Royal Flying Corps, the members of which at first lived at home and worked at nearby RFC units. Later their terms of service were changed, so that some members were designated 'Mobiles' while others were enlisted as 'Immobiles'. Later still some of these ladies, together with volunteers from the Women's Auxiliary Army Corps, the Women's Legion Motor Drivers and the curiously named Women Civilian Subordinates, would come together to form the Women's Royal Air Force, which by mid-1918 was about 25,000 strong.

LONG-RANGE BOMBING

But all these developments still lay well into the future in the autumn of 1915, and it was a time when the war was going badly. Allied troops had become bogged down at Gallipoli; the spring offensive in France had failed with heavy casualties; and there was political uproar over the fact that industry could not meet the rising demands of the war, particularly in terms of ammunition supplies. In this atmosphere the commander of the RFC in France,

Left: Fabric workers of the Women's Royal Air Force. (AHB)

Opposite page: Major-General Sir David Henderson, who commanded the Royal Flying Corps in France. (RAFM).

Major-General Sir David Henderson, returned to London to look after the interests of the Military Aeronautics department. His command was taken over by Major-General Hugh Trenchard, a distinguished soldier and one whose frustration with peacetime soldiering had induced him to qualify as a pilot three years earlier.

Meanwhile the notion of long-range air attack was attracting attention among the warring nations, and its possibilities had not escaped the Germans — whose first raid on Britain has been made as early as December 1914, when on the 24th of that month a single aircraft dropped a bomb on Dover. This solitary effort was followed in January 1915 by probing flights over the East Coast made by three Zeppelins, and then much more seriously by a Zeppelin attack on London on 31 May 1915, in which seven people were killed and 35 injured. By this stage of the war, little had been done to establish defences against air attack on Britain, and only nine aircraft of the RNAS took off in a forlorn attempt to intercept the raider. One result of this and other raids during 1915 was that, in February of the following year, the RNAS was given the task of air defence over the sea, but over the British Isles the responsibility was transferred to the RFC. This then led to the formation of a number of Home Defence squadrons equipped with BE2cs — the origins of all the later developments in the air defences of the United Kingdom.

Further raids by airships followed, including an attack on Hull on 6 June which caused rioting in the streets of that city. Then on the night of 2/3 September 1916 came the heaviest attack that would be attempted against London by these craft. Sixteen airships set out for the capital, but one was engaged by an intercepting fighter. The huge ship was set alight, to crash in spectacular fashion, whereupon the other Zeppelins turned back without reaching their target. Three more Zeppelins were brought down before the end of the year, and thereafter the airship attacks tailed off. Their physical impact had been very modest; but there was seen to be something uniquely horrible about these great black craft cruising almost silently over the countryside, causing random death and destruction, and they had had a very powerful psychological effect.

One of the remarkable features of these raids is that the airships carrying them out were never meant for such a role. Their primary task was that of reconnaissance over the North Sea, and air attack on Britain was a minor part only of their activities. Nevertheless, and quite apart from the alarm that they caused to the Government and population alike, they had the important military

consequence of diverting to the air defence of Britain military resources that were desperately needed by the BEF in France. By the end of 1916 the handful of anti-aircraft guns and interceptors that had been deployed for defence in the United Kingdom in the early months of the war had grown to a force of twelve squadrons of the RFC, with 110 aircraft, and 12,000 officers and men serving in anti-aircraft artillery formations. Altogether these defensive deployments absorbed 17,340 officers and men who could have been better employed elsewhere.

During this time the Germans had been forming a specialized unit of heavy bomber aircraft, and the diminishing airship raids were now followed by aircraft attacks. These began with one bomber making a tentative lone raid on 28 November 1916, but a much more serious attempt followed in May of the following year when 23 Gotha GIVs set out for their targets, fortunately being turned back by bad weather. Then on 13 June twenty attacking aircraft took off for a more telling raid on London. Fourteen of the bombers reached the capital in broad daylight, to drop 72 bombs into a square mile of the city, devastating Liverpool Street station in the process, killing 162 people and injuring another 432.

This bold assault on the centre of the capital was a profound shock to the whole country.

On 7 July sixteen bombers repeated the raid, and this time 78 pilots of the RFC as well as seventeen from the RNAS took off to intercept. No fewer than 21 different types of fighter were involved, and 36 machines got into a position to attack the bombers. But despite this greatly improved level of reaction by the defences, only one German aircraft was shot down, though four more crashed in high winds on their return to base. The result of the attack was another powerful upsurge of public opinion against the authorities, who had been made to look helpless, as indeed they were, in the face of such audacious enemy incursions. During August, however, the luck of the Germans making these attacks began to run out, and in that month alone a combination of more efficient defences and a spell of poor weather saw the loss of 22 enemy bombers. In September the German attacks switched to the hours of darkness, and at the end of that month the bombers were over the capital on six successive nights. These raids led to another

Below: Aloft on the engine nacelle of an RNAS airship during a patrol over the North Sea. (AHB)

reorganization of the defences, including among other measures the establishment of separate gun and aircraft defence zones, the construction of an 'apron' of tethered kite balloons and the deployment of numerous searchlights to work with the interceptor aircraft. Gradually, like the Zeppelin raids, these bombing attacks tapered away, the last of them being made on the night of 19/20 May 1918, when casualties on the ground totalled 203 for the destruction of seven attacking aircraft. A final Zeppelin raid followed three months later over the East Coast on 5 August 1918, when five of the airships set out, one being shot down; but that was the end of what had been a very worrying air offensive for the British Government. All told, there had been 51 airship raids, causing 557 deaths and 1,358 other casualties; and a total of 52 raids by aircraft, leading to 857 fatalities and 2,058 other casualties. Twenty years later, as we shall see, these figures were an important factor in the British defensive preparations for the Second World War.

THE WAR AT SEA

In the war at sea, it had long been clear that the aircraft of the RNAS could not only carry out reconnaissance flights and spotting missions for warships, they might also be invaluable in countering another new and, to the Royal Navy, very threatening weapon, the torpedo-carrying submarine (or, more precisely, since its ability to remain submerged was strictly limited, the submersible). This was an ideal role for dirigible airships, of which Britain produced some 200 during the war; but seaplanes, too, proved to be a useful counter to the U-boat, an outstanding example being the Felixstowe F2A aircraft which carried a crew of five and had a wing span of around 100ft. Seaplanes carried bombs and guns with which to attack U-boats, but since the submerged range of these craft was only some 60 to 80 miles, air patrols could often force them to remain below the surface for long enough to exhaust their batteries, making them virtually helpless — at least until they could again run on the surface using their diesels and recharge the batteries.

Airship operations were, however, often hindered by bad weather, and even seaplanes were difficult to handle once away from the shelter of their bases. An obvious solution was to deploy aircraft on board ships of the Fleet, and indeed experiments had been carried out along these lines as early as January 1912 when a Short biplane had been flown from the foredeck of the battleship HMS *Africa* while anchored at Sheerness. A major step forward was taken in 1917 when the light battlecruiser HMS *Furious* was modified in the course of

Felixstowe Flying Boats

The first flying boats to enter service with the RNAS were the American Curtiss H series and they were joined in 1917 by the first of the British-built Felixtowe series of aircraft. After the war the F5 variant became the standard Royal Air Force flying boat. Its biplane construction then became the forerunner of a whole family of similar machines such as the Blackburn Iris and the Singapore, Calcutta, Southampton and Stanraer, all built by Shorts. The Felixtowe was armed with four manually operated Lewis guns and it carried a bomb load of 920lb on wing points. Its endurance of seven hours made it a useful patrol aircraft, while its top speed of 95.5mph was creditable for its time. One of the late production models of the type was built with an all-metal hull — a pointer for the future.

construction to carry a complement of three Short seaplanes and five Sopwith Pup landplanes, and to operate them from a deck 228ft long that had replaced the intended forward gun turret. Forward of the bridge the ship was thus a kind of aircraft carrier; but aft of it she was still a battlecruiser. It was this ship that made the first carrier strike in history when, on 17 July 1918, seven Sopwith Camels took off from her deck to attack the German airship sheds at Tondern — which they did with great effect, destroying two Zeppelins. Because it had been found to be almost impossible, and certainly very risky indeed, to attempt to land back on board, when the crews returned from their successful mission they all ditched their machines alongside *Furious*.

AIDING THE ARMIES

Meanwhile, in France, the great battles of attrition continued on the ground, accompanied by air activity that was at first comparatively modest in terms of the forces engaged though of growing importance as the war progressed. By the end of 1916, for example, offensive action on the ground was sometimes postponed if unfavourable weather prevented supporting aircraft from taking part. At first, this air activity in support of the armies on the Western Front had, as we have seen, been limited to reconnaissance and then to reconnaissance and artillery spotting. Even at the Battle of the Somme, from July to November 1916, RFC air activity was, apart from a handful of missions, confined to reconnaissance flights, contact patrols to report the position of friendly troops on the ground, and raids in the enemy rear so as to keep enemy squadrons engaged in combat in areas away from

the ground fighting. These efforts, together with air combat over the front itself, were essential if superiority in the air were to be achieved, a condition that would allow British aircraft to operate freely over the lines while preventing the enemy machines from doing the same.

At first the efforts on the Somme to draw the opposing aircraft away from the battle on the ground were highly successful and, just as important, British losses were minimal. But by the third week of the offensive, German air reinforcements arrived in large numbers from other sectors of the front, and by October more than one-third of the total German air strength in the West was engaged, including specialized Schlachtstaffeln or ground attack units. Not surprisingly in this campaign of increasing intensity, aircraft losses rose steeply. During the whole period of the offensive the RFC struck off charge a total of 782 machines. Even more serious, 308 pilots and 191 observers were killed, wounded or missing in action in the same period.

A different pattern emerged during the Battle of Arras in April 1917, when the RFC opened an air offensive against German airfields five days before the ground offensive was launched. Although this was a largely successful effort to draw the enemy fighter aircraft away from the front so as to allow British observation aircraft free rein, it was not without high cost. Because the Germans at this time had superior aircraft, and because most of the air fighting took place behind the enemy lines rather than behind their own, the RFC lost 75 machines in the first four days of the offensive and over three hundred during the month of April (known to the RFC thereafter as 'Bloody April'). It was to be the highest RFC casualty rate of the whole war. Some belated relief was, however, to hand as new and much more battleworthy machines began to arrive in France. No 56 Squadron, for example, re-equipped with SE5s during April, No 48 took over Bristol F2s in March and No 70 Squadron received Sopwith Camels in the July of that year.

Unlike the German Air Force, whose Schlachtstaffeln tactics were concentrating air efforts at decisive points on the battlefield, the RFC had been attacking targets of opportunity rather than those of immediate concern to the ground forces. Strenuous efforts were therefore now made to improve the techniques of co-operation, and, for example, special courses for army unit commanders in ground-to-air co-ordination were organized. There was some improvement, but only in the context of the static and attritional warfare that had so characterized the fighting on the Western Front for the preceding three and a half years. But the early stages of the next major campaign were to produce rather different circumstances. In March 1918, with Russia knocked out of the war, the German Army was able to concentrate massive reinforcements on the Western Front, amounting to a total of over 200 divisions. In the air, the Germans could muster 730 aircraft for the offensive they were preparing — over one-third of the total German front-line air strength at that time. Opposed to them in the sector against which the main German thrust was directed, the RFC held 579 machines.

On 21 March, taking advantage of foggy conditions, specially trained German shock troops broke through the British Fifth Army, which collapsed. Telephone lines were destroyed or overrun, communications quickly became almost impossible and the limited artillery spotting that was attempted proved ineffective. Most of the effort by the RFC was instead devoted to attacks on enemy airfields so as to gain air superiority, to sorties against road and rail transport, and to sorties against German front-line forces, in that order of priority. Eventually the German advance was halted, but only after enormous losses on both sides.

For the air forces engaged, the return to a campaign of manoeuvre had for the first time in many months exposed troops on roads and in bivouacs to effective air attack. At the same time, however, troops on the ground had by now become well accustomed to the activities of hostile aircraft, and they frequently opened fire on them, often to good effect. This factor, combined with the losses in air-to-air combat, led to very high casualty rates. Major John Slessor, much later to become Marshal of the Royal Air Force Sir John, who was commanding No 80 Squadron at this time and flying close air support missions in the face of new levels of ground fire, records that '[the Squadron's] average strength was 22 officers, and in the last ten months of the war no less than 168 officers were struck off strength from all causes — an average of about 75 per cent per month, of whom little less than half were killed'.

In August 1918 it was the turn of the Allies to take the offensive, and on the 8th of that month the Battle of Amiens began. No 5 Brigade of the Royal Air Force, as the Service had by now become, supported the operations by the BEF with seventeen squadrons, which between them fielded 332 aircraft to cover a front of only 25 miles. Opposing them in this same sector was a force of some 365 German machines. On that sector of the front as a whole, there were about 800 British aircraft together with around 1,000 French machines. By now the employment of RAF aircraft in support of the army

had been developed to the highest pitch that it would reach during the war, and it is instructive to examine just what roles were undertaken by the RAF — and with what success — during the Battle of Amiens.

The infantry attack was launched in fog at 0420 hours on 8 August and air activity was hampered by the poor visibility until around 0900 hours. Nevertheless, some aircraft were airborne before the fog lifted, and, as planned, the noise of their engines successfully concealed the clatter of British tanks moving up to take part in the attack. As the visibility increased the aircraft were able to take on their more direct combat roles. For example, eight squadrons, four by day and four by night, were allocated to attacks on German airfields, while others raided rail centres behind the enemy lines so as to prevent the timely arrival of reserves, or else they attacked enemy artillery positions and the retreating German troops. As the fog lifted the squadrons began to concentrate on three main tasks over the battlefield itself. One of these was the familiar artillery patrol, in which the aircraft identified enemy artillery positions and directed counter-battery fire against them. A second task involved what were known as counter-attack patrols. For this role, two squadrons of aircraft had been detailed off to detect enemy attempts to concentrate forces for a counter-attack, whereupon the aircraft were to drop flares to attract the attention of nearby friendly forces and then fly directly towards the enemy concentration to indicate its position to the British troops. Third, there were contact patrols. These were intended to identify friendly troops on the ground, and to report their position back so as to give commanders some idea of what was happening in the general confusion of battle. But here the problems of poor communications intervened. In an attempt to overcome this serious deficiency, various measures had by now been introduced. For example, these aircraft carried coloured streamers on their struts so that the troops below would know that they were on contact patrol duties, and when the air crew wished the units on the ground to identify themselves they would sound a klaxon. The troops were then expected to show their whereabouts by using flares, metal discs or canvas shutters laid out on the ground and operated rather like venetian blinds. Sometimes even rifles were used to signal to the aircraft. Laid along the parapet of a trench, and parallel to the trench itself, the rifles indicated that our troops had advanced beyond that line.

These contact patrols met with only modest success, however, even after the fog had lifted to make visual signalling possible. Experience had shown that the indications given by the British troops on the ground to the RFC crews were equally visible to German reconnaissance aircraft, who would then call down artillery fire on to the British positions. The result was a natural reluctance by the troops to co-operate with the contact patrols. In other efforts to overcome the pervasive difficulties of communication, more wireless sets were by now in use. The aircraft concerned carried transmitters only, and these were used to signal down the fruits of aerial observation by Morse code to what was called a Central Information Bureau. But it was a laborious process, and by the time the information had been sent by the CIBs to units able to take advantage of it, as often as not the situation had changed.

The use of aircraft in more direct attacks on enemy assets on the ground sometimes showed useful results, even if it cost considerable effort. During the first thirty-six hours of the Battle of Amiens, for example, the nine

fighting squadrons of V Brigade RAF dropped 1,563 small bombs and fired 122,150 rounds of machine-gun ammunition at ground targets. As the battle continued, however, the German defences recovered and the RFC aircraft found themselves drawn away from the ground combat and into battles for air superiority. At the same time, as the advance of the Australian and Canadian troops leading the assault slowed down, it became clear that low-flying attacks of opportunity on the enemy were achieving progressively less and less but at increasing cost. Offensive air activity was therefore switched to attacks on the enemy bridges over the Somme in the hope of preventing his reinforcements from crossing the river, or his retreating units from escaping.

The heaviest bombs available were, however, only 112lb in weight, and even with a direct hit this was nothing like the capacity necessary to bring down a bridge. German movements were thus little hindered by the attacks, but they were successful in quite another way: the German Air Force rose in considerable numbers to defend the bridges, and in the air-to-air fighting that followed, it suffered a defeat from which it had still not

Below: The Bristol Fighter was the most successful fighter of the First World War. Here the gunner is demonstrating his Lewis gun on its ring mounting. (AHB)

recovered by the end of the war three months later.

That German defeat can be attributed largely to the sheer exhaustion of her fighting services, including the attrition of her air arm. On the Western Front alone, the German Air Force had been opposed not only by the RFC and the RNAS but also by the very large French Air Force, and, once the United States entered the war in April 1917, it had faced a steadily increasing number of American squadrons as well. Sources are confused about the exact numbers of aircraft on the inventories of the combatants, but some idea of the imbalance against the Germans by the end of the war can be given. Even ignoring the total of 3,300 RAF aircraft in that Service's widely scattered operational squadrons, there were 4,511 aircraft available to the French and another 1,481 combat aircraft in United States squadrons in France. Against these numbers, the German Luftstreitkräfte on the Western Front and in Germany itself could muster only 2,390 machines.

In summary, four years of fighting on the Western Front had seen the emergence of most of the main roles and missions of air power in support of ground forces, and these would be refined and consolidated in the decades that followed. Air reconnaissance over the battlefield, offensive counter-air (i.e., attacks against enemy airfields and air infrastructure), interdiction of lines of communication, air-to-air battles for air superiority — many of the foundations for later developments had been laid. There was, however, the glaring if understandable omission of effective close air support, that is, accurate and timely air attack on enemy positions at the request of friendly troops. The reasons were twofold: first, the lack of effective communications made it almost impossible to issue such requests or to act upon them; and second, even when a suitable target was identified, the weight of weaponry available and the accuracy with which it could be delivered meant that, with very few exceptions, little real influence on the situation could be exerted.

It followed that the best use that could be made of aircraft in the battle area was in supporting the army with other air roles such as reconnaissance and spotting for the artillery, particularly since it was the guns that wreaked havoc over the battlefields. In the Battle of Amiens, for example, no fewer than 2,650 British artillery pieces were engaged. Of those, 998 were 18pdrs, which meant that there was an average of one such gun for every 22yds of front. These weapons were used to lay down a barrage covering a depth of 4,500yds in just over two hours. Added to that there was a bombardment by 4.5in howitzers 200yds further on, and beyond that heavy artillery was engaged in counter-battery work and in bombarding German-held villages and redoubts in the rear. Compared with this dense carpet of fire, the air attacks, once the lifting fog had made them possible, can best be assessed as a valuable contribution to the offensive, but it was by no stretch of the imagination a decisive one.

By the end of the war, the accumulated experience of air support for armies emphasized, first, the importance of air superiority over the battlefield and second, the value of such roles as artillery support, reconnaissance, interdiction and liaison work. The concept of jointly planned and executed land/air operations lay a long way into the future. This somewhat limited scope for air power in support of ground forces during the great campaigns of the First World War was to have a formative impact on the operational doctrine of the RAF, as well as a retarding influence on the types of aircraft that were procured for army co-operation right up to the outbreak of the Second World War.

CREATION OF THE ROYAL AIR FORCE

Those formative factors in France were paralleled by some very important developments in London that came about as a result of the air raids over Britain in June and July 1917. These raids had not only caused a serious diversion of air defence resources that might otherwise have been dispatched to France, they had also brought to a head the whole question of the air defence of the British Isles. As a result, General Jan Smuts, a distinguished South African soldier and statesman, was brought in by the British Government to examine the question of the future of the air arm — a matter in which organization clearly played a very important part. In a little over a month, on 19 July 1917, Smuts produced the first of his two reports. The first dealt with the pressing question of the air defence of the London area, and it recommended the creation of a single unified command that would include all the fighter aircraft in Britain, all the searchlight and anti-aircraft gun batteries and all the observation posts that had been set up so far during the war. The second report, dated 17 August, was more seminal and dealt with the best way of reorganizing the whole of the British military air effort. Its conclusions rested on three premises: first, that aircraft had become weapons of strategic importance; second, that this was appreciated by the Germans, who had by then started an air campaign to bomb the British into capitulation; and third, that the home air industry had by now developed to a stage at which it could not only continue to give full

Right: WRAF members of the British occupation forces, seen at Cologne in May 1919. (AHB)

support to the Army and the Navy, but also support a British bombing campaign against Germany. The British military air organization as it existed, Smuts concluded, was inadequate to support the expansion of effort that was foreseen by the other findings.

In a key sentence, the Report said that 'Unlike artillery, an air fleet can conduct extensive operations far from, and independent of, both armies and navies. As far as can be foreseen, there is absolutely no limit to the scale of its future use, and the day may not be far off when aerial operations, with their devastation of enemy lands and destruction of industrial and populous centres on a vast scale, may become the principal operations of war, to which the older forms of military and naval operations may become secondary and subordinate...'. The same report also included these words: 'In our opinion, there is no reason why the Air Board should continue in its present form....and there is every reason why it should be raised to the status of an independent Ministry in control of its own war services.'

It was a report that aroused a great deal of hostility. Some opponents of the proposals, such as Haig, were against the whole principle of a separate air force. Others, including most of the senior ranks of the Royal Flying Corps and the Royal Naval Air Service, opposed not the proposal itself but its timing. They were adamant that

the middle of a desperate war was no time for such an upheaval. Trenchard's view was that one of the main assumptions on which the report rested, that of adequate home production facilities to support an independent bombing force, was flawed. He later wrote, '...that if anything were done at that time to weaken the Western Front, the war would be lost and there would be no air service, united or divided. I wanted to unify it, but later on at a more suitable opportunity.' Fortunately, his views did not prevail, and he himself was later to concede that Smuts and Henderson had been more far-sighted than he had been on the question of an independent air force.

The British Government now acted. On 16 October it was announced in Parliament that a Bill to constitute an Air Ministry had been prepared with the title 'The Air Force (Constitution) Act', and this Bill then went through its stages of acceptance until on 29 November it received the Royal Assent with the altered title of 'The Air Force Act.' An Order in Council on 17 December then laid down the composition and duties of the new Air Council, which came into being on 2 January 1918. The actual merger, and thus the foundation of the Royal Air Force, took effect on 1 April 1918.

The effect of this was that the Royal Naval Air Service, with almost 3,000 aircraft and a strength of 67,000 officers and ratings, was absorbed into the new service. The Royal Navy retained its two fleet carriers, HMS *Argus* and HMS *Furious*, together with the seaplane carriers *Ark Royal* and *Pegasus* which were employed mainly as aircraft transports. Later, during 1920, the carrier aircraft squadrons would be brought on the RAF inventory and allocated numbers in the 200 series; Nos. 210, 205 and, during 1921, No. 203 Squadron. These four squadrons marked the beginning of an era in which the Royal Navy operated the carriers, but the Royal Air Force operated the aircraft that flew from them. Thus it was that after considerable hesitation, and in the face of serious reservations even by its own supporters in principle and inspired as much by political pressures as by purely military considerations, the Royal Flying Corps and the Fleet Air Arm came together to form the Royal Air Force. The final step was taken on 1 April 1924, when all the remaining air units of the Royal Navy were absorbed into what was called the Fleet Air Arm of the Royal Air Force.

Trenchard was recalled from command of the Royal Flying Corps in France in 1918 to prepare for the amalgamation, and to take over as head of the Royal Air Force as Chief of the Air Staff. But Trenchard and his Secretary of State for Air, Lord Rothermere, a difficult and devious man, soon proved to be incompatible to such a degree that Trenchard felt obliged to resign from his post. He submitted a letter to this effect on 19 March, but since the Royal Air Force was to come into being on 1 April, he agreed for the sake of appearances that he would remain in office until 13 April, when Rothermere formally accepted the resignation. He was offered, and after much hesitation accepted, command of the infant Independent Bombing Force being set up in France. Although this force was never to achieve the size that had been hoped (a figure of 100 squadrons had been discussed), it was able to play a useful part in the later stages of the First World War. Its nine squadrons mounted over 200 raids between 6 June and 11 November 1918, dropping 543 tons of bombs on enemy industrial targets and on a number of his airfields. It was a costly business. The force lost 352 aircraft in the same period, or, in other words, one aircraft for each 1.54 tons of bombs dropped.

Meanwhile in place of Trenchard as Chief of the Air Staff, Brigadier General Sykes (who, it will be recalled, had been thought too junior to command the handful of aircraft of the RFC in 1914) now found himself in April 1918 unexpectedly promoted to Major-General and appointed to command what was at that time the largest air force in the world. He stayed as CAS until April 1919, and although this was a very brief term of office, it covered both a critical stage of the war and a time when the new Service had to be wrought from the amalgamation of the Royal Flying Corps and the Royal Naval Air Service. Apart from the high level concerns that all this involved, the year was also one during which a number of distinguishing features of the Royal Air Force were put in place. These included the decision to introduce a light blue uniform with effect from October 1919, fortunately rescinded and changed to the present dark blue-grey shade before that date; and the introduction of distinctive medals for services in the air, the DFC, DFM, AFC and AFM, all four of them instituted by King George V on his fifty-third birthday, 3 June 1918.

DEVELOPMENTS OVERSEAS

On the much wider scene, other developments had meanwhile taken place outside Europe during the third year of the war. One key measure already mentioned had been to set up in Canada part of the huge wartime machinery for training British airmen and for producing aircraft. Nor was this scheme the only source of trained air crew from overseas. For some time during the early stages of the war, American citizens had been accepted, quite unofficially of course, into the Royal Flying Corps; but with the entry of the United States into the war on 6 April 1917 this picture changed. The US Army Air Corps, a fledgeling organization, needed a great deal of support before it could deal with the new demands being placed upon it, and in October 1917 five squadrons of the pilots from the Canadian training schools moved down from Canada to set up schools in Texas. From this beginning, ten American squadrons were eventually formed, and they crossed to France where they were at first attached by Flights to Squadrons of the RFC. They later formed up into their own units, and played a very distinguished part in the later stages of the war in Europe.

There were other important training schemes for the RFC at that time. The Middle East had seen a detachment of three Maurice Farmans arrive in Egypt as early as November 1914, a tiny force that would constantly expand over the next four years. One aspect of that expansion was a decision by the War Office in August 1916 to take advantage of the good winter weather in Egypt and to set up in that country a training establishment for pilots. As a result, three reserve squadrons were formed which were soon producing 100 pilots on each course, though it has to be remembered that the flying amounted to only 15 hours' solo, the

De Havilland DH4

It was not until 1916 that the Royal Flying Corps received its first aircraft designed specifically as a bomber, the DH4. Although soon superseded by the more successful DH9, no fewer than 1,449 DH4s were produced in Britain alone, while another 4,846 were built in the United States. Some of these aircraft were still in service with the US Army as late as 1932. The DH4 was powered by a 375hp Rolls-Royce Eagle, which gave the aircraft a top speed of 136mph at 6,500ft, and it had a service ceiling of 20,000ft.

remainder of the very modest amount of flying training thought necessary for each pilot in those days being carried out in the United Kingdom. With the decision in July 1917 to double the size of the RFC, another training wing of five squadrons was formed in Egypt, and by 1918 the commitment had grown to a very large command in its own right, with repair depots, a flying instructors' school, an air fighting school and a school of navigation and bomb dropping, as well as extensive stores parks, a seaplane base and various support facilities.

It was from the RFC base in Egypt that a detachment of four aircraft was dispatched to Mesopotamia in May 1915 in support of General Townsend's ill-fated expedition against the Turks. By April 1916, after advancing towards Baghdad, the army of 14,000 British troops and 3,700 Arabs found itself besieged at Kut-el-Amara, and the RFC force, which had by now grown to fourteen aircraft, was engaged in desperate attempts to resupply the expeditionary force by air. But it was a forlorn hope with such slender resources, and although in a pioneering attempt to build an air bridge some 19,000lb of food was dropped, the troops were obliged to surrender on 29 April.

Other units of the RFC operated with considerable success in Palestine, particularly during the Third Battle of Gaza in late October 1917, in which 72 aircraft were engaged, and during the final stages of the campaign in September 1918. By the middle of that month, the Turkish position in Palestine stretched from the Mediterranean coast north of Jaffa inland to the River Jordan and beyond. A major offensive was begun by British and Imperial forces on 19 September, and the retreating Turkish columns found themselves under heavy air attack. The Turkish Eighth Army was shattered by the British advance, and the Seventh Army was cut off from all lines of retreat except for the most important one along the Wadi el Fa'a leading to the River Jordan. A large Turkish column was discovered by

reconnaissance making its way through the wadi, and heavy air attacks were launched against it. Escape was blocked, and in scenes of great panic and disorder the Turkish column was wiped out by air attack. When British troops came up to the scene they found 100 guns, 59 motor vehicles and 929 horse-drawn waggons wrecked or abandoned. Those Turkish troops who managed to escape were later engaged by cavalry and again by air attack, and about 9,000 were captured as a result. The Seventh Army had been destroyed, and with it the last Turkish hopes of holding Palestine. Turkey sued for an armistice, and one was duly brought into force on 31 October.

In the other theatres of war aircraft of the RFC or the RNAS, or both, saw action in the Dardanelles, on the Italian Front, in German East Africa and in German South-West Africa. Their part in all these peripheral campaigns was confined mainly to reconnaissance and spotting, but these activities, particularly against opponents unfamiliar with the potential of aircraft, brought very useful dividends. A more distant but less successful series of operations was seen when units of the newly formed Royal Air Force were dispatched to Russia in mid-1918. Early that year a peace treaty had been signed between the Bolshevik government of Russia and the Central Powers led by Germany. This left Germany free to devote all her military effort to the Western Front, a prospect that led the Americans, the French and the British to send aid to the anti-Bolshevik forces that were still holding out. The British contribution included two detachments of the Royal Air Force, one being sent to northern Russia and the other to the Caucasus region in the south.

In the north, a modest force made up of DH4 bombers, five Fairey Campania floatplanes, two Sopwith Baby floatplanes and a solitary Sopwith Camel were landed, later to be reinforced by Fairey IIICs, DH9As and Sopwith 1½-strutters. They were engaged from August 1918 until September in supporting Allied infantry in action some 100 miles to the south of the main airfield at Bereznik, near Archangel. In the south, the Allied forces were sent in after the end of hostilities to help occupy and stabilize the territory surrendered by the defeated Turks and Germans. The British contingent here included No 221 Squadron, formed from 'D' Squadron of No 62 Wing RNAS, later to be joined by No 266 Squadron from Malta. Both squadrons took part in operations from May until September 1919, when disquiet in the British Parliament about the operational role of these units in a country no longer at war led to their being withdrawn and disbanded. Meanwhile, and in

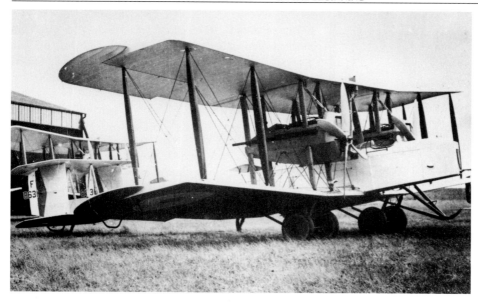

Left: A Vickers Vimy bomber of No 9 Squadron RFC. This was an aircraft of 1917 vintage, but some examples were still flying in 1929. (AHB)

Opposite page: A Victoria Mk V of No 70 Squadron over Iraq between the wars. (R. C. Sturtivant)

the forlorn hope of even now being able to reverse the Russian Revolution, a replacement military force was being assembled in Britain under the guise of a training mission. As part of this effort, No 47 Squadron of the Royal Air Force, renamed 'A' Squadron for the purpose, was deployed from October 1919 until March of the following year. Its role of general support for the Allied forces alongside the anti-Bolshevik troops included bombing missions, aerial photography, attacks on shipping in the Caspian Sea and air-to-air fighting against aircraft of the Bolshevik forces.

It was claimed by the Squadron Commander that No 47 Squadron had made an effective contribution to the anti-Bolshevik cause; but it was a cause championed by fragmented and badly organized forces and the effort was ultimately doomed. It had been a failure that was expensive both in men and in supplies, most of the latter being lost during the evacuation that took place from Novorossisk and Theodosia in early April. But it had nevertheless been a very active campaign, and some idea of its intensity can be gained from the honours and awards that were later made to members of the small air force element: these included four DSOs, three AFCs, and seventeen DFCs as well as a number of other lesser awards.

Further afield, the first RFC unit to arrive in India, 'A' Flight of No 32 Squadron, had come ashore in Bombay on 26 December 1915 with an inventory of five BE2cs. Three of these aircraft were sent on to the North-West Frontier province where, in the autumn of the following year, they were in action against tribal insurgents threatening the Khyber Pass. It was to be only the first of very many air actions along the frontier in support of the Army over the next two decades.

The end of the First World War brought profound changes to the Royal Air Force in these as in all other theatres of operations. Its size and shape over the next decades would contrast strongly with the massive resources that it had accumulated by November 1918. At the end of the war, the Royal Air Force had about 30,000 officers and over 263,000 other ranks on strength, and the 23,000 or so aircraft that have already been mentioned. There were 401 airfields in the United Kingdom and another 274 overseas. No fewer than 185 service (i.e. active) squadrons had been formed, 53 of them stationed in Britain, and there were also 200 training squadrons. During the four-year conflict, aviation as a whole had made remarkable progress, and at the technical level the war had seen the emergence of more powerful, more manoeuvrable and far more reliable machines than had been available in 1914.

Moreover, specialized equipment such as bomb sights, synchronized machine guns, airborne wirelesses, survey cameras and a host of other technologies had all been produced during the war, developments that laid the foundations for later progress in many fields. At the level of air power in its very widest sense, because of the huge numbers of people who had been involved in flying or in the support of flying, or who had simply worked in the many aircraft and component factories that had been set up during the war, there was now a widespread awareness of aviation and its potential — which helps to explain the enthusiasm for the subject that was to characterize the years that followed.

CHAPTER 2

WINGS IN THE SUN

After the national election that followed the Armistice of November 1918, Winston Churchill became Secretary of State for War and Air and he invited Trenchard to accept the appointment of Chief of the Air Staff, the post from which Trenchard had resigned less than a year before. He accepted on 15 February 1919, and thus began his ten-year stewardship of the Service. Unlike Sykes, his predecessor, who had visions of a large peacetime air force, Trenchard saw that in the post-war period there would be very little enthusiasm for military expenditure, and he realized that the ambitions of the Royal Air Force would have to be modest in the extreme. In 1918 another major war seemed virtually inconceivable, and when today we talk of the inter-war years we do so with hindsight: in the 1920s and 1930s they were simply the post-war years. There was no perceived threat to the United Kingdom itself, and, apart from an occupation force of modest size in the Rhineland, there was no reason to station British air units on the continent of Europe.

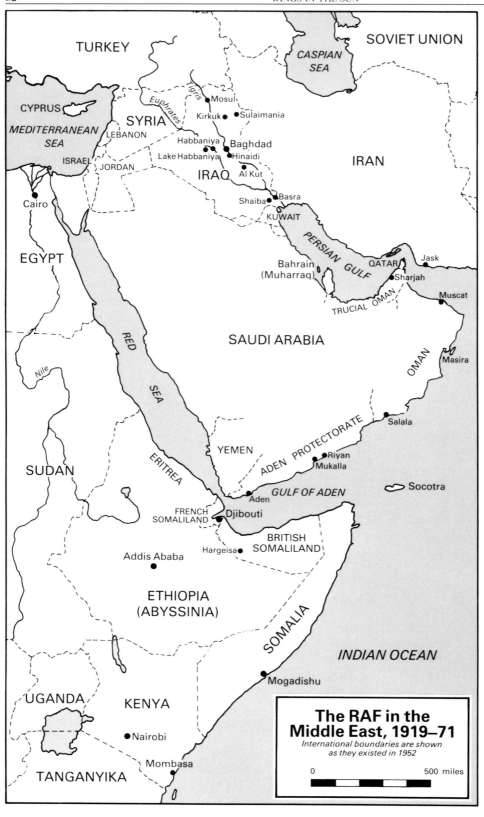

TURKEY

SOVIET UNION

CASPIAN SEA

CYPRUS

MEDITERRANEAN SEA

SYRIA

LEBANON

Tigris

Euphrates

Mosul

Kirkuk · Sulaimania

ISRAEL

JORDAN

Habbaniya

Lake Habbaniya

Baghdad

Hinaidi

IRAQ

Al Kut

IRAN

Cairo

EGYPT

Shaiba · Basra

KUWAIT

PERSIAN GULF

Bahrain (Muharraq)

QATAR

Sharjah

Jask

TRUCIAL OMAN

Muscat

SAUDI ARABIA

OMAN

RED SEA

Nile

Masira

YEMEN

ERITREA

ADEN PROTECTORATE

Salala

Riyan

Mukalla

Socotra

SUDAN

GULF OF ADEN

FRENCH SOMALILAND

Aden

Djibouti

BRITISH SOMALILAND

Hargeisa

Addis Ababa

ETHIOPIA (ABYSSINIA)

SOMALIA

INDIAN OCEAN

UGANDA

KENYA

Mogadishu

Nairobi

TANGANYIKA

Mombasa

The RAF in the Middle East, 1919–71

International boundaries are shown as they existed in 1952

0   500 miles

Against this background, and at Churchill's request, Trenchard drew up a paper setting out his first thoughts on the future size and shape of the Service. Its central features were, first, an emphasis on high quality, and second, an ability to expand the force to double its initial size should that prove necessary. The paper formed the basis of a more detailed scheme for the future, on which Trenchard and his principal advisers now began work.

The final product was a White Paper of prime importance to the future of the Service, entitled *An Outline of the Scheme for the Permanent Organisation of the Royal Air Force* and dated 11 December 1919. The document was put before Parliament by Churchill and accepted, though with a budget of only £15 million (£322 million at 1992 prices) it was clear that the RAF would by no means find it easy to meet its commitments.

It will be enough here to say that the paper laid down certain broad principles, including the need for rigid economy in order to release funds for a large building programme; it gave the proposed deployment of the limited number of squadrons that were being retained; and it devoted almost half its total length of seven pages to the 'extreme importance of training', so as to create a cadre for the future. In one significant passage the value of air force squadrons as a substitute for expensive overseas garrisons was mentioned: '...it is perhaps not too much to hope that before long it will prove possible to regard the Royal Air Force units not as an addition to the military garrison [in India] but as a substitute for it'. In another passage, the paper referred to Egypt as the Clapham Junction of the air between east and west, which it continued, was 'situated within comparatively easy reach of the most probable centres of unrest... making it the obvious locality for a small Royal Air Force reserve'.

It was a thesis that was to be tested almost at once by operational necessity, and because of their influence on future policy the events that followed deserve some examination. The training aspects of Trenchard's paper will be dealt with later. As we have seen, the Royal Air Force had been engaged in a modest way in support of the Indian Army against dissident tribesmen on the North-West Frontier in India as early as 1915. In May 1919 there was more serious fighting in the same region during what became known as the Third Afghan War, when the son of the hereditary ruler, Amir Ammanullah, tried to rally his divided people by launching an invasion of India.

During the four-week war that followed, Nos 31 and 114 Squadrons flew many missions in direct support of British Army columns in the area, and they also carried out bombing raids against rebel towns and villages. One of the more notable of these air attacks was that launched on the capital, Kabul, by a Handley Page V/1500 on 25 May, four bombs from which hit the palace of Amir Ammanullah. Duly impressed by this and by other military action against him, in August the Amir himself sued for peace. But many Pathan tribesmen in the frontier region remained hostile to the British, and as a consequence of their continuing depredations further military operations were launched against the Mahsuds and the Waziri tribes in November 1919.

In the first stage of this campaign, independent air attacks were made on the dissidents in an effort to bomb them into submission, but after a month of daily raids it became clear that the tribesmen had not only adapted to aerial bombardment but had also become worryingly proficient in hitting the attacking aircraft with rifle fire. In one particular raid, that against Pathans on 14 January 1920 in the Ahnai Jangi Gorge, no fewer than three aircraft were shot down and another three had to be written off when they managed to make their way back to base. Eventually, a field force of more than 29,000 men, with a supporting host amounting to almost 34,000 non-combatants as well as tens of thousands of animals, had to be sent into Waziristan before the uprising was finally quelled.

During these operations the RAF squadrons again flew many missions in support of the ground forces, and, despite the enormous difficulties of movement and supply in the wild and inhospitable terrain, by early May 1920 the punitive expedition had completed its task of subduing the worst of the uprising, though sporadic guerrilla warfare continued along the frontier for many years afterwards. By now the decision to deploy the greater part of the Royal Air Force overseas was taking effect, and three extra squadrons equipped with Bristol F2Bs and DH9As had reached India at the end of June 1919, bringing the total strength up to six squadrons. But even this was by no means a strong force to deal with all the demands that would be made in the years that followed.

UNREST IN THE MIDDLE EAST

That same year, 1920, saw the use of RAF aircraft against tribesmen in British Somaliland. During the years of the Great War, a tribal leader, Mohammed bin Abdulla Hassan, known to the British as the Mad Mullah, had extended his long-standing anti-British activities to cover most of the country. In the earlier years of the century, four expeditions had failed to remove him from the scene, and now the advice of the Army was that a new expedition would call for about two divisions of troops, and that a railway would need to be constructed behind the British advance so as to prevent any recurrence of trouble.

Clearly this was going to be a very expensive and thus a highly unwelcome business; but when Trenchard was asked by the Colonial Secretary, Milner, what might be done to reduce this expenditure, he saw a timely opportunity to put his belief in air policing to the test. He offered to employ Royal Air Force aircraft against the Mullah, supported only by the modest Imperial forces already in Somaliland, which amounted to a battalion of The King's African Rifles, 500 men of the local Camel Corps and 1,500 tribal levies. Trenchard's suggestion was accepted and, as a result, in December 1919 eight DH9 aircraft of the Royal Air Force were shipped from Egypt to Berbera on board HMS *Ark Royal*, followed by two more of the same type of machine fitted out as air ambulances. The attack aircraft were in action from 21 January, when the Mad Mullah's main camp at Medishe was bombed, with the Camel Corps following up on the ground. As the dissidents retreated, they were pursued by the aircraft and harassed by the tribal levies, until eventually the Mullah's main fort at Tale was attacked and captured, compelling him in early February to flee to Abyssinia, where he was killed in 1921.

Leopold Amery, who by now had become Colonial Secretary, was to say later that 'All was over in three weeks. The total cost, including transport of The King's African Rifles, extra pay for the Camel Corps and petrol for the Royal Air Force, worked out at £77,000, the cheapest war in history.' To an extent Trenchard's views about the possibilities of colonial policing had been vindicated by this brief campaign, though it has to be said that the dissident forces in Somaliland had already been greatly weakened by some six years of intermittent fighting against the Camel Corps.

Within only a few months there was to be a further opportunity to develop this new role of colonial policing by the Royal Air Force. In the unsettled Middle East, Britain had garrisons that totalled over 80 battalions spread across Palestine, Transjordan, Persia and Mesopotamia, territories that had been mandated to her by the League of Nations as part of the efforts to stabilize the region at the end of the Great War. Armed opposition to the British presence by the indigenous population was, however, soon in evidence both in Palestine and in Mesopotamia, but particularly in the remote northern areas of the latter, a region inhabited by warlike Kurdish tribes.

Churchill, as Secretary of State for War and Air, had already warned in August 1919 that a way would have to be found to reduce the costly garrison of 25,000 British and 80,000 Indian troops in Mesopotamia. His first suggestion had been to use fixed garrisons at key points, supplemented by mechanized units to cover the outlying

Left: A Nieuport Nightjar of No 203 Squadron being repaired near Constantinople during the Chanak Crisis of 1922. (AHB)

areas. This proved to be impractical, and in 1920, when Churchill had taken over as Colonial Secretary from Milner, he asked Trenchard whether he might be 'prepared to take Mesopotamia on', the inducement being an extra £5–7 million added to the budget of the Royal Air Force.

Trenchard needed no persuading. Military expenditure of any kind was by now very unpopular politically, and the extreme pressures on the Defence Budget, together with the rapidly growing determination by the two older Services to dismantle the Royal Air Force, made it highly desirable to find an independent air force role. The result was a plan drawn up by the Air Staff to station in Mesopotamia ten of the 33 squadrons by then making up the Royal Air Force, this air arm to be supported by only small forces on the ground. Predictably, it was a concept that drew heavy fire from the critics of the Air Force, an attitude perhaps best illustrated by a comment made in his diary at the time by Field Marshal Sir Henry Wilson, the CIGS, who noted on 7 May that 'The sooner the Air Force crashes the better... It is a wicked waste of money as run at present'.

A new urgency was brought to the problem of holding Mesopotamia in the summer of 1920, when a full scale uprising took place along the lower Euphrates river. The rebellion quickly spread until there were an estimated 130,000 or more tribesmen under arms. By early December 1920 it had been necessary to expand the Imperial garrison to a strength of 17,000 British and 85,000 Indian troops at an estimated annual cost of nearly £30 million. To resolve this and the many other problems of sustaining the British position in the Middle East, Churchill now called a conference for March 1920 in Cairo of the senior officials involved. At that conference it was agreed to pacify several of the key frontier areas of the region by paying subsidies, that is to say bribes, to local leaders so as to keep them under control, thus facilitating the withdrawal of most of the expensive British and Indian Army garrisons. This would then open the way for the far less costly option of air control, and since it was also agreed that the Royal Air Force was to play the principal role in these arrangements, supported by only a minimal force of troops on the ground, the overall commander would be an air force officer.

In the face of continuing opposition, in August Churchill put his proposals before the Cabinet in London and, no doubt impressed by the economies that were promised, the Cabinet endorsed them. At this same time, arrangements for the future of two other former Turkish territories, Transjordan and Palestine, were being made. At the request of the British-sponsored ruler, the Amir Abdullah, three airfields would be built by the British in Transjordan, an air route across the desert would be marked out linking that country with Iraq (where Abdullah's brother Faisal had been similarly installed by the British) and units of the Royal Air Force would be stationed in the country to underwrite the new regime. Thus after almost three years of financial debate and acrimonious inter-service dispute, the principle of air control was brought to the Middle East on 1 October 1922.

But it was always clear that the use of aircraft for colonial policing of this kind would on its own not be enough; forces on the ground, however modest in size, would be needed to support and to complement air action. And since the British Army, understandably, refused to make any more resources available for the garrison in Iraq, the Royal Air Force was obliged to raise a small army of its own to supplement the troops drawn from the British Army in India. As it happened, the basis for local levies already existed. An irregular force had been raised in Mesopotamia during 1915 to serve as bodyguards for political officers in the southern and central part of that country, and by 1918 there were over five thousand local men so engaged. They were reconstituted as the Iraq Levies in 1919 and placed under RAF command in October 1922 to augment the squadrons in their task of air policing. A useful element of mobility for the ground forces of the RAF was provided by armoured cars, the first unit of which, No 1 Armoured Car Company, was formed at Heliopolis, near Cairo, on 19 December 1921 for operations in Mesopotamia. The initial deployment of the Royal Air Force to Iraq, as Mesopotamia was renamed from 1922, was thus made up not only of eight flying squadrons but also of the Iraq levies, the armoured car unit (later expanded to a force of six armoured car companies), numerous pack animals and nine battalions of British and Indian infantry. The whole force was a charge on the Government of India, under which Iraq was administered, rather than on that of the home establishment in London. As had been agreed at the Cairo Conference, overall military command in the country was exercised by an airman, and Air Vice-Marshal John Salmond was appointed. He of course had already played an important role during the days of the RFC and during the formation of the Royal Air Force.

One of the first tasks of the RAF Command in Iraq was to deal with incursions in the north by Turkish troops, who were covertly trying to reassert the control over the country that they had forfeited at the end of the

Great War, partly by using some of their own troops but also by fomenting unrest among the local tribes. Salmond began by launching a small-scale bombing campaign against Turkish troops, and this was highly successful in driving them out of five of the northern districts that they had improperly occupied. This was by no means the end of operations in Mesopotamia, but nor was this initial engagement the only instance of recalcitrant Turks causing difficulties soon after the end of the war.

After the Armistice, the Allies had established a neutral zone at the Dardanelles so as to safeguard access to Constantinople, and as part of the peace settlement Greece had been given a mandate over the Smyrna district and Eastern Thrace. But the leader of what were known as the Young Turks, Mustapha Kemal Bey, later better known as Kemal Ataturk, had taken up arms against the Allies with the aim of regaining all these lost territories. In August 1922 he defeated the Greek garrison in Anatolia, occupied Smyrna amid much bloodshed and moved towards Constantinople. By mid-September his army had reached Chanak, just inside the neutral zone established by the Allies, and a confrontation became almost inevitable. This crisis caused the zone to be reinforced, notably by units of the Royal Air Force. An RAF troopship en route to Mesopotamia was diverted to Chanak, the seaplane

carrier HMS *Pegasus* sailed into Chanak on 9 September with her five Fairey IIID aircraft, and the aircraft carrier HMS *Argus* arrived on 22 September with five Nieuport Nightjar fighters of No 203 Squadron and another seventeen IIIDs. During late September and early October this force was then joined by further reinforcements: No 4 Squadron (Bristol F2Bs), No 25 Squadron (Sopwith Snipes), No 207 Squadron (DH9As), No 208 Squadron (Bristol F2Bs) and No 56 Squadron (Snipes), all from the United Kingdom, as well as by No 267 Squadron from Malta.

This considerable force established its HQ in Constantinople while the Aircraft Park and the main operating base were set up at San Stephano, some seven miles south-west of the city, with another base at Kilia on the Gallipoli peninsula opposite Chanak. Nos 25, 56, 207 and 208 Squadrons seem to have been based at San Stephano, with Nos 4, 203 and 267 Squadrons at Kilia. The arrival of these units coincided with the onset of the winter season. A brief spell of very hot weather and frequent duststorms was swiftly followed by rains and then gales, which in turn gave way to floods, ice and snow. Conditions became so bad at Kilia that the units

Below: RAF armoured cars during operations against Sheik Mahmud in Iraq. (AHB)

moved out to Kilid el Bahr, though even there things were not much better. Weather permitting, the aircraft carried out reconnaissance, surveillance and general patrol missions throughout their deployment as Kemal's forces made ready to attack the British positions. At the last moment, however, and after the British commander had made it plain that he would not surrender the neutral zone at any cost, the Turks rather surprisingly agreed to a local truce which was later to be ratified in a formal peace treaty at Lausanne in August 1923.

No actual fighting thus took place, and the threat of a major international incident, and perhaps even a war with Turkey, receded. For the units of the Royal Air Force it had been a difficult and uncomfortable deployment from first to last, with hopelessly insufficient logistic backing at its launch, compounded by totally inadequate support once the force had arrived in theatre. Nevertheless, and despite all the difficulties, it demonstrated that air force elements could move with what for those days was considerable dispatch in reaction to a crisis, and that they could operate under extreme conditions once they had arrived.

Although, as we have seen, the Turks had been prevented from re-establishing themselves in northern Mesopotamia, unrest in the area continued. There were at that time several rebellious tribes in Kurdistan, and a principal player among them was Sheik Mahmud, who had been appointed Governor of the Sulaimania district to replace the British administration when it had been judged that the area had been pacified. But in early 1923 intelligence showed that Mahmud had reneged and that he was planning a military attack on the city of Kirkuk, an assault that was to be the signal for a general uprising against British rule.

By now the Royal Air Force was well established in Mesopotamia. Salmond had under command eight squadrons in Mesopotamia itself, three at Hinaidi (Nos 1, 8 and 45), two at Mosul (Nos 6 and 55), two at Baghdad West (Nos 30 and 70), and one, No 84, at Shaibah. When Mahmud ignored a British summons to appear in Baghdad to answer for his actions, air operations were started against him. At first delayed-action bombs were dropped near Sulaimania, his main town, and then his own quarters in Sulaimania were attacked. Mahmud thereupon fled into the hills with many of his followers, and a joint land and air operation was then launched against him using two columns of troops on the ground and RAF squadrons in support. By the middle of May the rebels had been defeated, the town of Sulaimania occupied and Mahmud himself driven to seek sanctuary in Persia.

Although the operation had been a joint one, the RAF squadrons had played a prominent part in its success, bombing the tribesmen, ferrying troops, evacuating wounded and dropping supplies. But this was not the end of Mahmud, and in the summer of 1923 he was back in Sulaimania again, proclaiming himself to be the King of Kurdistan. After some minor actions against the Imperial forces, he now proclaimed a *jihad*, or holy war. This had to be taken seriously and a force of forty-two RAF aircraft launched a 48-hour air assault against his forces in Sulaimania. When Turkish troops tried to take advantage of the renewed fighting to re-enter the Kurdish areas, they too were attacked by RAF aircraft. With the strengthened force available to Salmond, and with the increasing experience that they had gained of fighting him, Mahmud was by now no longer the serious threat to stability in the region that his earlier efforts had made him, and the operations that continued against him sporadically until May 1931 were minor affairs, particularly after the Turks had finally accepted in 1926 the loss of their old provinces in the country.

Thus by early 1925, although occasional fighting continued both in the north and in the south of Iraq, it was clear that the policy of air control had succeeded. Not only that, but it had proved to be highly cost-effective. From a peak of military spending of over £20 million in 1921–22, the cost had now fallen to less than £3.4 million a year. One result of this outcome was that the Royal Air Force retained responsibility for the internal and external security of Iraq until the end of the League of Nations' mandate in October 1932.

One reason for the minimal cost of operations in Iraq had been the frugality with which personnel and aircraft were deployed and supported by a parsimonious administration in India. And this attitude was also reflected in the conditions of service that were endured by the forces involved. Service life in Iraq, and indeed on the outstations in India at this time, was hard and demanding. Very few families accompanied the married men, leisure facilities away from the major camps were virtually non-existent and the climate was often intolerable. At the RAF station of Shaibah near Basra, for example, the temperature in August occasionally rose to as high as 125°F. Soldiers on board troopships in the Gulf had been known to die of simple heat exhaustion. Tropical medicine was still a developing science, so that sickness on quite a large scale was not unknown, and even the medical recommendations for dealing with the extremes of climate were questionable. One curious result was that troops working in the open during the hot season in Iraq and India wore an item of equipment

called a spine-pad, a four-inch wide length of felt suspended from a cord round the neck, and hung down to the belt so as to protect the spine from the supposedly deleterious effects of the sun's rays!

As to the aircraft in these overseas stations during the 1920s and early 1930s, the squadrons were still equipped with Bristol F2Bs or DH9As. Both of these

machines were First World War types that had been very little modified since then, except that they had been adapted locally to carry all manner of extra equipment made necessary by operating over the desert. Some of the DH9As, in particular, can be seen in contemporary photographs to be carrying a spare wheel under or alongside the fuselage, a spare tropical radiator, water

bags at the wing tips so as to provide a cool drink on landing, two auxiliary fuel tanks mounted under the top mainplane and five-gallon drums of drinking water on the bomb-racks. Stowed internally would be engine and cockpit covers, screw pickets, ropes, tools, rations, bed-rolls and groundsheets. Other items of equipment might include one of the bulky hand-held cameras of the time, or even spare parts for armoured cars. It was as well that high speed and manoeuvrability were less important in these campaigns than simple load-carrying.

It was not until 1931 that the last of these obsolete aircraft left Iraq, usually to be replaced by Westland Wapitis. This new aircraft resulted from an Air Ministry requirement in 1927 which, so as to save money, specified that as many parts as possible from the DH9A should be incorporated in the design. Since Westland had been involved in the design work for the earlier machine, they had a considerable advantage over the other six manufacturers who tendered, and they won the contract. Westland were given the order for the first 25 Wapiti Mk Is in December 1927. This was a mixed metal and fabric machine, though the definitive version (of which 415 were built) was the Mk IIA, an all-metal aircraft powered by a 550hp Jupiter VIIIF engine. Wapitis served as general-purpose aircraft in India with Nos 5, 11, 20, 27, 28, 31, 39 and 60 Squadrons and in Iraq with Nos 30, 55, and 84 Squadrons. Although its top speed was only 135mph, it was a sturdy and popular aircraft, and a type of which about eighty were still in service in India as late as 1939; indeed, a handful were still engaged in target-towing until 1943.

POLITICAL PROBLEMS

This brief account of events in the Middle East has taken us well ahead of developments at the political level in London, events that came to threaten the very existence of the new Service. In May 1921 the Army had put forward the view that aircraft must essentially act as auxiliary arms to the Navy and to the Army, and that aircraft must therefore be organized, trained and employed as integral parts of those Services. No less an authority than Marshal Foch was quoted in support of this assertion. At the same time the Royal Navy was still pressing for its own air service, and the whole matter was therefore considered by the Standing Sub-Committee of the Committee of Imperial Defence in July 1921, under the chairmanship of Balfour.

The Committee was, not surprisingly, unable to reconcile the claims of the two older Services with Trenchard's restatement of the doctrine of the strategic air offensive, and Balfour was therefore obliged to produce an independent report. This report pointed out that there were certain very important types of military operations, including air defence, for which the Air Force was mainly responsible. While it was the case that there were other situations in which the Air Force must either be subordinate to, or work in close co-operation

Left, top: A DH9A of No 84 Squadron over Iraq, showing some of the externally carried equipment. (R. C. Sturtivant)

Left: A bombed-up Wapiti, ready for a raid against the Mahsud, at Miramshah, July 1930. Under the wings can be seen four 112lb and four 20lb bombs. (AHB)

Right: Bombs falling from a Wapiti over the North-West Frontier. (RAFM)

Sopwith Cuckoo

July 1918 saw the introduction into RAF service of one of its first torpedo bombers, the Cuckoo, which equipped two squadrons. It was an aircraft powered by a Wolseley Viper or Sunbeam Arab engine, either of which gave the Cuckoo a maximum speed of 100mph at 10,000ft. The machine had an endurance of four hours and a service ceiling of 12,000ft. The last of these aircraft went out of service in 1923.

with, the other Services, nevertheless it was essential that the Royal Air Force be autonomously administered and trained. To relegate it to an inferior position would greatly hamper its development, and might put Britain at a serious disadvantage compared with other nations.

Despite vigorous protests by the Army and the Navy, the Cabinet accepted Balfour's view, and in March 1922 the existing status of the RAF was confirmed. This was not enough for the Royal Navy, however, and only four months later, in July, the Admiralty again sought authority to establish its own Naval Air Unit for work with the Fleet, independent of the RAF. The controversy rumbled on, with Beatty, the First Sea Lord, threatening in February 1923 to resign over the issue. This, together with a certain amount of alarm that followed the French occupation of the Ruhr in the

previous month so as to enforce its claims for war reparations, led to an inquiry into national defence as a whole, this time under the chairmanship of Lord Salisbury. A sub-committee chaired by Balfour was to examine once more the specific claims of the Admiralty on the Royal Air Force. The hearings lasted for several weeks, with an agreed assumption that France might be treated as a potential enemy. Trenchard was able to point out that only 242 tons of bombs had been dropped on Britain during the late war; but if the expansion of the French Air Force that was at that time in prospect indeed came about, then the French would be able to drop as much as 325 tons on Britain in a single day. Trenchard went on to argue that the first essential in these circumstances was to gain air superiority, and to point out that although fighters could inflict some losses on an attacking air force, the only sure means of wresting the initiative from the opponent was to destroy his airfields by bombing them.

It was at this very point that the campaign being led by Air Vice-Marshal Salmond in northern Iraq reached its successful conclusion. The five-month campaign had cost the remarkably modest sum of £100,000 (just over £2 million at 1992 rates), and as a gesture of gratitude Salmond was promoted to the rank of Air Marshal. It is not clear just how much influence the events in Iraq had on the Salisbury Committee, but it can safely be assumed that the campaign was in the minds of its members when

Left: Vickers Vimys at No 4 Flying Training School, Egypt, during an AOC's Inspection in the late 1920s. (AHB)

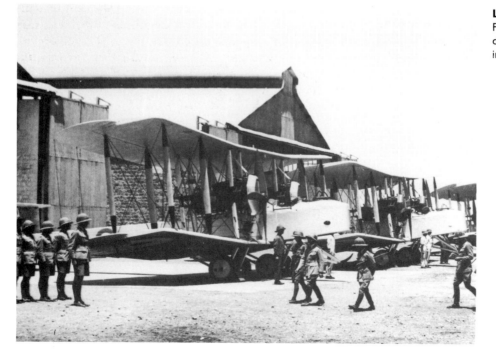

it now recommended that the Royal Air Force should be expanded. Trenchard himself was in no doubt about Salmond's contribution to this satisfactory outcome, saying in a letter to him, 'I cannot emphasize too much the value that your successful command in Iraq has been to us'.

Meanwhile the Salisbury Committee had also drawn up details of a scheme to expand the Home Defence Force to a strength of 52 squadrons, 'to be created with as little delay as possible'. In this context it should be explained that the Home Defence Force embraced all the fighting elements of the RAF based at home, and not merely what we would today regard as air defence units. A completion date of 1928 for the programme of expansion was intended, but for several reasons the momentum behind this revival of the Air Force quickly drained away. First, it soon became clear that, despite the short-lived alarm over French actions, there was no obvious threat to the United Kingdom. Second, the 'Ten Year Rule' (see Chapter 3) was in force. Third, the national economy was in no state to support such an ambitious scheme. And fourth, these years were an era of peace and of a public enthusiasm for peace, a sentiment given formal international recognition in the Treaty of Locarno of December 1925. As a result of all this, the Air Estimates were held down to a level below £20 million and the first of many Air Force expansion schemes was allowed to lapse.

At this point the Army again raised its claim for a separate air arm, which, it was suggested, could be sliced off from what was going to be the larger Air Force proposed by the Salisbury recommendations. This proposal was quickly turned down by the Government, but meanwhile the sub-committee set up to examine the Naval case was still in fitful session. After several inconclusive meetings, the members decided to visit the aircraft carriers *Argus* and *Eagle* to see for themselves how the new Service was managing its maritime element, and its members came down in favour of matters being left as they were. As a result, on 2 August 1923, Baldwin, by now Prime Minister, announced that the Fleet Air Arm would remain part of the RAF. Various concessions were made by Trenchard, including an agreement that up to 70 per cent of the pilots in the Fleet Air Arm would be naval officers, but the main principle was established.

It was a decision that was still resented by the Royal Navy, who took every opportunity in the years that followed to raise the subject again. One such opportunity presented itself in August 1925 when, because of the very poor shape of the national economy, another committee, this time chaired by Lord Colwyn, was set up to consider

Fairey Swordfish

Between the wars the Royal Navy was reluctant to concede the potential effectiveness of aircraft against surface ships, while the Royal Air Force, which was until 1937 responsible for all carrier-borne aircraft, devoted its limited resources to other roles. The result was that for many years little progress was made in the development of maritime attack aircraft, and it was only in 1935 that a requirement was drawn up for a more modern type. The resulting specification produced the Bristol Beaufort. Meanwhile, even as late as 1942, the obsolete Vildebeest and Swordfish, both of them biplanes, were still operational in the role. Of the two types, only the Swordfish proved to be combat-worthy, though Vildebeest crews at Singapore fought with determination against heavy odds. With its 750hp Pegasus engine, the Swordfish had a top speed of only 138mph, and the aircraft had a range of 564 miles. It could carry a 1,610lb torpedo or a 1,500lb load of bombs or mines. Despite its antiquated appearance, in the hands of very gallant naval aviators the Swordfish achieved some remarkable successes during the Second World War.

possible economies in the fighting Services as a whole. Both the Navy and the Army pressed the case once more for their own air arms, but the Colwyn Committee could not accept that savings would be made by dismantling the Air Force, and indeed it reported that such a step would actually prevent the savings in military expenditure that the Air Force was expected to make possible. Trenchard now asked that this final vindication of his views be formally endorsed, and on 25 February 1926 Baldwin announced in the House of Commons that the Government had no intention of reviving the question of a separate air arm, adding, 'It is in the interests of the fighting Services that controversy upon this subject should now cease.' Looking back at this running dispute during the first half of the 1920s over the independence of the RAF, it is clear that four factors had come together: the severe pressure on the British budget, Churchill's ambition for political advancement, the need to stabilize Mesopotamia and Trenchard's search for a peacetime Air Force role. It was a fortunate conjuncture.

Even now, however, the argument was by no means at an end. The whole dispute was revived yet again in late 1927 by the incoming First Sea Lord, Sir Charles Madden. Once again the case was reviewed, this time by Lord Salisbury who was appointed to arbitrate between the two Services, and once again the naval case was rejected. For the next nine years, the arrangement under which the Royal Navy operated the carriers but the RAF was responsible for their aircraft worked well, as indeed it had from the first. In 1937, however, in one of the many examinations of policy carried out by Sir Thomas Inskip, who had been appointed to the new post of Minister for the Co-ordination of Defence, the whole question of the status of the Fleet Air Arm was again aired. This time the decision went to the Royal Navy in what was known as the Inskip Award dated 21 July 1937, and although it would not be until 24 May 1939 that the decision could be fully implemented, the Fleet Air Arm was no longer under the control of the RAF.

Those same years of the 1920s that saw the RAF struggle for its existence had also been marked by deep parsimony on the part of British Governments, one result of which was that many aircraft were obsolete. This was particularly true of the overseas units, and most marked of all in India where the squadrons, funded by the Indian Army, were starved even of the most basic resources needed to keep their worn-out aircraft in the air. The state of the aircraft there is well illustrated by the comments of Squadron Leader Arthur Harris (later Air Chief Marshal Sir Arthur Harris, the Commander-in-Chief of Bomber Command), who was in command of No 31 Squadron at Cawnpore. He recorded that it was not unusual for aircraft to take off on the naked rims of their wheels because there were no tyres for them, and he describes how axles were sometimes lashed to the undercarriage struts with local rope of doubtful quality because the necessary elasticated material was not available. Even more serious, given the nature of the terrain over which the squadrons were operating, was the fact that the aircraft engines still had single ignition systems, long discarded everywhere else as unreliable and unsafe.

Eventually, growing public concern about the state of the overseas units, and especially those in India, led to heated exchanges in the House of Commons. The outcome was that Trenchard, anxious to see that the blame for this deplorable state of affairs was put where it belonged — on the Indian Government rather than on his own Service — sent Air Vice-Marshal John Salmond (as he still was) out to India on a tour of inspection in the summer of 1922. Salmond produced a report that was highly critical of what he found. Among other things, he pointed out that with 70 aircraft on strength in India it would be reasonable to expect two-thirds of them to be serviceable on any given day. In fact he found that, on one particular day, only seven were serviceable, and some squadrons could scarcely put anything at all into the air.

He concluded that the Royal Air Force in India was 'to all intents and purposes non-existent as a fighting force at this date'. He went on to make a number of recommendations, one of them being to stress the potential of a properly supported air force to act as 'the sole punitive weapon for the control of tribesmen in Waziristan with resulting economy in both the numbers and cost of maintenance of troops of occupation, and in the cost of punitive operations'. It amounted to a restatement of Trenchard's belief in the concept of air control, dispensing with the use of large and expensive army garrisons or field forces — in other words a re-affirmation of the decision of the 1921 Cairo Conference. There followed in political circles what amounted to a token acceptance of Salmond's report, but little was actually done to modernize the equipment in India nor even properly to extend the life of the inadequate equipment that was to hand, and it would be some years before any real improvement was brought about.

PALESTINE AND ADEN

Once air control was seen to be successful in Iraq in the early 1920s, it was extended to two other British-controlled territories in the Middle East, Palestine and Aden. Palestine proved, however, to be a quite different challenge from that posed in the remoteness of the North-West Frontier, or even that of northern Iraq. For one thing, it was a comparatively well developed territory, and it included large modern cities such as Jaffa, Tel Aviv and Jerusalem. Internal security was more a matter for a police force in such circumstances, with, if necessary, support from the Army; flying units could act only in the most extreme contingencies. Nevertheless, the Royal Air Force took over command in the country and deployed the first RAF operational unit there by reforming No 14 Squadron at Ramleh in February 1920 equipped with Bristol F2Bs. During the next sixteen years the squadron was variously in action against Arab raiders within Palestine and Transjordan, Arab tribesmen making incursions across the border from French-controlled Syria, or, as happened in 1926, Druze tribesmen who had fled across the same border and then set up armed camps on British-administered territory. Most of the flying operations were conducted in support of the Transjordan Frontier Force or the armoured cars of the Royal Air Force, and they usually took the form of reconnaissance missions or demonstrations of air power, though attacks against ground targets, using not only machine guns but also bombs, were by no means uncommon.

This kind of air activity continued on and off until 1936, but by then the picture had changed from one in

which dissident Arabs were occasionally threatening law and order to one in which antagonism between Arabs and Jews was threatening the security of the whole country. Serious disturbances grew and spread to such an extent that British Army and Air Force reinforcements were sent in. Nos 6 and 33 Squadrons were deployed to Palestine, but the nature of the inter-communal fighting, and the fact that the settlements of the two adversaries were often so intermingled, meant that the ability of aircraft to intervene effectively was very limited.

Meanwhile the crisis in the country, referred to by the British authorities as 'disturbances', by the Jews as 'riots' and by the Arabs as 'a revolution', grew worse. Finally, in September 1935 further British Army reinforcements had to be sent in, and in recognition of the predominant presence of ground forces RAF command in the country was relinquished in favour of the Army, with Lieutenant General J. G. Dill taking over. It was clear to all that the concept of air control had been stretched beyond its practical limits by the unusual circumstances in Palestine, though the lesson that the direct application of air power is no panacea in internal security situations was not one that was fully absorbed at the time or even in later decades.

Heavy fighting continued up and down Palestine during 1936, followed by a year marked by acts of terrorism rather than any large-scale engagements. In 1938 the situation again worsened and further reinforcements were dispatched to the garrison, which by now amounted to two infantry brigades, the Transjordan Frontier Force, No 6 Squadron, No 2 Armoured Car

Company of the RAF and No 14 Squadron stationed across the border at Amman in Transjordan. By the autumn No 33 Squadron with Hawker Harts had also arrived, together with No 211 Squadron from the Canal Zone, equipped with Hinds. The limited use to which combat aircraft could be put in such a situation led in late 1938 to the adoption of a new technique in the Internal Security operations known as 'air cordoning'. Villages, towns and even on one occasion Jerusalem itself were blockaded by aircraft flying round the outskirts to prevent movement away from the inhabited areas, while police and troops on the ground carried out sweeps for arms and for wanted men. By early 1939 rebel activity against the security forces was again less of a concern than the continuing terrorism, but then as the year wore on the shadow of far more ominous events in Europe led to a sharp reduction in the level of instability, and to a relatively peaceful period that would last until the years immediately after the Second World War.

The other and more successful use of the RAF in policing operations following the effectiveness of the technique in Mesopotamia during the early 1920s was seen in Aden. A handful of aircraft of the Royal Naval Air Service had arrived in Aden as early as 1916 aboard HMS *Raven II*, and they had been employed in reconnaissance missions, leaflet-dropping sorties and occasional bombing attacks against Turkish positions in the area. The following year saw a permanent Flight established in Aden; this had been formed at Lahore, India, from No 31 Squadron and its offshoot No 114. The Flight continued the modest level of operations

BAY OF BISCAY

FRANCE

GERMANY

CZECHOSLOVA

● Prague

● Paris

● Vienna

AUSTRIA

● Berne
SWITZERLAND

ITALY

● Milan

● Turin

PORTUGAL

Marseilles

CORSICA

● Rome

Foggia

SPAIN

● Madrid

Anzio ●

● Naples
● Salerno

BALEARIC
ISLANDS

SARDINIA

Tangier ●

GIBRALTAR

Palermo ●

● Messina

SPANISH MOROCCO

● Algiers

SICILY

● Gela

Oran ●

ALGERIA

Tunis ●

See Inset B

MOROCCO

TUNISIA

MALTA

ME

Mareth ●

Tripoli ●

■ Idris

TRIPOLITANIA

Inset A

Gamil ● Port Said

Suez Canal

El Firdan ■

Abu Sueir ■ ■ Ismailia

Abu Sultan ■

Fayid ■ ■ Deversoir

Abyad ●

Fanara ■

Nile

Heliopolis ●

Kabrit ■

Kasfareet ■

El Hamra ●

Cairo

Shallufa ■

■ Suez

0   50 miles

Inset B

GOZO

COMINO

MALTA

Sliema

Takali ■

Valletta

Luqa ■

Hal Far ■

Kalafrana

0   5 miles

POLAND

SOVIET UNION

Budapest

HUNGARY

RUMANIA

BLACK SEA

Novorossisk ●

● Theodosia

Belgrade ●

● Bucharest

YUGOSLAVIA

BULGARIA

Sofia ●

Tirana ●

● Constantinople
(Istanbul)

● Ankara

TURKEY

ALBANIA

Chanak
(Cannakale) ●

GREECE

● Athens

SYRIA

CYPRUS ● Nicosia

IRAQ

■ Akrotiri

LEBANON

Beirut ●

● Damascus

Iraklion
■

Haifa ●

● Mafraq

CRETE

ISRAEL

● Amman

Jerusalem ●

MEDITERRANEAN SEA

JORDAN

Tobruk ●

Benghazi ●

*See
Inset A*

■ Benina

El Adem ■

SAUDI ARABIA

CYRENAICA

El Alamein ●

LIBYA

EGYPT

The RAF in the Mediterranean, 1920–93

■ Airfields   ▲ Flying boat bases

0   100   500 miles

against the Turks until the Armistice, when it returned to India. Military air activity in Aden was then confined to sporadic sorties by small detachments of the RAF and the Fleet Air Arm, the machines operating against dissident tribes in the hinterland around what had previously been Turkish Aden but was now under British protection. This pattern of occasional air activity was eventually changed by the deployment to the colony of No 8 Squadron, a unit that was destined to remain in Aden for the next fifteen years until 1942 and then to return there from 1946 until the British withdrawal in 1967.

The arrival of No 8 Squadron in 1927 was timely, for at the end of that same year Yemeni irregulars launched a foray into the Aden Protectorate and almost simultaneously inter-tribal conflict broke out. Following the example set in Iraq, a Royal Air Force officer, this time Group Captain W. G. S. Mitchell, was appointed overall military commander in early 1928. A detachment of armoured cars was deployed from Baghdad to become 'D' Flight of No 8 Squadron and a force of local troops six platoons strong, the Aden Protectorate Levies, was raised for use up-country. On 21 February No 8 Squadron, flying DH9As, began air operations against the tribesmen that continued through until late August. It was hard pounding for the solitary squadron, which

flew 1,260 hours, dropped over seventy tons of bombs and fired off more than 33,000 rounds of ammunition in operational sorties.

By then re-equipped with Fairey IIIFs, No 8 Squadron was again in action against dissidents during January and March 1929, but thereafter matters quietened down and its flying activities in the Aden area were confined almost entirely to survey work, communications duties and the delivery of mail to the scattered administrative centres of the Protectorate.

This uneventful routine was interrupted in September 1935 when Italian forces from Somaliland invaded Abyssinia, thereby provoking an international crisis. The British Government, concerned at the potential threat to the stability of the whole region, reacted by reinforcing the garrison of Aden. Three squadrons flew in, No 203 with Short Singapore flying boats from Basra, No 12 Squadron with Hawker Harts from Andover and No 41 Squadron equipped with Hawker Demon fighters from Northolt. All were in place by October 1935, but the crisis subsided and the units found themselves flying uneventful patrol and surveillance missions both in Aden and in British

Below: Fairey IIIFs of No 202 Squadron at Khartoum in 1934. (AHB)

Somaliland until the last of the detachments was withdrawn again in August of the next year, leaving No 8 Squadron once more as the sole representative of the Royal Air Force in the area.

INDIA AND THE NORTH-WEST FRONTIER

During all these developments in the Middle East the Royal Air Force had maintained its presence and its efforts in India. Life on the Frontier was very rarely quiet, and in July 1924 operations were again undertaken against troublesome tribes in the region. All six squadrons stationed on the Frontier took part in reconnaissance and bombing flights against elements of the Mahsud tribes in south Waziristan, and by October most of their leaders had been persuaded by political officers to accept peace terms. One tribe, however, the Abdur Rahman Khel, together with supporters from three other tribes, would not submit and in January they began to raid outlying Army posts.

When the raids showed no sign of ending, it was decided by the AOC India, Air Vice-Marshal Sir Edward Ellington, to launch air operations against the rebels, but this time without the customary dispatch of an Army field force. This was the first independent air action of any size on the Frontier, and not only did it become a case study of some interest at the time, it was also to have an impact on the whole question of the future allocation of resources. The operational commander for the campaign was Wing Commander R. C. M. Pink, OC No 2 (India) Wing, and the operation became rather whimsically known as 'Pink's War'. After agreeing the outline of his intentions with the Northern Command of the Indian Army, Pink followed the usual procedure of dropping leaflets on the dissidents warning them what they could expect, and when after a week this had produced no result, aircraft from Nos 5, 20, 27, and 60 Squadrons began to deploy forward in preparation for the air assault. On 9 March the 40 or so aircraft involved began their attacks, using bombs up to a weight of 230lb, against targets such as tribal caves and other strongholds. After 54 days of operations during which 2,700 hours were flown by day and night and more than 250 tons of bombs were unleashed, the tribal leaders agreed to the terms that were put forward at a local peace conference.

Once the brief campaign was over, opinions on its effectiveness tended, predictably, to divide along single service lines. The C-in-C India, Sir Claud Jacob, believed that the same result could have been achieved more quickly had ground forces acted in co-operation with the Royal Air Force; Ellington on the other hand claimed that the use of aircraft alone had been less costly in manpower and in other resources than would otherwise have been the case. Pink's War was thus by no means the last word on independent air operations for colonial policing, but the outcome of the campaign gave Trenchard additional support in his fight for increased resources for his Service. He now drew up a scheme for air control on the Frontier that would increase the number of RAF squadrons deployed there from six to ten, offsetting savings being made by reducing the number of battalions in the Frontier Province — and at that time there were no fewer than 46 of them deployed in the region. In the event the scheme came to nothing, and instead the Royal Air Force found itself playing an increasingly significant role on the Frontier but using no more than the very limited resources that were already to hand.

Typical of the minor engagements that erupted over the next twelve years on the Frontier were the operations against a Mohmand lashkar (that is, a small force of tribal warriors), which was attacked and dispersed without loss in June 1927; and the engagement in November of the following year when bombing raids against a group of dissident Mahsuds compelled them to release the Hindu captives they had been holding. But even when the Frontier was relatively quiet the RAF squadrons were fully occupied. The almost inaccessible nature of much of the wild terrain necessitated the reconnaissance and surveillance of areas likely to house future trouble, and vertical photography was constantly undertaken as a basis for mapping these almost untrodden tracts. The regular delivery of mail and supplies formed another important feature of squadron life, as did contact flights and visits to the many outposts scattered among the mountains and valleys of the region.

At the same time, this period of relative quiet made it possible to consolidate and to improve the landing strips from which the squadrons had largely been operating, turning them into more or less permanent airfields. Training also absorbed a large part of squadron efforts, but the pattern of activities also included a number of interesting diversions such as long-range flights, some of them undertaken by whole formations of aircraft — for example, from the Frontier region down to Singapore. Other variety was offered by practice deployments to forward airstrips, or by bombing and gunnery practice flights, and on at least one occasion, at Risalpur on 21 February 1927, a major air display was arranged. On that day, and in front of a very enthusiastic audience, all six squadrons in India took part in demonstrations of airborne skills that included immaculate displays of formation flying and other aeronautical spectacles.

In 1928, six years after Salmond's report, the two extra squadrons he had recommended be added to the establishment finally began to arrive, which made it possible to reorganize the Royal Air Force in India into three Wings each of two squadrons. One of the other two squadrons was placed directly subordinate to No 1 India Group and the eighth was assigned to Air Headquarters. Even more important in the light of past parsimony, by May 1929 all the squadrons in India were at last up to full strength, and at the same time many of the long overdue support items also arrived. These included air crew oxygen equipment and aircraft WT and RT radios (used mainly to improve co-operation with units on the ground), and, in common with the rest of the Service world-wide, the first general issue of parachutes was now made to the air crews of the squadrons in India. (It is of passing interest that the first emergency use of a parachute from an RAF aircraft was not made until 17 June 1926, when a pilot officer, E. Pentland, abandoned his aircraft from an inverted spin.)

The comparative peace of the Frontier was to be broken yet again in late 1928, leading to a rather different reaction by the Royal Air Force. King Ammanulla of Afghanistan had returned from a seven-month-long tour of Europe, very impressed by the many features of modern Western life to which he had for the first time been introduced. His enthusiasm now led him to move towards the introduction of some of these new ideas into his own country, including advanced theories about the place of women in society. Such notions came as a deep shock to the very religious members of the community in Afghanistan and resistance to these innovations soon took the form of open rebellion against the King. Before long Kabul itself was under threat, and on 14 December 1928 the British Embassy, situated two and a half miles west of the city, found itself cut off and surrounded by rebel tribesmen. The minister, Sir Francis Humphrys, radioed to India asking for the Embassy to be evacuated of all the women and children who had taken refuge there.

In response, early on 23 December, five RAF aircraft, including a Vickers Victoria transport that had been hastily dispatched from Hinaidi in Iraq, arrived in Kabul and began ferrying out passengers and baggage. Three more transports joined the operation very shortly, and soon the RAF was flying out to safety not only the King, who abruptly abdicated under the pressure of events, but also his brother, Inayutullah Khan, who held the throne for only three days before joining the evacuation accompanied by his harem.

With the co-operation of the leader of the rebels, a certain Habibulla, the evacuation of the remaining British and other foreign nationals now continued, assisted by another five Victorias that had also been flown in from Iraq. Fighting in and around Kabul among the various Afghan factions competing for power had meanwhile spread and intensified, but not before the final RAF evacuation flights were completed, in freezing weather, on 25 February 1929.

During the operation 84 evacuation sorties had been flown, a large quantity of baggage had been brought out and 586 passengers had been brought to safety. For its time it had been a unique airlift operation, and it commanded a great deal of attention worldwide, not least because among those rescued were nationals of eleven different countries, not including those from Britain and British India. One practical result of the experience was that a number of Handley Page Clive transport aircraft arrived for the use of the RAF in India. These machines, together with the Handley Page Hinaidi already on strength, formed the basis of the Heavy Transport Flight in that country, though it was to be some years before India saw the use of transport aircraft to move troops and supplies as a matter of routine.

The next year saw another upsurge in operational activity on the Frontier. On 23 April 1930 a local anti-British political leader, Abdul Ghaffar Khan, held a huge and potentially rebellious rally in Peshawar, as a result of which he was arrested. This provoked savage rioting, and dissension quickly spread into the surrounding tribal areas. From mid-May onwards the RAF was in action against many of the centres of unrest that now emerged, and against a body of rebels which attempted to advance against Peshawar itself. These tribesmen were defeated and eventually driven back by a series of air attacks against them. Then in July there was another Mahsud uprising in Waziristan, and this led to daily air attacks on the tribesmen by the RAF for the next six weeks until most of the rebel groups broke up and made their way into the mountains, the last of them, the Badinzai Mahsuds, finally surrendering at the end of the month. Hostilities in other parts of the Frontier region continued, however, until the onset of winter, and took on a new intensity in March 1931 when Abdul Gaffar Khan was released from prison. The RAF was heavily involved in all these operations, which continued until early October 1931 when the main body of rebels finally accepted defeat and Khan himself was arrested and deported from the country.

This period on the Frontier was one that eventually saw the long overdue re-equipment of some of the

Above: Aircraft of Nos 5, 20, 28, and 39 Squadrons at Peshawar in 1930. (R. C. Sturtivant)

squadrons involved, four of which had been as late as early 1931 still operating Bristol F2Bs of First World War vintage. Nos 5, 31, and 28 Squadrons all received Wapitis by September 1931, and No 20 Squadron finally exchanged its F2Bs for Wapitis in February 1932 — fifteen years after the type had entered service. Two other squadrons, Nos 11 and 39, exchanged their Wapitis for Hawker Harts, faster machines and possessing a longer range though having about the same payload as the slightly older aircraft. Almost anything, however, would have been an improvement on the antiquated types with which these squadrons had, for over a decade, struggled to carry out their demanding roles.

Sporadic fighting in the Frontier region meanwhile continued against various recalcitrant tribes, with RAF units being engaged in virtually every action, particularly in March, July and September of 1932 and during a serious outbreak of trouble once more in Mohmand territory during August 1935, when the squadrons mounted attacks by night as well as by day as part of a wider campaign directed against dissident tribesmen. The contribution by the Royal Air Force in these operations tended to be restricted in scope by the customary hot-weather dispersal of some aircraft to the

hill stations, but it was also hampered by a tragic earthquake which struck the large cantonment of Quetta on 31 May 1935. Within a very few minutes all the RAF buildings except the aircraft hangars were demolished, all the aircraft except two belonging to the two resident squadrons, Nos 5 and 31, were rendered unserviceable and fifty-five RAF personnel and dependents were killed while hundreds of others were injured. In the city of Quetta itself, about half the population of 60,000 lost their lives. One notable survivor of this catastrophe was the then Wing Commander Slessor, and he and other RAF personnel did valuable work in rescuing casualties and repairing damage in the immediate aftermath of the earthquake; but it was to be many months before the RAF in India was able to claim that it was back to its full strength of eight operational squadrons.

In 1936 the relative peace of the north of India was again broken, this time by Mirza Ali Khan, also known as the Fakir of Ipi, who took advantage of local religious differences to launch a *jihad* against the British and their supporters. The resulting uprising was to last on and off right up until the outbreak of the Second World War. The first engagement against the Fakir took place in November 1936, when two Army columns supported by two squadrons of aircraft drove the Fakir and his supporters into the hills. He was there continually harassed by air attacks and by ground force action that gradually escalated in scale until, by the middle of April

1937, there were about 45,000 regular troops and militia forces deployed against him, while six RAF squadrons were based forward at Miranshah to mount intensive air operations in support. By mid-May the Fakir had been driven from his area of refuge, but he now moved between the various disaffected tribes, spreading anti-British propaganda and generally keeping the rebellion going, which he managed to do, though with diminishing effect, throughout the next two years and indeed for several years afterwards. The Fakir's long defiance of authority and his skill at evading justice not only proved to be a serious embarrassment to the authorities in India but also earned him a place in the 'paper exercises' of the RAF Staff Colleges, so that when in April 1938 he died, a suitable notice from his 'students' appeared in the obituary column of *The Times* in London.

VALUE OF COLONIAL POLICING

In retrospect, the era of air policing had been a testing time in the life of the new Service. But despite great difficulties posed by extremes of climate, by obsolete aircraft, by inadequate logistic support and by financial stringency throughout, the officers and men had carried out their task with conspicuous success within the limits that the task itself imposed. That caveat is important, for the concept of air policing was applied almost exclusively at the margins of the British Empire, notably on the North-West Frontier and in Aden. In Iraq and in Transjordan the RAF presence certainly held the line against possible Turkish reoccupation until local Governments could be established. But in Palestine, where, as it turned out, wider issues were at stake, air policing collapsed by 1936 and the concept had to be replaced by more conventional internal security methods.

There is also the moral aspect of the concept of air policing. A vocal minority of Members of Parliament consistently denounced the concept of using air bombardment against tribesmen and their families as unworthy of any civilized nation, and at least one senior RAF officer resigned his post in Iraq in protest at the practice. Salmond defended the concept robustly, offering in a letter to Trenchard arguments that he said should be used to justify the concept against its critics and pointing out that the air attacks were in any case directed against property rather than against people, and that the number of casualties caused in Iraq had been 'most remarkably small'.

To take issue with Salmond's justification of air policing 70 years later would be to apply contemporary values to a quite different era. But it must be said that if

Left: Wapitis of Nos 27 and 28 Squadrons at Kohat in the 1930s. (AHB)

better communications had existed in the 1920s, and had there been a wider public awareness of the often harsh effects of air policing, it might not have continued for as long as it did.

A final point to be made about these colonial campaigns is that they played no part in formulating RAF doctrine. It was clear at the time that they had no relevance to a conventional war, and the aircraft that were employed were quite obviously unsuited to any conflict with a first class military power. With the single exception of the Vildebeest aircraft, a machine introduced as a compromise air policing aircraft and torpedo bomber for the defence of Singapore, the design of aircraft intended for major warfare tended to diverge sharply from the obsolete craft that we have seen employed in roles overseas. What air policing did do was to contribute decisively to the independence of the RAF at a time when its continued existence was often in doubt; and the operations that were involved provided a training ground of sorts for a generation of servicemen, particularly the air crews, many of whom would gain high distinction in the years ahead.

Above, left and right:
The RAF lines at Quetta before and after the earthquake of 31 May 1935. (AHB)

Right: Harts of Nos 11 and 39 Squadrons over the Himalayas in the late 1930s. (AHB)

CHAPTER 3

TO BUILD AN AIR FORCE

Except for the very last years of peace, the story of the Royal Air Force between the two World Wars is one of repeated attempts by the other two Services to claim back their own aviation units, and, not least, it is a story of severe and continuous financial restraint. This last became a crippling inhibition on defence spending with the introduction in 1919, at the behest of the Treasury, of the 'Ten Year Rule'. In fact it was not a rule but a planning assumption. It presupposed that there would be no major war involving Britain for ten years. That was bad enough, but it was turned into a rolling assumption — in other words, it was carried forward each year. This meant that in 1932, when the 'Ten Year Rule' was finally abandoned, it was still being assumed for planning purposes that there would be no major war until 1942 at the earliest.

Nor was that all. As we will see later in this chapter, even with the end of the `Ten Year Rule', the British Government failed to take seriously the evidence from 1933 onwards of growing German militancy: only in 1935 do we see even the start of serious preparations to meet the escalating threat of war. Not without good reason, Sir Thomas Inskip, the Minister for the Co-ordination of Defence from March 1936 until January 1939, characterized the period from 1931 to 1935 as 'the years of the locust'. It was a reference to the Old Testament, Joel 2:25, where we read, 'And I will restore to you the years that the locust hath eaten, the cankerworm, and the caterpillar, and the palmerworm, my great army which I sent among you.' Those five years had been permeated by an almost wilful blindness to the dangers facing the country on the part of a British Government and an electorate intent on pursuing disarmament, and further eroded by severe economic crisis.

Trenchard's greatest contribution to the Royal Air Force during its very early days was simply that he kept the Service alive. But there were many other threads running through his ten-year term of office and through the decade that followed which explain the development of, and help to account for the state of, the RAF when

war finally came. These threads can be conveniently dealt with under four headings: first, the founding of RAF institutions; second, the need to keep the fledgeling Service in the public eye; third, contemporary concepts of air warfare and what this meant for equipment; and last, the structure of the RAF itself.

Trenchard's 1919 paper, *Permanent Organisation of the Royal Air Force*, contained numerous proposals, including the outlines of no fewer than five institutions that would become formative elements of the Service for many years ahead. One of these foundations was an RAF cadet college. There was as yet no such school at which future officers of the RAF could be trained, and to suggestions that RAF officers should be trained at the existing Navy and Army cadet establishments of Dartmouth, Sandhurst and Woolwich, Trenchard's reply

was that such an arrangement would prevent the RAF cadets from being taught to fly during their training because of the lack of aerodromes and suitable surrounding countryside. In fact he also feared that it could too easily lead to an erosion of the independence that he was so anxious to preserve. He would find a site for the Air Force to create its own cadet college.

CRANWELL

Although there exists today very little documentary evidence about the early days of flying at Cranwell, it seems that the Admiralty Aerodrome Selection Committee originally chose the location in late 1914 or early 1915 as one of a chain of air stations along the south and east coasts of the country. Its first role was as a training centre for the RNAS forward bases closer to the coast; but by April 1916 the station had expanded both in size and in function, and all RNAS officers and men, whether destined to serve with aeroplanes, kites, balloons or airships, would go to Cranwell to complete a finishing course and graduate. By late 1916 Cranwell was a fully established training base, and by the time of the Armistice in 1918 not only had it become a vital source of trained air crews and mechanics for the RNAS but it was also one of the largest aerodromes in the world. It was,

incidentally, in these very early days of the Royal Air Force that the Royal Family became closely involved with the new Service, and here a diversion from the Cranwell story is necessary.

Prince Albert (later the Duke of York, before becoming King George VI) had been trained at Osborne and Dartmouth for a career in the Royal Navy, and he served at sea during the First World War. But in January 1918 ill-health led to his being given a shore appointment with the RNAS at Cranwell, where he was appointed Officer in Charge of Boys and later OC No 4 Squadron. When the RNAS merged with the RFC to become the Royal Air Force, he automatically transferred. Prince Albert then remained in the Royal Air Force, moving in August 1918 from Cranwell to St Leonards-on-Sea, where he became involved in the programme of officer training. He gained his 'wings' on 31 July 1919 and received his permanent commission the next day. Though his service ceased on 1 July 1920, he remained on the Active List, being promoted in June 1921 to the rank of Group Captain, to Air Vice Marshal in June 1932, Air Chief Marshal in January 1936 and to Marshal of the Royal Air Force in December 1936 when he became monarch.

It was, incidentally, a Royal interest in flying later in the 1920s that contributed to the formation of what is

Left: Major-General the Rt. Hon. Sir Frederick Sykes, the first Chief of the Air Staff. (RAFM)

Right: Air Marshal Trenchard, Chief of the Air Staff, inspects the first entry of Aircraft Apprentices to pass out from Halton, 17 December 1924. (RAFM).

Left: Prince Albert, later Duke of York then King George VI, as a serving squadron leader with the RAF. (RAFM).

Right: King George V at his Silver Jubilee Review of the Royal Air Force at Mildenhall, 6 July 1935; the Prince of Wales and the Duke of Kent are in the centre of the photograph. The aircraft about to be inspected is a Handley Page Heyford, a type that entered service with No 99 Squadron in 1933. (RAFM)

absorbed into No 161 Squadron at Newmarket in February 1942. It did not re-form until May 1946.

That account of the origins of the Royal Flight has taken us somewhat ahead of the main story. To return to the origins of Cranwell itself, Trenchard saw the air station as an ideal site for the proposed college. He accepted that the college would have to be accommodated temporarily in the simple huts that had been erected during the war, but these would be replaced as soon as possible by permanent buildings. As to the cadets who would be trained there, because the Service would need a large number of officers in its junior ranks, and because there would be a comparative paucity of higher appointments, only 50 per cent of the RAF officer corps would be granted permanent commissions, and Cranwell would receive most of them. Others on permanent commissions would come in from universities or be commissioned from the ranks. For the rest of the

now the Queen's Flight, a subject that is also best mentioned here. Two Wapitis based at Northolt were being used from June 1928 onwards to fly VIP passengers, including Edward the Prince of Wales. The enthusiasm of the Prince led him to buy a Gipsy Moth of his own, followed by the purchase of other contemporary machines. In 1931, the aircraft belonging to the Prince were moved to Hendon, where they constituted what was known as the Royal Flight, though it was not at this time a Service unit. Aircraft that appeared on the Flight included a Vickers Viastra, a small twin-engine transport, and later on there were two de Havilland Rapides.

When the Prince succeeded to the throne in January 1936 he assumed the rank of Marshal of the Royal Air Force, and the Service agreed to fund the support his Flight required, with its machines, giving it official status as 'The King's Flight' of the Royal Air Force on 21 July 1936. Five months later, however, the King abdicated and the privately owned Rapide aircraft that made up the Flight by then were withdrawn. In May the following year the picture changed again when an RAF Airspeed Envoy of No 24 Squadron was allocated to the King's Flight, putting the unit at last on a permanent basis within the Royal Air Force. Its existence was interrupted three years later by the start of the Second World War, which saw the Flight disbanded and

officer corps, Trenchard introduced short-service commissions, another of his innovations.

The new college opened in the old huts on 5 February 1920 with 52 cadets, two of them sub-lieutenants of the Royal Navy, fifteen of them midshipmen transferred from Dartmouth and the remainder direct entrants from school. They would spend two years at Cranwell pursuing a very broad syllabus of military, academic and practical subjects, including in this latter category the assembly from stripped-down parts of a Phelan and Moore motorcycle, which the cadets could then use for their own recreational purposes. There seems to have been comparatively little flying practice, perhaps no more than sixty hours over the whole two-year course. For the privilege of sending a cadet to the College, parents were expected to pay a fee of up to £75 a year, a £35 entrance fee and another £30 at the start of the second year towards the cost of uniforms and books. This total of

Left: Three monarchs in Royal Air Force uniform: King George V, the Prince of Wales (later King Edward VIII) and the Duke of York (later King George VI). Mildenhall, July 1935. (AHB)

£215 represents £3,240 at 1992 prices, and for some parents at that time it was a considerable sacrifice.

In those early days the routine for the cadets was demanding and the conditions were spartan. Although the accommodation was by no means as wretched as the crowded huts at Halton, where serious epidemics of disease had broken out during the hard winter of 1917, it was clear that permanent buildings should be provided as soon as possible. It is, however, an interesting comment on the Service definition of the term 'temporary' that the last of the old huts at Cranwell was not taken out of use and demolished until June 1953, and even then one of these First World War structures survived as the College Post Office until as late as 1960. (At Halton meanwhile, the original workshops, built by German prisoners of war in 1916, are still in use today!)

Because of the extremes of financial stringency under which the Service laboured in the 1920s, the approval for a new College building, estimated to cost £299,550 (£6 million at 1992 prices), was not forthcoming until May 1929. In that same year the College was granted its arms (which, incidentally, are based on those of the de Cranewell family, discovered in the local church during the seventeenth century). By

September 1933 work had progressed far enough for the cadets to move into the still unfinished building, and the College was officially opened by HRH The Prince of Wales on 11 October 1934. The main building is much in the spirit of those days: it is basically built of red brick dressed with neo-Georgian features, and it occupies a frontage of over 800ft. The central dome, 140ft above the ground, is surmounted by a revolving light that can be seen for about twenty miles.

By 1936 the College had settled down with an average number of 133 cadets and by now the Avro 504Ks (1920–27) had been followed by Bristol Fighters (1920–30), DH9As (1920–30), Avro 504Ns (1927–33) and finally, before the outbreak of war, Avro Tutors (1933–39). The cadets from the entries of January and April 1939 found themselves on a much shortened course, and in July of that year the last of the pre-war formal inspections took place. These late pre-war cadet entries were to pay a high price over the following years: of the 65 young men who joined in 1939, no fewer than 39 would lose their lives during the course of the war. In September the Cadet College closed down for the duration of the war, the facilities then being taken over by No 17 Service Flying Training School, which soon became just one element in a greatly expanded training base at Cranwell, much along the lines of what had existed there during the First World War.

CENTRAL FLYING SCHOOL

To return to Trenchard's paper on the future of the Service, another feature that it contained was his support for a Central Flying School; this was something that in name at least was already seven years old when Trenchard drew up his scheme in 1919, but he now stressed its importance for the future of the Service. What he had in mind, however, was not merely the flying training school which the CFS had originally been; instead it was by now a school for flying instructors. The first such school had been opened at Gosport in August 1917, and it is not too much to say that this school and its successor turned the art of flying into a science. This was so important a development that it deserves a brief digression.

The idea of a school for flying instructors originated with Major Robert Smith-Barry while he was commanding a squadron in France towards the end of 1916. His enthusiasm led General John Salmond, who had been an instructor at CFS when Smith-Barry was a student there, to take up the notion of a special school, and Smith-Barry was brought home to command No 1

Above: An Avro 504K of No 4 Flying Training School. This aircraft was the RAF basic trainer from the formation of the Service until the mid-1920s. (AHB)

Reserve Squadron at Gosport to put his ideas into practice. Once there, he got rid of the old aircraft that were then in use at the school and brought in dual-control Avros, on which budding instructors were given twelve hours of dual flying and eighteen solo before advancing to Avro 504Js, to Blériot monoplanes and then to Bristol Scouts or Moranes.

The main principle on which the instruction of pilots was based was that of dual flying, and even after an *ab initio* pupil at a flying school had gone solo, half his instruction was given in a dual-control machine. A

Avro 504N

First flying in 1913, the Avro 504 entered service with the RFC as a reconnaissance and light bomber aircraft but by 1915 it had begun its long career as a training machine. The 504K version appeared in 1918 and the aircraft remained the standard trainer for the RAF until 1927, when the 504N was produced. This version served with four Flying Training Schools in the United Kingdom, and with No 4 FTS in Egypt as part of Trenchard's scheme to take advantage of the high weather factor in that country. The 504N was powered by one 160 or 180hp Armstrong Siddeley Lynx IV or a 215hp Lynx IVC. Its maximum speed was 100mph and it had an endurance of three hours and a service ceiling of 14,600ft. The Avro 504 remained in service for twenty years, until 1933 when it was replaced by the Avro Tutor.

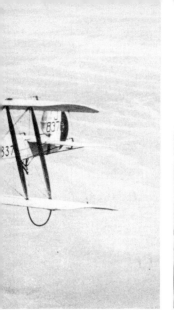

second principle was that of flying an aircraft to its limits. By thus exploring what is known as the flight envelope of an aircraft (that is, the boundaries of speed, height, wing loading and so on within which the aircraft can be flown), a pilot was taught to recover his aircraft from any difficulties encountered in the air, including a manoeuvre that was at the time still causing many fatalities — the spin.

In a spin, the lifting surfaces of the aircraft are stalled, i.e. they are providing very little lift, and the aircraft controls become largely ineffective. If the stall is allowed to develop fully, or if coarse rudder is applied, the aircraft will wing-over, pitch nose-down and begin to auto-rotate. This is a manoeuvre not unlike the gyrations of a falling sycamore seed. Instinct suggests that if the control column is now pulled back, the nose of the aircraft will rise and thus make recovery possible. In fact, moving the control column back actually increases the rate of rotation in the spin. The correct recovery, in a normal as opposed to an inverted spin, is to apply full rudder in the direction opposite to the spin rotation, and ease the control column forward. The spin then stops.

It was instruction in these and similar aspects of flying that made the Central Flying School so important a feature of the developing Service, and the new approach to flying was so successful that all the RAF flying schools adopted its principles. Gosport became the School of Special Flying, and a booklet, *Flying Instruction*, was produced which, although only 50 pages long, contained all the elements of instruction as well as the original version of what is still known as CFS 'patter', that is, the running commentary with which an instructor explains to the student what he is doing and why. In March 1920 the school moved from Gosport to Upavon,

where the principles laid down by Smith-Barry were combined with the traditions of the old Central Flying School.

HALTON

A third institution in Trenchard's 1919 plan for the future of the Royal Air Force was a training scheme for apprentices, and, like the Service itself, this had its origins in the Royal Flying Corps. During the early stages of the Great War, both the incoming stream of volunteers for the Army and the existing ranks of the Army had been combed for the many tradesmen that were needed to maintain the aircraft of the RFC.

As time went on, the demand for such men increased but fewer of them were available, so much so that the Corps was obliged to set up its own training schools in various parts of the country and to subsidize the training of mechanics at existing civilian technical schools. When this too proved to be inadequate, it ws decided to consolidate the training of mechanics at one large school, and the choice fell on the sizeable tented and hutted camp at Halton Park, one of the estates belonging to the Rothschild family. Another important measure was to expand a scheme under which 100 boys had already been taken in by the RFC for training as mechanics at Farnborough. By July 1917 there were 535 boys aged between 15½ and 17½ under training, and when in August and September the training for all fitters and riggers moved to Halton, these young trainees occupied what was called the Boys' Depot at West Camp. A very substantial expansion then followed, until by 1918 there was a staff 1,700 strong at Halton engaged in training 6,000 airmen, 2,000 boy mechanics and 2,000 women. These women trainees were, incidentally, members of the much larger Women's Auxiliary Army Corps, who were serving with the RFC. By the autumn of that same year, 10,500 women in the various WAAC companies of the RFC, together with women from the Women's Royal Naval Service and the Women's Legion, would be serving in the newly formed Women's Auxiliary Air Force, where they filled places in no fewer than 43 different trades.

Meanwhile the boy mechanics under training at Halton Park were the foundation on which Trenchard built his scheme to train apprentices for the Royal Air Force. In February 1920 the first group of 235 boys, selected by competitive examination, arrived at Cranwell, where training would take place until permanent facilities were constructed at Halton. By January 1922 the new buildings at Halton were ready, the term 'boy mechanic' was replaced by that of Aircraft Apprentice, and another of Trenchard's foundation stones was in place. So successful did the scheme prove to be that it was later expanded to include Administrative Apprentices, Boy Entrants (who were trained as mechanics rather than as fitters) and even, in much later years, Dental Technician Apprentices.

Not the least important question in this whole far-sighted plan for the future was that of a staff college for the Royal Air Force. Trenchard originally proposed that one should be opened at Halton in the house that had, until his death, been the seat of Alfred Rothschild, but this would have caused delay and extra expense, so Andover was chosen instead. The Staff College opened there in disused war-time huts on 4 April 1922. Twenty RAF officers were taken in annually for a one-year course, with eight or ten other students being drawn from the Royal Navy, the Army, the Indian Army and the Dominions.

AUXILIARY AIR FORCE

Another of Trenchard's clear-sighted proposals was that for the creation of an air force reserve, to be raised on a territorial basis. At a time of very heavy pressure on Government finance, a cadre of this kind would, he saw, be essential in preserving any kind of expertise for eventual expansion. The Paper gave no details of what was planned, but in fact this was to be the basis of the

Vickers Vimy

As the First World War progressed, more capable bombers such as the DH10 were produced, an aircraft with twice the bomb-load of the DH9, though these machines entered service only in the final months of the conflict. The Vickers Vimy was another of the newer bombers, designed to be able to reach Berlin. In the event the Vimy was too late to take part in operations, but it became the main heavy bomber for the Royal Air Force in the years that followed. It was powered by two Rolls-Royce Eagle VIII engines, which gave the aircraft a top speed of 100mph at 6,500ft. It carried a bomb load of 2,476lb, it had a range of about 900 miles and its defensive armament was made up of twin Lewis guns in the nose and midship positions. The type was finally withdrawn in January 1929, from No 502 (Reserve) Squadron.

Auxiliary Air Force. Although provision had been made for an Air Force Reserve and Auxiliary Air Force in the Air Force Constitution Act of 1917, the topic had not been pursued. There had been, first of all, a natural post-war apathy towards military innovation of any kind — people were anxious to return to a peacetime routine — but there had also been outright opposition to the notion that air crew, and especially pilots, could achieve and retain proficiency in the air as a part-time and mainly weekend activity. Amid continuing ministerial doubts about the proposal, a parliamentary Bill authorizing the formation of RAF reserve units was passed in 1922, but it was to be another two years before it became law. At last, in 1924 provision was made under the Auxiliary Air Force and Air Force Reserve Act to raise six Auxiliary squadrons and seven Special Reserve squadrons, the eventual aim being a force of twenty Auxiliary squadrons all told. Of the first seven Special Reserve Squadrons, four were to be in the single-engine bomber role and the other three would be equipped with twin-engine bombers. They would all be commanded by a regular officer and given a nucleus of regular SNCOs and airmen to support the two-thirds or so of the unit strength drawn from reservists living nearby. The Auxiliary Air Force was to be given a different style. These units were to be raised and maintained by County Territorial associations and manned by local personnel with only a small cadre of regulars as permanent staff; the commanding officers would themselves be Auxiliaries.

May 1925 saw the formation of the first of these squadrons, No 502 (Ulster) Squadron of the Special Reserve, which was initially equipped with two Vickers Vimy bombers. By October of that year four of the new

Auxiliary Air Force squadrons had also been raised, all of them flying a mixture of DH9As, Avro 504Ks and Avro 504Ns. Another four AAF squadrons were to follow by 1930, and three more were raised in 1936 as part of the wider air rearmament programme, all of them units in the '600' series. The squadrons in the '500' series, i.e., those of the Special Reserve, went through a less straightforward development, but the eventual outcome was that by the outbreak of war in 1939 there were 21 Auxiliary Air Force squadrons in existence, Nos 600 to 605, 607 to 616 and 500 to 504.

In an era when flying was a growing sport and air displays a popular form of public entertainment, the reserve units had little difficulty in attracting recruits. Many squadrons ran an active social programme, and some took on the characteristics of a club; indeed the members of No 601 Squadron would claim that their unit was actually founded not at RAF Northolt but at White's Club in St James's. If they were clubs, then they were often clubs with a membership of high social standing. For example, Lord Edmond Grosvenor was the first commanding officer of No 601 Squadron, and its distinguished membership included Sir Philip Sassoon, later to become Under-Secretary of State for Air. The Marquis of Clydesdale flew with No 602, Lord Willoughby de Broke with 605 and Viscount Runciman with No 607.

But beyond the social activity centred on them, these squadrons honed their flying skills and trained for war. Apart from the routine of weekend flying, regular summer camps were held on major RAF airfields, with Auxiliary Air Force and Special Reserve Squadrons taking part in the national Air Exercises of those pre-war years. Although the aircraft of the reserve squadrons were usually obsolescent or even obsolete and the war-fighting equipment far from adequate, the personnel at least were of the highest standard and they lacked nothing in dedication or enthusiasm.

Once embodied into the regular Air Force, as all units of the AAF were between September 1938 and the summer of 1939, then the squadrons lost their special status and became gradually merged into the wartime pattern of frequent postings between units, whether regular or reserve. Nevertheless, and before leaving the events of the Second World War to later chapters of this book, it is worth recording here that the squadrons of the AAF played a most significant part in virtually all the campaigns of that six-year conflict, and particularly in the air warfare of the first year or so when the squadrons retained much of their pre-war identity. Perhaps the most telling tribute to their efforts is the fact that of the 80 fighter squadrons that took part in the Battle of Britain, no fewer than fourteen were from the Auxiliary Air Force.

One institution that does not appear in Trenchard's paper, though he does refer to officer entry through the universities, is that of the University Air Squadrons. The squadrons at Cambridge and Oxford were formed in October 1925, and others followed in later years. The first units took the form of three Flights, one a Research

Right: An Avro Tutor of Oxford University Air Squadron. This aircraft became the standard trainer for all Flying Training Schools, starting in 1933. It was still in service in 1939. (AHB)

Left: The Royal Air Force
Central Band at its first
engagement. (AHB)

Flight, one a Technical Instruction Flight and the third dealing with flying, military studies and military duties. Flying was carried out on a handful of aircraft at first; in the case of Cambridge UAS, for example, the establishment comprised one Bristol Fighter and two Avro 504Ks. One of the odd features of the early days of these squadrons was that they had little real military character. The student members were not expected to hold any rank in the RAF, while as to uniform, if it can be so called, a dark blue blazer was worn bearing the RAF eagle crest on the breast pocket, set off with the squadron tie. This arrangement continued right up to the outbreak of war in 1939, when the UASs closed down. They were quickly reopened, however, in October of the following year, though with the changed role of pre-entry training units, with no flying at all provided. During the Second World War the former members of the various University Air Squadrons served with very great distinction, the fact that no fewer than four of them won the Victoria Cross perhaps testifying most eloquently to the contribution made by these young men.

PROMOTING THE SERVICE

In a field that was little connected with aerial warfare, and yet had an important place in Trenchard's schemes for keeping the Service in the public eye, were the Bands of the Royal Air Force. There had been many unofficial and part-time bands in the Royal Flying Corps from the earliest days, but affairs were put on to a regular basis in the new Service with the creation on 2 July 1918 of the Royal Air Force School of Music, based first at Hampstead and then at Uxbridge. The Central Band was

formed on 1 April 1920 and it quickly gained a high reputation both at home and in concerts abroad. Distinctive music was composed for the Service, including the well-known piece by Sir Walter Davies and Sir George Dyson, the 'Royal Air Force March Past', often erroneously called the 'RAF March'. Two other pieces written for ceremonial parades, this time by Wing Commander Sims, later joined the repertoire. One is the 'General Salute', the other is the 'Advance in Review Order', while a third item, 'Point of War', was borrowed from the British Army. Beyond these ceremonial pieces there are still in occasional use the Authorized Trumpet Calls for the Royal Air Force, which include not only the 'RAF Call' itself, but forty other calls by which camp life between 'Reveille' and 'Lights Out' was for many years regulated.

As another important means of publicizing his new Service in an age when there was such widespread enthusiasm for flying as a sport, Trenchard saw the attractions of air displays. The main one for the RAF was arranged to take place at Hendon, in the 1920s a grass airfield on the outskirts of north London. Before the First World War, Claude Grahame-White had held flying displays there and it had become one of the several RFC and then RAF airfields near the capital. It was on this airfield that the first so-called RAF Tournament was held on 3 July 1920, under the supervision of Sir John Salmond.

On that sunny day, a crowd estimated at 60,000 strong (quite apart from the many thousands who watched from outside the airfield) flocked in to witness a remarkable display of formation flying, aerobatics and items such as mock bombing attacks. It was a day of

Right: Hendon in 1932, showing the targets built for 'attack' by RAF aircraft. (AHB)

Below: Hendon on 25 June 1932, showing the 'New Types Park', the forerunner of the later Farnborough Air Displays. (AHB)

flying that drew high praise even from those elements of the Press opposed to the idea of an independent Air Force. Later known as the RAF Pageant and then as the RAF Display, the Tournament was held on the first Saturday in June of each year until 1937, by which time the airfield at Hendon was too small to accept all of the more modern aircraft types that should have taken part. As the years went by, the programme for the day was widened and modernized, so that parachute descents became common, formation flying was performed to musical accompaniment or with aircraft's wing tips tied

together, races were held and coloured smoke was used from 1929 onwards so that the crowd could better follow the aerial manoeuvres.

In the 1920 and 1921 displays there had been a set-piece attack which drew its inspiration from the battlefields of Flanders; but in 1922 a 'native fort', 100ft high and made out of scrap aircraft mainplanes, became the target for attack. By 1927 this event had grown to a display involving the rescue of women and children from hostile natives, involving supply-dropping by parachute and the air transport of troops; but by the time of the

display in 1930 the use of air power against tribesmen was becoming a more sensitive topic, and in that year the air assault was made against 'pirates'! One feature that had been introduced with the first Tournament was the 'New Types Park', where the latest aircraft were put on show. From 1932 onwards the Park was left in place after the RAF show until the following Monday, when it was used by the Society of British Aircraft Constructors as their showpiece for important guests and prospective purchasers. This was the origin of the later Farnborough Air Displays.

A more practical field of peacetime flying activity for the Royal Air Force during those difficult inter-war years was that of opening up and then operating air mail routes. This responsibility began with a request by the Foreign Office in November 1918 for the Air Ministry to organize a twice-daily messenger service by aeroplane from London to Paris, where the British delegation to the peace talks would be based. As a result, the Communications Squadron was formed at Hendon, equipped with DH4s, Avro 504s and a handful of other machines for the use of Air Ministry staff officers. As the demand for freight space and passenger seats grew, so did the unit, until by the summer of 1919 it was a Wing, No 86, holding no fewer than 36 machines, some of them converted Handley Page O/400 bombers, based at Kenley. This service to the Continent was later extended

to include mail runs to the headquarters of the Armistice Commission at Spa in the Ardennes, and to the British military headquarters in Cologne. Despite the lack of reliable navigation aids, the often adverse weather and the problems of operating aircraft that were less than robust, the service was a considerable success. It was brought to an end only when the reduced size of the British delegations and staffs on the Continent made it possible to transfer the work to civil operators during the late summer of 1919.

Beyond Europe, other air routes were being opened up. The first through-flights to India had been made in December 1918 by a Handley Page V/1500, a type that had been constructed with the bombing of Berlin in mind. This was the beginning of long-range route flying by the Royal Air Force across many challenging areas of the world, but one particular stretch of terrain became noteworthy among all the other sectors that were pioneered during these early years — the link between Cairo and Baghdad. The route covered about 860 miles, of which the 540 beyond Amman were over extremely inhospitable desert terrain. It was not the sand desert of fiction, but an arid rock plateau lying about 2,000ft above sea level and rising to over 3,000ft before gradually falling to the valley of the Euphrates. If worthwhile loads were to be carried by the aircraft of the day, intermediate refuelling stops along the route would be needed, and in the absence both of navigation aids and of easily recognized features on the ground, some means of marking the route was needed. A plan was therefore drawn up to dispatch vehicle convoys to survey the route, starting simultaneously from Amman and Baghdad and working towards each other. The party from Amman would mark out suitable landing grounds every 20 miles or so, giving them letters from A to R (omitting I and Q). Meanwhile the Baghdad party would do the same in a westerly direction, giving their strips Roman numerals from I to XI. (Apart from the official landing strips, certain others later came to embellish the route, strips with names such as Loui's Lapse, Titche's Tumble and Wo's Wallop, a telling commentary on the hazards of this operation!) In May 1921 the two convoys set out, supported by DH9As of Nos 30, 47 and 70 Squadrons, which carried supplies for the surveyors. The landing fields were at first marked out using whitewash and painted petrol tins; but when these methods did not provide the necessary conspicuousness, the survey parties marked the perimeters of the strips by using the tracks of vehicles, which, the DH9A pilots had found, stood out well against the floor of the desert. Later on, a plough was used to mark with its furrow the line of the most difficult section of the route, that between Baghdad and Landing Ground 'R', which lay on the borders of Transjordan and Mesopotamia.

The desert route opened in June 1921, operations during the first twelve months being conducted by DH9As and converted DH10 bombers. Vickers Vimys and then Vernons took over the route in 1922. The ugly Vernon — the first RAF transport aircraft actually designed for that role — was based on the Vimy bomber, and its capacious fuselage could hold twelve passengers, though in some discomfort. Despite its lumbering

Vickers Vernon

This twelve-seat passenger transport was the first RAF aircraft built specifically for troop-carrying. Its design was based on the Vimy bomber of 1917, and the first Vernon joined No 45 Squadron at Hinaidi in 1922. It was not a machine remarkable for its performance: the two Napier Lion II engines gave the aircraft a cruising speed of 80mph, and it could carry its two crew and twelve passengers over a range of 320 miles.

performance, particularly with the original Rolls-Royce Eagle engines which gave a cruising speed of only 70mph or so, the aircraft did valuable work on the route for almost two years until more powerful Napier Lion engines could be fitted. Vickers Victorias replaced the Vernons during 1927, aircraft not unlike their predecessors but now able to carry twenty passengers, and these operations continued until January 1927 when the Cairo to Baghdad route was absorbed by Imperial Airways flying DH Hercules right through to India on scheduled services.

A third arena in which during the inter-war years the Royal Air Force sought both to shine in public and to hone its operating skills was that of record-making flights. From 1919 onwards, various individual flights were made around the countries of the Mediterranean, but really long-distance attempts began in the mid-1920s when, for example, three DH9As flew from Cairo to Kano in Nigeria and back in October 1925, to be followed in March of the succeeding year by an epic flight from Cairo to Cape Town and back made by four Fairey IIIDs. This latter pioneering effort was successfully carried out between 1 March and 27 May,

Above left: The 'Service Types Park' at Hendon on 25 June 1932, showing 125 aircraft of the Royal Air Force drawn up. (AHB)

Right: The DH9A, which entered service in the last months of the First World War, was the only home-based bomber in the early 1920s. Overseas, it equipped squadrons in Iraq, Aden, Palestine, Egypt and India. (AHB)

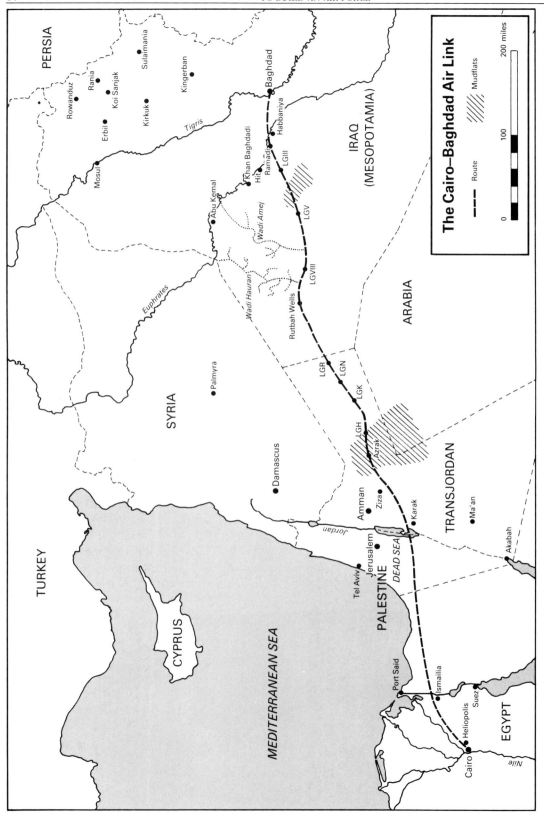

The Cairo–Baghdad Air Link

Right: Supermarine
Southamptons over Cowes,
Isle of Wight. Aircraft of this
type made many
long-distance formation
flights during the 1920s.
(RAFM).

Below: Air Marshal Sir John
Salmond with Flt Lts
Nicholetts and Gayford, in
front of the Fairey
Monoplane in which the two
latter broke the world
long-distance record with a
flight from Cranwell to
Walvis Bay in February
1933. (AHB)

despite the almost total lack of facilities or aids along the route, and it was then capped by flying back to Lee-on-Solent, having substituted floats for the aircraft's wheels in Egypt — a total journey of some 14,000 miles.

In 1927, in another famous episode, four Southampton flying boats of the Far East Flight travelled out to Singapore via India, and then went on to Hong Kong and Australia before returning to Singapore, where they remained to form No 205 Squadron at that base in

January 1929. Other long-range efforts followed during 1929, one of them ending in a fatal crash in Tunisia during a flight to South Africa, and then in February 1933 the world non-stop long-distance record was broken by Squadron Leader Gayford and Flight Lieutenant Nicholetts who flew a specially designed and purchased Fairey Long-Range Monoplane from Cranwell to Walvis Bay in South-West Africa, having covered 5,309 miles in 57 hours 25 minutes.

The Schneider Trophy races will be mentioned later in this chapter, but apart from speed and long-range records to be broken there were also altitude records. Because of the special equipment that would be necessary to survive at very high altitudes, it is perhaps not surprising that attempts at height records were somewhat less prominent than efforts in other dimensions, but nonetheless in September 1936 Squadron Leader F. R. D. Swan, flying a specially built Bristol 138 monoplane, set a world record of 49,967ft and nine months later Flight Lieutenant M. J. Adam, flying the same aircraft, raised the record to a remarkable 53,937ft.

THE WARTIME ROLE OF THE AIR FORCE

At the same time as the Royal Air Force was seeking a high profile in record-breaking and other activities, the Air Staff was devoting its efforts to the far more serious business of how the Service intended to conduct operations of war. In the years after the Armistice, quite separate theories on the role of air forces had been developed by the major military powers. In France and Germany, for example concern with land frontiers during the later inter-war years led to an emphasis on tactical air forces. The major maritime nations, on the other hand, tended to see air power as an instrument of blockade. But there were also more radical views, holding that air forces should have an independent or strategic function.

The most extreme of these theories was that put forward by the Italian Air Force General Giulio Douhet, who, in a book that was little noted outside Italy at the time, suggested that an independent air force should have two roles. The first was to seize command of the air, that is, make it possible to fly against the enemy while depriving him of the ability to do likewise. And then, said Douhet, in a second and quite separate phase of the air war, an air force should deliver such a massive air assault on the enemy's vital centres that he would be compelled to submit. Armies and navies would be rendered obsolete. At about the same time, Brigadier General 'Billy' Mitchell, in the United States, was advocating the centralized control of an independent air arm, with all its capabilities being placed under autonomous command — a command that would not only embrace strategic bombardment but also include all the means with which to dominate surface warfare.

Air doctrine in Britain emerged along rather different lines. One of its origins is to be found in a paper by Major-General Sir Frederick Sykes, the then Chief of the Air Staff, written in early 1919 and entitled *Review of the Air Situation*. Together with other proposals for the future size and roles of the Air Force, Sykes put forward the idea of 'strategic interception' for the Royal Air Force. He believed that while the Army and the Navy forced the enemy into relying on the consumption of massive war resources, the Air Force should deprive him of that support by destroying the sources from which it came, and by cutting the communications with which he would move his war-fighting resources up to the areas of combat. Bombers, said Sykes and his supporters, could exploit the vastness of the air to avoid any confrontation with opposing defences, striking instead directly at the key enemy targets and at the morale of his civilian population. These were bold assertions, and although it is the case that air defences of that time were still at a very rudimentary stage of development, it seems not to have been grasped by the authors of this concept that the importance of these centres would be equally obvious to

the enemy, and that he could be expected eventually to deploy effective air defences to protect them.

This view that air power on its own could not defeat an enemy was also held by Trenchard. He believed that the Air Force would need to be engaged as part of an integrated land, sea and air strategy, with air power being applied when and where it was required, including the task of assisting the Army and the Navy in their roles should that prove necessary. The emphasis was to be firmly on the offensive use of the air, an approach that would be relied upon to throw the enemy on to the defensive and to keep him there. It would not be necessary, according to this view, directly to attack the enemy air defences. These could be avoided; and if it did prove necessary to attack some of the opposing defence resources as part of the overall strategy, then that would be a bonus. In Trenchard's own words, taken from his Minute to his fellow Chiefs of Staff in 1929, 'intense air fighting will be inevitable [i.e. during an air offensive], but it will not take the form of a series of battles between opposing air forces to gain supremacy as a first step before the victor proceeds to attack the other objectives...The gaining of air superiority will be incidental to this main direct offensive upon the enemy's vital centres and simultaneous with it.' This emphasis on the primacy of the offence in air operations was to be was maintained by the Royal Air Force right through the 1920s and for all but the last eighteen months of the 1930s.

In 1933 Hitler became Chancellor of Germany, and he soon embarked on an extensive rearmament programme, which included the creation of a powerful air force — a move that caused particular alarm in Britain. By the late 1930s there were three reasons for what turned out to be grossly exaggerated fears in Britain about the likely potential of the new and growing

Right: The remarkably advanced Fairey Fox two-seat day bomber of 1925. Because of financial pressures, only twenty-eight of these machines were built, and only one squadron, No 12, was equipped with them. (AHB)

Below left: Cockpit instruments of a Hawker Fury I, an aircraft introduced in 1931. The thumb-operated levers on the control column are the firing buttons for the twin Vickers .303 machine guns mounted over the forward fuselage. (AHB)

German Air Force. First, memories were fresh of the relative ease with which London and other cities had been bombed during the First World War. Second, Press and film reporting of contemporary bombing atrocities in China from July 1937 onwards had caused anxiety, as had similar events closer to home during the Spanish Civil War, particularly the air attack on Guernica on 27 April 1937. Third, official predictions of the number of casualties that might be suffered if an assault from the air were to be launched against cities and towns in Britain were sobering. In these predictions, extrapolations had been made from `worst-case' and sometimes isolated incidents during the First World War, so that by 1937 the Home Defence Committee of the Committee for Imperial Defence, using the statistics from the First World War, was calculating that the German Air Force might be capable of a maximum effort of 3,500 tons of bombs dropped per day by 1939, and that this would cause up to 58,000 deaths and 116,000 hospital cases in each 24 hours. In fact, during the whole of the first year of the war, Britain suffered only 257 fatalities and 441 hospital cases. To be sure, casualties increased as the air war developed; but even so the total number of British civilians killed in air raids during the whole six years of war amounted to 60,595, not all that much higher than the forecast for a single day.

EXPANSION

In the hope of persuading Germany not to rearm, particularly in terms of the much-feared bomber, and to rely instead upon diplomacy to redress German grievances over the Treaty of Versailles, the British Government decided to build up the front-line strength of the RAF. It was not intended to be an arms race, nor even at first was it a purely military deterrent to any possible German attack on Britain: it was as much a kind of diplomatic deterrent to German rearmament as anything else. But when it became clear that Hitler would not be deflected, then the emphasis was indeed put on deterring him by military strength in the air from using his expanding air force against Britain. Although, as we have seen, the institutional foundations for a permanent Air Force had been successfully laid in the decade after the First World War, the severe lack of resources with which to build an effective air arm meant that the front line of the Service paid a heavy price in terms of its outmoded equipment. By the mid-1930s there was a very great deal of lost ground to be made up, and even now the emphasis would be on numerical parity with Germany rather than on very high quality aircraft.

The result of the realization that a new threat to national security was emerging was that the first of eight pre-war air rearmament schemes, Scheme A, was drawn up and approved by the Cabinet in July 1934. This was a plan to build by 1939 a front line of aircraft roughly equal to the number of aircraft that the Luftwaffe was expected to hold by that time. The Scheme laid down a total force of 138 squadrons with 1,544 aircraft; 41 squadrons were to be equipped with bombers and 28 would be fighter units. Some extra squadrons would be provided for the Fleet Air Arm, and very limited reinforcements would sent to Singapore in response to growing Japanese truculence in the Far East. Because the intention was simply at first to produce a convincing number of aircraft in the front line at all costs, the obvious need for reserves had to take second place.

Furthermore, because the Air Staff stressed the primacy of attack, the weight of emphasis in the Scheme was on bombers —even though 25 of the 41 bomber squadrons were equipped with light bombers. This was because it would clearly be less demanding on scarce resources to produce light rather than heavy machines, and since the intention was as much to deter further German rearmament as it was to develop the capability to attack that country, the short range of the contemporary light bombers was not thought to be very significant.

Scheme A was, however, to suffer an early and serious set-back when, in March 1935, Hitler announced to the Foreign Secretary, Sir John Simon, that he had already reached parity in the air with Britain, and that the Luftwaffe, formed just one month earlier with 1,888 aircraft of all types, was programmed to expand even further. This very startling news led to a hasty revision of the earlier plan, and to the birth in May 1935 of Scheme C, which envisaged the production by April 1937 of a front line of the same size that Germany was expected to field by that date. Again the emphasis was on bombers, 360 of which were to be light bombers. Because there was little else available to enter production at the rate required, the aircraft chosen to meet this demand was the Hawker Hind, a machine with an ancestry going back to the First World War. It was destined to equip thirty squadrons from 1935 onwards before more advanced designs such as the Blenheim medium bomber and the Battle light bomber could enter service. The last Hind was built as late as September 1938, and the type still equipped some squadrons of the Auxiliary Air Force until 1939.

Meanwhile, events in Europe were moving more quickly, and Scheme C was very soon to be overtaken. On 6 March 1936 Hitler remilitarized the Rhineland, greatly exacerbating an international tension that was already high as the result both of Italian aggression against Abyssinia in 1935 and of Japanese belligerence in Manchuria and then the fighting that followed in China from 1937 onwards. In this atmosphere, Scheme C was replaced by Scheme F (the missing letters in the sequence of schemes were plans that were never put forward), and the latter was endorsed by the Cabinet in February 1936.

Two factors gave Scheme F a quite different emphasis from that seen in Scheme C. First, it was by now fully appreciated that in order to attack the most obvious future opponent, Germany, aircraft such as the Hind, with its range of only 430 miles, would have to be stationed on the continent of Europe. But this implied the far from popular notion that a British Expeditionary Force would again be sent to France; and this in turn implied that a dedicated air force would be sent to work with it. Such a diversion from the commitment by the Royal Air Force to strategic interception was a very unwelcome prospect.

The second factor was the influence of the Abyssinian Crisis of 1935. The Italian aggression had caused the possibility to be discussed of attacking targets in the industrial north of Italy, and it was immediately clear that the light bombers of the RAF could not reach northern Italy even from bases in the south of France, let alone from the nearest permanent base in Malta. At this point personalities also took a hand in events. In late 1935 Group Captain (later Air Chief Marshal Sir Arthur) Harris took over the key post of Deputy Director of Air Plans. He reported direct to the Chief of Air Staff, and he was able to exercise considerable influence on decisions concerning the future of the Service. Harris pressed for a larger front line, and in particular for heavier bombers with which to equip it. The outcome was the important decision of the Air Council on 6 February 1936 to switch the emphasis in future procurement plans from light to medium bombers. At the same time it was decided to increase squadron establishments from twelve to eighteen aircraft, with the combined result that a bomber squadron would now be able to deliver 7½ tons of bombs instead of the earlier limit of 2½ tons. The aircraft specification settled upon for the medium bomber was B9/32, which had actually been drawn up in September 1932. But the delay caused by the cumbersome process of selecting aircraft from the designs put forward, together with a chronic shortage of funds, meant that the aircraft to this specification (upgraded by Specifications 29/36 and 30/36 of 1936), which became the Handley Page Hampden and the Vickers Wellington, did not actually enter service until mid-1938.

The first aim of the new Scheme was again parity with Germany, but this time with a completion date of March 1939. Scheme F turned out to be the only one of these pre-war plans that was completed, and it is therefore worth examining in some detail. The scheme differed from all the earlier ones in several important ways. First, it was a recognition that the attempt to deter German rearmament had failed. Mere numbers meant little, and it was now vital to deploy into the front line aircraft that could actually wage war. It was true that several hundred light bombers such as the Hawker Hart and the Hind were carried over from earlier programmes, but although no fewer than 360 of these biplanes had

Hawker Hind

Bomber performance took a considerable step forward in the Royal Air Force with the advent in 1925 of the Fairey Fox, a machine with a top speed of 156mph, though only one squadron, No 12, was equipped with these aircraft. In 1930 the achievements of the Fox were overtaken by the 184mph performance of the Hawker Hart; but within two years even more ambitious aircraft such as the Wellington were being planned, and it was decided to fill the gap until more effective bombers could be brought into service with an interim machine; this was the Hawker Hind. It was to be the last biplane light bomber in the RAF. Hinds joined No 21 Squadron in December 1935 and the type remained in the front line until mid-1939. It was powered by a fully supercharged 660hp Rolls-Royce Kestrel V engine, giving a top speed of 186mph. Armed with a Vickers gun forward and a Lewis aft, it carried a bomb load of 500lb.

appeared in Scheme C, there were none at all in Scheme F. There were to be 48 medium bomber squadrons (350 aircraft) and twenty medium/heavy squadrons (240 aircraft), a shift that can be seen as a compromise between the political imperative still to field high numbers in the front line and the military requirement to deploy an effective striking force. In the longer term it can thus also be seen as a move towards really heavy bombers, a move that was to be accelerated with the adoption, also in 1936, of Specifications B12/36 and P13/36, which would eventually lead, respectively, to the Short Stirling, the first four-engine bomber to enter

service with the Royal Air Force, and to the Halifax and Manchester bombers, the latter being the direct forerunner of the Lancaster.

The second major change running through Scheme F was its emphasis on reserves. It was planned that, by 1941, a total aircraft reserve of 225 per cent of the front-line strength would be held, 75 per cent of it either with squadrons or in the supporting engineering units. As to personnel, it was by now clear that the reserves of the Auxiliary Air Force would not on their own meet the likely needs of war, and the Royal Air Force Volunteer Reserve was therefore formed. This differed from the Auxiliaries because it was a general reserve for the whole of the Service; it was not formed into units as were the Auxiliaries, and it was thus the first step towards the citizens' air force that would prove to be essential during the coming conflict.

Finally, there were the airfields and other facilities to be considered. In 1934 there had been only 52 airfields in Britain, but another seven were built in 1934–35, eight the next year and six the following year, and a total of 89 were available by 1938 (another 389 would be built between 1939 and 1945). Even by the outbreak of war, however, there were still only nine airfields in the country with tarmac runways, and a massive effort would eventually be needed in order to operate the more modern and heavier aircraft that would be deployed.

Meanwhile, estimates of the strength of the Luftwaffe and of its war potential continued to rise, and after only nine months the Air Staff was obliged to replace Scheme F by yet another plan to outbid the

Right: A Hawker Hind of No 44 Squadron. This general-purpose bomber was a development of the Hart, and during the rearmament programme beginning in 1934 it helped to fill an important gap in the front line of the RAF until Blenheims and Battles could be built to replace it. (AHB)

German Air Force, Scheme H. This latest scheme, in its original form dated November 1936, was a plan to achieve parity with the Luftwaffe in March 1939 by deploying a peacetime front-line strength of 1,256 bombers by that date, with a total bomber strength of 1,631 machines. During all this time, the cost of this whole process of rearmament continued to rise, so that Scheme H was estimated at £664 million (almost £17 billion in 1992 terms) between 1937 and 1940, and another £90 million (£2.3 billion) each year thereafter to maintain.

Nor was that all: the scheme called for 9,700 pilots and 73,700 NCOs and airmen as well as for 23,500 civilians in support, very many of them with the same skills that were by now so much in demand in the civilian sector itself as aeronautical firms tried to increase their workforce to manufacture the numbers of aircraft required. Before Scheme H was under way, however, further intelligence suggested that German aircraft production rates were even higher than feared, and in December 1937 Scheme J went before the Cabinet, calling this time for a force mainly of bombers, 896 heavy and 546 medium, but all of them capable of reaching targets in Germany from bases in Britain. Only 532 fighters, of which about a quarter of those were for co-operation with the Army, were planned.

One of the expedients adopted at this stage by the Air Staff to build up the front line of the Service as quickly as possible was to scale down the planned expansion of the Fleet Air Arm, because, it was argued, the aircraft concerned could easily switch from their home defence duties to roles in support of the Fleet. Not unnaturally, this assertion revived the old quarrel about an independent air arm for the Fleet, and Sir Thomas Inskip adjudicated in the dispute. This led to the Inskip Award, discussed earlier. But now the strain on national resources, combined with the realization that the pursuit of parity had failed to halt German air rearmament, led during the second half of 1937 to a Treasury Review of Defence Expenditure, which in turn caused a complete reappraisal of British overseas and defence policy to be undertaken. This review also was carried out by Sir Thomas Inskip, and it was submitted to the Cabinet on 15 December 1937. The Air Staff meanwhile were maintaining their view that bombers should continue to be given priority in yet another revision of their plans, Scheme K dated January 1938, which took account of the growing concern over costs by reducing expenditure on reserves. It was to be the last Scheme based on the notion that the best defence in the air was attack, and it was rejected by the Cabinet in favour of a new order of priorities introduced by Inskip.

Inskip's review, his Interim Report on Defence Expenditure and his Aide-Memoire to the Secretary of State for Air dated 9 December 1937 mark the start of a fundamental change in Britain's pre-war preparations for war in the air. Inskip held the view that Britain did not need to have anything like the same number of long-range bombers as did Germany, and he proposed that many of them could be replaced by cheaper light and medium bombers. (In fact, the early stages of the war were to find the Royal Air Force with too many light bombers, most of them obsolescent and of very little military value.) But Inskip also argued that the role of the Royal Air Force should not be to deliver an early 'knock-out blow', 'but to prevent the Germans from knocking us out', as he succinctly put it.

This was of course a complete reversal of the priorities on which the Air Staff had insisted right from the formation of the Royal Air Force. From now on, the emphasis would be on fighter production. Bomber strength would have to be conserved for a second phase of the coming war, a phase in which the massive resources of Britain and her Empire would enable her to overcome what was thought to be the comparatively modest industrial strength of Germany. No account seems to have been taken of the possibility that Germany might have all the resources of continental Europe at her disposal, and little thought was given to the prospect of a major and coincident war in the Far East.

The practical result of this for Air Force planning was that the next scheme, Scheme L, approved by the Cabinet four months later in April 1938, contained roughly the same number of bombers as had Scheme K (around 1,360) but increased the number of fighters from 532 to 600. Far more significant than mere numbers, however, was that the fighters were to have priority. In May the threat of war came much closer with the start of the Munich Crisis. Hitler had marched into Austria two months earlier, and although the resulting union with Germany was a clear violation of the Treaty of Versailles it was an event that brought little reaction from the rest of the world. But now Hitler made his next move by insisting on 'self-determination' for the three million ethnic Germans living in Czechoslovakia. This was a country created after the First World War, and one whose security was guaranteed by France and the Soviet Union. Self-determination for the German Czechs was a very clear threat to the post-war settlement, and in 1938 war thus seemed imminent. Scheme M was now produced, the last of the pre-war plans, and one that called for 638 fighters and 812 bombers by 31 March

1939, and a total of 3,185 aircraft of all types by March 1942. Particular effort was to be concentrated on three heavy bombers, the Stirling, Halifax and Manchester, and, above all, on three fighter types, the Hurricane, the Spitfire and the Defiant.

One other important type came to be added when doubts began to arise about the ability of the new generation of medium and heavy bombers to survive aerial combat. Ludlow-Hewitt, the Commander-in-Chief of Bomber Command, said in a report dated March 1939 that he had been pressing for the previous eighteen months for what he called a 'speed bomber', an aircraft that would be able to carry out harassing missions and photographic reconnaissance at such speeds and heights that it would be able to outrun any fighters sent against it. His strongly held opinion struck a chord with Air Marshal Sir Wilfrid Freeman, the Air Member for Research, Development and Production on the Air Council, and he gave authority for de Havilland to start design work on a light bomber that would carry a 1,000lb payload of bombs and cameras over a range of 1,500 miles. By chance, de Havilland had already been thinking along similar lines, and the result was that work began in December 1939 on an aircraft whose design was strongly influenced by the success of the de Havilland 88 Comet racer of 1934. To its critics in the Air Staff this machine was known as 'Freeman's Folly'; it would in due course become much more widely known as the Mosquito.

RE-EQUIPMENT AND REORGANIZATION

Thus were plans laid to meet a war that had been a remote possibility at the start of the decade but which only seven years later had become a very real probability. But they were only plans, and despite very determined efforts to catch up, the actual strength of the Royal Air Force even by the time of the Munich Crisis of 1938 was quite a different story. Fighter Command, for example, had only 100 operational Hurricanes, and just three Spitfires; only five radar stations had been completed, and none of the planned underground operations rooms nor the necessary communications were ready. It would be another year before all the dedicated efforts that had gone into building a modern air force during the previous few years actually bore full fruit.

All these many schemes of the 1930s were the stuff of Air Force Board meetings, of Cabinet discussions and of Treasury concerns about what the national economy could actually stand. At another level of activity, that of technology, some striking achievements had meanwhile been emerging. Marshal of the Royal Air Force Sir John Salmond had taken over from Trenchard in 1929, and despite the lack of finance, the opposition of the other two Services and the pacifist climate of the time, he had managed to take some steps forward that were to prove invaluable later on. To give but two examples, the Schneider Trophy race was won outright by the RAF in 1931, a field of high-speed aviation which led eventually to the emergence of the Spitfire. And in 1932, the year before Salmond retired, the specification for the Wellington bomber had been issued by his Air Staff.

Under the little-remembered but very effective Marshal of the Royal Air Force Sir Edward Ellington, who was Chief of the Air Staff from 1933 to 1937, several more measures were taken that would be highly significant when war came in 1939. In the first of them,

Left: The Supermarine S6B in which Flt Lt J. N. Boothman won the Schneider Trophy outright for Britain on 12 September 1931, and in which Flt Lt G. H. Stainforth gained the world speed record on the 29th of that month. Stainford's 407.5mph meant that the S6B became the first aircraft in the world to fly faster than 400mph. (AHB)

Above: Marshal of the Royal Air Force Sir Edward Ellington. During Ellington's four and a half years as Chief of the Air Staff, from 1933 until 1937, the RAF put in place many of the foundations for later success, including the specifications that led to aircraft such as the Halifax and the Lancaster. (AHB)

the remarkable improvements in aircraft performance that had recently been seen, particularly in the Schneider Trophy Race of 1931, made it clear to a small group of enthusiasts that aviation was entering a new era.

From these high-speed machines of the first half of the 1930s evolved the designs that were to lead at the end of the decade to the eight-gun high-speed fighters, with all that these meant for the capabilities of the Royal Air Force during the Second World War. This development came about when analysis suggested that at these revolutionary new speeds of flight, interceptors would have to destroy their targets in a single pass, and that the time available for aimed firing might be as little as two seconds. Ballistic studies meanwhile indicated that it would take over 250 rounds of .303 ammunition to destroy a bomber, and since the rate of fire of contemporary machine guns was about 1,000 rounds per minute, this suggested an array of eight guns. Furthermore, such a high rate of fire meant that it was no

longer possible to synchronize the gun to fire through the propeller arc, which meant that the guns would have to be installed in the wings. This new concept was successfully championed by two relatively junior Royal Air Force officers, Wing Commander A.T. Williams and Squadron Leader (later Air Marshal Sir Ralph) Sorley.

Meanwhile the chief engineer at Hawker, Sydney Camm, and the chief designer at Supermarine, Reginald Mitchell, had each been working to produce a mock-up of an aircraft to Specification F5/34, which was based on this thinking as well as on the expected availability of a new engine from Rolls-Royce, the PV12 of 1933, later known as the Merlin. These designs emerged as the Hurricane and the Spitfire. It is worth pausing here to note the almost parallel state of military aeronautical development in other countries at about this same period. In the United States, for example, the first all-metal monoplane fighter for the Army Air Corps, the Boeing P-26, was in production in 1934; in Japan a first, though not very successful, version of the Mitsubishi A5M all-metal monoplane was built early that same year; and, particularly significant in view of future developments, in Germany the Bf 110 first flew in 1934, while the very important Bf 109 was designed in the same year, making its maiden flight in October 1936.

In Britain, all the moves towards an entirely new generation of aircraft were being paralleled by a second decisive technical development in air warfare, that of radio-direction finding (RDF), or radar as it became known in 1942. It is an oft-told tale, but very briefly the first elementary but successful demonstration of the potential of radar was given in early March 1935 to Air Marshal Dowding, then Air Member for Supply and Organization, and this led to his bold decision to construct the first chain of twenty air defence radar stations in Britain. With this as the foundation, a complete infrastructure for the ground control of fighter aircraft was devised and put into place during the following three years, so that by 1940 a highly reactive and very efficient air defence system was in place. Not only that, but it was radar that brought operational practice into line with the conceptual move away from bombers and towards the reliance on fighter defence that Inskip had initiated at the end of 1937.

The system was operated by Fighter Command, one of four commands that had been formed in July 1936, and a word should be said about this reorganization and its background. In 1918 there had been three RAF Commands in the United Kingdom; Coastal Area Royal Air Force, which embraced all units working with the Royal Navy; and two others, Southern and Northern

Areas, which in that year were amalgamated to form the Inland Area. There were also two small local Commands at Halton and at Cranwell. In January 1925 a new Command was set up, the Air Defence of Great Britain. This formation included Anti-Aircraft Artillery, Searchlight and Listening Posts provided by the Army, while the RAF portion of the overall Command embraced a Bombing Area and a Fighting Area as well as all the Special Reserve and Auxiliary Air Force units. This organizational framework was inadequate to the demands of the expansion that took place from the mid-1930s onward, and in 1936 four new Commands were created, the three other than Fighter Command being Bomber, Coastal and Training. Other developments followed later. Maintenance Command was formed in April 1938, and Balloon Command in November of the same year. To complete the story of these commands here, Training Command was split into Flying Training Command and Technical Training Command in May 1940 as the expansion of the Service continued, and three further Commands were created, Army Co-operation Command in December 1940 (which in June 1943 became the 2nd Tactical Air Force or 2TAF), Ferry Command in July 1941 and Transport Command in March 1943. It is one of the oddities of this wholesale reorganisation of the Royal Air Force that although the need for technical excellence was already clear, no Engineering Branch was formed to nurture it. It was not until early 1939 that Portal, then Air Member for Personnel, recommended the creation of a Technical Branch to bring together the existing Engineering, Armament and Signals specialists of the General Duties Branch, and only in 1940 was the Technical Branch actually formed.

Many other organizational developments had taken place during the years since the end of the First World War, including the transfer of the Observer Corps from Army control in January 1929; the formation of a Royal Air Force Nursing Service in June 1918, to become Princess Mary's RAF Nursing Service in June 1923; and, not least, the creation of the Women's Auxiliary Air Force on 28 June 1939, nineteen years and three months after the Women's Royal Air Force had been disbanded.

As a result of the comprehensive expansion that was now taking place, by 3 September 1939 the strength of the Royal Air Force had grown to 11,753 officers and 163,939 other ranks (about 15 per cent of what it would be by the very end of the war). As far as aircraft were concerned, because production lines were by now getting into their stride, the numbers of aircraft available in the United Kingdom had also shown a great improvement

Above: Hawker Fury IIs of No 25 Squadron. The Fury was a standard RAF fighter of 1937. (AHB)

over the totals of only a year before. In 1938 a total of 2,827 machines had been manufactured, while in 1939 the figure rose to 7,940. To be sure, some of these aircraft (and the Fairey Battle was certainly one such type) were of very dubious operational value. They were being produced because they were better than the alternative, which was to halt production altogether and leave some of the production lines idle until the designs and then the jigs for more modern aircraft were complete and meanwhile leave the squadrons with nothing to fly.

As to the numbers of squadrons, Fighter Command by now had 39, made up of 25 regular Air Force units, fourteen Auxiliary units and one or two squadrons that were not yet fully operational. Twenty-six squadrons held Hurricanes or Spitfires, but the others were equipped with a variety of less impressive types including outmoded Gladiators, Gauntlets and even a few Hawker Hinds. Within a few days of the outbreak of

Above: An air gunner of No 23 Squadron in flying kit in 1937. The aircraft is a Hawker Demon, this particular example being fitted with a Frazer-Nash hydrualically operated turret with a 'lobster-back' shield to give the gunner some protection from the aircraft's slipstream. The Demon had a top speed of about 190mph. (AHB)

war, four squadrons of Hurricanes would be dispatched to France, leaving only 22 squadrons of first-class fighters in the country. This should be weighed against the target of 50 squadrons laid down in Scheme M of the previous year, and the 46 fighter squadrons that the Commander-in Chief of Fighter Command, Air Chief Marshal Sir Hugh Dowding, had said was the minimum force necessary for a successful air defence of the UK.

Bomber Command at this time, 3 September, held 920 aircraft in 55 squadrons. But this impressive total is not by any means the whole story. Ten squadrons of Fairey Battles had been earmarked to join the Advanced Air Striking Force in France, together with two squadrons of Blenheims. Far worse in the short term, no fewer than seventeen squadrons were withdrawn from the front line at the outbreak of war in order to form Operational Training Units. This was a bold investment in the future, but one that left Bomber Command with an operational strength of only 25 squadrons, holding, all told, 352 aircraft — eight squadrons of Blenheims, six of Wellingtons, five of Whitleys and six of Hampdens. Clearly, there was a long way to go before the hopes of the pre-war plans for a powerful bomber force stood any chance of being realized. To complete this picture of the Royal Air Force front line as war began, Coastal Command, always something of a 'Cinderella', had a strength of 20 squadrons: eleven held Ansons, one was equipped with Hudsons recently purchased from the United States, two were flying Sunderlands and there were several other units manning a variety of obsolete types, mainly older flying boats, that need not concern us here.

For the purposes of a very rough comparison, it is important to consider the number of first-line aircraft held by the Luftwaffe in September 1939, and here the picture is not entirely clear. One estimate from German sources, quoted by Wood and Dempster, gives a total strength of 4,204 machines, of which 3,609 were serviceable. The German history published by the Militärgeschichtliches Forschungsamt in 1979 gives 4,093 aircraft, of which 90 per cent were serviceable, deployed in 302 squadrons making up 21 Wings.

It was against this background of partial recovery from the years during which the pressure for disarmament held sway, of hasty re-equipment and of reorganization and expansion that the Royal Air Force now faced the test of war. What no one could tell was whether it would all be enough.

CHAPTER 4

INTO BATTLE

During the late 1930s, fears in Britain about the likelihood of a 'knockout blow' by the German Air Force were matched in some quarters by expectations that a bombing offensive by the Royal Air Force would decide a future war against Germany. This belief in RAF circles led the Directorate of Plans in the Air Staff, headed by Group Captain Slessor (whom we last saw in India), to draw up a series of outline plans for such an offensive. Known as the 'Western Air' Plans, some of these were recognized by their authors at the time as resting on future hope rather than on present capability, and, for example, one or two of them depended for their success on the availability of longer-range aircraft or on heavier bombs than were actually to hand.

Others were thought to be more realistic, and three in particular deserve mention here. Plan W.A.1 was concerned with an air offensive against Luftwaffe air bases and against the installations that supported the German Air Force. This plan commanded only ambivalent support from the Air Staff. It was agreed to

be a possible means of reducing the impact of the expected German air offensive in the West, when what was actually required by RAF doctrine was an assault by bombers against key areas of the German war-making industries. In the event it mattered little: the plan had to be shelved when it was realized that most of the Luftwaffe targets were in any case well beyond the range of the available bomber aircraft.

More attractive, not only to the Air Staff but also to the Army, who saw it as more directly relevant to a land campaign, was W.A.4. This plan involved air attacks on road, rail and canal links in western Germany and the Low Countries with the aim of stemming any German invasion. W.A.5 also took account of Army concerns by targeting the industries of the Saar, the Rhineland and in particular the Ruhr, including the transportation facilities in the Ruhr, thereby, it was hoped, causing serious disruption to German efforts to concentrate their armies in the West. There were variations on this basic plan, notably W.A.5c, which concentrated on the German oil industry and its dependent branches such as

Right: Avro Ansons of No 48 Squadron. This aircraft was the first monoplane to enter service under the pre-war Expansion Scheme, which it did in 1936. It did good work with Coastal Command in the early days of the war and proved to be a very useful trainer and communications aircraft. The last examples were not withdrawn until June 1968.

the chemicals sector. This was thought by the Air Staff to be a particularly attractive option. Plan W.A.5, with its variations, eventually became an all-purpose basis for the air offensive because it met both the doctrinal requirements of the Air Force and the concerns of the Army..

In fact, however, even this plan bore no relation to the capabilities of the Royal Air Force in the late 1930s. As we have noted, on the outbreak of war the Battles, together with two squadrons of Blenheims, left Bomber Command to join the Advanced Air Striking Force in France, and another seventeen squadrons were pulled out of the front line to become training units. Nor was that all. The level of operational training was hopelessly inadequate, and it had failed to exploit even the out-of-date equipment that was available on which to train. Partly this was a result of the rapid expansion of Bomber Command that was under way, and partly it was caused by the repeated and inevitable process of re-equipment with new aircraft types. But, even so, only a minimum of all-weather training had been carried out, and even in good weather the standards of navigational skills were abysmal, no doubt because the duties of navigation were frequently conducted by Air Observers, who were airmen carrying out these responsibilities part-time, and also because there were no navigational aids. Trials in 1937 had shown that, even when an aircraft had made its way successfully to its target area, the average crew could not place its warload closer to the intended mark than about 250yds. In air-to-air gunnery the picture was if anything even worse, not helped by the fact that some of the part-time gunners had not been properly trained to operate their new turrets.

It was not until a month after the outbreak of war that decisive steps were taken to rectify these and other grave deficiencies, when three institutions very important for the future of the Service were set up, the Bombing Development Unit, the Central Gunnery School, and the Aeroplane and Armament Experimental Establishment. Meanwhile the condition of Bomber Command as late as May 1939 was summarized by the Commander-in-Chief himself, Air Chief Marshal Sir Edgar Ludlow-Hewitt, a highly capable, clear-sighted and greatly respected airman. He informed the Air Council in a letter that his Command 'could not within any predictable period attain the strength or efficiency to declare it ready for war'. It was a damning indictment of the 'years of the locust', and although a great deal had been done in the short time that was left before Europe was engulfed in war, yawning gaps of inadequacy remained.

Thus when war actually started Bomber Command was in no state to launch the strategic air offensive that had played so prominent a part in pre-war theories, nor indeed was it politically advisable to do so. On 1 September 1939 Britain and France had announced, in response to an appeal by President Roosevelt to avoid all civilian targets, that strategic bombing would be restricted to targets of military importance. Germany followed suit on 18 September, in other words at the end of her short campaign in Poland. Both sides thus found themselves exercising restraint. For the RAF, instead of the intended strategic bombing campaign, and despite misgivings by Ludlow-Hewitt about the likely balance of risk and value of the attacks, the Command now turned its attention to the military targets offered by the German Fleet and its bases on the North Sea coast. As far as operations over land were concerned it contented itself with leaflet raids.

LESSONS OF WAR

These operations by the Royal Air Force during the very early days and months of the war are worthy of rather more detailed coverage than many of the later activities of the Service, since they illustrate with devastating clarity two things: at the strategic level, they show how far reality diverged from conceptual expectations; and at the tactical level, they show how far divorced from practicabilities were the pre-war intentions of the Air Force.

On the very first day of the war, eighteen Hampdens and nine Wellingtons took off to attack German naval units that had been reported in the Schillig Roads outside the naval port of Wilhelmshaven, but bad weather hindered their approach and the aircraft returned to base without having made contact. On the next day, 4 September, fourteen Wellingtons took off to attack two German battleships that reconnaissance had shown to be off Brunsbüttel, while fifteen Blenheims set course for Wilhelmshaven. Five Blenheims and two Wellingtons failed to return from raids that caused minimal damage to the German ships, partly because the bombs that did hit their targets were fused for an eleven-second delay, which meant that they bounced off the armoured decks without exploding. It was a poor start to offensive air operations.

Leaflet raids also began on the night of 4 September, and these questionable activities continued on and off until 23 December, by which time 113 sorties had been flown on 22 nights. Even Sir Arthur Harris, AOC No 5 Group of Bomber Command from 11

Right: The first production Wellington Mk I, photographed in June 1936. The specification to which the Wellington was designed was issued as early as September 1932, and later marks of this aircraft were still in service as crew trainers with Flying Training Command in 1953. (R. C. Sturtivant)

September, referred to them as a supply of toilet paper. If these 'Nickel' operations, as they were known, had any lasting value, then at a tactical level they accustomed crews to night missions over hostile territory, while at the level of higher strategy the low number of losses sustained showed a possible way forward for the future of the bombing offensive.

At the same time sporadic attempts to attack the German Fleet continued, though the sortie rate was greatly restricted by bad weather during October and November. With an improvement in conditions during December, a total of 233 daylight sorties were flown, starting with an attempted raid by 24 Wellingtons on 3 December against two cruisers near Heligoland. This was

Vickers-Armstrong Wellington

This bomber represented one of the most striking steps forward in aircraft procurement during the 1930s. The specification for the aircraft was issued as early as September 1932, though the prototype did not make its maiden flight until June 1936. The first production model flew in December 1937 and Mk II and Mk III versions were flying before the outbreak of war in 1939, by which time six squadrons of Wellingtons were in the front line. In the early days of the war the IC was the most common version in service, an aircraft powered by two Bristol Pegasus XVIII engines rated at 1,000hp. The IC had a top speed of 235mph at 15,500ft, a range of 1,200 miles carrying 4,500lb of bombs, and a service ceiling of 18,000ft. The Mk III eventually became the main variant in service with Bomber Command and 1,519 of this particular version were built. All told there would be eighteen marks of the Wellington before deliveries ended in October 1945, by which time 11,461 of the type had been built..

unsuccessful, but all the attacking aircraft returned to base despite being intercepted by enemy fighters. On 14 December 44 aircraft set out on shipping searches, and the twelve Wellingtons airborne attacked a convoy in the Schillig Roads, losing five of their number to enemy fighters and one more aircraft that crashed on landing at base.

Serious concern now grew about the validity of the theory that daylight bombers could defend themselves against attacking fighters, but worse was to come on 18 December. In a cloudless sky, 22 Wellingtons reached their target area, Wilhelmshaven, where they were met by a combination of flak and fighter defences that had been alerted by an early version of the 'Freya' radar equipment. Twelve Wellingtons were shot down and three more were obliged to make crash-landings at base. This loss of 55 per cent of the attacking force was confirmation, if any were needed, that, at least in daylight, unescorted bomber formations were highly vulnerable to interception.

The fact was that although the Wellington, the best armed of the bombers available, carried a twin .303 turret in the nose, another in the tail and two manually operated .303s in beam stations, this firepower was hopelessly outclassed by the two 20mm cannon and two machine guns of the Bf 109E, and even by the two 20mm cannon of the Bf 110, particularly when the fighter could manoeuvre with a distinct speed advantage. In the case of the Bf 109 it was a speed margin of about 100mph over the bombers, more than enough to allow flexible tactics against the less manoeuvrable British aircraft.

These disastrous bombing raids were not the only serious set-back for the Royal Air Force during the early stages of the war. The German High Command was

Right: The Handley Page Hampden, like the Wellington, was designed to a 1932 specification. It entered service in August 1938, operated with Bomber Command in the early days of the war and later saw service with Coastal Comand in the torpedo bomber role. (R. C. Sturtivant)

anxious to protect the country's northern flank from any attempt by the Allies to cut off supplies of iron ore from Sweden. Most of the iron ore was exported through Narvik, on the Norwegian coast about 120 miles inside the Arctic Circle, and on 3 April 1940 the first German military units sailed for Norway, landing at seven points around the coast from 9 April onwards. The move north of the ships concerned had been reported by reconnaissance aircraft of Coastal and Bomber Commands, but although Wellingtons and Blenheims were sent to attack them, no success was recorded. Meanwhile the first British and French forces went ashore to the north and south of Narvik on 28 April.

The reaction by the Royal Air Force to the start of the campaign included an attack on 9 April by Hampdens on two German cruisers at Bergen, though without success; and the dispatch of a force of 83 aircraft on 12 April, 36 Wellingtons, 24 Hampdens and 23 Blenheims, against various targets on and near the coast. On that day six Hampdens and three Wellingtons were shot down during what had been the largest bombing operation of the war thus far; but losses on this scale could not be tolerated, and it was to be the last major daylight bombing raid of the war by Wellingtons or Hampdens. The pre-war notion that unescorted bombers could operate by day in reasonable safety was at last recognized to be unfounded, at least for these aircraft types, and apart from occasional raids in daylight by the Blenheims of No 2 Group, the Command as a whole now turned almost completely to operations at night. For the rest of the campaign in Norway itself, Bomber Command operated mainly against enemy occupied airfields, for

example on the nights of 17/18 April and 20/21 April, flying a total of over 200 sorties in these and other missions, including minelaying operations from the night of 13 April onwards.

Because there were no airfields left from which air cover could be flown in support of Allied troops now landing in central Norway, the aircraft carriers *Glorious* and *Ark Royal* were recalled from the Mediterranean to operate offshore. It was, however, decided also to embark No 263 Squadron, flying Gladiators, which, it was hoped, would be able to operate from makeshift airstrips in central Norway. Lake Lesjaskog was chosen for this venture, and the Gladiators landed on the thick ice during 23 April. The very next day the lake was attacked by Ju 88s and He 111s in a raid that destroyed ten machines on the ground before they could overcome the difficulties of making a scramble from so unpromising a site, and only 30 Gladiator sorties were flown. The following day the five remaining aircraft of the squadron flew down to a small strip near Aandalsnes, but in the very poor operating conditions they all quickly became unfit for flying, and the pilots were withdrawn by sea without achieving any useful results. The Allied ground forces in the area were also obliged to re-embark, starting on 2 May, and RAF activity was then confined to long-range attacks from the United Kingdom against targets such as Sola airfield, where on the night of 30 April/1 May five bombers were shot down.

Meanwhile No 263 Squadron had re-formed and re-equipped in Britain, and the resurrected unit was transported to the Norwegian coast on board the carrier HMS *Furious*, which was to act in support of the Allied

Right: The last Gladiator of No 263 Squadron, at Aandalsnes in Norway in April 1940. (IWM)

forces still fighting in the Narvik area. The aircraft flew off to Bardufoss on 22 May, to be joined by No 46 Squadron with Hurricanes which arrived in the same way at the same airfield four days later. During the following fourteen days the two squadrons between them flew 638 sorties, claiming 37 enemy aircraft destroyed, and although this air cover played an important part in the successful capture of Narvik by the Allied forces, it was only a local triumph in a campaign that was already lost.

The eight Gladiators that remained after these actions were flown out to HMS *Glorious*, and when orders were received to destroy the Hurricanes because it was thought that they could not be landed on the carrier, ten pilots volunteered to save the valuable machines and all ten of them landed safely in the first deck landings that they had ever made. But it was all to be in vain: *Glorious* was intercepted at sea by the German battlecruiser *Scharnhorst* and sunk with the loss of 1,474 officers and men of her crew, 41 airmen and all but two

of the RAF fighter pilots. It was the final tragedy in an ill-conceived campaign, one that had seen the errors of committing a weak force at the end of uncertain lines of communication compounded by an almost total lack of air cover.

THE BATTLE OF FRANCE

Other grave disappointments lay in store for the Royal Air Force in these early days of the war, particularly during the campaign in France and the Low Countries. Fighting in this theatre of the war had begun in earnest in May 1940, and events were to show that the hopes placed in the two elements of the Royal Air Force dispatched to the Continent were ill-founded. The first of these was the Air Component of the British Expeditionary Force, which was made up of five squadrons of Lysanders for tactical reconnaissance and photographic survey, four squadrons of Blenheims intended for strategic reconnaissance up as far as the Rhine, and four squadrons of Hurricanes for air defence — a fighter force that would later be increased to ten squadrons at the request of the French. This force of thirteen (later nineteen) squadrons was assigned to operate only on that part of the front occupied by the BEF.

The second element dispatched to France was the Advanced Air Striking Force. This was made up of ten squadrons of Battles and Blenheims, which were to attack advancing German columns, and four squadrons of Hurricanes, allocated for air defence. Unlike the Air Component squadrons, the fourteen squadrons of the

Gloster Gladiator

This aircraft was the last of a very long line of biplane fighters to serve first with the RFC and then with the Royal Air Force. It joined the front line in February 1937 and it was in production until 1940, by which time over 480 of the machines had been delivered. Its 840hp Bristol Mercury IX engine gave the Gladiator a top speed of 253mph at 14,500ft, and the aircraft was armed with four .303 machine guns.

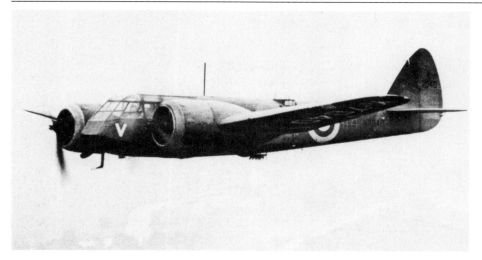

Left: A Bristol Blenheim Mk I of No 114 Squadron. The Blenheim was one of the first of the new generation of monoplane bombers ordered by the RAF under the pre-war Expansion Scheme. (R. C. Sturtivant)

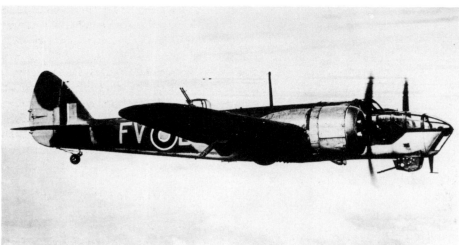

Below left: In 1938, production of the Blenheim Mk I was switched to the Mk IV, with a redesigned nose and improved armament. Some aircraft were fitted with a ventral pack of four .303 machine guns and employed as night fighters. As a bomber, the aircraft was disappointing, though it remained with Bomber Command until August 1942. Thereafter it saw service in the Western Desert. The aircraft shown was with No 13 Operational Training Unit. (R. C. Sturtivant)

AASF could be tasked anywhere along the Allied fronts. In addition to those air units actually in France, the Blenheims of No 2 Group in the United Kingdom could be called upon, as well as the sixteen squadrons of Wellingtons, Whitleys and Hampdens of Nos 3, 4 and 5 Groups. To some extent the UK-based squadrons of Fighter Command could also be drawn upon.

A comparison of the total air forces available to each side on the Western Front itself helps to explain much of what followed, though it is not the whole story. The Germans held the initiative and the advantage of surprise. Beyond that, the Luftwaffe had gained invaluable experience during the Spanish Civil War, and it had been able to translate this into appropriate aircraft procurement, so that, for example, Ju 87 dive bombers were able with great skill to operate in direct support of advancing German columns; the Allies had no equivalent capability with which to try to halt them. With the notable exception of the Hurricanes, many of the Allied aircraft were fit only for museums; for example, out of the French bomber force of 242 aircraft, only about twenty could be considered modern types. Finally, the German forces had been able to increase their combat experience and to hone their fighting tactics during the brief campaign in Poland only a few months earlier. In effect they were operating almost entirely as the kind of tactical air force that would be developed by the Allies some three years later during the campaign in North Africa. With all that in mind, we can contemplate the opposing strengths, drawn from the German history of the campaign:

	RAF	French	Belgian/ Dutch	Total Allied	German
Fighters	261	637	152	1,050	1,736
Bombers	135	242	21	398	2,224

Right: Fairey Battles over France in January 1940. Although this aircraft carried twice the bomb-load twice as far as the Hart and Hind biplanes it was designed to replace, it was already obsolescent in 1939 and it suffered disastrous losses in the early days of the war.

Air hostilities had actually begun for the Royal Air Force in France on 30 September 1939, when five Battles carrying out reconnaissance over the Franco-German border were intercepted by fighters, four of them being shot down and the other so badly damaged that it was written off. During the following months, as what became known as 'the Phoney War' set in, there was little air activity by either side; but then, on 10 May 1940, the expected German invasion in the West at last began, accompanied by massive air activity by the Luftwaffe — on such a scale that the Germans were able to seize the initiative in the air and retain it throughout the brief campaign.

On that first day nine of the RAF airfields in France were attacked and the whole force found itself heavily engaged. Thirty-two sorties were flown by the Battles, though for negligible results at the targets, thirteen of these aircraft being shot down and every one of the others being damaged. The force of Blenheims fared little better. Six of the aircraft were dispatched against Waalhaven airfield near Rotterdam which, together with other key points, had been taken by German parachute troops. The Blenheims were intercepted by Bf 110s and five of the bombers were lost. The results on 11 May were equally disappointing: of eight Blenheims dispatched, four were lost and two damaged. Eight Battles of Nos 88 and 212 Squadrons were launched and only one returned to base; while at about the same time all the Blenheims of No 114 Squadron were destroyed on the ground by German air attack. Finally, on 12 May nine Blenheims of No 139 Squadron set out to attack an enemy column near Maastricht and seven of them were lost, leaving so few serviceable machines that this virtually meant the end of the AASF Blenheims as an operational force.

On 12 May, as the German advance continued, it became vital to cut the bridges over the Albert Canal near Maastricht, and in No 12 Squadron volunteers were called for to carry out what was obviously going to be a very difficult mission for their Fairey Battle aircraft. Nevertheless the whole squadron volunteered and six machines were dispatched. One became unserviceable, and the other five pressed on to their targets. One of the two of the bridges was put out of action by the 250lb bombs that were carried, but all five aircraft taking part in the operation were shot down, with four crews killed or captured.

This desperate operation earned the first VCs of the war for the Royal Air Force, Fg Off D. E. Garland, the pilot, being awarded one, and the other going to his observer, Sgt T. Gray, an ex-Halton apprentice. Both awards were posthumous. Because the only possible posthumous award is the Victoria Cross, and two of them in one crew was already highly unusual, the third crew member, LAC Reynolds, received no recognition. In a further operation on 12 May, 24 Blenheims, this time from Bomber Command, flew to attack bridges over the River Maas, losing ten of their number for very little appreciable result, while fifteen Battles engaged in attacks elsewhere also failed to return.

Losses at this rate had, by the end of that day, 12 May, reduced the original force of 135 bombers in the AASF to only 72. The Battles had suffered particularly badly. Their losses on 10 May had amounted to 40 per cent of those dispatched; on 11 May all the aircraft engaged were lost; while on 12 May the loss rate was as high as 62 per cent. The very next day the German armies broke through the Allied defences, and in this critical situation 32 more pilots for the Hurricanes, the equivalent of two squadrons' worth, were sent across to

France as reinforcements. On 14 May all bomber effort
was concentrated on German pontoon bridges near
Sedan in the hope of halting or at least slowing down the
enemy advance. The result was again disastrous, the
numbers of Blenheims engaged, and their losses being as
follows:

	Dispatched	Lost
No 12 Squadron	5	4
No 105 Squadron	11	6
No 150 Squadron	4	4
No 139 Squadron	6	4
No 218 Squadron	11	10

This represented an overall loss rate of 75 per cent. At
this point it was decided to employ the AASF Battles and
the Blenheims only by night, leading to the dispatch of
28 Blenheims of Bomber Command against targets in
France on the night of 14/15 May, which cost another
nine aircraft shot down.

On 14 May the character of the air war as a whole
began to change when the Luftwaffe launched a heavy
bombing attack on the centre of Rotterdam. Great
damage was caused, and there were numerous civilian
casualties. This incident was decisive in persuading the
War Cabinet in London to lift the severe restrictions that
had been imposed on target selection for bombing raids,
and thus air attacks on the Ruhr (which as has been
explained, was the preferred area for attack by Bomber
Command) now became politically possible. Thus was
opened a second phase of the RAF's part in the campaign
on the Continent: on the night of 15/16 May a force of
96 Wellingtons, Whitleys and Hampdens was dispatched

against the Ruhr, with oil facilities in particular as their
targets, but in the poor visibility over that heavily
industrialized area only 24 crews claimed to have found
their targets, and certainly the heavy damage on which
the planners had placed so much hope failed to
materialize. Over the next few days bombing attacks were
therefore switched, part of the force continuing to attack
bridges over the Meuse and part seeking out targets that
were more easily distinguished by the nearby coastal
features in the area of Hamburg and Bremen. It was a
very unpromising start to the strategic bombing
campaign against Germany.

Meanwhile the hard-pressed French had requested
the transfer of another ten squadrons of Hurricanes from
their bases in the United Kingdom, and on 15 May
Dowding appeared before the War Cabinet, persuading
its members that such a step would be folly in the light of
the needs of Home Defence. This decision was reversed
the very next day, and eight half-squadrons were flown
across to join the uneven battle. Churchill, who had
travelled across to Paris, signalled for yet another six
squadrons, but he was eventually persuaded that there
were not enough serviceable airfields to accommodate
them, and the compromise reached was that three
squadrons of Hurricanes should fly to France to operate
there each morning, being replaced by three different
squadrons in the afternoons. This arrangement held for
only three days. All this time bombing raids, and bomber
losses, continued. On 17 May, No 82 Squadron of
Bomber Command set out to attack German columns in
France, but en route the formation was intercepted by
fifteen Bf 109s and eleven of the twelve Blenheims were
shot down. Only the squadron commander, Wing

Westland Lysander

In the twenty years after the First World War, army co-operation duties were carried out at home first by the Bristol Fighter, next by the Hawker Audax (a derivative of the Hart from the same stable), and after that by the Hawker Hector. Most overseas squadrons in this same role meanwhile relied upon the Westland Wapiti. In 1938 the first monoplane aircraft for army co-operation appeared, the Lysander. This two-seat machine was powered by a Bristol Mercury XII engine, delivering 850hp and giving the aircraft a maximum speed of 219mph at 10,000ft. It was armed with two fixed, forward-firing .303 machine guns and one manually operated .303 in the rear cockpit. The Lysander could also carry six light bombs on sponsons attached to the wheel spats, but its parasol wing and the very large cockpit transparencies clearly indicated its primary intended role, that of observation over the battlefield. However, even before the Lysander entered service, the kind of static warfare for which it was designed was being replaced by highly mobile armoured warfare, and this aircraft marks the end of an era in army co-operation aircraft. In 1941 it was withdrawn from its original role and relegated to such duties as air/sea rescue, target-towing and special duties, which in this case meant the clandestine insertion and recovery of agents and other personnel from enemy-occupied territory. The last examples of the Lysander Mk III(SD) were not withdrawn until late 1945, when No 357 Squadron in the Far East was disbanded.

there was no choice but to pull out to bases further south and west. In four stages the whole force withdrew across France, and then on 19 May began to embark for the United Kingdom. By 21 May only a handful of Hurricanes and Lysanders were left on the Continent, the latter carrying out liaison duties with the retreating units of the British Army, which by 26 May were heading for the Channel ports.

The reverses thus far sustained were bad enough, but there was yet to be a final disaster. It was perhaps to be expected that most of the RAF vehicles and equipment would have to be abandoned in France; but the combat aircraft were irreplaceable, certainly in the short term. Out of the 261 Hurricanes that had gone to France, 75 had been shot down or written off as too badly damaged to be repaired. Another 120 Hurricanes, however, were damaged but recoverable, and now even these machines had to be destroyed so as to prevent their falling into enemy hands. Thus it was that only 66 of these valuable aircraft returned to Britain, which meant that almost one quarter of the whole inventory of Hurricanes in the Royal Air Force had been lost. The Hurricane pilots, meanwhile, had performed near-miracles in almost impossible circumstances and had managed to inflict substantial losses on the Luftwaffe, though at great cost. The experience gained by the survivors would later be invaluable when the air war moved to the skies over Britain.

Daylight attacks against targets in France from airfields in Britain now continued, made somewhat less hazardous because the shorter ranges involved made it possible to provide fighter escorts. In the case of the remaining Battles, however, their high vulnerability

Commander the Earl of Bandon, an ex-Cranwell cadet, returned to base, where he managed to scrape together the makings of a revived Squadron for operations the very next day. By now the AASF was down to the equivalent of six squadrons of Battles and three of Hurricanes, the German advance was still unchecked and

Left: The Westland Lysander gave very good service in many varied roles but was quickly found to be of little value in that originally intended for it, army co-operation. The machine shown belongs to No 28 Squadron and is shown at Delhi in May 1939.

Right: Ground crew at work on a Hurricane in France, 1940.

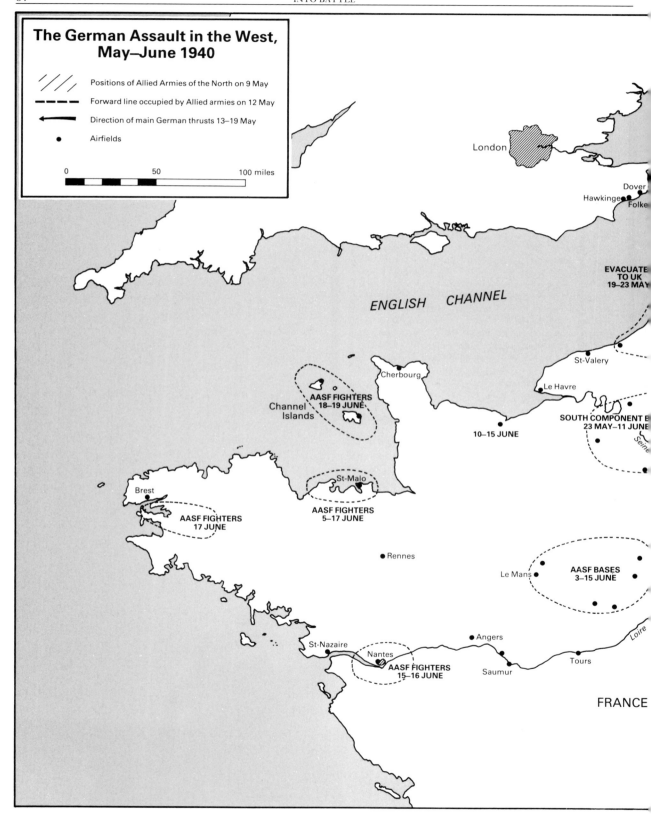

The German Assault in the West, May–June 1940

Positions of Allied Armies of the North on 9 May

Forward line occupied by Allied armies on 12 May

Direction of main German thrusts 13–19 May

• Airfields

0   50   100 miles

London

Dover
Hawkinge
Folke

ENGLISH CHANNEL

EVACUATE
TO UK
19–23 MAY

St-Valery

Le Havre

Cherbourg

AASF FIGHTERS
18–19 JUNE

Channel
Islands

SOUTH COMPONENT E
23 MAY–11 JUNE

Seine

10–15 JUNE

St-Malo

AASF FIGHTERS
5–17 JUNE

Brest

AASF FIGHTERS
17 JUNE

• Rennes

Le Mans •

AASF BASES
3–15 JUNE

St-Nazaire

Nantes

AASF FIGHTERS
15–16 JUNE

• Angers

Saumur

Tours

Loire

FRANCE

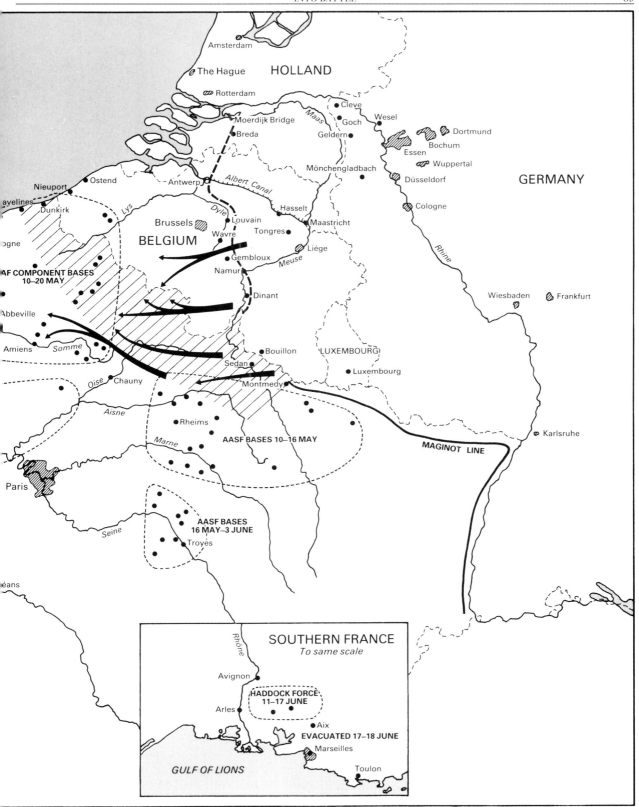

Amsterdam

The Hague   HOLLAND

Rotterdam

Cleve

Moerdijk Bridge   Goch   Wesel
Breda   Geldern   Dortmund
                                                    Bochum
Maas   Essen   Wuppertal
                          Mönchengladbach   Düsseldorf
Nieuport   Ostend   Antwerp   Albert Canal   GERMANY
ogne   Dunkirk   Cologne
                          Dyle   Hasselt
                  Brussels   Louvain   Maastricht   Rhine
                  BELGIUM   Wavre   Tongres
AF COMPONENT BASES   Gembloux   Liége
10–20 MAY   Namur   Meuse
                                              Wiesbaden   Frankfurt
Abbeville   Dinant

Amiens   Somme   Bouillon   LUXEMBOURG
                          Sedan   Luxembourg
Oise   Chauny   Montmedy
                                        MAGINOT   LINE   Karlsruhe
Aisne
        Rheims   AASF BASES 10–16 MAY
Marne

                                      AASF BASES
Paris   16 MAY–3 JUNE
Seine   Troyes

éans

SOUTHERN FRANCE
To same scale

Rhône
Avignon
                  HADDOCK FORCE
                  11–17 JUNE
Arles
                              Aix
                  EVACUATED 17–18 JUNE

GULF OF LIONS   Marseilles
                          Toulon

meant that they were still confined to night operations. But since they lacked even the most rudimentary bomb-aiming system, they were obliged to bomb on ETA, that is, on their estimated time of arrival over the target. With the navigational errors endemic at this time in Bomber Command, it would be difficult to imagine a more fruitless method of attempting to put bombs on targets, but the incident illustrates both the desperate situation that gave rise to the need even for this kind of effort, and it sheds another clear light on the inadequacy of RAF equipment at the time.

At last the efforts of the BEF had to be brought to an end, and on 27 May Operation 'Dynamo', the rescue of Allied troops from the beaches around Dunkirk, began, accompanied by the third phase of RAF operations. The story of that remarkable affair has been too often told to need repeating here, except to comment on the air aspects of the evacuation. The efforts of the Royal Air Force were criticized both at the time and in retrospect, and not only by the troops on the ground and at sea in the rescuing ships but also by Vice-Admiral Ramsay who commanded the operation from his headquarters in Dover. It was true that the whole strength of the Air Force was not engaged, but this was partly because of a lack of suitable bases within range and partly because Dowding recognized the clear need to conserve the bulk of his forces for the air battles over Britain that had by now become inevitable. As it was, Air Vice-Marshal Park, commanding No 11 Group, the southernmost Group of Fighter Command, had about 200 aircraft on which he could draw to support the withdrawal.

Because there was no means by which warning of enemy aircraft approaching the combat area over western France could be received in time to scramble fighters from their bases in the south of England, these aircraft at first resorted to standing patrols, a comparatively wasteful disposition of valuable assets. What is more, the position of the RAF bases that did exist, and the geography of the area, meant that the fighters had only enough endurance to stay on station for about forty minutes. These severe handicaps constrained the efforts by Fighter Command to prevent a total German mastery in the air, though matters were to improve somewhat when Park changed his tactics.

Instead of trying to maintain constant though weak patrols over the area of Dunkirk, Park decided to put up to four squadrons at a time into the air over the beaches during the hours when he judged that the Luftwaffe would appear in its greatest numbers. The effect of this was to maintain an air presence for eleven out of the

seventeen daylight hours, though none at all for the other six. On the whole, this approach was successful, and despite the criticisms of the RAF's efforts, it is not too much to say that the Luftwaffe suffered its first defeat at the hands of the RAF over Dunkirk. Some measure of the total effort by the Royal Air Force during the nine days of the evacuation is given by the number of sorties flown. These amounted to 2,739 fighter sorties in direct or indirect support, 651 bombing missions and 171 reconnaissance flights. Taking into account the pressing need to conserve as much effort as possible for the battles to come, it was by no means a discreditable contribution.

However, this was not quite the end of the campaign. As the Battle of France continued, such fighter cover as could be spared was maintained over the 51st Highland Division still gallantly holding out at St-Valery, until this formation had no choice but to surrender. And, finally, there was the near-farcical effort of Haddock Force. The plan was that this Force would assemble on two airfields near Arles, with the aim of launching a bombing attack on the industrial cities of northern Italy if that country should, as seemed likely, enter the war on the side of the Germans. Italy obliged by declaring war on the Allies on 10 June, and on the next day the Wellingtons of No 99 Squadron, a unit that had been earmarked for 'Haddock', arrived to come under the command of No 71 Wing in the south of France. Great confusion now arose, however, as to whether the proposed attacks had been authorized at Governmental level. When the aircraft of the Squadron attempted to take off on their mission on 11 May, the runway was blocked by French lorries while contradictory messages flew backwards and forwards

between the airfield and Paris and London, authorizing the mission and then forbidding it, the French fearing retaliatory raids and the British anxious to strike some kind of blow against the Italians.

Back in Britain, other units had previously been alerted for 'Haddock', and on this same day, 11 June, 36 Whitleys from Nos 10, 51, 58, 77 and 102 Squadrons set out for the Channel Islands where they were to refuel before continuing their missions to northern Italy. Most of them found that they were prevented from crossing the Alps by storms and severe icing, and only thirteen of them actually reached their targets in Turin or Genoa.

On 15 June another attempt was made by eight Wellingtons of Nos 99 and 149 Squadrons, this time operating out of Salon airfield, but again bad weather hindered the attack and only one aircraft made the flight to the target area. The next day nine Wellingtons set off on the same mission and five managed to attack; but then on 17 June the French Government surrendered to the Germans and any further operations by the short-lived Haddock Force were out of the question. If it served any useful purpose, then 'Haddock' gave notice to the Italians that their entry into the war had made them legitimate targets for strategic bombing attacks, and indeed those

Above left: Fairey Battles attacking an enemy column in France. (IWM)

Above right: A Flight of Hurricane Mk Is belonging to No 56 Squadron take off for a patrol over France, May 1940. (IWM)

Right: Pilots man their Hurricanes at an airfield in France. (IWM)

attacks would follow in good measure three years later. But like too many of the operations in France at this time, it is difficult to avoid the conclusion that `Haddock' was not worthy of the dedicated airmen who were obliged to carry it out.

Mention has already been made of the RAF's fighter losses during the evacuation from the beaches of northern France, but the total of losses in Western Europe during the months of May and June was of course even higher. The AASF lost 229 aircraft, the BEF Component 279, Fighter Command 219, Bomber Command 166 and Coastal Command 66, for a grand total of 959. More serious than those figures, however, was the fact that between 10 May and 4 June, when the evacuation from France ended, a very considerable proportion of the most valuable air assets, a total of 432 Hurricanes and Spitfires, had been lost.

TARGETS IN GERMANY

After the fall of France, the efforts of Bomber Command were directed against two quite separate sets of targets. First, and following pre-war doctrine, attacks were made against selected German industrial targets, particularly oil installations but also transport facilities and even forests and standing crops (attacks on which, it was hoped, would lead to widespread and destructive conflagrations). The second set of targets embraced those with a more immediate military significance, in particular at this stage of the war — German barges assembling in the Channel ports in preparation for Operation 'Sealion', the invasion of Britain, together with Luftwaffe bases and German aircraft factories supporting the German air offensive against this country. This division of effort illustrated once again the contradiction between the requirements laid down by the RAF concepts of strategic bombing and those of more pressing military necessity. It was a dilemma that would more than once cause friction between the Services as the war continued.

The part played by Bomber Command in the fighting at this stage of the war as the Battle of Britain was about to begin, is often overlooked; yet its targets were of vital importance. By 13 September the Germans had assembled 994 invasion craft in the newly captured Channel ports, and another 1,497 were on their way. From 7 September onwards, these barges and the port facilities were subjected to repeated attack, and many of the craft were sunk in their harbours. Attacks on German-occupied airfields were also pressed home, though not always with great success. The inadequacy of the Blenheims that were often employed in these raids

led to many losses, in particular on 13 August when twelve aircraft of No 82 Squadron took off to attack the airfield at Aalborg in Denmark. One aircraft aborted and returned to base; the other eleven pressed on but were intercepted by Bf 109s, and all eleven were shot down.

The first of the strategic raids against Germany had been launched on the night of 15/16 May 1940, when a force of 99 aircraft, made up of 39 Wellingtons, 36 Hampdens and 24 Whitleys, was sent against sixteen targets in the Ruhr, though some of the aircraft attacked alternative targets and bombs fell on Cologne and on Munster. On every night but one from now until the end of June, Bomber Command dispatched aircraft against targets on the Continent, as often as not against strategic targets in Germany, though usually the numbers taking part were small. One feature of these early raids was that each aircraft carried out its own navigation. This depended upon what is known as 'dead reckoning'. The expression comes from deduced reckoning (abbreviated to 'ded. reckoning'), a technique in which the position of the aircraft is plotted from its heading and the forecast winds, updated if possible by accurate wind measurements during the flight. But unless the winds can be forecast with high accuracy, and unless the aircraft is flown with great precision, then over long distances

Below: Air Marshal Sir Wilfred Freeman, seen with General 'Hap' Arnold of the United States Army Air Corps. Freeman was responsible for much of the pre-war re-equipment programme, being Air Member for Research and Development from April 1936 until August 1938, and then Air Member for Development and Production until October 1942. (IWM)

Right: Marshal of the Royal Air Force Sir Cyril Newall, Chief of the Air Staff from September 1937 until October 1940. He presided over the most active period of RAF re-equipment and he sustained the many early defeats of the war, but he then saw the Service win the Battle of Britain.

large errors and sometimes gross errors can result. And so it proved during very many of these night bombing raids. For example, Wilhelmshaven was bombed on twenty-one occasions during that period, yet, according to German records, houses were destroyed on one night, seriously damaged on two nights and slightly damaged on four others. In the dock area very minor damage was caused on two nights, with four people being killed. It is true that records of this kind may be incomplete because the civilian reports on which they depend may not have included, for example, full details of the damage caused to military installations in the dockyard, but the general picture is undoubtedly one of trifling results from these continuing bombing raids. It seems odd in retrospect that so optimistic a view of bombing results was maintained by the RAF commanders. A few aircraft at this time were carrying bombing cameras designed to take a flash photograph at the estimated time of bomb detonation, and this should have given some indication of the wide gap between expectation and achievement, yet for too long this evidence seems to have been ignored.

Meanwhile the raids continued. Between the end of June and mid-October 1940, operations of one kind or another were flown on 105 days and 102 nights. Over 10,000 sorties were flown altogether in this period, 80 per cent of them at night, with losses of 246 aircraft, 64 per cent of which were sustained at night. Many of the sorties in daylight were sea-sweeps, mine-laying or shallow penetration raids, for example over France. There was a change in the pattern of the raids from August onwards when, following an air attack by the Luftwaffe on London during the night of 24/25 August, bombing raids against Berlin were sanctioned. On the night of 25/26 August, 103 bombers were dispatched on operations, and about half of them headed for Berlin. It was not, however, a successful raid. The city was covered by thick cloud, the winds were not accurately forecast and most of the bombs released fell into country districts to the south of the city. Although this raid against Berlin and many of those that followed it were failures, they played an important part in the decision by the German High Command to switch the Luftwaffe effort, which at this time was being directed against the airfields of Fighter Command, from those vital targets to that of London. Indirectly, and of course quite unknown to these bomber crews at the time, they had inadvertently made a most important contribution to the success of Fighter Command in the Battle of Britain.

On the night of 23/24 September the pattern of RAF operations changed again when, instead of making attacks on many scattered targets, the whole bomber force was dispatched against a single city, Berlin. Out of 129 aircraft dispatched against targets that included seven marshalling yards, six power stations, three gas works and two aircraft factories, 112 crews claimed to have bombed successfully. Although the German records are incomplete, it seems clear that once again this bombing raid, a considerable effort given the modest size of Bomber Command at the time, had actually caused very little damage.

From mid-October onwards, bad weather in that harsh winter of 1940 hampered bomber operations, but at least the political restraints against attacks on cities had been removed and the need for attacks such as those against the Channel ports and German airfields on the Continent had faded away. The way was thus open for the strategic bombing campaign to begin in earnest. This change in direction coincided with moves in the higher command of the Royal Air Force. Air Chief Marshal Sir Charles Portal left Bomber Command on 5 October 1940 to relieve Sir Cyril Newall as Chief of the Air Staff. Newall had completed three years as CAS, and although he had attracted criticism because of the early disasters of the war and the incomplete preparedness that had contributed to them, he had presided over the period of the most intense expansion of the Service leading up to the war, and, as the previous chapter has shown, a massive effort had been needed in order to fill even the least glaring gaps in the capabilities of the Royal Air Force.

Portal was replaced at Bomber Command by Air Marshal Sir Richard Peirse, who soon after his appointment received a Directive from the Air Staff for the future conduct of the bombing offensive. In its final form, dated 11 November, the Directive nominated oil as the priority target and listed other facilities such as railways and certain industries which were to be attacked if the opportunity arose. Although the difficulties of accurate attack by night were by now becoming clear, it was still expected that the bombers would be able to strike very specific facilities, and with one exception, that of the night of 16/17 December 1940 when an attack on Mannheim was carried out in retaliation for the German raids on Coventry and Southampton, no one was yet thinking of area bombing.

It should be stressed that Bomber Command was still of very modest size at this stage of the war. Peirse had taken command of a force of about 500 aircraft, made up of 217 Blenheims, 100 Wellingtons, 71 Hampdens, 59 Whitleys and 85 Battles. In fact, of this number, only 230 aircraft were suitable for night operations, and when allowance is made for unserviceabilities and for the fact that crews were at this stage still being converted to operational status on squadrons, a more realistic estimate of the number of bombers that could be dispatched was about 150.

The size of this force, and the fact that its efforts were so often spread across many targets, makes it all the more surprising that optimism about the results of the bombing offensive was still maintained. A report by the Lloyd Committee, for example, which had been set up to make a systematic assessment of results, reported that the 539 tons of bombs that had been directed against German synthetic oil production had reduced total output by 50 per cent, an estimate which turned out to be wildly inaccurate. The first real indication that something was seriously wrong came with a report on 28 September 1940 from the Photographic Interpretation Section on recent air raids against two synthetic oil plants at Gelsenkirchen. Although almost 300 sorties had been directed against these targets, the photographic evidence showed that no major damage had been caused. A similar lack of effect was found after attacks on Mannheim, when 102 crews claimed to have been over the target. Photographs taken soon afterwards by the Spitfire-equipped Photographic Reconnaissance Unit, which was formed on 21 December of that same year, showed that very little damage had in fact been caused.

Nevertheless the attacks continued, though on a much reduced scale because of unusually poor weather. The intention was, however, still optimistically clear. In a new Directive to Peirse dated 15 January 1941, all seventeen of the German synthetic oil plants were specified as targets, and attention was particularly drawn to the first nine on the list, the destruction of which, it was said, would cut Germany's internal supply of oil by about 80 per cent. These targets were to be the sole primary objective for future strategic bombing attacks.

But now another diversion arose to take the bombing effort away from strategic targets. British shipping losses to U-boats and to German long-range aircraft operating beyond the reach of shore-based fighters had reached intolerable levels by the spring of 1941, and the shipyards could neither build replacements fast enough nor construct sufficent escort vessels. At Churchill's instigation, therefore, a new Directive, dated 9 March 1941, went out to Peirse, this time ruling that for the following four months the priority was to defeat the enemy's attempt to strangle Britain's food supplies and her connection with the United States. One significant feature of this Directive was that, in selecting U-boat and aircraft factory targets, it gave priority to those facilities lying 'in congested areas where the greatest moral [sic] effect is likely to result'. It was the start of a shift towards area targets that would develop further over the coming months.

Bombing attacks followed during the next four months against boat yards in Kiel, Bremen, Hamburg and other ports, as well as against U-boat bases in Lorient, St-Nazaire and Bordeaux, though the effectiveness of these last was greatly reduced because the Germans were by now constructing massive concrete pens to protect the boats in harbour. Including other operations, for example against warships in Brest, aircraft factories and various other targets in Germany, the four-month period saw a total of 12,721 sorties flown by Bomber Command, 10,532 of them at night, with a total loss of 321 aircraft, 73 per cent of these at night.

By July the threat to the Atlantic sea routes had somewhat receded, and the Air Staff was free to return to a strategic bombing campaign. The problem was which targets to select. It had at last become clear that little damage had been caused to German oil production during the earlier efforts, and attention was therefore turned, in yet another Directive, this one dated 9 July 1941, to the dislocation of the German transportation

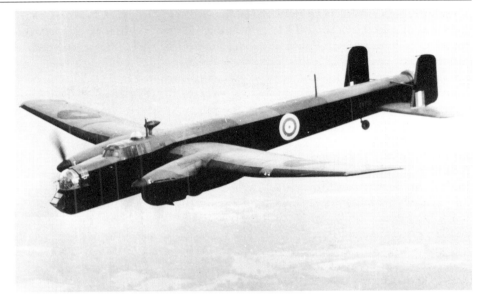

Right: The Armstrong Whitworth Whitley, chosen by the RAF in August 1935 to re-equip the heavy bomber squadrons. It continued in that role until the spring of 1942, later seeing service with Coastal Command.

system and to 'destroying the morale of the civil population as a whole and of the industrial workers in particular'. On moonlit nights, when bombing accuracy was believed to be within 600yds, railway installations around the Ruhr would be attacked so as to isolate the region and prevent the forward movement of war materials. When there was no moon, city areas standing on the Rhine, and thus easily identifiable, would be attacked; and if weather over western Germany as a whole were poor, then more distant targets such as Frankfurt, Mannheim and Stuttgart would be bombed.

The assumptions about bombing accuracy on which this part of the offensive and much else were based were at last brought sharply into question in mid-August by the emergence of the Butt Report. Mr D. M. Butt, the author, was a civil servant in the secretariat of the War Cabinet, and he had been deputed by Lord Cherwell, scientific adviser to the War Cabinet, to examine all the available photographs taken by camera-equipped bombers in an effort to establish just how successful the bombing offensive had so far been.

The results were far worse even than those at which earlier photographic interpretation had hinted. Mr Butt analyzed 4,065 photographs from 100 raids carried out during June and July 1941. It turned out that of those crews that claimed to have bombed their target in Germany, only one in four had been within five miles of it. On moonless nights, only about one in twenty crews claiming success had been within the five-mile radius, and for targets in the smog-covered Ruhr the results were even worse. Even this was not the whole story, for cameras were fitted only to aircraft flown by the most

proficient crews. And, finally, two-thirds of all the crews dispatched on bombing missions did not claim to have been over the target in the first place, which meant that, out of every hundred aircraft dispatched, an average of only eight had bombed within an area of 75 square miles round the target.

Despite these dismal findings, the July directive remained in force until November 1941, and during those four months attacks were made on 83 days and 92 nights against a variety of targets in Germany. Because of concern about the maritime situation, this period also saw several other raids mounted, at considerable cost, against Brest, where enemy battlecruisers and other warships were harboured. A formative operation then took place on the night of 7/8 November, when after a lengthy period of bad weather and questionable bombing results, a force of 392 bombers was dispatched, 169 of them against Berlin. It was the heaviest effort by Bomber Command so far, but its results were disappointing and its cost was disastrous. In the very poor weather that night, only 73 aircraft actually reached Berlin, where very little damage was caused; but 21 aircraft were lost in that raid alone, or 12.4 per cent of aircraft dispatched and no less than 28.8 per cent as a proportion of those that had bombed the city. The loss for the whole force had totalled 37 aircraft, a rate of 9.4 per cent, and more than twice as much as had so far been sustained in a single night.

Peirse was summoned to Chequers by Churchill, and the War Cabinet discussed the way ahead. The result was that there would be no further major effort against Berlin for the next fourteen months, and indeed the

November raid was the end of this whole phase of operations by Bomber Command. On 13 November 1941 another Directive went to Peirse, this time informing him that 'the War Cabinet... have stressed the necessity for conserving our resources in order to build a strong force to be available by the spring of next year'. Operations continued during the next few months, sometimes involving up to 90 or more aircraft in a single raid; but the level of activity was less than half what it had been during the previous four months as Bomber Command sought to recover during the winter and awaited the arrival of the new navigation and bombing aids that were by now under urgent development.

THE 'CHANNEL DASH'

Strategic bombing had, in these last few months, been the principal, but not the only, activity of Bomber Command. Over western France a considerable number of 'Circus' operations were flown. These were excursions by bombers in daylight escorted by fighters to draw into action the German air defence fighters, which would then be engaged and destroyed. It was hoped in this way to reduce the German fighter strength to such an extent that deeper penetrations by the bombers, perhaps even by day, would be made possible. These efforts were controversial and ultimately unsuccessful, as were attempts to penetrate the German air defences in daylight by using small forces of the new four-engine bombers, the Halifaxes and Stirlings now starting to come into service.

The failure of these efforts over the nearby parts of France was then overshadowed by a more serious tactical failure with the escape of the German battlecruisers *Scharnhorst* and *Gneisenau* and the heavy cruiser *Prinz Eugen* from Brest to German ports on 12 February 1942. Taking advantage of bad weather and low cloud, these ships, together with an escort of six destroyers and a small fleet of torpedo boats, minesweepers and other lesser craft, set off up the Channel covered by an umbrella of low-flying fighters. The force was not detected until late morning, when a Spitfire of Fighter Command reported the ships off Le Touquet. It so happened that most of Bomber Command had been stood down because of the weather, but frantic efforts were now made to launch aircraft from Bomber, Coastal and Fighter Commands as well as from the Fleet Air Arm. No fewer than 242 sorties were flown that day by the aircraft of Bomber Command, but in the poor visibility few aircraft were able to find the German warships, and those that did were unable to score any hits

on these well-defended and fast-moving targets. Although *Scharnhorst* and *Gneisenau* were forced to slow down after striking mines that had been laid by aircraft off the Frisian Islands a few days before, they managed to reach German harbours before dawn on 13 February. The attempt to stop them had been an embarrassing failure — *The Times* used the word 'mortifying' to describe it — but in the long term the escape of these vessels meant that at last the aircraft of Bomber Command were no longer obliged to carry out attacks on these ships in Brest — attacks which had cost 127 aircraft — and, even more important, the ships themselves ceased to be a threat to the South-Western Approaches.

It is of more than passing interest that mines turned out to be one of the most serious threats to the German ships during their passage. Minelaying had played a significant part in the activities of both Coastal and Bomber Command since the early days of the war, and, for example, during March 1943, at the same time as comparatively heavy bombing raids were being made on the major German cities, aircraft of Bomber Command were also out on minelaying operations on at least twenty of the nights on which the Command flew missions. The score of successes attributed to mining from April 1940 up to that same month of March 1943 was already 369 enemy vessels, and it was a campaign that would continue throughout the war. It was an effort that also had value in two indirect ways. First, it caused the enemy to devote something like 40 per cent of his naval personnel to minesweeping work; and second, minelaying from the air not only gave new air crews a useful introduction to operations, but these operations could often be carried out by bombers that were reaching obsolescence.

HARRIS TAKES OVER

During the last few months of 1941 the Air Staff drew up a new plan for the strategic air offensive against Germany. It was proposed to attack forty-three of the main industrial centres in Germany, employing a force of 4,000 bombers and relying upon new navigational aids that were being brought into service to carry out the attacks successfully. Although the proposal to create so large a bomber force was ultimately rejected, the continuation of Bomber Command's strategic role, despite the many failures thus far, was confirmed. It was a role that would be shared within a few months with the United States Army Air Corps. The United States had entered the war in December 1941, and plans already existed for the creation of a US strategic bomber force to be based in the United Kingdom. By March 1942 a plan had been drawn up to station no fewer than 115 USAAF groups in Britain, aircraft soon began to arrive in substantial numbers and the first US operational mission was flown on 4 July of that year. It was the start of a huge combined air offensive that would continue until 8 May 1945.

At the same time, and in a very important change of RAF policy, the concept of bombing specific industrial targets was abandoned, and instead a Directive was issued on 14 February 1942 promulgating the policy of 'area bombing'. This laid down that the primary objective would henceforth be the morale of the enemy's civil population, and in particular that of his industrial workers. The fact that the Directive contains no fewer than nine references to TR.1335 equipment, later to be known as 'Gee', illustrates the great importance that was attached at this time to the use of navigational aids in future operations. Gee was to be the first of four important systems introduced into the Command during the war, and it will set the scene for many of the operations of the Command if these systems are briefly mentioned here.

The main problem in navigation by dead reckoning is, as has already been mentioned, that of measuring the speed and direction of the wind. In order to make accurate measurements of wind during a flight, it is essential to take frequent fixes of the aircraft's position. Map-reading is the most obvious means of doing this, but at night or in bad weather it is far from a reliable procedure. It was to help overcome this problem that the Gee system was introduced. It depended for its operation on pulse transmissions from three stations on the ground about 100 miles apart. One of the stations transmitted a radio pulse, and simultaneously triggered transmissions from the other two stations. The minute difference in time taken by the radio waves from the two stations to reach an aircraft flying, say, over the Continent, was measured and displayed to the navigator on a cathode-ray tube, and by referring to a special grid printed on Gee charts the position of the aircraft could be fixed to within perhaps as little as half a mile, depending on the range from the stations. It was originally hoped that Gee might be used for blind bombing, but at anything beyond the most modest ranges it proved to be too inaccurate for this purpose. Its other weakness, and one that was never rectified throughout the war, was that it was susceptible to jamming. Nevertheless, Gee was regarded as essential equipment. It was employed operationally for the first time in August 1941; by August 1942 80 per cent of the force was carrying it, and by January 1943 it had been fitted to all aircraft in the operational force.

It was at this same time, February 1942, that Peirse was replaced by Harris as Commander-in-Chief, Bomber Command. Peirse had been in command for sixteen months over a very difficult period, but confidence in him had waned, partly because of the Berlin fiasco two months before, and he was removed from command and dispatched to India. But despite the fact that the bomber offensive under Peirse had shown so little in the way of tangible results, it had produced other benefits. First, it had been a visible means of striking back at the enemy at a time when no other was available. Second, after June 1941, when Germany invaded Russia, it was seen as at least a partial response to Soviet demands for a Second Front. Third, the offensive had already compelled Germany to devote extra resources to air defence, resources that might otherwise have appeared on the battlefields of North Africa and Russia. And finally, Bomber Command was accumulating operational experience that would prove invaluable as and when more resources became available with which to press home heavier air assaults.

Harris would remain as commander-in-chief for the rest of the war, becoming linked in the public's mind not only with Bomber Command but with the policy of area bombing against German cities. But, as we have seen, this policy had in fact been developing for some time in the Air Staff, and when it was finally laid down in the various Directives it was done so with the full support of the War Cabinet. Harris took over a Command that was still little stronger than it had been a year before. There had been heavy operational losses, training losses were also high and the needs of Coastal Command and the Middle East had combined to reduce the size of the force even further. On 1 March 1942, as Harris assumed command, the aircraft available to him, ignoring 78 Blenheim and Boston day bombers, comprised 221 Wellingtons, 112 Hampdens, 54 Whitleys, 29 Stirlings, 29 Halifaxes, 20 Manchesters and 4 Lancasters — a total of 469.

Far more significant than the mere numbers, however, were the new aircraft types that were now beginning to enter service. Lancasters were starting to arrive in the Command in place of the inadequate Manchesters; the Hampdens would be progressively withdrawn, and the last of the Whitleys would be transferred to Coastal Command duties. These changes in equipment would be matched by new tactics under Harris's direction. Instead of directing aircraft to carry out several simultaneous raids, inevitably made by small numbers of bombers, he would concentrate his efforts

over a more restricted number of targets and compress the duration of the attack. This produced a density of attack that had two consequences: it reduced the length of time that the bomber force was exposed to enemy flak

Above: A Halifax Mk II of No 35 Squadron.

defences, and, by increasing the intensity of a raid, insoluble problems were imposed on the German passive defence organizations such as fire-fighting teams — they would be simply overwhelmed by the number of calls on their services, particularly since Harris favoured a greater use of incendiary bombs than had been customary in the payloads of the force hitherto.

With all these changes, though there was a long way yet to go, Bomber Command was approaching a stage when it could begin the strategic campaign against Germany in earnest. Harris began cautiously, though he also launched several attacks that can best be described as experimental. In what had become more or less routine operations, night attacks continued on such targets as Essen, Kiel, Hamburg and smaller cities. On the whole these were less than successful, bombs often being scattered over a very wide area. Particularly disappointing results were seen in early May 1942, when Stuttgart was attacked on three successive nights by a total of 295 aircraft dispatched. On two of the three nights, not a single bomb fell on the city; most were later thought to have been directed at a nearby decoy site.

There were four exceptions to this general pattern of attack during the first four months with Harris in command. The first was a raid on the Renault factory at Billancourt, when 235 aircraft were dispatched in three waves to bomb the works at very low level so as to avoid

Avro Lancaster I

The Lancaster was one of the great aircraft of all time, and it was the introduction of this bomber that gave the Royal Air Force its main striking arm during the Second World War. Its advent followed the failure of its immediate predecessor from the same stable, the twin-engine Manchester, an aircraft designed to meet Specification P13/36. In June 1942 the last of the Manchesters was scrapped, by which time the four-engine Lancaster (originally called the Manchester Mk III) had proved to be an exceptionally good machine. Deliveries of the aircraft began in early 1942 to No 44 Squadron at Waddington, and by the end of the production run in 1946, 7,377 of these aircraft had been built. The last Lancaster was withdrawn from service with the Royal Air Force as late as February 1954. Various marks of the Lancaster eventually saw service, but the real breakthrough in bomber capability came with the Mk I aircraft. This version was powered by four 1,460hp Merlin 20s or 22s, or by the 1,640hp Merlin 24. These engines gave the aircraft a top speed of 287mph at 11,500ft, and it had a range of 1,040 miles with its maximum bomb load, the 22,000lb weapon, or 1,660 miles when carrying 14,000lb of bombs. Defensive armament consisted of twin .303 guns in the nose and dorsal turrets and four .303 guns in the tail turret.

It is at this point that Trenchard began to form his views on operation and organisation that would later affect the formation of the R.A.F.. In April 1915 Trenchard paid a business visit to London and found that the Royal Aircraft Factory at Farnborough had a monopoly on the design and supply of all aircraft and engines for the Army whereas the Admiralty had freedom to order from private contractors where the best machines were available. Even if the Farnborough monopoly could be broken, the Navy had cornered the market in the scarce raw materials. This problem was to fester over the next two years and eventually precipitate the formation of the RAF

Trenchard's Air Wing also formed the first Photographic Reconnaissance Section which had a dramatic effect on the attack at Neuve Chapelle on 6th February 1915. This episode together with successful spotting from the air for the artillery established Trenchard as an expert on Army Co-operation. From this time on Haig and the rest of the Army accepted the RFC as a useful adjunct to the Military forces.

The problems with the supply of machines for the RFC had become increasingly serious and the necessity for a very senior and experienced fighting officer to head the Military Aeronautics Directorate in London became paramount. Sir David Henderson, then head of the RFC in France decided that he was best placed to fill this role. With the agreement of Haig and Kitchener, Trenchard was appointed General Officer Commanding the Royal Flying Corps on 19th August 1915. With the appointment, Trenchard was promoted Colonel.

It was during the chaos of the Battle of Loos in September 1915 that Trenchard, finding his Squadrons had lost touch with the front line, put RFC officers and NCO's in the front line with the attacking forces. A tradition that has been largely followed ever since. At the end of the Battle Trenchard was promoted to Brigadier- General.

In the Autumn of 1915 a new German fighter began to appear in the skies over the British lines. The Focker, a monoplane with tremendous firepower, had the ability to fire through the propeller arc. The RFC machines were slow and unarmed and their casualties soared. This was the period of Max Immelmann, the German Ace

In September 1903 Trenchard voluteered for service in Nigeria, much of which had not been explored or pacified. After mapping and taming the territory, he returned to England on sick leave early in 1910. Upon his recovery he was posted to his regiment at Londonderry where he met Kathleen Boyle who he would marry many years later.

Trenchard and the RFC

Bored with the stagnation of Londonderry, Trenchard applied for a transfer to the Royal Flying Corps. The limiting age for qualified pilots who wished to join the R.F.C. was 40 and Trenchard was now 39 and unqualified. He had four weeks in which to fly solo. On 13th August 1912 Major Hugh Trenchard received his Royal Aero Club pilots certificate No. 270.

The Royal Flying Corps had come into being on 13th May 1912 and Trenchard joined on the 16th August, reporting to the Central Flying School at Upavon. Shortly after joining he was appointed adjutant to the Commandant and later graded an instructor (Squadron Commander). In August 1913 he was appointed second-in command with the temporary rank of lieutenant-colonel and met for the first time Winston Churchill who was First Lord of the Admiralty who was taking flying lessons.

The head of the R.F.C. in 1913 was Brigadier Sir David Henderson, Director of Military Aeronautics. The appropriations at this time were so small that the R.F.C. had no money for research and development and precious little for new machines. At the end of that year the Navy split away from the Military Wing and founded the Royal Naval Air service and a struggle commenced for control of the meagre air resources available.

In August 1914 Henderson took the R.F.C., comprising four squadrons, to France and Trenchard was left behind to recruit pilots and build up the squadrons strength. In October Henderson re-organised the R.F.C into three operational wings, one for each Army Corps, and Trenchard was offered command of the First Wing and appointed second in command to Henderson.

as far as possible hitting the surrounding town. Using massed flares to illuminate the target, the bombers attacked with high success, destroying an estimated 40 per cent of the buildings and halting the production of vehicles for the German forces for four weeks. It must, however, also be recorded that over 300 French civilians lost their lives in the raid, and as many again were seriously injured. A second raid of note was that on Lübeck on the night of 28/29 March, when 234 aircraft were sent against this old Hanseatic city. In moonlight and good visibility, 191 aircraft claimed to have bombed on target from a height of only 2,000ft, and very great damage was caused by the fires that quickly spread through the closely packed buildings. About 30 per cent of the built-up area was estimated to have been destroyed. In a third raid of this period, and one that was clearly experimental, on 17 April an attack was launched on the MAN diesel engine factory at Augsburg in daylight and at low level by twelve of the new Lancaster aircraft. The target was successfully struck, but four Lancasters had been shot down en route and another three were lost near the target. No further raids in daylight against such distant targets would be launched

by Bomber Command again until the very end of the war.

The fourth raid came about when, at the end of May 1942, Harris conceived a plan to dispatch 1,000 bombers against a single target in one night, and with the approval of Churchill and Portal and the co-operation of Coastal and Flying Training Commands it was found that the necessary number of aircraft could be assembled for the operation. Clearly a raid of this size would call for careful tactical planning and this was now carried out. By this stage of the war the Luftwaffe's air defences facing Britain were organized into territorial 'boxes' stretching in a line from Denmark in the north to the middle of France in the south. In each box a controller could direct by radar up to six simultaneous interceptions by German fighter aircraft.

In a major tactical innovation Harris decided that all the aircraft taking part in the raid would take the same route and fly at the same speed to and from the target using height bands to avoid collisions. So as to fly through the German air defence boxes as quickly as

Below: Lancasters at dusk. (IWM)

possible and to minimize the exposure time to flak over the target area, the stream of bombers would be compressed into as short a length as possible. In the raid on Lübeck a concentration of 234 bombers over the target during an attack lasting two hours had been thought revolutionary; but now only ninety minutes were to be allowed for the passage of 1,000 bombers over Cologne.

At a late stage of the planning the Royal Navy, not unreasonably in the light of the Atlantic struggle being desperately fought, vetoed the use of Coastal Command aircraft for the raid, and the units of Bomber Command were combed out to make up the numbers. In the event, 1,047 aircraft were dispatched, although this included 365 from Nos 91 and 92 Groups, which were made up of Operational Training Units. Many aircraft took off with pupil pilots at the controls. During the raid 1,455 tons of bombs, two-thirds of this tonnage made up by incendiaries, were dropped by the 868 aircraft that claimed to have bombed the main target. Massive damage was caused to industrial facilities, to many public services and particularly to domestic buildings. Nearly 500 people were killed, over 5,000 were injured and over 45,000 were rendered homeless. The raiding aircraft lost 41 machines or 3.9 per cent — not an unusual rate of loss at this period of the war. In terms of the new policy of area bombing which Harris had inherited, the attack was an undoubted success.

A second raid by such a large force, actually 956 aircraft, followed two nights later against Essen, but this time the target area was obscured by cloud or haze, and the bombing was widely scattered in and around the Ruhr. The raid must be considered a failure, though the tactics of compressing the bomber stream into the shortest possible space again proved successful, and this tactic would later be improved to a stage where up to 800 aircraft would pass over a target city in as little as twenty minutes. These new tactics, together with the sheer size of the raiding force, marked a turning point in the air war against Germany. It was also a time when the unsatisfactory Manchester aircraft was being withdrawn from the front line, the Lancaster was arriving in greater numbers and, for the first time an entirely new type of aircraft was seen on operations: in the early morning after the Cologne attack, five Mosquito aircraft overflew the city on a reconnaissance and harassing raid.

During the rest of the summer of 1942, night attacks were made, usually by forces of between 200 and 300 aircraft, against numerous targets such as Emden, Bremen, Duisburg, Düsseldorf and Essen. On the night of 25/26 June there was another raid by the 'Thousand Force', this time in fact 960 aircraft, against Bremen. Once again this target turned out to be covered by cloud, but aided by Gee the leading aircraft were able to start fires that guided the rest of the force to the city. Though the results were nothing like as spectacular as those concerning Cologne had been, they were better than those of the earlier raid on Essen three weeks before. Losses against Bremen, however, were not light: a total of 48 aircraft were lost, or 5 per cent of the Bomber Command aircraft dispatched.

Though of course it was not realized at the time, the war had by now run half its course. The bombing campaign had been waged for over two years and a great deal of progress in operational techniques had been made. But the problem of delivering really accurate attacks by night even against large cities had by no means been solved. Successes like those at Cologne had been offset by the far more numerous failures such as those at Stuttgart and Essen. Despite the navigational assistance now provided by Gee in at least enabling aircraft to reach the target area, something over half the bombs dropped were falling outside large cities designated as area targets.

For some months past, Bomber Command had been using the concept of what were termed 'raid leaders', experienced and proficient crews who could be relied upon to lead the rest of the force to the target, and the suggestion had been made as early as 1941 that these crews should be brought together in a specialized target-finding force. When this idea was first put to him Harris was strongly opposed to any notion of an élite force within his command, but after lengthy discussions about the proposal he was overruled by Portal, and on 11 August 1942 Harris was instructed to form what would become known as the Pathfinder Force. This was to be a force of specialized squadrons brought together under the command of the then Wing Commander D. C. T. Bennett, a distinguished pilot and navigator of pre-war days.

In a noteworthy coincidence, on the same day that the Pathfinder Squadrons were assembling at their newly assigned bases, twelve B-17 Flying Fortresses of the US Eighth Air Force carried out their first heavy bomber operation, a raid on railway yards at Rouen. These two events mark a very important turning point in the air war. Bomber Command would henceforth continue to develop new and highly successful tactics for attacks by night, and a US force was forming what would complement this offensive by carrying out its operations in daylight. That part of the story of the Royal Air Force during the Second World War will be taken up in Chapter 7.

CHAPTER 5
BATTLE OVER BRITAIN

This account has taken us some way into the bombing offensive against Germany; but we now need to go back to the consequences for Britain of the fall of France. After Dunkirk, Hitler was convinced that Britain was defeated. He believed that the only thing preventing the British from accepting the compromise peace offer he made in a speech in Berlin on 19 July 1940 was the hope by the Cabinet in London that the United States or the Soviet Union might intervene to shift the strategic balance against Germany. In fact, at the end of May the British Chiefs of Staff had made an assessment in which they had looked at the implications of a possible French collapse. In the light of information from the Ministry of Economic Warfare, they had concluded that, provided American economic and financial assistance were forthcoming to support a continuation of the war, Germany would face an economic crisis by mid-1941. It was a classic case of reciprocal misappreciation.

From the Germans' point of view, there was every reason to feel optimistic about the ability of their army to destroy the British land forces, provided the troops could be projected in safety across the Channel. The German Army was by now 120 divisions strong, and fresh from its triumphs in Poland and France. In Britain, on the other hand, there were but 21 divisions, nine of them hastily formed 'county divisions' for coastal defence and all of them seriously short of arms and equipment. In aircraft, the Luftwaffe held over 3,000 fighters and bombers, while the strength of the RAF at this time was around 1,200 combat machines. Only at sea did the British have superior forces. Against a Royal Navy which, admittedly worldwide, could count fifteen capital ships, five aircraft carriers, 60 or more cruisers and almost 250 destroyers or escort vessels, the Kriegsmarine could deploy only five capital ships, six cruisers, fewer than 40 destroyers and no more than 60 submarines. Even the considerable Italian Fleet, in any case largely restricted to the Mediterranean, could not affect the balance; and the French fleet at Mers-el-Kebir, Algeria, which might at the very least have caused a later and serious diversion of

British maritime effort, had been effectively put out of action by the Royal Navy on 3 July.

It was hoped by the German High Command that this overall disparity at sea would be offset by German air power, and the importance of air superiority was acknowledged in Hitler's Directive No 16 on Operation 'Sealion', dealing with plans for the invasion dated 6 July. This laid down Hitler's intention to 'prepare a landing operation against England and if necessary carry it out'. Under the conditions necessary for the operation, he specified that the RAF 'must be so crushed that it would be unable to offer any resistance worth speaking of to the German crossing of the Channel'. The German Navy was less enthusiastic about the whole venture than the other two Services, and this concern contributed to the contradictory aims set out in Hitler's Directive No 17 dated 1 August, which said that the Luftwaffe was to 'use all means in its power to destroy the RAF and its . supporting industries in the shortest possible time' but was at the same time to 'remain altogether combat effective for Operation "Sealion".'

COMMAND AND CONTROL

On the other side of the Channel, although inferior in terms of numbers of aircraft, the Royal Air Force had meanwhile been building a highly effective system for defence. After the modest experiment in 1935 that had convinced Dowding of the potential of radio direction-finding, later to be called radar, work continued under the guidance of H. T. Tizard and Watson-Watt, two distinguished physicists, notably at the specially created Ionospheric Research Station at Orfordness on the coast of Suffolk. The success of this work led to the construction of the first of the 'Chain Home' RDF stations in the late spring of 1937, and by the outbreak of war another nineteen such sites had been constructed in the United Kingdom, as well as three overseas.

These RDF stations were able to detect aircraft flying at medium altitudes from around a hundred miles away, and it was possible for experienced operators to give the approximate size of a formation of aircraft, as well as some indication of its height. One weakness with the CH network was that the stations offered virtually no cover at low level, and it was to plug this important gap that a second chain of stations, known as Chain Home Low, was erected during 1939 to monitor the airspace below 3,000ft. By the start of the German air offensive proper, twenty-seven CH stations were in place and the same number of CHL sites.

Another problem was that of distinguishing friend from foe. Here, too, important progress had been made. During 1939 and 1940 a small transmitting device for aircraft had been brought into service that responded to the CH radar beams by emitting a signal producing an elongation of the radar 'blip' on the screen being monitored by the operators on the ground. This device, called IFF (identification friend or foe), was invaluable in assessing the often busy and confused air situation.

This warning coverage by RDF did away with the need for impossibly wasteful standing patrols by the defending fighters, but its success hinged crucially on good communications and on a responsive means of control. To meet this need, two main systems had been installed. The first was the Defence Telecommunications Control Organization, a Post Office facility that linked radar sites, operations rooms and airfields using primary and fall-back telephone lines. The second system was the Defence Teleprinter Network, which had been introduced in March 1939, again to link the key features of the whole air defence network.

Right: Ground crew arming a Hurricane during the Battle of Britain. (AHB)

Overall command of the air defences, including the static defences, was exercised by Dowding from his headquarters at Bentley Priory, Stanmore. Anti-Aircraft Command was also under Dowding's operational control, with its own headquarters and its commander, General Sir Frederick Pile, nearby. By the start of the Battle of Britain this Command, with its seven Divisions, held about 1,000 heavy AA guns and 600 light pieces, which was in fact a quite inadequate total, being just over half the number that had been assessed as necessary two years earlier. These guns were supplemented by perhaps 3,000 machine guns, and supported by around 4,000 searchlights.

Stanmore was also the headquarters of the Observer Corps, a body of civilian volunteers with a history going back to 1917 and an organization that had been transferred from War Office to Air Ministry control in 1929. By the middle of 1940 this important Corps had expanded to a strength of 31 Groups, each with between 30 and 50 observation posts covering the whole of Britain and particularly the Eastern Approaches. Something like 3,000 observers made themselves available to man the 1,000 or so posts up and down the British Isles. The Corps was called out for standing duty on 24 August 1939, and it was to man all its posts continuously throughout the next six years of war.

Stanmore was also the headquarters of Balloon Command of the RAF. In June 1940 this Command held about 1,400 barrage balloons, and for the next five years these would become a familiar sight in British skies and

over Channel convoys. The greatest concentration of balloons was to be found around London, where about 450 were deployed. It must be said that their utility in the air battles to come was only marginal; but they could be winched out to altitudes as high as 5,000ft, where they could deter bombers, and especially dive-bombers, from making accurate low-level attacks. They could also have the useful effect of forcing enemy aircraft up to heights at which they were exposed for a longer period to the attentions of the anti-aircraft gunners.

Although he held overall command, Dowding could not be expected to exercise close control of the whole complex air defence system. His function was, for example, to move whole squadrons from one Group to another as the tide of battle ebbed and flowed, to pull squadrons out for rest or replacement, to oversee the operations of his Groups generally and to address longer-term issues such as the problems of air defence at night. To manage the more detailed challenges that would need to be met day by day, there were four Groups under Dowding's command: No 13 Group commanded by Air Vice-Marshal Richard Saul, covering the north of Britain; No 10 Group, under Air Vice-Marshal Sir Quintin Brand, looking after the south-west of the country; No 12 Group, commanded by Air Vice-Marshal Trafford Leigh-Mallory, responsible for the defence of the Midlands and the Wash; and No 11 Group, responsible for the area between the East Anglia and West Dorset, including the London area and the Home Counties. It was this Group, commanded by Air Vice-Marshal Keith Park, a New Zealander, which was to bear the brunt of the coming battle.

Each Group was divided up into sectors for the close control of the battle, No 11 Group, for example having seven such sectors. Each sector controlled a number of fighter airfields, and No 11 Group, which faced the largest German formations, held about 350 aircraft in 22 squadrons. Thirteen of these units were equipped with Hurricanes, six with Spitfires and three with Blenheims. No 12 Group had around 210 aircraft in thirteen squadrons, six of Hurricanes, five of Spitfires and one each of Blenheims and Defiants. No 13 Group held 220 or so aircraft in six Spitfire squadrons, six of Hurricanes and one each of Blenheims and Defiants. Finally, No 10 Group in the south-west, recently formed to face Luftflotte 3, the Luftwaffe formation that had just completed its deployment to western France (from where it might have outflanked the RAF dispositions originally planned), held about 60 Hurricanes and Spitfires in four squadrons.

The focal point of the whole system was the Operations Room, together with the neighbouring Filter Room, at Bentley Priory. Into the Filter Room came all the reports from the radar stations, so that duplications and conflictions could be resolved before the plots of incoming raids were passed to the Fighter Command Operations Room and, simultaneously, to the operations rooms at Groups and sectors, together with the direct reports from Observer Corps posts. Thus all operations rooms at the three levels of control were seeing the same air picture. It was left to Groups to allocate raids to sectors, and to scramble appropriate squadrons or Flights of aircraft, which were then controlled to a point from which they could engage the enemy aircraft. The controllers responsible for actually guiding the fighters were key players in the whole system. A really competent controller would take every advantage of factors such as the relative position of the sun to manoeuvre the fighters into the best possible position for attack; a less experienced controller could on occasions waste favourable opportunities.

There was one additional factor that was helping Fighter Command to make some of its preparations and dispositions by this time. For the previous four months, and quite unsuspected by the Germans, the British had been reading enemy radio transmissions that made use of the German cipher machine known as 'Enigma'. This was, of course, by no means a complete breakthrough since a great deal of communications traffic on the Continent was conducted by means of land-line. Nor, it seems, was Dowding given direct access to the deciphered material. But certainly some of the assessments and deductions were passed to him, and they helped to build up the wider intelligence picture, particularly in terms of orders of battle. Receiving also other material, such as intercepts of tactical radio traffic by the Y (Interception) Service, he does seem to have been well served, though the official history of British Intelligence in the Second World War tells us that 'For all his major decisions, C-in-C Fighter Command depended on his own strategic judgement with no direct assistance from Enigma'.

EQUIPMENT

Although Bomber Command and Coastal Command would also be engaged in vital operations as part of the wider air war during the coming weeks and months of the Battle of Britain, everything would ultimately depend on the forthcoming struggle for air superiority over the British Isles, and that meant, above all else, fighter aircraft. During the Battle of France, the RAF had lost

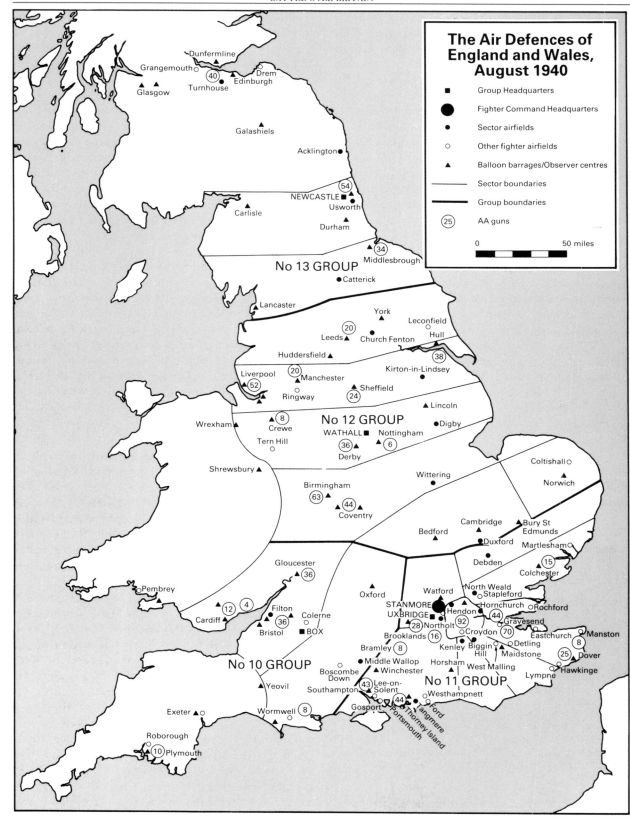

The Air Defences of
England and Wales,
August 1940

■ Group Headquarters
● Fighter Command Headquarters
● Sector airfields
○ Other fighter airfields
▲ Balloon barrages/Observer centres
— Sector boundaries
— Group boundaries
(25) AA guns

0   50 miles

Dunfermline
Grangemouth
(40)
Drem
Glasgow   Turnhouse   Edinburgh

Galashiels

Acklington

(54)
NEWCASTLE ■
Usworth
Carlisle
Durham

(34)
Middlesbrough
No 13 GROUP

Catterick

Lancaster

York   Leconfield
(20)   Hull
Leeds   Church Fenton
Huddersfield ▲   (38)

Liverpool   (20)   Kirton-in-Lindsey
(52)   Manchester
Ringway   Sheffield
(24)
No 12 GROUP   Lincoln

Wrexham   (8)   Digby
Crewe   WATHALL ■ Nottingham
Tern Hill   (36)   (6)
Derby
Shrewsbury ▲

Coltishall ○
Birmingham   Wittering   Norwich
(63) ▲
(44) ▲
Coventry
Cambridge   Bury St
Bedford   Edmunds
Gloucester   Duxford   Martlesham
(36)   Debden   (15)
Colchester
Pembrey   Oxford   Watford   North Weald
Stapleford
STANMORE ● Hornchurch   Rochford
(12) (4)   UXBRIDGE ■ Hendon   (44)
Filton   Colerne   (28) Northolt (92)   Gravesend
Cardiff   (36)   Brooklands (16) Croydon (70)   Eastchurch   Manston
Bristol   ■ BOX   Kenley Biggin   (8)
Bramley   (8)   Hill Maidstone   (25) Dover
No 10 GROUP   Middle Wallop Horsham West Malling Lympne Hawkinge
Boscombe   ▲ Winchester
Down   No 11 GROUP
Yeovil   Southampton (43) Lee-on-
Solent (44)   Westhampnett
Wormwell   Gosport Ford
Exeter ▲○   (8)   Portsmouth Thorney Island
Tangmere
Roborough ▲
(10) Plymouth

almost 300 fighter pilots, about a third of the total available; and although very welcome Czech and Polish personnel had joined the Command after the destruction of their own air forces, Dowding would still be 154 pilots below strength in the middle of August. His margins were very narrow.

As to aircraft, there had been two months after Dunkirk during which many of the losses over France could be made good, and although the actual number of squadrons had scarcely changed, the number of machines available showed a heartening increase. On 4 June only 446 operationally ready fighters had been available to Fighter Command, but by the start of the Battle of Britain in the second week of August there were just over 700 aircraft to hand, of which 620 were Hurricanes and Spitfires. And more aircraft were on the way. During June 1940, 446 fighters were produced, in July 496 and in August another 476. So vital were the industrial establishments from which these new aircraft were coming that many of the available anti-aircraft guns and barrage balloons were deployed in close defence of aircraft factories rather than at military sites. These factories, together with the whole of the maintenance, repair and salvage organization that had been built up, formed a little known but essential part of the whole air defence infrastructure. At squadron level, for example, procedures had been developed to turn aircraft round in the shortest possible time. At station level, maintenance staff had been pooled so that they could be directed to where they were most needed. Supporting the network of stations was the Civilian Repair Organization, which had been set up in 1938 and later transferred to the Ministry of Aircraft Production. Together with the repair depots of the Royal Air Force, the CRO was taking in damaged machines from the salvage units to such an extent that, of the total number of aircraft issued to squadrons during the Battle of Britain, 65 per cent were deliveries from factories but the other 35 per cent were machines that had been repaired, many from a seriously damaged state.

The force of RAF fighters, though substantial compared with what had been available only two years earlier, was still only modest when compared with the extensive resources ranged against it by the Luftwaffe in Western Europe. In Norway and Denmark, Luftflotte 5 held about 130 bombers, as well as thirty-five Bf 110 long-range fighters, 50 reconnaissance aircraft and some Bf 109s for local air defence. The other two Luftflotten, 3 in northwest France, and 2 based in northern France, the Low Countries and north Germany, together held a force of around 1,130 long-range bombers, made up of Ju 88s, He 111s and Do 17s, together with perhaps 320 Ju 87 dive bombers as well as about 800 Bf 109s and 250 Bf 110 fighters. The total combat strength of these three Luftflotten is given in the Militärgeschichtiches Forschungsamt German history as 1,481 twin-engine bombers, 327 dive bombers, 289 twin-engine fighters and 934 single-engine fighters. Average levels of availability in the Luftwaffe at this time were around 75 per cent, and the total number of combat-ready aircraft is given by the German source as 2,288 machines.

FEATURES OF THE BATTLE

Many accounts of the Battle of Britain have been published over the years, and it is not proposed to offer a detailed treatment here of what is one of the most important air battles of history. Nevertheless, it was a battle with many interesting features, some of which were seminal to the future development of the Service. A brief coverage of the main features of the battle, and of the thinking behind developments during that summer of 1940, is thus essential to our main story.

Sporadic attacks on inland Britain were made by the Luftwaffe during June and July 1940, though heavier air engagements resulted during the following weeks as German aircraft launched determined assaults on the convoys that continued to ply around the east and south coasts of Britain. The character of these early air battles made it clear to many of the defenders that there was something wrong with the tactics that they were employing, as indeed there was. To begin with, the pre-war training evolved by the Royal Air Force had as much, or more, to do with spectacle at air displays as it did with the realities of air combat. Not nearly enough thought had been given to the possibility that bombers might be heavily escorted by fighters — an omission that

---

Supermarine Spitfire I

Although the Hurricane entered service first, the classic piston-engine fighter of the Second World War was the Spitfire. The Mk I version was the first of a long line of variants, and it joined the front line with No 19 Squadron in June 1938. It was powered by a Merlin II engine, which gave a top speed of 355mph at 19,000ft and a rate of climb of six minutes to 15,000ft. The Mk IA was a modified version that carried eight .303 machine guns, while the Mk IB was armed with two 20mm cannon and four .303s. More advanced models soon followed, notably the clipped-wing Mk IX, which became the most numerous variant in service with a total of 5,739 built.

almost certainly had its origin in the plans for unescorted bomber attack by the RAF itself. Air combat had thus been seen before the war as a question of fighter against bomber, and somewhat stereotyped attack manoeuvres had been worked out. These were largely based either on the use of elements of aircraft in line astern or on units of three fighters in close arrowhead, or 'vic' formation. Larger formations would be made up of elements stepped back into, say, three vics of three aircraft each. It may all have looked well at air displays, but in action the pilots had to spend most of their time simply maintaining formation at the cost of their look-out for enemy aircraft; and if formation were indeed lost, then each pilot was likely to find himself entirely alone in a hostile sky.

The German approach was quite different. Drawing on the extensive air fighting experience that they had gained during the Spanish Civil War, Luftwaffe fighter pilots used a formation based on a pair of aircraft, known as a Rotte, in which the second aircraft, the Rottenhund (wingman), had the primary duty of guarding his leader's rear, leaving the leader to direct all his attention to the sky around him and to any intended interception. Larger formations could be built up on this basis. The main one was the Schwarm, which consisted of two Rotten. Seen from above, the Schwarm has the layout of the four fingernails of an extended hand, and is now known for this reason as the 'finger-four' formation. It is flown loosely, with perhaps as much as 300–400yds between element leaders and 50–100yds between the aircraft in each pair. It is a highly flexible formation for air combat, making it possible for all four pilots to keep a good look-out and yet be able to stay together. Furthermore, by using cross-over turns to change direction swiftly (a manoeuvre in which the finger-four changes from one hand to the other), the formation can swiftly change heading but at the same time retain its cohesion.

Once the intense air fighting that characterized the Battle of Britain began, it was too late to re-train the whole of Fighter Command. The result was that some squadrons developed their own loose formations, others made the best they could of the pre-war drills, modifying them so that perhaps one of the vics was detailed off to weave behind the rest of a formation giving cover to the rear, but in almost all cases the vic formation was abandoned for any actual attack. Instead, the aircraft in

the vic were brought into line astern and led into combat in a stream.

At a higher level of command, there was another difficulty with tactics in what became known as the 'Big Wing' controversy. It arose from the fact that the basis of Dowding's system was the close control of fighters, an arrangement which ensured that they could be directed quickly from the ground to where they would be most effective. For No 11 Group, covering the south-east of England, this was an appropriate and highly successful method of intercepting incoming raiders. In No 12 Group, however, whose squadrons were deployed behind No 11 both to defend targets in the Midlands and to act as a reserve for No 11 Group, this led to periods of frustrating inactivity. One of the leading squadron commanders, Douglas Bader of No 242 Squadron, and his Group commander, Air Vice-Marshal Trafford Leigh-Mallory, took the view that the fighters of No 12 Group would be far better employed if they were called off the ground several squadrons together as soon as an incoming raid was identified, so that the enemy would be confronted by overwhelming numbers. But the use of such large formations, named 'Balbos' (after the Italian

Left: Hurricanes of No 501 Squadron scramble from RAF Gravesend on 15 August 1940. Both these aircraft were lost three days later. (AHB)

Marshal Balbo, who had pioneered long-range flights by formations of aircraft before the war), ignored two things. First, many targets on the ground were left entirely unprotected by such a concentration of effort in only one or two areas; and second, the essential reserves for No 11 Group were not available when they were needed, having already been committed. If there is a criticism of Dowding's handling of the battle, it is that he failed to resolve this dichotomy of views in his principal subordinates.

As to the opposing aircraft in the Battle of Britain, each side could show advantages and disadvantages. The Bf 109E, for example, was less manoeuvrable than the Spitfire but the German aircraft had a better performance at altitude. It had a fuel-injection DB 601 engine which gave sustained power under negative g, while under similar conditions the Merlin engine with its float-chamber carburettor would cut out. Against that disadvantage, however, the British fighters had started to use 100 octane fuel, giving them a very valuable boost in performance; the German aircraft continued to burn 87 octane fuel. Range was an important limitation on the Bf 109E: the aircraft's effective combat radius was around 125 miles, and the Luftwaffe failed to employ drop tanks, which meant that although from bases on the coast of France these fighters could escort bombers as far as London, there was little or no fuel then to spare for combat.

The twin-engine Bf 110 Zerstörer, or heavy fighter, on the other hand had both the range that the Bf 109E lacked and the heaviest armament of any of the fighters in the battle, five machine guns and two 20mm cannon; but it had nothing like the manoeuvrability needed for fighter-to-fighter combat. There were also some inadequate fighters on the inventory of the Royal Air Force. The Boulton Paul Defiant proved to be a disaster, while the Blenheim was marginally useful but only at night. German bombers were, on the whole, reasonable machines, though their payload was nothing like that seen in Allied bombers during the next few years. There was one exception — the Ju 87 dive bomber, which had been such an asset in France. Against well-directed fighters, however, the losses in Luftwaffe units flying this aircraft became so high during the third week of August that the Ju 87 was, as we shall see, withdrawn from first-line operations.

One other difference between the two air forces — and it was a crucial one — was that despite the excellent air defence system that had been built up in Britain, there was still bound to be an administrative time delay between the first sighting on radar of an incoming raid —

requiring its assessment, its allocation to a sector and the order to scramble aircraft — and the time taken for the fighters to climb to height and engage. The attacking aircraft were meanwhile already at height, and the opportunity actually to intercept them could be very short-lived. Against that, however, a disparity of a different kind was working for the defenders. Any Fighter Command pilot who baled out of a damaged aircraft over England without serious injury stood a good chance of rejoining the battle; a German pilot in similar circumstances was out of the war. Many pilots of both air forces came down in the English Channel, and each side developed a rescue organization. The Germans at first employed Heinkel floatplanes with Red Cross markings; but it was clear that the crews of these aircraft could report the positions of British convoys, and they were little used once the RAF announced that it would shoot them down. For the Royal Air Force, it soon became clear that the existing organization, which depended entirely on marine craft, was not enough. Air Vice-Marshal Park therefore borrowed a number of Lysanders to help locate downed air crews and direct rescue launches to them, a system that proved to be the first step in creating a comprehensive, valuable and eventually a world-wide Air/Sea Rescue Service and one that continued to use RAF-manned launches until as recently as the 1980s.

Meanwhile, at the strategic level, Admiral Raeder, head of the Kriegsmarine, had declared that preparations for the intended landing in England could not be completed before 15 September, and Hitler had then set that date for the completion of all other arrangements. His final decision on the invasion had been made conditional on the success of the air campaign, allowing one to two weeks for this part of the enterprise, which was timed to start on or about 5 August. Broadly, the German plan was to launch harassing attacks from the air against British shipping, ports and other targets in the south of the country during late July and early August, and then, on a date to be determined, the Luftwaffe was to 'overpower the English air force with all the forces at its command, in the shortest possible time', as the Directive put it.

For five days the attacks were to be directed at targets in an arc 150 to 100km to the south of London, moving for the next three days on to targets in a radius of 100 to 50km, and then for the final five days of the offensive targets within 50km of the capital would be bombarded. The aim of this whole operation was laid down in Hitler's Directive No 17, 'For the Conduct of the Air and Sea Campaign against England', dated 1

August. The Luftwaffe was to 'destroy the Royal Air Force using all available force against primarily the flying units, their ground facilities and their support, but also against the aviation industry, including that manufacturing anti-aircraft equipment'. At a later stage, the Luftwaffe staff would add radar stations to the list of targets to be attacked. The weight of this whole offensive would, it was expected, turn the intended invasion of Britain into a virtually unopposed landing, or perhaps even, by forcing the British to sue for peace, make an invasion per se unnecessary.

The date eventually selected for the major German air assault was 10 August; but poor weather intervened and it was not until two days later, in less than ideal weather, that the Luftwaffe began its systematic attacks. Heavily escorted formations of bombers attacked airfields and radar stations near the English coast, the deliberate lack of penetration inland giving the air defences little time to react. All five of the British radar stations attacked on 12 August were damaged and put out of action, though fortunately all but one of them, Ventnor, were back in operation within a few hours. Manston airfield was put out of action, and at Hawkinge and though Manston airfield suffered a surprise low-level attack and even the customary night penetration attacks by fifty or a hundred bombers against aircraft and other factories failed to materialize; Generals Kesselring and Sperrle, the commanders of, respectively Luftflotten 2 and 3, had been instructed by Goering to conserve their main effort for the following day.

On 15 August a concerted assault was launched by all three Luftflotten. For the first time Luftflotte 5, commanded by General Stumpff and based in Denmark and Norway, was ordered to take part in the air offensive. The Germans were confident that the bulk of Fighter Command had by now been drawn into the air fighting in the south of England, but when the first wave of German attackers, sixty or so Ju 88s from airfields in Denmark, coasted in over Yorkshire they were met by the often experienced pilots of squadrons that had been rotated to the northern sectors to give them a break from combat. Driffield airfield was hit and ten aircraft destroyed on the ground, but the unescorted attackers were severely mauled by fighters as they eventually made their way back out to sea.

Further north, about seventy He 111 bombers from bases in Norway, escorted by twenty-one Bf 110 heavy fighters, headed for the Tyne–Tees area, while at the same time a force of Heinkel seaplanes was to make an approach towards the Scottish coast about 80 miles to the north of the attack so as to draw off any fighters. But the German formation made a navigational error that took the aircraft 75 miles north of their intended track, so that the defending fighters were alerted in good time and intercepted the genuine attack. Seven Bf 110s were shot down as well a number of bombers, for no losses to the defending squadrons.

In the south of England, the simultaneous assault that had been planned for Luftflotten 2 and 3 was delayed by unfavourable weather and finally got under way in the late morning. First blood was drawn when, at 1130, 60 Ju 87s escorted by about 50 Bf 109s attacked airfields in the south-east, badly damaging Lympne, which fortunately was being little used. In the early afternoon a three-pronged raid was launched, one formation penetrating into Suffolk and attacking, among other targets, the airfield at Martlesham Heath where over twenty aircraft bombed without suffering any loss. A second prong of about 100 aircraft was plotted approaching Deal, and Ju 87s then split up to make dive-bombing attacks on the airfields at Hawkinge and Lympne. Manston suffered a surprise low-level raid when a force of Bf 110s attacked, causing casualties and damage. A third, with nearly 150 aircraft, coasted in near

Above: Spitfires of No 610 Squadron during the Battle of Britain. (AHB)

Lympne take-offs and landings were confined to strips between the bomb-craters.

'Adlertag', 13 August, and the day from which the Germans count the start of the Battle of Britain, began with the postponement of the planned air assault from early morning until the afternoon because of unfavourable weather. Two powerful attacks were then delivered against targets in south and south-east England, mainly airfields, causing scattered damage except at the minor airfield of Detling, which was very badly hit, suffering 68 fatal casualties and many more injured. It served as a clear demonstration of what the Luftwaffe might achieve against the more vital airfields if its efforts were not successfully countered. By the end of the day, one in which weather continued to hamper operations, the Germans had lost 45 aircraft in action, three more in accidents and almost 40 more seriously damaged. The Ju 87 Stukas had been particularly hard hit. Thirteen RAF fighters were lost, three of them with their pilots. The next day, 14 August, was much quieter,

Folkstone. The strength of the fighter opposition and the heavy air fighting that resulted deflected these raids from most of their principal targets, notably the airfields, though heavy damage was caused to some of the raided aircraft factories.

Later in the afternoon seven enemy formations amounting to a total of between 200 and 300 aircraft were detected heading towards Hampshire and Dorset. Fourteen squadrons of fighters from Nos 10 and 11 Groups, almost 150 machines, took off to intercept, with air combats taking place all along the coast, from Kent to Exeter, and inland. This wave of raids had very little effect, though at Middle Wallop two hangars and a handful of aircraft were damaged. At 1815 hours a further raid, this time amounting to about 90 Dorniers with an escort of 130 Bf 109s and a diversionary force of another 60 109s trailing their coat over Kent, crossed the Channel and, although a total of ten squadrons of fighters were sent up, some of the attacking aircraft managed to penetrate well inland. West Malling and Croydon airfields were bombed, as well as three factories in the area, but with this raid the day came to a close.

It was a day that had seen 1,750 sorties launched against Britain by the Luftwaffe, 520 by bombers and 1,270 by fighters. In the confusion of battle and the haste to publicize the favourable results of the day's fighting, the RAF claimed to have destroyed 182 enemy aircraft, with another 53 probables. More careful research later caused this figure to be revised down to 76 attacking aircraft destroyed, though the German history admits to only 57. Fighter Command had lost 34 aircraft, but only sixteen of the valuable pilots were killed with three more being taken prisoner.

While the day's fighting was going on, Goering had, extraordinarily enough, been holding a conference with his three Luftflotten commanders at his distant country seat, Karinhall near Berlin. At this meeting Goering emphasized the overriding importance of concentrating the weight of future attack against the Royal Air Force, its support and the factories that were supplying it. This was very much to the point; but then in a fateful misjudgment, he also suggested that since attacks on the British radar sites had produced so little effect they should be discontinued. The result was that, apart from two more raids, the radars were left to operate without hindrance.

On the very next day, 16 August, the Luftwaffe offensive was renewed when three major assaults were launched. The first came just before midday with an incursion over Kent, followed by an incoming force from Luftflotte 2 estimated at 300 aircraft further west. Eighty

fighters were scrambled and intense air-to-air fighting soon spread over the whole of south-east England. As the aircraft of Luftflotte 2 began to make their way home, another large raid, this time from Luftflotte 3, approached the Isle of Wight from the south, hoping to catch the defending aircraft being refuelled and rearmed on their airfields after the earlier raids. But the fighters of No 10 Group in the west of England had not so far been engaged at all, and nor as it happened had those of the Tangmere Wing in No 11 Group. A force of Stuka dive bombers made straight for Tangmere airfield just as several of the Hurricanes were taking off, destroying two hangars, damaging the other three and destroying thirteen aircraft inside, seven of them Hurricanes. Seven of the attacking dive bombers were shot down by fighters and one by anti-aircraft fire.

These six days of unremitting action were followed by one day, 17 August, of unreal calm. Only a handful of aircraft were airborne on either side of the Channel, and at the RAF airfields the opportunity was seized to repair landing surfaces and communications and, above all, to produce as many serviceable aircraft as possible for the further action that was bound to follow. This was vital, for between 8 and 17 August Fighter Command had lost 154 aircraft in combat and another 30 on the ground, yet the fighter production rate at this time was only just over 100 a week. Although the German losses over the same period were an encouraging 292 aircraft destroyed, Fighter Command was beginning to eat up its reserves.

Even more serious were the losses of air crew. In the period 8 to 18 August, for example, 96 fighter Command pilots had been killed, were missing or had been severely wounded. The number of replacement pilots arriving during the same ten days was only 63, and most of these were without operational experience. Because they had to be thrust so hastily into the front line, many of these new pilots would soon become casualties in the intense fighting that lay ahead. Fighter Command had already been supplemented by volunteers from Blenheim and Battle squadrons, and in the search for even more reinforcements some pilots about to join bomber squadrons were given hasty conversion courses on to Hurricanes or Spitfires and put into the front line. All these new arrivals were joining a Command that already held a surprisingly large number of pilots drawn in form other sources, including many who had come from overseas. The Commonwealth had provided a very high number of volunteers. No 242 Squadron, for example, was still largely made up of Canadians, though a number had been lost during the fighting in France, and No 1 Squadron of the Royal Canadian Air Force came to Britain as a complete unit, being declared operational on 26 August. There were also 22 South Africans (not least among them 'Sailor' Malan), 21 Australians and an astonishing 129 New Zealanders (among them Colin Gray and Al Deere).

Nor was that all. As well as French and Belgian pilots, there were the Poles and Czechs who were briefly mentioned earlier. All told, there were 87 Czech pilots in the Command by this time, and no fewer than 141 Poles; indeed, the Czechs manned two complete squadrons, Nos 310 and 312, while the Poles formed a further two, Nos 302 and 303. There were even seven gallant volunteers from the United States, a country which was, of course, still at peace. Finally, a very welcome reinforcement was provided to the Command by the Royal Navy, from which 58 high-quality air crew were detached, in addition to two squadrons of the Fleet Air Arm. Yet despite this talent — and over 2,800 air crew took part in the Battle of Britain — air crew losses from all causes, and their replacement, remained the most serious of the problems that faced Dowding as the battle continued through the summer and autumn of 1940.

On 18 August, the battle was resumed at high intensity by the Luftwaffe, but with different tactics. Instead of attacking RAF airfields across the southern counties, almost all the available effort was to be directed against Kenley and Biggin Hill during the morning. During the early afternoon, a formation of 111 Ju 87 dive bombers, escorted by about 50 Bf 109s, approached the English coast east of Portsmouth. As they flew in they split up to attack the radar station at Poling to the east of Tangmere, and the next station along the south coast, Ventnor, as well as the airfields at Thorney Island, Ford and Gosport, wrongly believing them to be front-line bases of Fighter Command. The attack on Poling was particularly serious, and put this CHL station out of action for a fortnight. Since Ventnor was still non-operational after the raid on 12 August, and Kenley sector control had been knocked out, these losses created a worrying gap in the air defence system, though some relief was at hand from mobile radars that were now set up to replace those destroyed.

For the Luftwaffe, however, the raid had been little short of disastrous. Eighteen Ju 87s had been shot down, and about the same number severely damaged. This was a particularly serious blow to German hopes of an invasion, since it was the dive bomber which was intended to be a principal weapon of attack against the British Fleet, as indeed it was to be the following year in the Mediterranean. But losses at this rate could not be supported, and it was at this stage that the Ju 87s were withdrawn from the battle.

In the late afternoon of this same day, 18 August, a third wave of attacks by the Luftwaffe was launched against the fighter airfields near London. Once more a large force of Hurricanes and Spitfires took off to intercept, breaking up the incoming formations which, confused by falling visibility and cloud that came in to cover much of south-east England, tried to bomb secondary targets but succeeded only in scattering their efforts over a wide area. Many civilians were killed as a result. The day's fighting had resulted in 64 Luftwaffe aircraft being destroyed, for a cost to Fighter Command of 25 Hurricanes in air combat, plus three on the ground, and seven Spitfires.

A period of very cloudy weather from 19 to 23 August now intervened to restrict Luftwaffe operations, though many sporadic raids were made, and both sides took advantage of the pause to redeploy some of their operational assets. In Fighter Command, two squadrons had already been pulled out of No 11 Group to be replaced by units from the quieter sectors, and now another four were similarly replaced. On 24 August the Luftwaffe was able to resume its heavy daylight attacks, and from then until 6 September there was only a single day when fewer than 600 sorties were flown against targets in Britain.

NIGHT ATTACKS

But now another feature of the air assault was seen, as German attacks by night became a significant part of the overall attack. Some scattered raids by night had been made as early as June, but on the night of 19/20 August Liverpool was bombed by a force of twelve He 111s, and on the night of 23/24 August over 300 bombers attacked targets in areas ranging from South Wales to Liverpool and East Anglia. One force of bombers bound for Rochester and Thameshaven instead dropped their bombs inadvertently over central London, the first raid on the city since those in 1918. It was this attack that caused the British War Cabinet on 25 August to sanction the first bombing raid on Berlin, which was carried out on the night of 25/26 August, though without hitting any targets of value. These German attacks by night posed a very serious problem for the defences. Only a handful of anti-aircraft guns were at this stage of the war laid by radar, and even when so directed the guns were far from effective against manoeuvring aircraft. During these night raids in September and October 1940 some 250,000 rounds of ammunition were expended, bringing down a total of only fourteen enemy aircraft — an

Above: The height of the Battle of Britain. As a pilot leaves his aircraft, the ground crew are already turning it round for its next flight. (AHB)

average kill rate of one for every 18,000 rounds. Later in the war, with much improved equipment, the average rate would fall to around one kill per 1,000 rounds, but in 1940 that kind of success seemed a very long way off.

As to night fighters, the only machines available were the Blenheims, but since their top speed, 260mph, was almost exactly the same as aircraft such as the He 111 bomber, the operational effectiveness of the Blenheim as a night fighter was no better than it had been in the day bomber role. Even more serious, the airborne interception radar available to the night fighters up to this stage of the war was primitive; most of the available radar research effort had, not surprisingly been directed to the construction of the ground-based network of stations. It was not until September 1940 that the first Beaufighters entered the front line, and only in November was the greatly improved AI Mk IV airborne interception radar fitted as standard to production machines. With its top speed of over 330 mph, together with a radar that was effective between about three miles and a minimum 400ft, and armed with four 20mm Hispano cannon (it was the only RAF aircraft so equipped at this time), the Beaufighter was a serious adversary for the night bomber. All that was missing to make the night fighter system a deadly weapon was an efficient means of directing the aircraft to a position

where the navigator could take over the final stage of the interception using the on-board AI radar.

After intense efforts by the Air Ministry Research Establishment, more effective ground radars were produced using a much enhanced rate of circular sweep, thus giving a more accurate picture of the relative position of target and interceptor. This improved radar capability, together with the developing skills of the controllers, gradually brought ground-controlled interception up to a fine art. The improvements were not, however, very swift to emerge. In the first two months of the Blitz proper, which began in early September, only eight raiding aircraft were shot down by night fighters during something like 12,000 sorties by the Luftwaffe. It would not be until March the following year that higher kill rates were achieved, and it was not until the later stages of the Blitz in May 1941 that the system became deadly to the attacking bombers.

The lull in the daylight raids lasted until 24 August when the airfields at Manston, Hornchurch and North Weald came under attack as well as Dover, Ramsgate, Portsmouth and other centres — a pattern of raids that was to continue for the next fourteen days. The whole ring of airfields defending the approaches to London, Kenley, Biggin Hill, Hornchurch, North Weald and Northolt — all came under repeated and often very damaging attack. Many other airfields were also struck, particularly Debden, Croydon, Hawkinge, Eastchurch, Rochford, Martlesham and Lympne. Manston was taken out of use, Kenley was badly hit and operating at much reduced effectiveness, while Biggin Hill had most of the buildings still standing rendered unsafe by raids that sometimes took place twice or even three times in a single day, as they did on 2 September. The scale of the air battles that raged daily over the Home Counties is best seen in terms of the very high losses on both sides. Between 24 August and 6 September, the Royal Air Force lost 286 aircraft; but the Luftwaffe suffered the loss of 380 machines and, because virtually all the fighting was taking place over British soil, nearly all its crews.

This last fact is of crucial importance. It is sometimes said that by 6 September Fighter Command was so exhausted that had the Luftwaffe kept up its attacks on the RAF airfields for another fortnight the defence might well have collapsed. But reinforcements could have been brought down from the north where, because that part of Britain was well outside the range of Bf 109s, the attackers were in any case at a serious disadvantage; and as to replacing the very large numbers of aircraft lost, both in combat and in accidents, the production rate for British fighters was by now double that which the Germans were managing. Pilots were still the key factor. At the end of August, the pilot establishment of Fighter Command was 1,558 while the actual strength was 1,377, a deficit of 181. It actually rose to a total of 1,752 on strength by 12 October. Against that, German single-engine fighter pilot strength, according to the German Military Research Office, was always some 400 less than the RAF figure, and the Luftwaffe continued to lose these valuable air crews over Britain and in the Channel. Finally, the Luftwaffe pilots could not be moved to a quiet sector for a break from the fighting, and their constant efforts in the air led to what the German crews knew as Kanalkrankheit ('Channel sickness') — in other words combat stress. It seems likely that only the quite erroneous belief by the Germans that Fighter Command was down to its last 150 to 300 aircraft made it possible for them to maintain their efforts.

Nevertheless the pressure on Fighter Command was severe, and it was this that led Dowding to introduce what he called his 'Stabilization Scheme'. This scheme, brought into force on 8 September, divided the fighter squadrons into three categories. Category A, those squadrons operationally fit, were deployed into No 11 Group and the two adjoining sectors of Nos 10 and 12 Groups, Middle Wallop and Duxford respectively. Category B squadrons, those partially fit for operations, were placed in Nos 10 and 12 Groups ready to replace the Category As. Category Cs were those squadrons with only a handful of experienced pilots, and these units were deployed further back, mostly in No 13 Group. Within the scheme, cross-postings between squadrons now became frequent, leading to turbulence that is always unwelcome in close-knit fighting units, and had Dowding been obliged to continue with it for much longer than was the case it might well have had a serious effect on morale.

TARGET LONDON

On 7 September, however, the whole shape of the battle changed when, during the late afternoon, unprecedentedly large German formations appeared on the radar screens; but this time, instead of heading as expected for their usual airfield targets, they headed steadily for the London area. With the adequate warning that this straightforward routing allowed the defence, 21 of the 23 squadrons sent up to intercept managed to engage the enemy formations. The result was that 41 German aircraft were destroyed for the loss of 28 fighters. The precise reasons for the German switch away

from airfield targets have never been determined, but the attack on Berlin on 25/26 August that has already been mentioned, together with other raids on subsequent nights, almost certainly played a part, as did the German belief that Fighter Command was by now so weakened that it could be finally defeated over London. It is also possible that Churchill had seized upon the unintended Luftwaffe raid on London on 24/25 August as a reason for bombing Berlin, correctly assuming that this would lead to reprisals against London but a reduction of the pressure on the airfields of Fighter Command.

These first deliberate attacks on London focused on the city's docks and on industrial targets, for example at Woolwich, causing extensive damage and many serious fires. The urban areas in London's East End were also badly hit. In the early evening, and while the emergency services were still fully stretched in dealing with devastation, about 250 bombers returned to the scene of the attack with an even heavier raid, dropping a mixture of high-explosive, delayed-action and incendiary bombs. Many more fires resulted, some of them huge conflagrations, particularly among the warehouses lining the Thames. Casualties for the day and night of bombardment were 436 fatalities and about 1,600 people severely injured. No enemy aircraft were brought down during the night attack, either by fighters or by the 92 heavy anti-aircraft guns deployed around the capital.

Attempts by a hundred or more enemy aircraft to penetrate to the London area during the following three days and nights were only partly successful, though again London itself and other targets were hit. On 12 and 13 September heavy cloud hindered Luftwaffe operations, though again bombs fell on many parts of London, including the Admiralty, the War Office and Buckingham Palace. The weather cleared on 14 September, and London was raided twice by daylight and twice that night, though nothing like the intensity of the first major attack was seen. On the 15th, however, the date now celebrated as Battle of Britain Day, a huge German formation gathered over France during the late morning and coasted in at Dungeness at 11.30 a.m. Twenty-two fighter squadrons rose to meet the attack, and heavy fighting took place over the Home Counties as the bombers made their way to London. Later in the afternoon three more waves of attackers came in, a total force of about 150 to 200 bombers escorted by 300 or more fighters. The first two waves were largely turned back by the strength of the opposition, but the third wave, despite the fact that there were by now no fewer than 31 squadrons of RAF fighters airborne, reached the London area, causing widespread damage and casualties.

Greatly exaggerated claims were made at this time of enemy aircraft losses; at first the figures announced were 188 certainly destroyed, 45 probably destroyed and 78 damaged. In the confusion of battle, with many duplicate claims, and with the need to proclaim 15 September to be the outstanding air victory that it undoubtedly was, the errors are understandable. Later and more careful research showed that, for an RAF loss of 26 aircraft, the Luftwaffe had lost 60 machines.

This was a somewhat lower German loss than the 76 enemy aircraft that had been destroyed on 15 August, but far more important than the arithmetic was the fact that, after two months of combat over hostile territory, and with the Channel separating them from the safety of their own bases, the German crews were still being met by up to 300 aggressive fighters every time they crossed the English coast. With this latest and serious reverse, there were now clear signs on the German side of an erosion of the will to carry on the struggle. In a campaign characterized by mutual attrition and exhaustion, the Luftwaffe had started to crack: it was the turning point in the Battle of Britain. Even more significantly, Hitler, after three days of hesitation, now decided to postpone Operation 'Sealion' indefinitely.

After launching a handful more of heavy attacks, the Luftwaffe now restricted its bomber force to night operations, leaving almost all daylight activity to be carried out by high-flying fighter-bombers and fighters. Like the earlier switch to night raids, these daylight attacks posed new problems for the defence, this time because they were being flown at heights up to as much as 33,000ft, an altitude that only the Spitfire could match. What was more, a new variant of the Bf 109E was being employed on these raids, with an uprated engine and in some cases a long-range fuel tank. Although only a single 250kg bomb could be carried by these fighter-bombers, the sheer weight of numbers, sometimes amounting to a stream of 1,000 sorties in a single day, made this phase a particularly wearing one for the pilots of Fighter Command. The strain imposed upon them was made worse by the fact that the defence radars could still not accurately measure the height of incoming raids, and since the available warning time was not enough to allow for a climb to the heights often required, Park had to resort in many cases to wasteful standing patrols. But the many efforts by the Luftwaffe to sustain its daylight assault were by now fading, and indeed the Royal Air Force counts 31 October as the official end of the Battle of Britain. The battle *over* Britain, would now move almost entirely to the hours of darkness in what became known as the Blitz.

The nightfighting capability of the Royal Air Force was still quite unable to deal with the raids of the Blitz, and during the period from 7 September to 13 November night fighters were able to claim only eight enemy aircraft shot down. The overall loss rate suffered by the Luftwaffe to fighters, guns and barrage balloons together was less than 1 per cent of sorties dispatched. Meanwhile the night attacks were causing considerable damage and not a little alarm. Not least among these raids was the attack on Coventry during the night of 14/15 November, in which 554 people were killed and 865 seriously injured. In comparison with some of the casualty lists later in the war, these figures may be thought modest; but, at the time, this night raid and the many others that were being directed against British cities in the winter of 1940 were a very serious problem. It was crucial that the defences should be able to deal with this new threat.

One set of measures that was adopted was designed to counter Luftwaffe navigation aids, including their Knickebein radio beam, a system that had been unmasked and to a great extent countered by British scientists, notably by Dr R. V. Jones. A more advanced aid to navigation, the 'X' Gerät, used by a special Luftwaffe pathfinder unit, was similarly discovered and an effective jamming apparatus to deal with it was soon in use. In another passive counter to the German night attacks, dummy targets were constructed up and down the country. Known as 'Starfish' sites, these were carefully constructed so as to simulate the lights of a town being dimmed on the approach of raiders, and even the effects of blast furnaces and the sparks from tramlines could be reproduced in some of them. Once the bombers began releasing their loads, reasonably convincing explosions and fires could also be produced on the ground by the use of various pyrotechnics. By 1942 there were 209 Starfish sites operational up and down the country, and there were several occasions when they succeeded in drawing off some of the weight of enemy air attack, notably at Cardiff on the night of 4/5 March 1941 and Portsmouth on 17/18 April.

This same period also saw the start, on a very small scale, of what became known as intruder operations, in which RAF aircraft flew long-range patrols over German territory hoping to catch the bombers by surprise near their bases, which were normally well lit so as to aid the returning aircraft. This task had been allocated in December 1940 to No 23 Squadron of Fighter Command, though it was not until March 1941 that the first success was scored using newly arrived Havoc aircraft that had replaced the earlier and unsuccessful Blenheims.

More important than all the passive measures and the early intruder operations, however, were the improvements now beginning to appear in the night fighter force itself. Not only were the newly formed Operational Training Units producing better trained crews, but by March 1941 five of the six Blenheim squadrons had exchanged their machines for Beaufighters, and all of them carried the more effective Mk IV airborne interception radar. The pilots of the eight Hurricane and Defiant squadrons on night fighter duties had at the same time been gaining more experience, and, finally, the number of GCI stations to control the force had grown to eleven. The effect of these developments is shown by the number of enemy aircraft claimed by the night fighters during the early months of the year: in January, three attackers were shot down, in February eight, in March 22, in April 48, and in May no fewer than 96.

Most of these Luftwaffe losses were suffered during what turned out to be a campaign to cripple British ports and shipyards by night attacks, while in the Atlantic the German U-boat fleet sought to cut the sea lines of communication. These raids, together with occasional attacks on the British aircraft industry, would, it was hoped, bring the country to its knees before German military might was switched to Eastern Europe for the forthcoming invasion of the Soviet Union. Between mid-February and mid-May 1941 there were 61 raids in which more than 50 Luftwaffe aircraft took part. Forty-six of these attacks were directed at ports such as Bristol, Swansea, Cardiff, Hull and Southampton, while major raids were also launched against London, Coventry and Birmingham. The two attacks on London on 16/17 and 19/20 April were the heaviest that the city had seen, and extensive damage resulted. A final raid on the city during the night of 10/11 May was almost as severe, but by then the Luftwaffe had begun to redeploy to bases closer to eastern Europe, and attacks on Britain gradually subsided until most raids took the form of small harassing attacks against seaside towns.

It had been a powerful German offensive, and one that in its early stages had caused significant damage to the British aviation industry and also some loss of production, both because plants had been hit and because the factories had been compelled to disperse. Other industries such as shipbuilding, vital in order to counter the losses being sustained at sea, as well as the steel industry, communications and other parts of the national infrastructure, had also suffered damage. Many urban areas had been quite severely hit, and apart from the resources that were consumed in mitigating the worst effects of the raids, about 40,000 civilians had been killed and around 46,000 injured. These figures are of course nothing like those predicted before the war, but they were none the less very serious. From a strategic point of view, the diversion into the defence of manpower, of fighters and of guns that were badly needed in the Middle East was an even more telling consequence of the air war over Britain. Nor had the air offensive been particularly costly to the enemy. The Luftwaffe had lost around 600 aircraft in the night attacks, but this represented a rate of only 1.5 per cent of sorties dispatched — a figure that Bomber Command would come to see as highly satisfactory during its own bombing offensive over the following years.

In retrospect, it is clear that at the strategic level the whole German air campaign against Britain was ill-conceived and poorly executed. The first stage of the campaign was intended to gain air superiority over the intended invasion area, yet attacks were made against many airfields that had no role in the battle and the Luftwaffe thus failed to concentrate the weight of its efforts on the airfields that were crucial to the defence. A great deal also depended on the operation of the British radar chain, but the importance of these sites was either not recognized or it was ignored. Faulty intelligence also played a part. The Germans not only underestimated the strength of Fighter Command, but they also chose to overlook the importance of British aircraft factories in making up combat losses. British fighter production at the time was almost twice the rate being achieved in Germany, yet little effort was devoted to destroying these sources of new aircraft, and instead the Luftwaffe attacks were directed against a whole range of industries and facilities, with little clear logic behind them. Finally there was the German switch from the assault on British airfields to bombing raids against cities, and especially against London. This not only relieved the direct pressure on Fighter Command, but it meant that the fighters of the Luftwaffe could remain in the combat area for only a very limited time, yet the deeper penetration over England that was entailed meant that the defences were given a better opportunity to intercept the raids.

THE 'BAEDEKER RAIDS'

For most of 1941 and for the whole of 1942 the Luftwaffe was heavily committed in Eastern Europe, the Mediterranean and North Africa. Only about a quarter of its operational strength was deployed in Germany itself and in occupied Western Europe, with the result that the pressure on the air defences of Britain was greatly reduced. To be sure, during the latter months of 1941 scattered raids still took place, most of them carried out by fighter-bombers, though, unlike the attacks by high-flying aircraft at the start of the year, these raids were made at very low level, with the attacking aircraft often coasting in below the coverage of the radar screen. Many targets such as railway installations, barracks and harbours were attacked along the South Coast, and the raids proved difficult to intercept until standing patrols of defending fighters were again introduced.

In April 1942, however, there was a change of pace. As we saw in Chapter 4, on the night of 28/29 March Bomber Command carried out a highly destructive attack on the historic city of Lübeck, and a month later the bombers raided Rostock on four consecutive nights. In retaliation, the Germans now began to attack similarly ancient towns and cities in Britain in what became known as the 'Baedeker Raids' (so named after the *German Handbook for Travellers to Britain*, first published in 1842 by Karl Baedeker). Bath, Exeter, Canterbury, Norwich and York were all attacked in turn, with the loss of over 1,600 civilian lives, a total of 1,760 people injured and very great damage to irreplaceable buildings.

But by now both the active and the passive defence measures in Britain had been greatly improved, so that the fourteen main raids that took place during this new offensive between April and early October cost the Luftwaffe about 40 bombers, which, though not a large number, was an important loss from the modest force by now still remaining the West. By the end of July three RAF squadrons of newly arrived Mosquito night fighters, with their high speed and formidable armament of four 20mm cannon and four machine guns, were providing a highly effective defence, while the German attempts to employ their 'X' and 'Y' beam bomber guidance systems were being countered with growing effectiveness by No 80 Wing of the Royal Air Force. Even the German use of pathfinders, a technique which they hoped would overcome the inexperience of many of their new crews, did not always produce the concentration of attack that had been expected.

A period of relative quiet followed the Baedeker Raids, to be broken in January 1943 when another series of air attacks was launched by the Luftwaffe. On the night of 17/18 January the heaviest raid since July of the previous year was made, followed by another attack, this time in daylight, three days later. But by now Fighter Command held twelve night fighter squadrons equipped with Beaufighters and another six with Mosquitos. Two squadrons of Bostons were operating in the night intruder role, and Anti-Aircraft Command had increased

Above: An enemy bomb fell without exploding on the parade ground of RAF Hemswell, Lincolnshire, during an attack on 27 August 1940. It is seen here being detonated by the station armament officer. (IWM)

its holdings to a total of 2,075 radar-laid heavy guns, 1,453 40mm Bofors weapons and numerous cannons for use against low-flying aircraft. The result was a series of engagements so unsatisfactory for the Luftwaffe that Hitler now appointed newly promoted Generalmajor Peltz to be Angriffsführer England (Attack Leader England), whose task it was to direct the whole air operation and to remedy the weaknesses in attack that had by now become so very obvious. But the Luftflotten facing Britain by this stage of the war were much weakened. Luftflotte 3, for example, showed a strength of only 124 serviceable aircraft on 30 September 1943, and the supply of new machines was barely keeping up with losses in combat and in accidents. Some modest successes followed, but on the whole the new offensive failed to make the impact that had been hoped of it, and on 6 June it came to an end. Many more scattered raids would take place during the following months, but it was not until the German V-weapons were first launched against Britain in June of the following year that enemy attack from the skies again posed a really serious threat to the British Isles.

CHAPTER 6

CRISIS ON THREE FRONTS

Despite the inter-service disputes of the 1920s and 1930s and in particular the arguments over the future control of maritime aircraft, when the Second World War began there was a very high degree of co-operation between the Royal Navy and Coastal Command, notably at the level of the operational headquarters. Coastal Command, which, it will be recalled had been formed in 1936, had three Groups, No 15 with headquarters at Plymouth, No 16 at Chatham and No 18 at Rosyth. Each of them was manned by a joint naval and air staff, sharing the same operations room.

This satisfactory arrangement was, however, not matched by a similar readiness for war in terms of equipment. Although the Inskip Award of 1937 had paved the way for the transfer of carrier-borne aircraft to the recreated Fleet Air Arm, land-based aircraft in the maritime role remained the responsibility of the Royal Air Force, and during the whole of the inter-war period maritime aircraft had to take their place in the RAF order of priorities. It was a very modest place, both because of RAF policies and because of Admiralty perceptions of the likely course of war at sea.

As to RAF policies, the meagre resources that were available for new equipment before the rearmament drive of the late 1930s meant that apart from a total of around a hundred flying boats such as the Short Singapore III and the Supermarine Stranraer, both of them elegant but ponderous machines dating from 1935, very few aircraft had been procured for the maritime role. One land-based maritime aircraft had entered the inventory, but this was the Vildebeest of 1928, a design that was a hopeless compromise between the demands of colonial policing and those of the seaward defence of Singapore. One other and more important maritime aircraft entered service during the later 1930s as rearmament gathered momentum, however, and this was the Short Sunderland. It was a military development of the 'C' Class Empire flying boat and had been designed to meet Air Ministry Specification R2/33, which called for a four-engine monoplane to replace the outmoded biplanes. Twenty-one of these aircraft were ordered by the Air Ministry in March 1936 to meet Specification 22/36, and the first examples in the front line arrived in No 230 Squadron in Singapore — another indication of the extent to which the overseas commitment of the

Right: A Vildebeest of No 36 Squadron over Singapore before the outbreak of war in the Far East. (RAFM)

Service, which had played so important a part in preserving its independence, still had an influence on procurement decisions. To mention that factor is by no means to decry the very real operational value of the Sunderland — indeed, it flew with great distinction throughout the Second World War and later. A total of 749 of the type were built, and some remained in front-line service until 1959. The last Sunderland was withdrawn in that year — oddly enough, in the light of all that had gone before, from No 205 Squadron, also in Singapore.

In another procurement decision of these pre-war years, 1934 saw the Avro company being asked to tender for the design of a twin-engined landplane for the maritime reconnaissance role, and the company adapted the Avro 652 six-passenger civil machine in order to do so. The only competitor to the Avro contender was a military version of the de Havilland Rapide, but this was an aircraft much inferior both in range and in endurance to the Avro submission, and what became known as the Anson was thus accepted by the Royal Air Force. It duly entered service with No 48 Squadron at Manston in March 1936, and it is worth noting in passing that in various marks and roles, just over 11,000 Ansons would eventually be produced. As a maritime aircraft, however, it was lacking both in range and in armament, and in the summer of 1939 the Lockheed Hudson, a military version of the Super Electra airliner, began to replace it in the front line. Two squadrons of Hudsons were available at the outbreak of war, and over two thousand of these aircraft would eventually be delivered to the Royal Air Force.

THE MARITIME REQUIREMENT

Other than these modest improvements in maritime capability, very little had been done even in the late 1930s to build up Coastal Command. Instead, as we have seen in Chapter 3, priority had at first been given to the procurement of bombers, with fighters coming second. Then, from April 1938 onwards fighters came first and bombers second. But in neither case did the maritime role play a part in the desperate efforts of those late pre-war days to build a modern air force on the debris of the disarmament years.

The second reason for the largely obsolescent state of Coastal Command's inventory of aircraft, particularly in anti-submarine capability, was that the principal threat to British seaborne trade in war was assessed by the Admiralty to be posed by surface raiders rather than by submarines. These raiders were seen as challenges with

Short Sunderland II

This military version of the Imperial Airways flying boat entered service in 1938, its rugged all-metal monoplane construction marking a decisive step forward from the mainly wooden structures of the biplane types in the maritime role. In the Mk V variant of the Sunderland, four Pratt and Whitney Twin Wasp radial engines delivered 1,200hp each, giving the aircraft a top speed of 213mph. On operations it had a maximum radius of action of about 450 miles. It carried a crew of thirteen, and its defensive armament was made up of eight Browning .303s. A war load consisting of 2,000lb of bombs, depth-charges, mines or pyrotechnics was carried internally, to be winched out for release along rails mounted under the mainplane. With its endurance of more than eleven hours (almost double that of its immediate predecessor, the Short Singapore III), this aircraft proved to be a valuable addition to Coastal Command.

which the Royal Navy would deal, employing its powerful surface forces together with its own fleet of submarines. Aircraft would be employed, if at all, in the reconnaissance and spotting roles. There was thus no pressure on the Royal Air Force to devote more of the scarce resources available to a role that was accepted by all concerned as being of rather marginal importance — and this despite the lessons of the First World War.

The result was that not only were effective maritime aircraft lacking, but the development of anti-submarine weapons had also been neglected, and the war stores that were available were virtually useless. This uncomfortable fact began to intrude on 3 December 1939, when a 100lb Mk III anti-submarine bomb was dropped in error by one of the Ansons on a British submarine, *Snapper*, and although the weapon struck the boat at the base of its conning tower the pressure hull was undamaged.

The other airborne anti-submarine weapons available at this time, the 250lb and the 500lb Mk III bombs carried by the Sunderland, were found to be ineffective unless they exploded within about six and eight feet respectively of a submarine's pressure hull, accuracies that were quite beyond the crude bomb sights then to hand. Even the Hudson, the only maritime aircraft until the end of 1939 with a bomb-release distributor that could lay down a stick of bombs, depended for aiming on the Mk IX bomb sight, which in turn required a steady run up to the target at a height not below 3,000ft. This mode of attack posed little threat to a manoeuvring submarine. Only when depth charges were modified for air-drop, as they were the following year,

Right: A Sunderland at Bathurst, Gambia, in March 1942. (AHB)

Right: Lockheed Hudsons began to replace some of the Ansons of Coastal Command in the summer of 1939. By 1942 some of the Hudsons were fitted with airborne lifeboats for air/sea rescue duties, as seen here. (AHB)

was this serious deficiency in anti-submarine capability rectified.

At the outbreak of war Coastal Command was thus in some difficulty. It held ten squadrons of Anson general reconnaissance machines, worthy aircraft but limited by their top speed of only 178mph and range of around 250 miles; one squadron of Hudsons, aircraft with a top speed of 246mph and an endurance on patrol of 6 hours; two squadrons of Sunderlands with a speed of 213mph, an endurance of over 13 hours and a payload of over 2,000lb, and, finally, two squadrons of older flying boats, one of Stranraers and one of Londons.

It was as well that the tasks at first given to the Command made only modest demands on so inadequate

a force. As it was, its duties during these early months of the war were mainly made up of reconnaissance patrols over the North Sea and convoy protection down the east coast of Britain. This relatively low-key start to operations came about largely because the German submarine threat was itself at only a modest level, and certainly nothing like the mortal danger in the Atlantic that it was to become two years later. At the outbreak of war the German Navy held a total of 57 U-boats, 32 of which were too small for operations in the Atlantic. Another 79 were at that time being built or were on order. Of the boats actually available on 3 September 1939, seven or eight were already on station to the west of the British Isles — indeed, a British liner, the *Athenia*, was sunk on that very first day of the war. Thereafter losses of British and Allied merchant ships continued at a steady rate: 53 in September, 46 in October, 50 in November and 72 in December. Of this total of 221 ships, 114 were lost to U-boats or were believed to have been sunk by mines laid by U-boats.

These losses were of course heavy, but they were by no means disastrous. On the other hand, over the same period the U-boat fleet lost nine boats, six of them to the Royal Navy; and since the rate of construction averaged only two new boats each month right up until mid-1940, this erosion of his strength gave Dönitz, the Commander-in-Chief of the U-boat fleet, cause for serious concern. It was a trend that would continue for some months to come. According to the Militärgeschichtliches Forschungsamt history, 27 boats were lost in the ten months of war up to mid-1940, while during the same period only 20 new craft joined the fleet. From the British point of view it was thus possible to conclude that the first phase of the war at sea had been reasonably successful.

Apart from commerce raiding, and the audacious sinking of the battleship *Royal Oak* in Scapa Flow by *U47* in October 1939, the first real test for the U-boat force came with the German invasion of Norway on 9 April 1940. Thirty-one boats were available for operations at this time, and they were able to make over thirty attacks on Allied targets that ranged from battleships to troop transports. The result of such a weight of underwater attack should have been an Allied disaster; instead, it was an almost farcical German failure. Nearly all the torpedoes fired by the U-boats failed to explode on their targets or else ran beneath them. It turned out that not only were the magnetic fuses disabled by the local geological conditions in northern waters, but the mechanical fuses were also faulty and so were the depth-keeping devices on many of the weapons. So serious were these weaknesses that the boats were actually pulled out of the campaign altogether on 17 April, eight weeks before the Allies themselves withdrew.

This German set-back was paralleled by a pair of technical disappointments on the British side, disappointments that were to have longer term consequences. Great hopes had been placed on two new aircraft types for Coastal Command, the Saro Lerwick twin-engined monoplane flying boat, which entered service in June 1939, and the Blackburn Botha strike aircraft, which began to replace the Anson in May 1940. Both types were utter failures. The results of this were twofold: Shorts, who were meanwhile busy switching the Sunderland production line over to Stirling bombers,

had to resurrect the flying boat jigs, with all the delays in delivery that this involved; and the planned maritime strike aircraft were not forthcoming at all, leaving a serious gap in front-line capabilities.

An even more serious set-back, this time at the strategic level of the maritime war, resulted from the fall of France. From now on German fleet units could operate from bases all down the Atlantic coast from northern Norway to the Spanish frontier. This entirely new strategic situation meant that U-boats could henceforth save a great deal of time on their passage to the operating areas in the Atlantic, and they could thus remain on patrol for longer periods. Not only did this represent the equivalent of an effective increase in U-boat strength of 22 per cent, but the availability of the excellent facilities in France meant that some of the pressure was taken off the German shipyards. The first U-boat arrived in Lorient as early as 7 July, to be followed over the next four years by a whole armada of submarines that would pose a very serious threat to Allied supply lines. The scene was thus set for the real Battle of the Atlantic.

By this stage of the war, the end of May 1940, fourteen U-boats had been destroyed by surface units of the Royal Navy, five had been lost through various other causes, one had been sunk by the Fleet Air Arm and another had fallen victim to an aircraft of Bomber Command. Coastal Command, at that time concerned

largely with North Sea patrols and with the watch for German surface raiders trying to break out into the Atlantic, had been able to do no more than force a handful of U-boats to dive once they had been spotted, and indeed the aircraft were too poorly armed, as we have seen, to do much else.

Even this was not, however, a wasted effort. In November 1939 German U-boats began laying the first magnetic mines around the east coast of Britain and in the North Sea. Air patrols by the RAF, even though some of them would be carried out by nothing more potent than Tiger Moths, were enough to drive the U-boats below the surface and thus hamper their operations, as well as to give some indication of where the mines had been laid. The mines themselves were soon overcome by means of two technical counters. In the first, degaussing gear was fitted to ships, which rendered the mechanism of the mine inoperative; and second, certain aircraft of Coastal Command were modified to carry a large magnetic hoop from nose to wing tips and tail, which, when flown low over a mine, caused it to explode below (and, it was to be hoped, behind) the aircraft.

With the Royal Navy heavily engaged during the summer of 1940 in the evacuations from Norway, Dunkirk and Brittany, and then with both the Navy and the Royal Air Force tied down by anti-invasion activities and the Battle of Britain, shipping in the South-Western

Left: A U-boat under attack by a Hudson in the Bay of Biscay, 9 April 1943. The anti-aircraft gun on the submarine's conning tower is in action. (AHB)

Approaches was exposed to the growing weight of attack by U-boats and by the Luftwaffe. Because of the limited range of the RAF aircraft available, air cover by Coastal Command fell off sharply beyond about 15° West, but the new bases on the French coast meant that the U-boats could operate out as far as 25° West. The result was a heavy toll of Allied shipping in the Western Approaches, and 153 vessels were lost to submarines alone from July to September for a penalty of only five U-boats destroyed. It was to be only the first of a whole series of Allied low points in the war against the U-boats.

U-boats at this time had a maximum speed of around 8kts when submerged, but only 4kts if they were to achieve their maximum underwater range of 80 miles. They therefore spent a good deal of time on the surface. By day this could expose them to air reconnaissance; but by night they were reasonably safe, because, without the surface-searching radars that became available at a later stage of the war, air patrols at night were virtually blind. Not only that, but asdic, in which the Royal Navy had invested such very high hopes during the inter-war years, was unable to detect U-boats on the surface. U-boats therefore tended to operate at night, and often made their attacks while surfaced. The problem for Coastal Command was that even if its aircraft had the range to reach the U-boat operating areas, they had no means of detecting the submarines by night; moreover, apart from the inadequate flares that were available, there was no means by which the U-boats could be illuminated for attack.

While the British maritime forces waited for the technologies and for the reinforcements that might reverse this unhappy situation, the sinkings continued into the autumn of 1940, and by October ships were being lost at an average rate of two each day. A particularly heavy loss was sustained by three convoys during the second half of the month, when a total of no fewer than 38 merchant ships went down in three days and two nights. This was capped at the very end of the month when the liner *Empress of Britain*, making a fast passage from the Middle East to Liverpool, was damaged by an attacking Focke-Wulf 200 and then sunk by a U-boat. Though operating in only limited numbers, the activities of these four-engine Luftwaffe aircraft, with their range of up to 2,150 miles and bomb load of over 4,000lb, were also a considerable threat to shipping at this stage of the war. Using the newly occupied airfields in Norway, Denmark and France, they were able to make sweeps deep into the Atlantic, where they could launch their own attacks on shipping or direct U-boats on to worthwhile Allied targets. It was as well that their numbers were limited, but as it was these aircraft managed to sink 48 ships during May 1940 — three times as many as were sunk by submarines during the same month.

In November 1940 there was a change of pace in the war at sea as ship losses to the submarines fell to 32 and remained at about that level for the following three months. Although of course not known to the British at the time, there were four reasons for this. First, after the intense actions at the end of October, most of the U-boat fleet returned to harbour to rearm and in some cases to refit. Second, the general shortage of boats available for operations was made worse by the withdrawal of a number of them in order to train up new crews so as to man the submarines expected from the shipyards in the coming spring. Third, during September 29 U-boats were transferred from the Atlantic to the Mediterranean, reflecting an increased German concern with that theatre of the war. Eighteen of the boats actually arrived. Five were sunk on their way and another six were so badly damaged that they abandoned the attempt. The fourth reason for the decrease in U-boat activity was that at last there was some increase in the number of maritime patrol aircraft available to Coastal Command. This growing strength of maritime air power contributed to a shift in U-boat operations in the Atlantic out to safer areas beyond about 15° West, a redeployment that had the effect of reducing the amount of time that the boats could spend on their operational station.

Nevertheless, the October losses had been severe enough to lead to a special meeting of the Defence Committee chaired by Churchill on the 21st of that month, at which several measures were decided upon to counter the alarming and growing threat to maritime trade. Among these was a shift in priorities from attacks on German preparations for the invasion of Britain to the German threat to the North-Western Approaches. At the same time, and in another very important decision, Coastal Command was to be reinforced. Taking into account the various technical improvements that were by now starting to come forward, the Command was thus at last to be prepared for a time when it would be able to make a more decisive contribution to the anti-U-boat campaign.

COASTAL COMMAND BUILDS UP

Already, by September 1940, the Command had grown to a force of twenty-eight squadrons, with a strength of 461 aircraft. The equivalent of five more squadrons, Wellingtons, Beauforts and Beaufighters, would shortly join the front line, and 57 Consolidated PBY-5 Catalinas would be added early in the next year. These American-built flying boats were to give excellent service. They offered a range of 4,000 miles and an endurance of over seventeen hours and they could carry a payload of over 2,000lb. Nine Coastal Command squadrons would eventually receive these aircraft, and they would also equip a further fourteen RAF squadrons overseas before the war was over.

As to other resources, the most serious problem at this time, as with the rest of the Service, was a shortage of trained air crews: in Coastal Command alone there was a deficiency of about 100 such crews. In terms of weapons, there had been some improvement in quality (though not quantity) with the introduction of the air-dropped depth charge. But even when the shortage of resources was overcome, there was still the overriding operational problem of finding the U-boats in the first place, and it would be some time before this difficulty was overcome. As in so many operational fields during the Second World War, the answer lay in radar. Trials of the very first air-to-surface vessel (ASV) radar equipment had taken place as early as 1937, and by January 1940 twelve Hudsons of Coastal Command had been equipped with ASV Mk I sets that could detect a submarine on the surface at about seven miles. One abiding problem in extending the use of this equipment was that precisely the same technical and industrial resources needed for the production of ASV equipment were also required for AI radars to counter German night bombing over Britain.

At the strategic level, the main concern by now was the 'Atlantic Gap', that stretch of the ocean between Iceland and Newfoundland, some 600 to 700 miles wide, in which no air cover at all was yet available for shipping. Some alleviation was provided by the formation of No 30 Wing in Iceland with its mix of Sunderlands, Hudsons, very doubtful Battles and Northrop seaplanes of No 330 Squadron Royal Norwegian Air Force. Further help was forthcoming with the loan of two Bomber Command squadrons in March, and then in September 1941, three months before she entered the war, the United States took over the responsibility for the active protection of ships out as far as Iceland. Yet another technical innovation seen at this time was the introduction of escort carriers, the first of which, HMS *Audacity*, joined the Fleet in that same September. But in spite of all these welcome palliatives, the North Atlantic gap remained, and it was a weak link that would be exploited by the U-boats for the next year and more.

A shift in the focus of submarine activity at this

Right: A Catalina over
Europa Point, Gibraltar,
March 1942. (AHB)

stage of the war now led in February 1941 to an organizational change in Coastal Command. The key area had become the Western Approaches rather than the North Sea, and No 15 Group moved up from Plymouth to Liverpool to fight the battle, while No 19 Group was formed at Plymouth facing the South-Western Approaches and the Bay of Biscay, an area that would see its full share of activity in 1943. The result of this change was that No 19 Group was co-located with the Headquarters of the Royal Naval C-in-C Western Approaches, an arrangement that would pay important dividends in the trials yet to come — for the crucial battles had not yet begun. Indeed, even up to the end of September 1941, although Coastal Command aircraft had carried out 245 attacks on U-boats, the score was still only one submarine sunk, another forced to surrender, three destroyed in collaboration with units of the Royal Navy and a total of perhaps twelve damaged.

All the same, and with the exception of September, when Dönitz had launched another offensive in the North Atlantic, the last four months of 1941 had shown a distinct shift in favour of the Allies in the war at sea. Quite apart from the gradual involvement of the US Fleet in escort duties, there were four main reasons for this. First, from June 1941 onwards German maritime signals traffic was increasingly being read by the British, making it possible to route Allied convoys away from the areas most threatened by U-boats. Second, high-frequency radio detection equipment was by now becoming available at sea as well as on land, making it possible rapidly to fix the position of a submarine's radio transmissions, even though those transmissions were extremely brief. Third, ASV radar was improving, and at the same time seaborne radars were being fitted to British ships. A fourth reason for the shift in favour of the Allies, and a factor that led to sometimes over-optimistic views on the success of the anti-U-boat campaign, was that the German U-boat dispositions were changed once more. This came about when, in June 1941, the German invasion of Russia caused Hitler to deploy boats to the Arctic and to the Baltic, leaving at one stage only eight to twelve U-boats at sea in the Atlantic. Then during August 1941, ten U-boats were sent to the Mediterranean in an effort to secure German lines of communication to North Africa, and fifteen more deployed to the focal point of Allied sea communications in the area of Gibraltar, with the result that, for a period, U-boat operations in the North Atlantic almost ceased, just at the very time when they had been causing grave concern in Britain about the future viability of the Atlantic routes. It was a missed German opportunity that ranks with the enemy's failure to press home his assault on Fighter Command in the summer of 1940.

To some extent this lost opportunity was balanced by a misappreciation in British operational decision-making. The Admiralty was urging that priority in the attacks by Bomber Command on German-occupied French ports be given to the capital ships harboured there, *Scharnhorst* and *Gneisenau*. This was at a time when enormously strong concrete pens for U-boats were beginning to appear in the French ports, and had these partly completed pens been bombed instead of the warships, it is just possible that significant damage could have been inflicted on the U-boat fleet both at the time

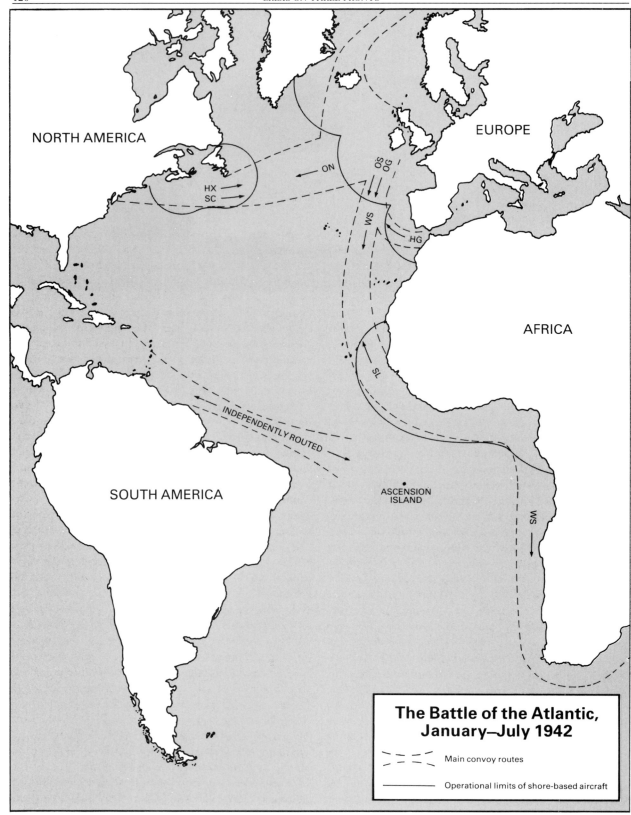

NORTH AMERICA

EUROPE

ON

HX
SC

OS
OG

WS

HG

AFRICA

SL

INDEPENDENTLY ROUTED

SOUTH AMERICA

ASCENSION
ISLAND

WS

**The Battle of the Atlantic,
January–July 1942**

Main convoy routes

Operational limits of shore-based aircraft

and later, though it has also to be remembered that Bomber Command was still incapable of delivering the tonnage of bombs that later years would see. In the event the pens were completed, and from the end of 1941 any effort against these structures was bound to fail, even employing the massive resources that eventually became available to the RAF.

Quite apart from the anti-submarine effort in which it was by now trying to play a full part, Coastal Command had been developing the capability for strikes on enemy merchant shipping, and by the middle of the year Beauforts, Hudsons and sometimes even Blenheims of No 2 Group were making frequent 'freelance' attacks on German vessels in the Channel and the North Sea. During the second half of 1941 Coastal Command, with some support from Fighter and Bomber Commands, attacked 698 enemy vessels, sinking 41 and damaging many more, for the loss of 115 aircraft. Although these activities were serious from the German point of view, and although they caused scarce resources to be diverted to the defence of German convoys, the losses to the Royal Air Force were also heavy, and the value or otherwise of the sacrifice became a matter of some controversy. By arming many of their merchant ships, and by providing often heavy escort for them, the Germans compelled attacking RAF aircraft to abandon low-level tactics from July 1942. The resulting lack of accuracy was a serious weakness, and one that led the Commander-in-Chief Coastal Command, Air Chief Marshal Sir Philip Joubert de la Ferté, to suggest the use of Beaufighters. Some of these would be armed with torpedoes (the aircraft then being known as 'Torbeaus') while others would rely on guns and bombs for attacks on shipping. The result was that a Strike Wing of Coastal Command was formed in November 1942, made up of three squadrons and based at North Coates in Lincolnshire. No 143 Squadron flew Beaufighters, No 236 was equipped with Beaufighters fitted out to carry bombs, while No 254 Squadron flew a mix of Beaufighters and Torbeaus. Operations began in April the following year, but aircraft losses continued at a high level. It was only in 1944 that a combination of improved tactics, better co-ordination and more aircraft would make it possible to halt enemy surface traffic.

While the maritime strike capability of Coastal Command was being improved during 1943, invaluable progress was being made in another field, and one that would be vital to very many types of operation — photographic reconnaissance. As early as 1940 a number of Spitfires had been equipped with cameras and painted a light blue colour so as to make them as inconspicuous as possible at very high altitudes, and during August that

Bristol Beaufort

A new generation of maritime attack aircraft was introduced by the Beaufort, an aircraft which joined the front line of the Royal Air Force in November 1939. It remained the standard torpedo bomber for the Service until 1943, when it was replaced by the torpedo-carrying version of the Beaufighter. The Beaufort was powered by twin 1,130hp Bristol Taurus VI engines, giving it a top speed of 265mph at 6,000ft, and the aircraft had a range of over 1,000 miles with an endurance of up to six hours. The last of the type was withdrawn in 1946.

year these aircraft had been busy photographing concentrations of German barges and other vessels in the Channel ports. By December 1942 the improved Spitfire Mk XI was available for this role and Mosquito Mk IXs had joined them. By the following year, aircraft of the Photographic Reconnaissance Unit (as this force had been designated) were operating as far afield as northern Norway, Budapest, Berlin and Vienna in a role that would play an outstanding part in the later Allied successes of the war.

With the German declaration of war on the United States on 11 December 1941 and the early Anglo-American decision that the strategic priority should be given to the war against Germany rather than that against Japan, the Atlantic became an even more important theatre of operations. Without secure communications across it, the huge military effort needed to free Europe could never be assembled. But, at the same time, this extension of the war also had the effect of releasing the U-boat fleet from any restraint in its attacks on American shipping, and Dönitz was quick to take advantage of the fact, inhibited only by a paucity of submarines. Although by now there were 249 German boats altogether, 158 were in the training role or on trials, 26 of the remaining craft were committed to the Mediterranean, six were off Gibraltar and eight more were assigned to the Norwegian coast. This left 51 submarines, but of that number around 30 were undergoing repairs or refit at any one time, so that the number actually available to operate in the Atlantic was only about 22, including those on passage to the killing zones.

Nevertheless Dönitz was able to launch an offensive on shipping off the fully lit east coast of the United States, and by the end of January 1942 some 23 ships had gone down. Total losses to the U-boats now continued to rise, until 95 ships were sunk during March, another 66 in April, 120 in May and 124 in June.

Against this, the Allies destroyed only eight U-boats during the first half of the year. It was a potentially disastrous attritional imbalance. By June 1942 it was clear to all, including the Admiralty, that ships alone were unable to maintain command of the sea. The problem was that Coastal Command was still struggling to develop the means to fill the glaring gaps in capability.

The Command was under very severe pressure. Aircraft were in demand in the Mediterranean, in the Far East and to help counter the U-boat threat off the American coast. Only five VLR (very long range) aircraft, Liberator Mk Is, were available even as late as August 1942 to cover the North Atlantic gap. Meanwhile that very month saw the start of 'wolfpack' attacks by U-boats on convoys in the North Atlantic once the ships were outside air cover, and heavy losses were sustained in a whole series of convoy battles. Further south there were signs of some relief. U-boats crossing the Bay of Biscay en route to their Atlantic stations did so on the surface and at night, and a technique was developed in Coastal Command by which the submarines were detected by ASV radar and then illuminated by a powerful airborne searchlight, the Leigh Light. These tactics were at first highly successful; but the submarines reacted by making the transit submerged, and in another response to the sudden effectiveness of night air attack by Coastal Command the Luftwaffe deployed a force of Ju 88 fighters along the Bay of Biscay, leading to a period that saw many small-scale air battles over these waters. Worse was to come during this same critical summer

Right: Spitfires parked at the foot of the Rock of Gibraltar in 1942. Work is in progress to extend this part of the airfield. (IWM)

when the Germans developed a 'search receiver' for submarines that could detect the ASV transmissions at around 30 miles, or twice the range at which the aircraft could detect a submarine. By October all U-boats were carrying the new equipment.

The result was a sharp fall in submarine sightings, greater U-boat freedom of action and heavy Allied mercantile losses. During November 1942, 134 ships were sunk, 83 of them in the Atlantic. The figure for the tonnage of shipping lost was even more alarming: over 800,000 tons had been sunk, making it the second worst month of the whole war, and more than 60 per cent of it had been lost in the Atlantic. It was a time of serious crisis, and until more aircraft with longer range and better equipment could be made available the outlook in the war at sea would remain very worrying.

MEDITERRANEAN OPERATIONS

Although, as we have seen in earlier chapters, the Middle East was intended during the inter-war years to be a focal point for RAF activity, when Italy entered the Second World War on 10 June 1940 there were very few modern RAF aircraft in the theatre. About 300 first-line aircraft all told in 29 squadrons were spread across the vague geographical area known as the Middle East. Under the command of Air Chief Marshal Sir Arthur Longmore, its boundaries included the Persian Gulf, East Africa, Aden, the Balkans and the Mediterranean Sea. Within those boundaries, nine of the fourteen bomber squadrons were equipped with the reasonably modern but short-range Blenheim and two of the four maritime squadrons held Sunderlands. None of the five squadrons of fighters had anything better than the Gladiator, the last biplane fighter in service with the Royal Air Force, while the tactical reconnaissance squadrons were making do with the slow and vulnerable Lysander. The rest of the force was made up of an extraordinary mixture of Battles, Wellesleys, Vincents, Audaxes, Harts and other machines of even older vintage. About half the entire force was based in Egypt, guarding the key route through to the Far East, with the rest stationed in Aden, the Sudan, Palestine, Kenya, Iraq and Gibraltar.

On the Italian side, there were some 282 aircraft based in the Libyan colony, and around 150 in Italian East Africa; but the main strength of 1,200 machines was held in southern Italy, from where the country's African

---

Consolidated Liberator V

In its day, the Liberator had a greater range than any other land-based aircraft in service anywhere in the world, and it soon became a candidate for the role of very long range maritime patrol, a capability that was sorely needed to counter the activities of U-boats in the mid-Atlantic. Mk I versions of this bomber entered service with Coastal Command in September 1941 with an effective radius of action of 850 miles, almost twice that of the Sunderland. As well as a substantial defensive armament of twin .50 guns in nose, tail and dorsal positions, and another three guns of this calibre in a ventral turret and at each waist position, the Liberator carried 12,000lb of bombs and depth charges. Some aircraft were also fitted with Leigh Lights for night work against U-boats. Although the Liberator was the most complex and the most expensive military aircraft of its era, in all its roles it was also one of the most successful and certainly it was the most numerous type in service. No fewer than 19,203 of the various marks were built altogether (this total including spares equivalents).

possessions could be rapidly reinforced. Fortunately the Italian Air Force was as poorly equipped as was the RAF in the theatre. Its best fighter, for example, was the Fiat CR42, like the Gladiator a biplane, with a top speed of 272mph or only 15mph better than the Gladiator. The main bomber in the Italian Air Force was the three-engine SM79, a 1937 contemporary of the Blenheim Mk I with a very similar top speed of 267mph and roughly the same range performance of 1,200 miles but able to carry almost three times the bomb load, 2,756lb of weapons.

Lengthy preparations would be needed before the Italian ground forces were ready to invade Egypt, but already, on 11 June, RAF squadrons began their air offensive with an attack on El Adem, the main Italian air base in Cyrenaica. Other attacks followed, but on a very modest scale because Longmore was holding back most of his strength for the main Italian effort. It was clear to him that, because of the desperate situation in Western Europe, he could expect little reinforcement from home, and even those modest resources that might be made available would have to run the gauntlet of Italian air power in the central Mediterranean. It was this last consideration that now led to the opening of a supply route 4,000 miles in extent right across Africa from Takoradi to Khartoum and thence north to Egypt. The first aircraft reinforcements to make use of what would quickly develop into a main supply artery, six Blenheims and six Hurricanes, were unshipped in West Africa on 5 September and a week later the first aircraft reached the

Canal Zone. It was the start of an air supply route that would be vital to the campaign in North Africa.

In East Africa the handful of RAF squadrons operating out of airfields in the Sudan, Kenya and Aden not only maintained air superiority over the vital sea lane through the Red Sea but also attacked Italian airfields, dumps and military concentrations with considerable success, despite their antiquated equipment (which included such relics as the Wellesley and the Victoria) and in spite of the persistent attempts by the Italian Air Force units in the area to destroy them. In terms of the main theatres of war this was a sideshow, but it was a campaign that the British could not afford to lose if the lines of communication to India were to be kept secure.

Even before the Italian Army in Libya was ready to launch its planned invasion of Egypt, Mussolini attacked Greece from his base in occupied Albania, and Longmore had little choice but to dispatch at least a token of support to the Greeks. This took the form of No 30 Squadron, equipped with a mixture of Blenheim bombers and fighters, which now took up station near Athens in defence of that city. By the end of November, and on instructions from London, two more squadrons of Blenheims and one of Gladiators deployed to Greece, initially finding themselves on very inadequate airfields near Athens. These fighters were able to make a useful contribution to the local defences against sporadic Italian air attack, and some limited offensive work was also possible in the difficult conditions of climate and geography. Some offensive activity in support was also launched from Malta, through whose airfields Wellingtons were by now being routed as reinforcements to Egypt.

This raised the question of the air defence of Malta, which held three well-founded airfields, a flying boat base and even one of the three radar sets that had been sent abroad before the outbreak of war; but there were no fighter aircraft. To fill at least a fraction of this gap, four Sea Gladiators, still in their packing cases as spares for the Fleet, were hastily assembled and were ready for action when the first Italian air attack was made on 11 June. At the end of the month four Hurricanes en route to Egypt were held back in Malta, and, together with the anti-aircraft guns on the island, this modest force was for six weeks all that faced the two hundred or so Italian aircraft based in Sicily. Matters began to improve in early August when twelve Hurricanes flew in from the aircraft carrier HMS *Argus*, followed by various bomber, fighter and reconnaissance machines over the next few months.

In Egypt, meanwhile, Longmore had brought together sixteen squadrons, including some equipped with Hurricanes, aircraft that outclassed any Italian machines in the region. Facing him in Libya, the Italians were still building up their forces for a major offensive,

---

Hawker Hurricane IID

The Hurricane had been the most numerous RAF fighter aircraft in the Battle of Britain, and its main success in operations will always be associated with that victory. It shot down more enemy aircraft in that conflict than the rest of the British defences put together. Later derivatives of the type gained further laurels in quite different roles. Although by 1942 the Hurricane was becoming outclassed by the newer aircraft appearing in western Europe, two developments in aircraft armament gave this 1935 design a new lease of life in the Western Desert and in Burma. One was the introduction of air-to-ground ballistic rockets, and the other was the adoption of the 40mm cannon as an aircraft weapon for ground attack. Hurricane IIDs carrying two of these weapons were the first RAF tactical aircraft capable of delivering heavy and accurate firepower in direct support of ground forces. This version of the Hurricane was powered by a Rolls-Royce Merlin XX engine, producing 1,185hp and giving the aircraft a maximum speed of 286mph. A later version, and the last of the line, was the Hurricane Mk IV, introduced in February 1943, which carried two 40mm cannon, or eight 60lb rocket projectiles or 500lb of bombs or long range tanks. Like the IID, this aircraft proved to be highly effective against a variety of targets, including enemy tanks. The last Hurricanes did not leave the front line until January 1947, when they were withdrawn from No 6 Squadron in Palestine.

---

but in the months since the start of the war in the Mediterranean General Wavell had been preparing a campaign that would pre-empt them. To support the planned Army operations, the RAF had assembled by the end of November a force made up of two squadrons of Wellingtons, two of Hurricanes and three of Blenheims. The Italians opened the campaign by making a tentative advance, but then on 9 December Wavell launched his assault. Very few Italian aircraft appeared over the battle, an unexpected development that made it possible to switch the Hurricanes from air defence duties to the ground attack role. Meanwhile bombers from Egypt attacked the Italian ports of Tobruk, Benghazi, Bardia and Derna along the North African coast, while Wellingtons from Malta attacked Tripoli and intercepted merchant ships crossing the Mediterranean to supply the Italian forces.

The successful British advance now swept along North Africa until the whole of Cyrenaica was captured and most of the Italian Army taken prisoner. A major contribution had been made by the squadrons of the Royal Air Force, supplemented by those of the South African Air Force — a total force of only some 200 aircraft yet one that had overcome an Italian air force in the theatre of twice that number. At the moment of this brilliant victory, however, the German High Command, impatient with the hesitant efforts of the Italians, intervened. A small but powerful element of the Luftwaffe, Fliegerkorps X, deployed forward to airfields in Sicily, where from a distance of only about 80 miles it could attack Malta. At the same time the leading elements of what would become the Afrika Korps disembarked in Tripoli. And, more immediately threatening in terms of the wider strategic situation in the theatre, on 6 April some 27 German divisions, together with a total of about another 23 from Italy, Hungary and Bulgaria and supported by around 1,200 aircraft of Luftflotte 4, now invaded Greece and Yugoslavia. German preparations for this move had already caused Longmore to dispatch additional squadrons to Greece, two of Blenheims, one of Hurricanes and one with a mix of Hurricanes and Lysanders.

Hampered by two days of bad weather over Greece, there was little that the Air Force could do against the advancing Axis columns. When the weather cleared, massive German air attacks were made against the RAF units until by 15 April there were only 46 battleworthy aircraft left. On 23 April the Greek Army surrendered, and the next day the last seven remaining Hurricanes were pulled back to Crete. Valuable evacuation work was

Above: RAF Sunderlands off Greece during the withdrawal. (IWM)

meanwhile carried out by some Sunderlands, Lockheed Lodestars, Bombays and two BOAC Short 'C' Class flying boats, which between them managed to bring out a useful number of British troops. But the brief campaign had been a total failure, causing the sacrifice of valuable British forces for no tangible gain and, as far as the RAF was concerned, writing off almost 200 aircraft that could not be spared. German losses were officially stated to be 164 aircraft.

The loss of Greece was followed by three weeks during which the Germans consolidated their positions in that country, while the British made preparations to defend the island of Crete. Among the British garrison were the remnants of three fighter squadrons and one squadron of the Fleet Air Arm, making a total force of twenty-five machines. In Greece, only 70 miles away, the Germans were assembling 650 combat aircraft, 700 transports and 80 gliders in readiness for their next assault. For more than a week the Luftwaffe bombarded the only two airfields and the only two landing strips in

Crete until, despite a trickle of Hurricane reinforcements from Egypt, the defending fighters were down to a strength of just three Gladiators and four Hurricanes. Clearly, these last few aircraft would soon be lost, and in such a hopeless situation they were flown out to Egypt, leaving the garrison with no air cover at all.

On 20 May 1941 the German invasion of Crete began when the first of about 15,000 airborne troops landed by glider or parachute around the British airfields. All too soon other German forces then landed on the airfields, and despite fierce resistance by the garrison the defence was soon overcome. The absence of air cover also exposed the ships of the Royal Navy to heavy attack by the Luftwaffe, as gallant elements of the Mediterranean Fleet struggled to evacuate what could be saved of the garrison. No fewer than three cruisers and six destroyers were lost in these efforts, while a battleship, an aircraft carrier, six cruisers and eight destroyers were damaged. For all the British forces engaged, the whole campaign had been an unmitigated disaster. The source of the failure lay in the lack of adequate resources, caused by the simultaneous demands of other theatres, and by the long British supply lines leading to the Eastern Mediterranean from the home base in the United Kingdom. Politically the British had perhaps been obliged to do what little they could to help the Greeks; but the result now was that Longmore and Wavell were deprived of the military strength needed to hold on to their gains in North Africa.

THE MIDDLE EAST

Nothing could conceal the fiasco of the British intervention in Greece and Crete. Yet at this same time there was one victory which, though minor, was heartening at the time and, in the longer term, became part of RAF legend. Well to the East of the dismal events just described there was a military coup in Iraq during April in which Rashid Ali, a man with strong pro-German sympathies, came to power. He determined to force the British out of the country, and one of his principal targets for action was the Royal Air Force station at Habbaniya, some 40 miles to the west of Baghdad. The station had been built between 1934 and 1937 as the permanent headquarters of the RAF in Iraq, and it was a very well-found facility which by now held some 1,200 RAF personnel within its seven-mile perimeter, as well as six companies of Iraq Levies, No 1 Company of RAF Armoured Cars and over 9,000 civilians. On the airfield there were about 70 Audax biplanes (variants of the Hawker Hart) and twin-engine Oxford training aircraft, which together made up the strength of No 4 Flying Training School.

It was clear from the first that the British position in Iraq was threatened, and preparatory moves included the evacuation of over 200 British civilians from Baghdad into Habbaniya, as well as the deployment into the cantonment by air of 400 reinforcing troops and the dispatch of a flight of Gladiators — all that could be spared — from Egypt. By 30 April Iraqi forces had closed on Habbaniya and the garrison found itself overlooked from a nearby ridge by 9,000 troops and 28 guns. Meanwhile the garrison had taken advantage of the time available to fit many of the training aircraft with makeshift bomb racks and with machine guns, in anticipation of the worst.

At the very end of April the local garrison commander was given clear guidance from London that the British position in Iraq was to be restored and that the Iraqis facing Habbaniya were to be forced to withdraw. This gave the initiative to the British, and at dawn on 2 May air attacks were launched against the Iraqi positions. Air Chief Marshal Longmore had meanwhile been recalled to London on 30 April for

urgent discussions on the unsatisfactory situation in the Middle East; but he was destined not to return, and Air Marshal Tedder now took over his responsibilities as Commander-in-Chief Middle East Command of the Royal Air Force. It was under this new commander that ten Wellington bombers were now deployed to Shaiba, the RAF base near Basra, and these aircraft led the air bombardment of the Iraqi forces, to be immediately followed into the attack by 35 assorted Audaxes, Oxfords and Fairey Gordons. By the end of the day, 193 operational sorties had been flown for the loss of five machines, two of them shot down and three destroyed by Iraqi artillery fire on the ground. The following day a flight of Blenheims arrived from Egypt to give some measure of air defence against possible attack either by the Iraqi Air Force or by German aircraft which were known to have deployed forward to bases in the north of the country.

On 4 May Iraqi artillery again opened up against targets on and around the airfield, but its fire was largely subdued by continuing air attack against the guns. After this the Iraqis took to firing at night, but patrols by the aircraft of No 4 FTS using very rudimentary night flying aids did much to counter even this bombardment. The following day the RAF air patrols kept enemy shelling to a minimum, while at the same time air attacks were launched further away against Iraqi airfields. More troops now arrived by air to reinforce the garrison, the base was evacuated of women and children and preparations were made for further fighting. The Iraqis, however, finding themselves the besieged rather than the besiegers, had had enough, and during the night of 5/6 May they abandoned their positions above Habbaniya. The crisis was over. Any opportunity there might have been for the Germans to turn the affair into a threat against the Middle East from that direction had now passed, and Rashid Ali fled the country. It had been a minor but heartening incident. A flying training unit, no less, with some outside support, had seen off a substantial hostile force by dispatching some 1,400 sorties in non-combat aircraft equipped only with makeshift armament.

REVERSES IN NORTH AFRICA

Meanwhile, in North Africa, a German light division, together with substantial Italian reinforcements and over 100 aircraft of the Luftwaffe, had arrived by the end of February; about 50 of these machines were Bf 109Es, aircraft that had been transferred with their experienced crews from the Channel coast, and their arrival quickly destroyed the air superiority which the RAF units had

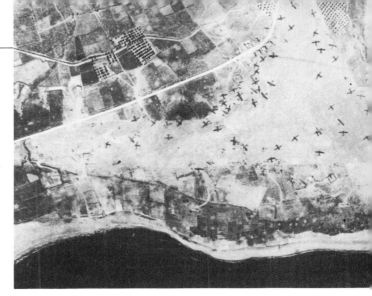

managed to gain. Within a few weeks the Axis forces as a whole were on the offensive and by 2 April it was clear that Benina and Benghazi might have to be given up. RAF Blenheims, Wellingtons and other aircraft made strenuous efforts against enemy airfields and troop concentrations, but the situation grew worse until by 3 April it was chaotic. Army reinforcements were brought up from Egypt to Tobruk and two squadrons of Hurricanes, Nos 6 and 73, were left to operate within the besieged perimeter while the remains of Nos 3 (RAAF), 45 and 55 Squadrons were pulled back into Egypt. An attempt to relieve the garrison of Tobruk during July failed, but meanwhile the advance of the Axis forces, hindered by growing logistic difficulties at the end of an increasingly lengthy supply line, had lost momentum and had halted at the border of Egypt.

Logistic difficulties were not, however, confined to the Axis forces, and the RAF in the Middle East was by this time suffering badly from a loose and incoherent technical organization. A particular weakness was that, apart from relatively straightforward repair work, virtually all efforts to put damaged aircraft back in the air depended upon replacement spare parts from the United Kingdom. In order to tackle this debilitating problem, Air Vice-Marshal Graham Dawson, an engineer and a man of remarkable energy, was sent out to Air Headquarters Middle East in May 1941. Showing very great drive, and with the full support of Tedder, Dawson created efficient maintenance units under a newly formed No 206 Group, established workshops that were capable of engineering work hitherto thought to be out of the question in the Middle East and separated the Maintenance organization from that of the Administration branch, to which it had until then been subordinate. These changes made an invaluable contribution to the increase in front line aircraft strength from about 200 in May to almost 600 in November, and

this was the month in which General Auchinleck, who had by now replaced Wavell, planned his offensive for what had by now been renamed the Eighth Army.

Other important changes in the organization of the RAF in the Middle East were also by now in train. In November 1941 No 205 Group took over the command of the long-range bombers in the theatre; No 201 Group was given the task of naval co-operation; No 202 Group became Air Headquarters Egypt, responsible for air defence; and finally, No 204 Group became Air Headquarters Western Desert. This last formation was made up of mobile Wings and it was the foundation for what later became the Desert Air Force. These improvements were complemented by agreements between the Air Force and the Army on the future use of air power in the theatre, and for example on the overriding need for air superiority. To translate principles into practice was, however, not easy while there were such severe shortages of equipment in radars, light anti-aircraft guns to protect forward airfields, trucks and radios. But gradually the principles were being

Above right: The RAF bombing Maleme airfield in Crete. Many German aircraft, a good number of them wrecked, can be seen on the ground. (IWM)

Right: Hurricanes at an airfield in the Western Desert. (IWM)

absorbed, and slowly the means of implementing them was assembled.

The keys to successful land/air co-operation were threefold: first, a mutual understanding of the concepts involved; second, a high mobility of air force units, that is, the ability to move operating bases swiftly so as to match Army movements in the open spaces of the desert, often by leap-frogging units of the two Wings of the Desert Air Force; and third, really good communications. As we saw in Chapter 1, this was the problem that had caused such difficulties in air-to-ground co-operation during the First World War. Very little progress had been made in the intervening quarter of a century, but at this stage of the campaign the first steps towards the creation of an effective system for close air/land co-operation were at last being taken. Units known as Air Support Controls were created. These were mobile, jointly manned units located at the Headquarters of each Army Corps, with rear links at HQ Western Desert Air Force and the HQs of the RAF Wings, their task being to co-ordinate requests by Army units for air support and relay them to RAF HQs and units for action. Communications were provided by newly formed Air Support Signals Units, which were organized to provide what were called 'tentacles', allotted to forward units of the Army. It was a good start, and it was a system that should have given appropriate priority and a rapid response to requests for air support; but technical teething troubles, combined with the pressure of events, meant that it was a less than successful innovation. During the retreat from Gazala, for example, when air support would have been invaluable to many hard-pressed units of the Eighth Army, only twelve requests for such support were received. The light bomber squadrons in particular were at a high state of readiness, but they were virtually unused. Only the fighters,

employing the 'sweep' (a technique acquired over France after the Battle of Britain), were really effective.

All this lay some way ahead, and meanwhile Auchinleck prepared his offensive and Tedder's command operated far and wide, searching out enemy troop concentrations and attacking ports, supply lines and in particular the sea lines of communication across the Mediterranean so as to disrupt any opposing build-up of combat strength. This was so successful that not only, as we have seen earlier, were German U-boats ordered into the Mediterranean, but Luftwaffe units were sent once again to Sicily with the express aim of subduing the island of Malta. Finally all was ready, and the British offensive in North Africa, codenamed 'Crusader', began on 18 November 1941. By this time Tedder had built his available air strength up to 660 machines in 49 operational squadrons, nine of them in Malta, eleven in the Canal Zone or the Delta and 29 in the Western Desert under the command of Air Vice-Marshal Coningham. It was a force that faced an estimated 642 enemy aircraft in North Africa, including 435 machines of the Italian Air Force — a narrow enough margin since the enemy might well bring in further reinforcements from across the Mediterranean.

Under conditions of air superiority, the advance of the Eighth Army drove ahead and Tobruk was relieved, but then the two Panzer Divisions of the Afrika Korps engaged and the ground fighting swung to and fro. Tobruk was at first again isolated, and then in early January the Eighth Army pressed forward as far as El Agheila, 300 miles to the west, where the opposing lines stabilized. Highly effective air operations continued through this advance, but now the Commonwealth forces were at the end of a supply line a thousand miles long, while the enemy had been driven back to his main port of Tripoli, shortening his supply lines to about half that

Left: An RAF Baltimore in its protective pen at an airfield on Malta. (IWM)

Opposite page, top right: American-made RAF Kittyhawks over Libya in 1942. (IWM)

distance. At this very time, when so much depended on sustainability the Eighth Army lost some of its momentum and the Germans went on the offensive right across the Mediterranean (and especially against Malta), while to add to the wider strategic difficulties, Japanese aggression in the Far East caused a serious diversion of troops and equipment from the Middle East to that more distant theatre of war.

A final factor in reversing the British success was the arrival in Tripoli of two large Axis convoys with reinforcements and large stocks of aviation fuel. The German commander, Rommel, seized this somewhat slender chance and launched a drive to the east. Airfields flooded by winter rains, numerous unserviceabilities and a general overstretching of resources at first hindered many attempts by the Royal Air Force to intervene, though when opportunities did offer themselves great damage was done to enemy columns moving forward. Partly for this reason, in mid-July Rommel came to a halt on a line between Gazala and Bir Hakeim, about 40 miles west of Tobruk, where the positions remained static for the next three and a half months.

Throughout January and February the Luftwaffe in Sicily had been pounding Malta, concentrating mainly on its airfields. By mid-March the number of aircraft defending the island had been reduced to thirty and the force of Wellington bombers on Malta had been obliged to pull out altogether. On 20 March a new phase of the air assault against the island opened when a force of about 150 Ju 88s and Bf 109s attacked Grand Harbour and the Maltese airfields in the first of a series of day and night attacks. This air offensive continued into April, sometimes with up to 300 sorties each day being directed against the island, causing among other things the withdrawal in the second week of that month of the destroyers and the submarines from their bases in Grand Harbour. By the middle of the month there were only six serviceable fighters available in Malta, and the airfields in particular were a shambles. At this crucial stage in the siege of the island, it now at last became possible to send in reinforcements and on 20 April 47 Spitfires were flown in from the aircraft carrier USS *Wasp*, and although many of them were quickly lost the Luftwaffe itself was by now overstretched: at the beginning of May most of the German aircraft based in Sicily and southern Italy were redeployed to France to oppose the growing efforts of Bomber Command or to North Africa in support of Rommel, or — and this was particularly significant — to the Russian Front to support the German summer offensive. Malta itself meanwhile had received another reinforcement of 62 Spitfires, and

although heavy air raids against the island continued, the first crisis was over. The Axis offensive against Malta had changed the island from an offensive base to one that was concerned largely with its own survival; but it had not been eliminated.

By the time the Malta reinforcements arrived, so had those for Rommel in North Africa, and on 26 May 1942 he began his offensive against the Eighth Army in the Gazala–Bir Hakeim position. During that first day Coningham's fighters launched more than 150 sorties in efforts to seize air superiority, but at the request of the hard-pressed ground forces the main effort was switched on the second day to their direct support. Very heavy and confused fighting now followed around Bir Hakeim and at a junction known as 'Knightsbridge', and although considerable resources had to be diverted to protect a convoy trying without ultimate success to make its way from Alexandria to Malta, the Desert Air Force continued its efforts throughout ten vital days while Bir Hakeim held out. On 10 June, however, Bir Hakeim fell, Rommel outflanked the British position and drove for the coast. A British retreat now took place that had all the appearances of a rout, and although the Desert Air Force flew very many sorties where the existence of suitable airstrips made this possible, it was not enough to stop the headlong drive of the Afrika Korps. The withdrawal continued for over 300 miles until it halted on a line between El Alamein and the Qattara Depression to the south. Fortunately, because of the concept of mobile squadrons and the practice of 'leap-frogging' one half of the ground support while the other half continued operations, the Desert Air Force came back to Egypt in reasonable order. But, like the Battle of the Atlantic in November 1942, the campaign in North Africa had now reached a dangerous point of crisis.

THE FALL OF SINGAPORE

This was a low point in the war as a whole, but there was yet a third crisis in British fortunes at this same period — in the Far East. During the early 1920s Singapore had been decided upon as the main British base in that region in preference to Hong Kong, and its defence was planned to depend upon coastal artillery and on torpedo bombers. The particular aircraft concerned were Vickers Vildebeests, which we met in Chapter 2, and by 1939 there were two squadrons of these machines based in Singapore, Nos 36 and 100, operating alongside No 205 Squadron equipped with obsolete Short Singapore flying boats. By late July 1940 the war in Europe was going so badly that the Chiefs of Staff were obliged to abandon a pre-war plan to reinforce Singapore with a handful of RAF squadrons and major elements of the Royal Navy, and they recognized that the defence of the base would have to rest entirely upon air power. It was decided that a force of 336 modern aircraft would be necessary to defend all of the British interests in the Far East, from Ceylon to Hong Kong — a figure that was confirmed by the Chiefs of Staff over the protests of the commanders in the Far East, who had asked for 566 aircraft.

In fact, when Japan launched her offensive across the Far East and the Pacific on 8 December 1941, only 362 RAF aircraft of all kinds were in the theatre of operations, and of those only 233 were serviceable. Of the total number of aircraft available, 158 were in the front line in Malaya, with another 88 in reserve. Apart from the two squadrons of antiquated Vildebeests in Malaya and Singapore, the bomber force was made up of Nos 27, 34, 60 and 62 Squadrons of the RAF equipped with Blenheims, backed by a reserve of fifteen machines. There were also Nos 1 and 8 Squadrons of the Royal Australian Air Force, flying Hudsons, with a reserve of seven machines, and three Catalina flying boats of No 230 Squadron, RAF. For the air defence role, there were four squadrons of Brewster Buffalos: these were No 243 Squadron of the Royal Air Force, No 488 of the Royal New Zealand Air Force and Nos 21 and 453 of the RAAF, backed by a total of 31 serviceable aircraft in reserve. The Buffalo had been rejected for the European theatre of war by the RAF as inadequate, and although local efforts were made in Singapore to improve its performance by substituting .303 machine guns for the heavier American .50 calibre guns, and by reducing the fuel load to only 84 gallons, the Buffalos were hopelessly outclassed by Japanese fighters, notably the Navy Type Zero. This Japanese machine had a speed advantage of almost 50mph over the Buffalo's 270mph, and it had a much better climbing performance. Another important factor was that most of the defending crews were fresh from flying training schools, and they had had very little experience even on the inadequate aircraft with which they were equipped. Japanese crews, on the other hand, were often veterans of several years of air combat in China.

Nor was the ground infrastructure for the defending air force in any better shape than the aircraft that relied upon it. There were 22 airstrips in Malaya, all but two of them, Penang and Alor Star, grass-surfaced despite the generally rainy climate, and most of the airstrips had only rudimentary facilities. On Singapore Island itself there were four airfields, but again they were less than adequate for the demands of war. Only one airfield, Seletar, out of the total of 26 in the whole peninsula had its full complement of anti-aircraft guns, and there were but five radar stations in the country to give any warning of approaching air attack. Finally, communications between the various elements of this overall deployment, including the aircraft radios themselves, were dated in style and inadequate in performance.

Tension in the Far East was high in early December 1941, and when on the 6th of that month Hudsons of No 1 Squadron RAAF sighted two large Japanese convoys 300 miles from the coast of Malaya and heading west, the threat became unmistakable. On the 7th all forces were brought to immediate readiness, and that night the air campaign opened with an attack by No 1 Squadron on Japanese ships off Kota Bharu, where enemy troops were landing. This invasion was timed to coincide with the other Japanese initiatives right across the whole Far Eastern theatre of operations, including the air attack on Pearl Harbor, thus putting intense and simultaneous pressure on the Allies at many points and denying them any opportunity to redeploy forces.

The Japanese assault at Kota Bharu succeeded in drawing most of the squadrons stationed in northern Malaya towards the scene of the landing, while the main Japanese landing took place at Singora just across the border in Siam. At the same time Singapore City was bombed by elements of the 300 or so Japanese Army aircraft based in southern Indo-China, while other aircraft, together with a force from the two available air flotillas of the Japanese Navy, raided airfields and other targets across Malaya. The attacks on airfields were particularly serious since the weapons used were anti-personnel and fragmentation bombs which all too often succeeded in killing personnel and destroying aircraft without damaging the airfield surfaces. They would soon be used by the Japanese themselves. Many of the squadrons lost valuable aircraft in these raids, and to make matters worse the Buffalos, which might have been expected to mount some kind of defence, were found to have defective guns. By the end of the day more than half the aircraft that had been based in northern Malaya were unserviceable, and when on 9 December more aircraft were lost in attacks on the Japanese-held airfields at Singora and Patani, the air commander, Air Vice-Marshal Pulford, called a halt to daylight bombing operations. It had been a disastrous start to the campaign — but worse was to follow.

Six days before the start of hostilities, naval reinforcements for Singapore had arrived in the shape of the battleship HMS *Prince of Wales*, a very modern ship of 35,000 tons carrying a main armament of ten 14in guns, together with the older battlecruiser HMS *Repulse*, armed with six 15in guns, and an escort of four destroyers. Their commander, Admiral Sir Tom Phillips, was well aware of the possible air threat to his force when he sailed into the South China Sea late on 8 December, but he believed that his speed would give him protection against high-level Japanese bombers, and that torpedo bombers were unlikely to operate more than about 200 miles from their bases in Indo-China. If, however, as he intended, he was to attack the Japanese landing forces off the north-east coast of Malaya, he saw that air cover would be essential. The air reconnaissance to the north of his ships for which Phillips asked was provided on 9 December, but the fighter cover for which he also asked depended, because of the short range of the Buffalos, on airfields in the north of Malaya. After Phillips had sailed, it became clear that these airfields were out of action, and that there could be no air cover for the fleet. This news was signalled to Phillips, who turned back for Singapore after dark on the 9th, but then diverted towards Kuantan on the strength of a report (false, as it turned out) that there was a Japanese landing force off that town. Meanwhile the position of the fleet had been reported by a Japanese submarine, and the Japanese prepared a sizeable striking force of aircraft with which to make an attack on the ships. Because Phillips was maintaining radio silence so as to conceal his whereabouts, Pulford had no way of knowing that the fleet was by now in a position where air cover could indeed have been provided from the airstrip at Kuantan itself, and the ships thus remained without air protection.

At first light on the 10th, a force of 88 Japanese aircraft, 61 of them torpedo bombers, headed south to scour the sea along the 105th Meridian, and at 1100 hours the British fleet was sighted. Attacks by Japanese bombers were followed by torpedo attacks from several directions at once, leaving the ships no opportunity to evade. After several hits *Repulse* sank at 1233 hours, and less than an hour later *Prince of Wales* also went down. A signal received by Pulford from *Repulse* at 1219 hours telling him that the fleet was under air attack resulted in a scramble by the eleven Buffalos at Sembawang that had been detailed off for fleet protection, but they arrived just as the second of the two capital ships was disappearing beneath the waves.

This catastrophe was accompanied by continuing air attacks on the airfields in northern Malaya, mounted with such effect that the handful of aircraft remaining were withdrawn further south and efforts both to attack Japanese-occupied airfields and to give close air support to the hard-pressed ground forces were soon abandoned. Attempts to send reinforcements from outside the theatre to the shrinking air force in Malaya resulted in the arrival of ten Hudsons and seven Blenheims by Christmas Day, but then, on 3 January 51 crated Hurricane fighters and 24 pilots arrived in a convoy that had brought Army reinforcements. By now the strength of the air forces in Malaya had been reduced to 75 bomber or reconnaissance aircraft and 28 fighters, and the arrival of the Hurricanes made it possible to put up a more effective air defence when Singapore was attacked by 27 unescorted Japanese bombers on 20 January. Eight of the Japanese aircraft were shot down, but on the following day the raiders returned with an escort of Zero fighters. This time five Hurricanes were destroyed without loss to the Japanese.

A Japanese landing at Endau on the East coast of Malaya on 26 January finally sealed the fate of the peninsula, despite very gallant efforts by the obsolete Vildebeests and their escorting Buffalos and Hurricanes to intervene. Thirteen of the attacking aircraft were lost in short order, the escorts being again outclassed by the Japanese air cover of Zeros. By 28 January there were only 21 serviceable Hurricanes, six Buffalos and a handful of bombers left, and with all the remaining defenders withdrawn to Singapore Island by 31 January the Japanese air effort could now be concentrated on targets in that more restricted area. Very soon the airfields on Singapore Island were almost continuously out of action. Finally, Japanese artillery from across the Strait of Johore joined in the bombardment of the airfields, and the decision was made to withdraw all the fighters except eight Hurricanes and the last six Buffalos from Singapore to Sumatra. Sporadic air fighting by the undaunted crews still in Singapore then continued until 10 February, when the last fighter aircraft left for

Right: Brewster Buffalos over Singapore. The Buffalo had been rejected by the RAF as inadequate for first-line fighter duties at home, and five squadrons of them were instead sent to the Far East, the first becoming operational in June 1941. However, the Buffalo was hopelessly outclassed by the Japanese Zero fighter. (IWM)

Sumatra. On the 15th Singapore surrendered. Pulford, who had managed to escape by boat two days earlier, took refuge from Japanese air attacks on one of the many small islands to the south, where he died while continuing to evade capture.

THE JAPANESE ADVANCE

The campaign had been perhaps the greatest disaster ever to befall British arms. Because of the demands of other theatres of war, the powerful fleet that should have gone to Singapore could not be dispatched, while because priority in the allocation of aircraft had been given to other pressing needs, including those of the Soviet Union, nothing like the strength of air power essential to the defence of Malaya had been made available. Without the air superiority that was clearly vital if an invasion were to be repelled, the efforts that were made at sea and on land were in vain.

An attempt was now made to carry on the unequal fight from the Dutch colonial islands of Sumatra and Java, but it is a story soon told. At the end of January, assisted by Singapore-bound reinforcements that had been diverted to Sumatra on their way from the Middle East, 48 bombers in various states of repair were operating out of Sumatra against Japanese shipping and against occupied airfields in Malaya. Forty-eight Hurricanes had also arrived in the theatre on the aircraft carrier HMS *Indomitable*, 28 of these machines flying safely to Sumatra from where they were able to offer invaluable air cover to the bomber force. On the very day that Singapore surrendered, a particularly successful series of air attacks was made against Japanese forces

attempting to land at the mouth of the Pelembang river, causing such serious losses among the enemy ships and troops that the invasion was for the time abandoned.

This was, however, a last throw, and renewed Japanese attacks caused the Allied forces to fall back on Java, to where by 18 February the remaining aircraft deployed. They made up a force of eighteen serviceable Hurricanes and eighteen Hudsons and Blenheims, which, together with a handful of gallant Dutch pilots, now continued offensive and defensive air operations in the face of the inevitable Japanese invasion of Java. By 6 March it was clear that nothing more could be done, and two Vildebeests that were, incredibly enough, still able to fly were ordered to try to make for Burma. Both crashed in Sumatra. The last two undamaged Hurricanes were demolished, and three Hudsons of No 1 Squadron RAAF which were also still operational were successfully flown out to Australia. Many hundreds of officers and airmen of the RAF, the RAAF and the RNZAF were unable to escape from Java in the chaotic circumstances of the premature collapse of the Dutch Army that now followed, and, as was the case with those taken prisoner in Singapore, very large numbers of them did not survive the appalling conditions of their captivity at the hands of the Japanese during the subsequent three and a half years.

During the Japanese assaults right across the Far Eastern theatre of war, Hong Kong and Borneo had quickly fallen, and now Burma could represent another valuable prize. Its capture would cut off supplies to China, and its natural resources would help make up for the almost total lack of them in the home islands of Japan. Two weeks after the start of the war in the Far

East, Japanese bombers attacked Rangoon and the defending forces prepared themselves to meet the inevitable invasion from the Japanese in Thailand. The main defence line was along the Salween river, and seven airfields together with satellite strips had been built ready to meet the expected attack from the East. Other strips had been hastily constructed at various points up and down the country, but the main problem was not the lack of bases but of aircraft to use them.

In the air the Japanese held an estimated 400 bombers and fighters, against which the defence could field only 37 front-line aircraft, out of the 280 that had been assessed as essential to a successful defence. Sixteen of the defending aircraft were the unsatisfactory Buffalo, while the other 21 were P-40Bs of Chenault's 'Flying Tigers', part of the American Volunteer Group serving the Chinese. We have already seen the Buffalo in the Malayan campaign, but the P-40B, known to the RAF as the Tomahawk Mk II, offered at least a reasonable combat capability, being an adequate though not brilliant machine for this stage of the war. Some improvement in this picture was made in January when 20 Blenheims and 30 Hurricanes arrived, followed by another squadron of each type in February. But the Japanese advance on the ground had by then occupied much of the south of Burma, thus depriving the slender air forces of airfields in that part of the country. Further Japanese air attacks were made on Rangoon between 23 and 29 January during which, despite an almost total absence of air raid warning, the defending fighters claimed to have shot down about 50 enemy machines. Two more days of air assault against Rangoon a month later led to over 60 enemy aircraft being claimed as destroyed, though these figures are almost certainly inflated. The air fighting over the city did, however, have two benefits. First, it made possible the landing through the port of reinforcements; and later, it gave time for the valuable port facilities and the oil storage farms to be destroyed by the retreating British forces.

Most of the surviving aircraft were now pulled back to Magwe in central Burma, or to Akyab on the west coast. But despite some valiant raids by Blenheims and Hurricanes on the airfields that were by now occupied by the Japanese, there was no real hope of gaining air superiority and attacks in turn by the Japanese on the remaining British bases had soon reduced the number of defending aircraft to six Blenheims and eleven Hurricanes, none of them now fit for combat. On the ground the Japanese advance meanwhile continued into central and then northern Burma; this caused the surviving air crews to fly out to Calcutta, while the ground staff, transporting much of their equipment with them, travelled to Chungtu in China. Once there, and lacking any soldierly training, they made themselves available to the Chinese forces in the role of technical instructors.

With the onset of the monsoon in May, the Japanese advance in northern Burma slowed down and then halted; but India and Ceylon were now open to air attack from the bases captured by the Japanese. To improve the defences, four squadrons of Hurricanes were dispatched to Ceylon, two of them from the Middle East, bringing the air force on that island by the end of March up to a strength of 50 Hurricanes, fourteen Blenheims, six Catalina flying boats and a handful of Fulmars and Albacores of the Fleet Air Arm. The British fleet based at Trincomalee, ready to meet any Japanese incursion into the Indian Ocean, was a substantial force consisting of three aircraft carriers, five battleships, seven cruisers, fifteen destroyers and five submarines, and when reports came in that a Japanese strike fleet was threatening to attack Ceylon on or about 1 April, the British force sailed to locate it. On 5 April, while most of the British fleet was refuelling in the Maldive Islands, the approaching Japanese force was sighted by a Catalina about 350 miles south-east of Ceylon. This gave time for most of the Allied shipping in the area to disperse, and when the Japanese air attack came in at dawn on the 5th the defences were waiting for them. Twenty-three enemy aircraft were shot down for the loss of fifteen Hurricanes and four Fulmars, and three days later another air assault resulted in 21 enemy aircraft being shot down for the loss of eleven defending fighters. Meanwhile the Japanese force managed to sink two British cruisers some 300 miles south of Ceylon, as well as the aircraft carrier HMS *Hermes* and two escorts just off the east coast of Ceylon, while a total of 28 merchant ships were lost to enemy action in the waters of the Indian Ocean. Much damage had also been caused to facilities ashore in Ceylon, and the whole episode was yet another triumph for the Japanese, causing the British fleet to withdraw out to the west. At the same time, however, while it was true that the Japanese ships were intact, their carriers had lost many of their best air crews, so that when the fleet returned to Japan, as it now did to re-equip and to take on board new crews, the result was that only two of Admiral Nagumo's five aircraft carriers were available to take part in the Battle of Midway on 4 June, the turning point in the whole Pacific War. In this way the heavy losses suffered by the British sea and air forces off Ceylon played an important if indirect part in a crucial American victory.

CHAPTER 7

BATTLE OVER GERMANY

Although it takes us somewhat ahead of the story, it will be convenient here to mention some of the important changes that were taking place in Bomber Command at about the same time as the shift in bombing policy mentioned at the end of Chapter 3 was coming into effect.

The first concerns the air crews. For the first two years or so of the war, bomber aircraft had carried two pilots together with an observer (whose duties were not always well defined) and gunners, one of whom also acted as the wireless operator. In March 1942 this pattern was changed. Henceforth only one pilot would be carried, and one member of the crew was designated as navigator. The bomb-dropping duties were assigned to an air bomber (or bomb-aimer, as he became known), wireless operators were no longer required to man the guns and gunners were no longer given wireless training. Finally, the new air crew category of flight engineer was introduced. These changes brought about both better training and higher efficiency through clearly defined specialization, and, very importantly, they released more pilots to man the aircraft by now arriving in larger numbers in the front line.

Flying Training Command produced all these specialists through the remarkable Empire Air Training Scheme, later known as the Commonwealth Air Training Plan. This scheme began when the first courses were opened in Canada, and at its peak in 1943 there were altogether 333 Flying Training Schools in Britain and the territories of the Empire, another six in the Middle East and five in the United States, these last under the Arnold Scheme. During the course of the war this whole training machine produced well over 300,000 air crew, most of them, incidentally, trained in Canada.

These men were not, however, formed up into crews until they reached Bomber Command. For this reason, and in order to convert crews on to the operational types of aircraft that they would fly on squadrons, Operational Training Units had been formed early in the war, in which a crew would complete some 80 flying hours together before going on to its operational

unit. The need for this training was to grow as the war continued until by September 1943, the OTUs made up three whole Groups, Nos 91, 92 and 93, with 22 OTUs between them.

Because of the obvious need later in the war to keep more aircraft such as the Halifax and the Stirling in the front line, a pattern of training was evolved in which new crews leaving Flying Training Command went first to an OTU to join together, and to fly interim aircraft such as the Hampden or the Whitley, machines no longer urgently needed for operations. They then finished their lead-in with a short course, of perhaps 45 hours, at what were called Heavy Conversion Units, where they flew an operational type, usually the Stirling or the Halifax.

With the arrival in service of the Lancaster, the training pattern became for a time more complicated. Clearly, few of these high-quality machines could be spared away from the front line, and a third stage of operational conversion was introduced. Crews would form up to undertake a first stage of training on, for example, the Wellington, followed by a second stage on the Halifax or Stirling and then a short third phase at what was called a Lancaster Finishing School. This arrangement continued until 1944, when at last there were enough Lancasters available to equip the Heavy Conversion Units, and training then reverted to the earlier two-stage pattern.

HITTING THE TARGET

None of this could do much to cure the operational problem with which we left Bomber Command at the end of Chapter 4, that of finding and then hitting targets with reasonable accuracy at night. But once approval had been given to set up the Pathfinder Force, Bennett, promoted within the year from Wing Commander to Air Vice-Marshal, acted with vigour and set up his headquarters at Wyton, with Oakington as his second base and using Gravely and Warboys as satellite airfields. All crews in the new force were to be volunteers, they would undertake a tour on operations of 50 missions instead of the 30 which was the rule on the other squadrons of Bomber Command, and they would automatically be promoted one rank for as long as they remained in the force, once they had been assessed as proficient in their role. As a distinguishing mark, a new badge was introduced — a gilt RAF eagle authorized to be worn just above the left breast pocket of the No 1 Home Service Dress tunic, though not on battledress. (This last rule was, predictably, often ignored.)

Five founder-member squadrons made up the original Pathfinder Force: No 7 Squadron with Stirlings, No 35 with Halifaxes, No 83 flying Lancasters, No 109 with two pressurized Wellington aircraft and No 156 also with Wellingtons. It was a force that would eventually grow to become No 8 Group in January 1943, and by the end of the war this Group had grown to a strength of nineteen squadrons. Between August 1942 and March 1943 Bennett and his crews worked to perfect the techniques that would later be so successful in the bombing campaign in Europe. There was much to do, as events were immediately to show on the first Pathfinder-led raid, against Flensburg on 18 August 1942. With 'Gee' jammed by the enemy, cloud over the target, inaccurately forecast winds and no special target-marking devices available even if the target could have been found, the attack was as bad a failure as had so far been seen, the bombs of the main force being scattered over a very wide area.

Improved equipment was, however, being developed and better tactics were being devised. In particular, three different methods of marking were introduced and soon became standard in the Pathfinder Force. One was blind marking on the ground, codenamed 'Parramatta'; the second was visual marking on the ground, known as 'Newhaven'; and the third was a method of blind skymarking called 'Wanganui' (these codenames recalled the birthplaces of Bennett and two of his personal staff). At first the role of the Pathfinders had been simply to find and to illuminate the general area of the target, and makeshift markers were devised for this purpose consisting of bomb cases filled with a mixture of phosphorus, rubber and benzol. Two sizes of marker were common; a 250lb case known as a 'Red Blob Fire' and a 4,000lb case called a 'Pink Pansy'. The technique was that the Pathfinders would lay down markers in the target area and crews of the main force were briefed to find their aiming point within the area lit up by the Pathfinder incendiaries. But this proved to be an unsatisfactory arrangement, even on nights when the target area could be found; and to make matters worse the Germans were highly successful in diverting the attentions of the main bomber force on to skilfully constructed dummy target sites.

From the beginning of 1943 the makeshift markers were replaced by specially designed target indicators (TIs). For ground marking, 250lb cases were employed, now filled with sixty 12in pyrotechnic candles, red, green or yellow in colour, which were ejected from the casing by a barometric fuse to burn for three minutes. These markers were first used over Berlin on the night of 16/17 January 1943. If a marker were fused for a height of 1,500ft, a ground pattern about 60yds in diameter resulted; from 3,000ft the pattern was about 100yds across. Later this device was adjusted to give a pattern that burnt for up to twelve minutes.

By May 1943, however, the Germans had developed simulated TIs that could be fired from the ground on their decoy sites, and to overcome this tactic as well as to give greater accuracy of marking, more advanced TIs were developed. Two main versions were

Right: A Wellington Mk VIII, illustrating some of the many modifications made on later models of this aircraft. (AHB)

known as 'Red Spot Fire' and 'Green Spot Fire'; these markers burnt with very high intensity though with a much reduced ground pattern, and they were used not only on smaller targets but also as route markers to guide the main force to the target area. Meanwhile German decoy sites continued to be a problem, with sometimes up to 30 per cent of main force crews claiming to have bombed on, for example, red TIs when no such colour had been dropped by the Pathfinders. More and more variations of the basic markers were therefore introduced: one carried 200 candles so as to give a larger ground coverage; another changed colour every 15 seconds; yet another actually emitted a two-letter signal in Morse code.

When the target area was covered with cloud, sky markers were employed. These were either parachute flares or candle TIs that had been specially fitted with parachutes. Here, too, various pyrotechnic effects were employed. Some sky markers had mixes of colours: one, the 'White Drip' sky marker, produced an illuminated tail up to 1,000ft long as it fell; another consisted of a group of 25 candles giving a candelabra effect in the sky. One other variation that was brought into use for daylight raids from the autumn of 1944 onwards was the 'Smoke Puff'. This, as its name suggests, produced a large cloud of coloured smoke either on the ground or in an air burst.

With the passage of time, and with growing experience, the Pathfinders developed a number of specialized roles within their broad task of illuminating and marking their targets. Special route markers were designated for their self-explanatory role, as were windowers; but there were also 'Blind Illuminators', 'Recenterers' and 'Backers-Up' who all played their part in the orchestrated activities over the target areas for the main force.

On their own the marking techniques were increasingly successful once the target had been found and identified by the Pathfinder Force; but in the frequently poor weather and reduced visibility over targets in Germany, particularly in the Ruhr, the difficulty was to find the target in the first place. Then in December 1942 another electronic aid, 'Oboe', was introduced which would play a large part in solving this long-standing problem. Gee remained in use as a valuable navigation aid, particularly at shorter ranges, but Oboe was something much more telling in the air campaign — a blind-bombing system.

Oboe was a device by which aircraft was guided from a pair of ground stations, each station transmitting radio pulses which were boosted by equipment in the aircraft, so as to give better range, and then re-transmitted. The system was so arranged that the bomber flew along an arc of constant range from one of the ground stations, known as the 'cat', the arc being laid so as to pass over the target and the ground station signalling corrections by transmitting dots or dashes to indicate deviations to the right or to the left of the required track. Meanwhile the second station, known as the 'mouse', situated on a baseline about 100 miles from the 'cat', was also monitoring the progress of the aircraft. When the aircraft reached its bomb release position, taking account of weapon ballistics, a release signal was transmitted from the 'mouse'.

Oboe was, like Gee, limited in range by the height of the aircraft. From 28,000ft a range of about 270 miles was usually possible; but at lower levels the curvature of the earth brought the range down sharply. The Germans never succeeded in completely jamming Oboe, but there was one serious limitation: because of the characteristics of the system's transmissions the number of bombers that could use Oboe simultaneously was limited. At first only one aircraft could be controlled by a pair of ground stations, though later some improvement was gained by opening more stations and by using more radio frequencies, but operational limitations remained.

Partly for that reason, Oboe was until late in the war fitted exclusively to Mosquitos of the Pathfinder Force. Another reason for selecting the Mosquito as the platform for Oboe was that this aircraft could operate at altitudes much greater than those familiar to the Halifaxes, Lancasters and other bombers of the main force, so that it was effective over a wider Oboe range. Finally, because the Mosquito had a much higher speed it was exposed to enemy defences for a much shorter period during the necessarily steady bombing run along the 'cat' arc up to the 'mouse' release point.

Oboe became widely used by the Pathfinder Force to lay down markers and the three techniques were then known as 'Musical' Parramatta, Newhaven or Wanganui. Whether employed as an aid to marking or as a bombing aid, Oboe was remarkably accurate and in good conditions an average error of about 300 yards could be achieved.

In January 1943, just a month after the first operational use of Oboe, a third bombing aid, H2S, was brought into use. This was an airborne radar system that scanned the ground over which the aircraft was flying, producing the result as a crude map on a cathode-ray screen. Because H2S did not, like Gee and Oboe, depend on ground transmitters, it was not limited in range; nor, since it was self-contained, could it be jammed. But the

Right: A Mosquito Mk XVI of No 571 Squadron. (AHB)

system had weaknesses. First, although it could pick out distinctive features such as coastlines and rivers, the radar screen was overwhelmed by a blaze of radar returns when the aircraft was over a large built-up area such as Berlin. Second, because the returns from smaller built-up areas often did not resemble the equivalent features on a topographical map, its success depended on a high degree of operator skill. Third, and more serious, the radar transmissions from the aircraft could be used by enemy night fighters to home in on the bomber stream. The Germans were not slow to realize this once an H2S set fell into their hands in a crashed Lancaster during March 1943, and they developed two devices to exploit this weakness. One was an airborne interception radar known as 'Naxos', with a homing range of about 50km. This system was first used by the Luftwaffe in January 1944 and by the end of the war some 1,500 German night fighters had been equipped with it. Even more serious from the point of view from Bomber Command, by July 1944 the Germans had also developed and deployed 'Korfu', a ground-based H2S monitoring system which could even detect H2S transmissions made by bombers on the ground at their bases in England. It was thus possible for German controllers to follow the progress of a bomber stream throughout its mission from take off to landing. This weakness was, however, suspected at Headquarters Bomber Command, and as a result a partial H2S silence was imposed in the autumn of 1944.

Most of these developments were of course still far in the future when Harris was about to start in 1942 what he described after the war as the preparatory phase of the bombing campaign. But now, at the very start of that year and just when all seemed ready for the opening of the next phase of the offensive, another diversion was imposed upon the efforts of the Command, again as the result of a worsening situation in the war at sea. This time Bomber Command was instructed, in a Directive dated 14 January 1943, to undertake area bombing raids against U-boat bases on the west coast of France at Lorient and St-Nazaire. This turned out to be both an error and a tragedy. The Germans had by now finished building the enormously strong concrete shelters for the U-boats and their essential facilities (mentioned in an earlier chapter) and the bombing had little military effect. The effect on the surrounding French cities, however, was devastating, and many casualties were caused among the civilian populations. This campaign against the U-boats was continued until the spring, and later extended to include submarine construction yards in Germany such as those in Hamburg.

We should pause here to consider the size of the force by now available to Harris, as new equipment arrived in his Command and as more squadrons of bombers were formed. By early February 1943 the original force of 33 operational squadrons (ten of them flying Battles and six with Blenheims) had expanded to

The Air Offensive over Germany, 1939–45

0   100   200 miles

62 squadrons, fourteen of them equipped with Halifaxes, seventeen with Lancasters and three with Mosquitos — a clear indication of the extent to which really capable aircraft were reaching the front line. The total force amounted to about 600 first-line machines, and very soon raids by up to 600 or even 700 aircraft in a single night would become commonplace.

BATTLE OF THE RUHR

After the diversion of effort in order to strike at the German submarine capability, Bomber Command was able from March 1943 to return to its campaign over Germany, and Harris began what he referred to at the time as the Battle of the Ruhr. It was during this stage of the offensive that the well-known 'Dambuster' raid against dams close to the Ruhr took place. Selected crews were drawn from squadrons in No 5 Group, and formed up in No 617 Squadron, where they trained for six weeks for this single operation. On the night of the raid, 16/17 May 1943, nineteen Lancasters set out at low level in three waves to attack four major dams just east of the Ruhr industrial area. One aircraft was damaged when it brushed the surface of the sea, losing its bomb and forcing it to return to base. Five others were shot down or crashed en route to the target, and a sixth was so badly damaged that it too turned back. Twelve aircraft made their way to the targets; five bombed the Möhne Dam, breaching it; three went on to breach the Eder Dam; and two attacked the Sorpe and one the Schwelme, but without success. Another three of the Lancasters were shot down or crashed on the return flight, making a loss of eight aircraft all told out of the original nineteen dispatched. No fewer than 53 gallant and valuable crew members were killed. It had been an unusually costly raid, but at the time it was also counted a successful one. Water from the dams flooded a large area, disrupting road, rail and canal communications as well as damaging electricity and water supplies in the Ruhr area. In retrospect, however, it is clear that the physical effects of the raid were transitory, the Möhne Dam itself being repaired by late September. The real effect was perhaps a psychological one: the raid caused dismay in Germany, while in Britain it was raised to the status of a legend at a time when good war news was still a scarce commodity. In the longer term, the specialized No 617 Squadron went on to apply its particular skills against several other very important targets as the war and the bombing campaign continued.

As to the Ruhr as a whole during the four months March to July 1943, this key industrial area held many large cities and numerous smaller targets, and the whole of it was within Oboe range. Furthermore, because of the relatively short distance from the bomber bases in Britain to the Ruhr, missions could be carried out wholly in darkness, even during the short nights of late spring and summer. During the four months of attacks a total of 43 major raids were launched by Bomber Command, about two-thirds of them on the Ruhr itself, with the rest being spread widely from Stettin in the north to Pilsen in Czechoslovakia, so as to discourage any tendency for the Germans to deploy their air defences only around the Ruhr.

The Ruhr battle proper opened with a successful attack on Essen on 5/6 March 1943 by 442 aircraft, during which fourteen bombers were lost, and the attacks continued until the third week in July. Duisburg, Dortmund, Bochum, Oberhausen, Wuppertal and Mulheim were all raided, some of them repeatedly, while in the same period other attacks were made on targets such as Berlin, Nuremberg, Munich, Stuttgart and Frankfurt. Not all the raids were successful, particularly over the more distant targets, but in most of the nearer ones, and particularly in Essen, Dortmund and Wuppertal, very extensive damage was caused. During the twenty weeks of the Battle of the Ruhr, 23,401 night sorties were flown by Bomber Command and over 57,000 tons of bombs were dropped. But at the same time the raids had cost 1,000 aircraft, a very discouraging loss rate of 4.3 per cent.

Although this loss rate was far lower than that sustained during the daylight bombing attacks at the start of the war, it is sobering to calculate the odds of an air crew surviving the two tours of operations that were by now normal in Bomber Command (the first tour being one of 30 missions, followed, after a break, by a second tour of another 20). A loss rate of just 1 per cent over 50 missions would have meant that, on average, just over 60 crews out of 100 could expect to survive the two tours; but a consistent loss rate of 4 per cent, for example, would mean that the chances of coming through were 13 in 100, representing odds of over 7 to 1 against. If we examine the statistics for the whole of the war, they are distorted by the large numbers of daylight sorties flown with little or no opposition during its final stages. A better impression is gained from the statistics for night operations only, and these show a loss rate for the whole war of 2.6 per cent. This equates to a survival rate of very roughly 25 men out of every 100 over their fifty missions. But averages can be very misleading, and even these figures do not tell the whole story. Some squadrons suffered relatively few losses, while others consistently took higher than average casualties. No 57 Squadron, the worst hit of the whole Command during the war, lost no fewer than 172 Lancasters, a rate over the 5,151 operational sorties flown of 3.3 per cent.

HAMBURG

After the Battle of the Ruhr, Bomber Command launched at the end of July 1943 a series of four major raids in ten nights on Hamburg, the largest port in Europe at that time, and the second largest city in Germany. Although it had so far been attacked on 98 occasions, Hamburg had suffered comparatively little damage. This was now to change in dramatic and even notorious fashion. Three important features distinguished the tactics that were employed against the

Below: Flak patterns over Hamburg on the night of 19/20 September 1943. Beams of light marked 'A' are searchlights, 'B' are bursts of heavy flak and arrows show other bursts of flak. (AHB)

city in these new attacks. First, although Hamburg was well beyond the range of Oboe, the coastline on the approach path of the bombers offered a distinctive outline for H2S operators, and the city itself, with features such as the Elbe river and the harbour, would also be recognizable on the radar screens. Second, 'Window' was used by Bomber Command for the first time in these raids. Window was the codename for radar-reflective aluminium foil backed with paper and cut into strips exactly 27cm long and 2cm wide. Metal strips with those dimensions, when dropped in large quantities, created false radar echoes not only on the German 'Würzburg' radars used to control the night fighters and on the radars used to lay heavy anti-aircraft guns, but also on the 'Lichtenstein' airborne interceptor radars carried by German night fighters.

Window had been prepared for use over a year earlier, and Harris had pressed for its operational introduction; but concern that this highly effective method of degrading radar might be copied by the Germans delayed its use over Germany until the first of these four attacks on Hamburg. In retrospect, this delay was a grave error. By this stage of the war the Luftwaffe was heavily engaged on the Eastern Front and incapable of mounting against Britain the kind of massive air attacks being inflicted on Germany, whether it used Window or not. But, even worse, the Germans had already developed their own version of Window, codenamed 'Düppel' after the site where successful testing of their metallic strips had been carried out. The Germans also were fearful that their secret might fall into enemy hands, and they too forbade its use. Meanwhile, during the period of the British embargo on the use of Window, over 2,000 aircraft of Bomber Command had been lost to defences that largely depended on radar for control and interception.

The third distinctive feature of these night attacks on Hamburg was that they were complemented by daylight raids carried out by B-17 Flying Fortresses of the US Eighth Air Force. As it happened, these raids, flown on the two days immediately after the first RAF night attack, were severely hampered by smoke over the target area. But this use of bombers from the two air forces in round-the-clock attack was a pattern that would be developed with increasing effect during the months ahead.

The objective of the Hamburg raids is given in Bomber Command Operation Order No 173 of 27 May 1943: 'destroy Hamburg'. There was clearly no longer any doubt about area bombing and its intended effect, and this will be a convenient point at which to mention the higher policy that was at this stage guiding the broad direction of the whole bombing offensive. An Anglo-American conference had been held at Casablanca in January 1943, and one outcome was what became known as the Casablanca Directive. In part this important document laid down that the primary objective for the bomber offensive from the United Kingdom would be 'the progressive destruction and dislocation of the German military, industrial and economic system, and the undermining of the morale of the German people to a point where their capacity for armed resistance is fatally weakened'. It was a formula that had been put forward to the British Chiefs of Staff by Portal three months earlier in October 1942, based on his belief that during 1943 and 1944 it would be possible to drop 1¼ million tons of bombs on Germany, which would have the likely effect of killing 900,000 of the enemy population, seriously injuring another million and rendering twenty-five million homeless. Such an offensive would, he thought, call for a force of between 4,000 and 6,000 heavy bombers. Portal's proposals were significantly watered down before being agreed by the Chiefs of Staff, but the episode illustrates the exaggerated belief in the power of the bomber at a stage of the war when losses in Bomber Command and the failure of many raids were already causing serious concern — a concern, indeed, that had led to the creation of the Pathfinder Force, at Portal's insistence, only two months before he produced his paper.

Quite apart from these inflated expectations, the question of the morality of area bombing directed against civilians cannot be ignored; but as Dr Noble Frankland, the official historian, pointed out in a lecture nearly two decades later, 'the great immorality open to us in 1941 and 1942 was to lose the war against Hitler's Germany. To have abandoned the only means of direct attack which we had at our disposal would have been a long step in that direction.'

Mention has been made of the combined nature of the bombing offensive, and although there is no space here to examine the vast American air effort that was by now building up, it has to be remembered that the night-time operations by Bomber Command were increasingly mirrored by the daylight efforts of the US Eighth Air Force in Britain, and from November 1943 by those of the US Fifteenth Air Force operating from bases in Italy. From August 1943, as the Eighth Air Force continued its expansion, it was putting an average of some 250 bombers into the air on every major raid. As these efforts increased, however, so did American losses, climbing in October 1943 when 175 bombers were lost in seven

operations, a rate of 7.3 per cent, and reaching a peak when 60 were lost out of 367 aircraft dispatched on the Schweinfurt raid on 17 August.

These losses, together with those being sustained by Bomber Command, led to the emergence of another Directive, this one dated 14 May 1943 and known to history as the 'Pointblank Directive'. It laid down six systems in the German economy for air attack, embracing 76 specified targets. High priority was now to be given to the destruction of the German Air Force, particularly its fighters, and the German aeronautical industry. In the event, the Americans shouldered most of this particular burden while Harris concentrated his attention on the German cities. Events were soon to show that the selection of targets in 'Pointblank' was based on well-founded fears about the growing threat from German fighters.

It is against this background of the explicit decision at the highest levels to carry out bombing against cities that the next stages of the strategic bombing campaign should be seen, starting with the first of the raids on Hamburg that were mentioned earlier. Cities were, after all, target complexes containing very many facilities of direct or indirect military value, as well as the inevitable civilian populations. In the night raids by Bomber Command that now followed, all the available heavy aircraft in the front line would take part, and it was estimated that 10,000 tons of bombs would be needed to complete the destruction of Hamburg.

On the first raid, during the night of 24/25 July, the Pathfinders marked an aiming point in the centre of the city, the intention being that the by now well established tendency of the main force to drop their bombs short, known as 'creep-back', would cause a carpet of bombs to be laid back from the centre of the city across the built-up north-western sector, the direction from which the attacking aircraft would approach. A force of 791 bombers took off for Hamburg and 729 of them dropped 184 flares, 261 target indicators, 1,346 tons of high explosive and 938 tons of incendiaries in the 50 minutes that the attack lasted. But the raid was not the success that had been hoped: less than half the bombs fell within three miles of the city centre, and the creep back extended for no less than six miles.

On the second attack, which took place three nights later, 787 aircraft were dispatched. The aiming point was again in the centre of the city but this time the approach was from the north-east. Although the target markers fell short of the aiming point, the extent of the creep-back by the main force was much less than in the first raid, and the result was a heavily concentrated attack on the north-eastern sector of the city. Meanwhile on the ground the temperature was unusually high for the time of year, 30° C at 6 p.m., and the humidity was unusually low at 30 per cent compared with a more normal seasonal figure of perhaps 45 per cent. There had been no rain for some time and everything was very dry; and the fire-fighting services were at the other end of the city still engaged in damping down fires from the earlier attacks. At 1.20 a.m., about twenty minutes after the first bombs had fallen, the many small fires started by incendiaries in a densely built-up part of the city began to spread, finally joining together until a large district was engulfed in a single huge blaze. The intense heat drew in air which fed the flames, increasing the draught until the whole area was a roaring inferno with winds rising to almost hurricane speed. It was a firestorm. The doors and windows of buildings fell out, spreading the fire even further and faster; large trees were uprooted by the force of the wind; and a blizzard of sparks and burning brands was spread into an even wider area as bombs continued to fall. The effect was a catastrophe for the city, and although no accurate figure could be ascertained, something like 40,000 people are estimated to have died.

Immediately after this raid over a million people fled the city in fear of further attack, and indeed another raid followed on the night of 29/30 July. This time 707 aircraft attacked, dropping 2,318 tons of bombs. Like the first raid, this one was made from the north-west with the aiming point again in the centre of the city; but manyof the Pathfinder aircraft were carried off track by a strong cross-wind and most of their markers fell some three miles to the east of the intended point. The result was that most of the bombs dropped by the main force fell in residential districts in the east of Hamburg, again causing extensive fires, though nothing like those of the previous raid. The fourth and last of this series of raids on Hamburg was carried out on the night of 2/3 August when 740 bombers set off from their bases in Britain. On this occasion, however, there was a very extensive and severe thunderstorm over north-west Germany, the turbulence and heavy icing from which caused about 300 bombers to abort the mission. Weather conditions also made Pathfinder marking at Hamburg impossible, with the result that most crews bombed on dead reckoning, scattering the intended raid widely over the German countryside. The attack missed the target altogether, and it had been a costly failure: thirty of the bombers did not return and two more crashed on landing. Nonetheless the series of raids on Hamburg had had a profound effect in Germany, leading to widespread apprehension about the possibility of more raids of this kind.

THE GERMAN DEFENCES

August was the most active month for Bomber Command during 1943. Targets included Milan, Genoa and Turin in an effort to hasten the withdrawal of Italy from the war — and indeed that country surrendered on 8 September. Just three weeks earlier there had been another notable attack by Bomber Command, this time a moonlight raid on the German rocket research establishment at Peenemünde, where V1 and V2 weapons were under development. Following earlier, more modest but successful efforts using Master Bombers to control from the air the work of the main force of bombers over the target, this technique was employed against Peenemünde. The Master Bomber was Group Captain J. H. Searby of No 83 Squadron, who was given three aiming points on a target that was only about two miles by one mile in extent. One aiming point was to be the rocket factory itself, another was the research station and the third was the domestic site for the scientists and workers. Certain Pathfinder crews were, for the first time, detailed off on this raid as 'Shifters', whose task it was to move the target marking from one part of the site to another as the raid progressed. The first bombs fell short by 1½ miles, but the efforts of the Pathfinders directed by Searby quickly corrected the error and the target was successfully attacked. Almost 1,800 tons of bombs were dropped by 560 aircraft, 40 of which did not return. This loss rate of 7.1 per cent was high, but it was judged by Bomber Command to be acceptable in view of the importance of the target and the effectiveness with which it had been put out of action. In fact, as in the raid on the dams, most of the physical results of the attack were soon repaired, though the production of missiles was certainly delayed.

Most of the losses during this night attack fell to German night fighters, but they might have been much heavier than was the case but for another tactic that was being increasingly employed by Bomber Command at this time — the use of diversionary aircraft to draw the night fighters away from the main target. During the Peenemünde raid eight Mosquito aircraft had made a diversionary attack on Berlin, and the Luftwaffe night fighters arrived over Peenemünde in time to catch only the last wave of attacking bombers. By coincidence this same raid also saw the first use of an important German innovation, the Schrägemusik weapons (literally 'slanted music', and a German expression for jazz). These were twin 20mm cannon mounted in the fuselages of German night fighters and firing upwards at an angle of about 10 or 20 degrees from the vertical. The fighter positioned

Above: Peenemünde before and after the air attack of 21 August 1943. (AHB)

itself in the blind spot underneath the bomber being attacked and fired upwards into the target, usually with devastating effect. Because ball ammunition was used without tracer, it was often the case that the bomber crew had no idea where the attack had come from.

After a late summer and autumn that saw heavy attacks on several major German cities, including four on Hanover alone and three on Berlin, Harris judged that his Command was now ready to launch an all-out air assault on the German capital. His bomber force would, however, meet unexpectedly stiff opposition, and it is necessary to pause here and consider the state of the German defences. By this point in the war German night fighter operations had developed to a new pitch of effectiveness. Until the introduction of Window, the German night fighters were controlled, as has been explained, in 'boxes' from the ground with the aid of radar. By blinding the radar coverage, Window had destroyed this system in a single blow, compelling the defending aircraft to operate more widely and more freely, and in the event this turned out to be a considerable bonus for the defenders.

With their release from the previous close control, the single-engine fighters, Bf 109s and FW 190s, using a tactic known as 'Wilde Sau' ('Wild Boar'), would make their way towards a city under attack and find their prey in the stream of bombers en route to or on the way back from the target. Particularly in the immediate area of the raid, the fighters would often find the bombers silhouetted against the glare of searchlights or the light of fires on the ground, or even against the flares dropped by the bombers themselves. This mode of operation by the night fighters was reasonably successful, but it was soon overshadowed by another approach to the problem of intercepting bombers at night, this time known as 'Zahme Sau' or 'Tame Boar'.

In this tactic, the German force of twin-engine fighters, made up of Bf 110F-4s and G-4s, but increasingly of Ju 88Cs and Ju 88Rs, took off once a raid was approaching and, using radio beacons as the navigation aid, made its way towards the bomber stream. Once near the stream the fighters searched visually for their target, staying above 15,000ft, a height below which the often dense concentrations of anti-aircraft guns were free to fire. To make matters worse for the bomber force, the Germans were by now introducing some telling electronic aids of their own, including the SN-2 airborne interception radar that operated on a frequency unaffected by Window; and for closer-range work the 'Lichtenstein' airborne radar was also being fitted to the twin-engine night-fighter force.

At about this same time 'Naxos', the German device for detecting Bomber Command's H2S transmissions, was now adapted for airborne use by the Luftwaffe, making it possible for the fighters to home in on the unsuspecting bombers as they used their radar to map-read. 'Flensburg' was yet another German airborne aid brought into operation at about this stage of the bombing campaign. This was a radar receiver designed to detect 'Monica', a tail warning radar device by now fitted to bomber aircraft, so that, far from detecting the approach from astern of an enemy night fighter, 'Monica' now acted as a beacon to guide the fighter into the attack. Finally, in addition to all these important qualitative improvements, the strength of the German fighter force was building up in a very impressive manner. By January 1944 there were 870 single-engine fighters facing the combined US and British air offensive and 780 twin-engine machines; this was an increase of almost 60 per cent on the total of a year earlier.

German ground defences were also being greatly improved at this time. During 1943 the number of heavy anti-aircraft guns, notably the 10.5cm and the very heavy 12.8cm weapons, had increased from around 600 to about 1,000 and batteries were now brought together in enlarged units so as to give more concentrated fire both against Bomber Command at night and against the formations of US bombers by day. Two other innovations must also be mentioned: 'Würzburg' early warning radars were modified by late 1943 to make them less vulnerable to interference from Window; and more resources were put into the construction of decoy sites. Some of the latter were highly effective. One of them, V500, was a huge affair lying some fifteen miles north-west of Berlin, in other words near the main approach path of the bombers to the city. It contained not only dummy fire sites but also whole districts of streets laid out to simulate those of Berlin itself. It was equipped with decoy markers, with devices to simulate the explosion of bombs, and in fact with everything possible to convince bomber crews that the site was their intended target. Only the skilful efforts of Pathfinder crews and Master Bombers could discount the ingenuity with which these decoys were constructed and operated.

On the British side, too, late 1943 was a period that saw several important changes before the offensive was renewed at an increased tempo. The Stirling bomber, never able to operate at the altitudes favoured by the Halifax and the Lancaster, began to suffer losses that climbed to a rate of 6.4 per cent during the period from August to late November 1943 and, like the Wellington shortly before, it had to be withdrawn to less demanding roles. A similar fate overtook the earlier versions of the Halifax Mk IIs and Mk Vs, which were restricted in the operations they undertook from September 1943. Their losses had climbed to 9.8 per cent in the winter of 1943–44 and in January, the worst month, losses in No

434 (Canadian) Squadron were at a horrifying 24.2 per cent. Harris had little choice but to withdraw these aircraft from operations over Germany, and ten squadrons, amounting to something like 250 aircraft (or one-third of the total number of 'heavies' in the Command), left the front line. The Halifax would not return to operations until February 1944 when the much improved Mk III became available.

THE BATTLE OF BERLIN

Despite the growing effectiveness of the German defences that has been described, Harris now began his all-out assault on Berlin, after claiming in a letter to Churchill on 3 November that 'We can wreck Berlin from end to end if the USAAF will come in on it. It will cost between us 400–500 aircraft. It will cost Germany the war.'

This grossly over-optimistic view may have had something to do both with the utter conviction by Harris that strategic bombing was the key to victory and with his realization that once the Allied invasion of Europe was under way (and it was now only seven months ahead) his force would no longer be given the very high priority for resources that it had so far enjoyed. In addition to that, he was concerned that the invasion of Europe would lead to further diversions of bomber effort away from the strategic campaign. Whatever the balance of these factors in his thinking, a new phase of the bombing offensive, this time lasting for four and a half months, now began. From mid-November 1943 thirty-four major attacks were launched, sixteen of them against the German capital, while numerous smaller raids were made during the same period, either as diversionary efforts or in attempts to destroy German flying-bomb sites in France. But Berlin was the focus of a substantial proportion of the effort of Bomber Command.

The attacks started modestly enough on the night of 18/19 November with a raid carried out over total cloud cover for the loss of only nine Lancasters out of a force of 440 despatched. On the 22nd/23rd the attack was repeated, this time by 764 aircraft, the largest force sent out during the period, and again losses were not unreasonable, amounting to 26 aircraft, or 3.4 per cent of the force. Despite a full overcast again in Berlin, the raid was accurately delivered in the central districts of the city and very heavy damage was caused. But on the third and subsequent raids losses began to mount: 42 aircraft out of 443 were shot down or crashed on the night of 26/27 November, 40 out of 458 on 2/3 December and so on until by the end of the most intense period of raids, late

Above: A Lancaster taxying at night. (IWM)

January 1944, fourteen attacks had been made and 384 bombers lost. During the whole period of the Battle of Berlin, from November to March 1943, 492 aircraft were lost and another 95 were written off — a total of 587 machines, almost all of them Lancasters.

At the very end of this period there also took place the disastrous attack on Nuremberg, and it is best dealt with here since the loss rate sustained formed part of the overall state of the bombing offensive and the change in approach that had become necessary. On the night of 30/31 March 795 aircraft were dispatched to raid this distant target in southern Germany, but several factors told against them. First, the bombers unexpectedly produced contrails in the cold air, and in the moonlight the progress of the stream of attacking aircraft was unmistakable. Then, by a fateful coincidence, the German controller of the 3rd Fighter Division assembled his aircraft over radio beacon 'Ida', to the south-east of Aachen, so that he could dispatch them against the bomber stream once its course became clear. In fact, and following the pre-arranged route for the mission, the stream altered course as planned over northern France and headed almost directly for the beacon.

The result was a running battle with night fighters all the way to Nuremberg and for most of the long return journey, with the fires of burning aircraft on the ground clearly marking the route. Out of a force of 795 aircraft despatched, no fewer than 94 were lost and another twelve crashed in Britain, making a total for the raid of

106, or 13.3 per cent. This was quite insupportable, and for this reason together with the fact that many crews had already been showing signs in the missions against Berlin of less than their earlier determination to press home their attacks, this whole phase of the bomber offensive was halted. The fact was that German morale had not cracked, the bomber crews could see little or no positive return for their hitherto willing efforts and, as post-war analysis was to show, far from German industry being crippled, production of key items such as tanks, aircraft and guns had actually increased during this period. The Official Historian was later to describe the Battle of Berlin as 'more than a failure, it was a defeat.' A tactical failure it undoubtedly was; yet it had caused a massive diversion of German resources into defence, thus not only giving a certain amount of indirect support to the Red Army but, more importantly helping to prepare the way for Operation 'Overlord', the invasion of France. At the strategic level, these efforts by Bomber Command had made an indispensable contribution.

SUPPORTING THE INVASION

Two weeks after the Nuremberg raid the control of Bomber Command was transferred to General Eisenhower, the Supreme Commander Allied Expeditionary Force, in preparation for the invasion of Normandy. Although attacks on cities in Germany continued, notably on Cologne, Düsseldorf, Munich and Duisburg, most of the effort of Bomber Command, together with that of the other Allied air forces, now switched to transportation targets in France with the aim of making it impossible for enemy reinforcements to move up once the invasion began. At the same time elaborate measures were taken to convince the Germans that the invasion would take place not in Normandy, but in the Pas de Calais, and as part of the deception plan bombing raids were carried out on transportation facilities such as marshalling yards and major rail junctions throughout northern France.

At the end of May coastal batteries were added to the target list, and once again, so as to conceal the intended invasion area, the sites attacked stretched from north of the Pas de Calais right down the French coast to Brittany. On 4/5 June, for example, just as the invasion was about to go in, 259 aircraft of Bomber Command attacked three gun positions in the northern sector; but only one, that at Maisy, lay in the invasion area, in this particular case between what would very shortly be known as 'Utah' and 'Omaha' beaches.

On the night before the landings in France, Bomber Command flew 1,211 sorties, its highest night total so far, most of them in support of the Allied invasion. During the first hours of the venture, no fewer than 1,012 bombers were meanwhile attacking enemy coastal batteries, dropping over 5,000 tons of bombs in efforts to neutralize these powerful defences. After the invasion, and as the build-up of Allied forces in Normandy began, enemy communications, airfields, ports from which his naval forces might sally to attack the invasion fleet and a multitude of other targets all received the continuing attention of Bomber Command.

Once the Allied forces were well established ashore, it then became possible to redirect a large part of the strategic bombing effort back to targets in Germany, and in particular to the priority oil targets in that country such as Gelsenkirchen, attacked on the night of 12/13 June, and Sterkrade, bombed four nights later. This last raid was again notable for a high loss rate sustained by the bomber force when, as in the Nuremberg attack the previous March, the route of the bomber stream happened to run close to a beacon at which German night fighters were being assembled by their controllers. Out of 321 aircraft taking part in the raid, 162 were Halifaxes, and this particular element of the force lost 22 aircraft, or 13.6 per cent.

But now yet another of the diversions to which Bomber Command was prone intervened. On 13 June ten V1 flying bombs, the first of 8,892 that would be fired at Britain during the next few months, left their launching rails in France, heading towards their intended targets. Three nights later Bomber Command began a campaign against the launching sites and the storage areas for these

weapons, continuing it throughout the rest of June and July. By late July 1944 there had not been a major raid on a German city for two months, but on the 23rd/24th the offensive was resumed with a very heavy and successful attack on Kiel, followed by a series of three devastating raids on Stuttgart.

Meanwhile the occasional employment of Bomber Command in tactical support of the Allied ground forces in Normandy continued. On 7 July 467 aircraft laid a heavy and concentrated carpet of bombs, at Montgomery's request, in the city of Caen. It was, however, an attack that caused little damage to the German units in the area and it created great destruction in the northern part of Caen itself. Ultimately the damaged urban area turned out to be a severe hindrance to Allied forces when they tried to advance. Two other similar attacks were made during the next month, though with equally disappointing results; and then on 14 August a force of 805 aircraft was dispatched to attack German positions facing the 3rd Canadian Division near Falaise. Despite every precaution being taken, and in spite of the fact that Master Bombers were conducting events over each of the seven targets to be attacked, half way through the raid bombs began to fall on a large quarry in which was deployed a Canadian artillery regiment. It appears that there was confusion between the yellow coloured identification flares being used by the Canadians, and the target markers being employed by the bomber force, which also happened to be yellow. The result was a loss of thirteen Canadians, another 53 injured and a large quantity of guns and vehicles destroyed.

As the campaign in North-West Europe progressed and the break-out from the Normandy beach-head began, preparations were made for a resumption of the full air offensive against Germany, starting on 15 August with raids against nine Luftwaffe night fighter airfields in Belgium and Holland. With Bomber Command released from the control of Supreme Headquarters Allied Expeditionary Force in mid-September, there was a choice of target systems in Germany that could be attacked by the massive power of Bomber Command and the US Army Air Forces, the latter by now based in great strength in the United Kingdom and at Mediterranean airfields.

The first option, supported by only a few senior RAF officers but including Harris, was to continue the bombing of German cities. A second option, favoured mainly by Tedder, who was Eisenhower's deputy for the campaign in North-West Europe, was to concentrate on transportation targets since these would have the most immediate impact on the ground campaign still to be fought across the Continent. The third option, supported by Portal and his Air Staff, was to go for oil targets because the destruction of these key facilities would not only affect German mobility on the ground but also halt operations by the Luftwaffe. The result was another Directive, this time dated 25 September 1944 and affecting Bomber Command as well as the US strategic air forces in Europe. It laid down the first priority for attack as the German 'Petroleum industry with special emphasis on petrol (gasoline) including storage'. The German transportation system, and German tank and truck production plants and depots, were made a second priority.

By now the German night fighter force was well past the peak of its effectiveness, while the Allied bomber force was continuing its inexorable expansion. The number of first line aircraft in Bomber Command, for example, rose by an extraordinary 50 per cent during 1944. Not only that, but bombing accuracy had greatly improved, particularly with the arrival of improved H2S. Many Lancasters were now fitted with the 'Gee-H' blind bombing equipment; and there was a higher technical capability in electronic warfare, largely exercised by a specialist squadron, No 100 — a capability that had now outclassed that of the enemy in this increasingly important field of air warfare.

In August 1944 attacks against French railway targets and on the V1 sites came to an end and the weight of the bombing offensive was moved on to cities such as Rüsselheim, Kiel, Darmstadt and Bremen among many others. One of the more notable efforts at this stage of the campaign, as Allied bombers began to range freely over Central Europe sustaining losses that averaged only 1.1 per cent at night and 0.7 per cent by day, was that set out in the so-called 'Hurricane Directive' of 13 October 1944. Here the aim of the attacks was 'to bring home to the enemy a realization of [the overwhelming superiority of the Allied Air Forces in this theatre] and the futility of further resistance'. Two outline plans were put forward. The main one was 'Hurricane 1', a concentrated effort in time and space against objectives in the Ruhr intended to 'achieve a virtual destruction of the areas attacked'.

'Hurricane' began in the early hours of 14 October 1944 against Duisburg, when 1,013 aircraft of Bomber Command, together with an escort of fighters, were dispatched for a daylight attack on that city. That same day 1,251 machines of the US Eighth Air Force, escorted by 749 fighters, attacked the Cologne area, and that night 1,005 aircraft of Bomber Command were again sent out to attack Duisburg, causing heavy casualties and very severe damage. Attacks were also made against a variety of other targets in Germany as well as a few in France, where some of the isolated German garrisons continued to hold out. Other raids were made against German gun batteries in the path of the advancing Allies, on dykes on Walcheren and on the Dortmund–Ems canal.

By now Allied air superiority was virtually unchallenged, and combat losses remained very low. The size of Bomber Command meanwhile had continued to grow, and an Order of Battle schedule from this period shows that there were by now 70 heavy bomber squadrons in the Command, all of them operating Lancasters or Halifaxes, as well as eleven squadrons of Mosquitos and another thirteen on bomber support duties in No 100 Group — in other words a force totalling 94 squadrons.

THE FINAL RAIDS

These closing months of the war saw a continuation of numerous and widely scattered attacks across the whole of Germany and her remaining occupied territories but three of the raids at this stage of the campaign deserve a particular mention. The first was that on 12 November 1944 when 30 Lancasters of Nos 9 and 617 squadrons

Left: A Halifax Mk III. (AHB)

Above right: Railway repair sheds at Kassel, seen on 29 May 1945. The sugar-cone shaped building in the bottom right-hand corner is an air-raid shelter. (AHB)

attacked the German battleship *Tirpitz* in Tromso Fjord. *Tirpitz* was struck by at least two 'Tallboy' (12,000lb) bombs, which caused a heavy internal explosion before the ship capsized with the loss of most of her crew. Only one of the attacking aircraft was hit by flak, and even this machine made a successful emergency landing in Sweden.

The second raid was the controversial attack on Dresden on the night of 13/14 February. Dresden, Leipzig and Chemnitz as well as Berlin had been suggested as targets in a letter from the Air Staff to Harris on 27 of January 1945 stating that 'a severe blitz will not only cause confusion in the evacuation from the east but will also hamper the movement of troops from the west'. This heavy blow, consisting of raids on several major cities, and with the code-name 'Thunderclap', would be delivered once the military situation in Germany had reached a critical point, and the expectation was that 'Thunderclap' would lead to a final collapse of the enemy war machine and his civil administration, thus ending the war. Dresden was selected as the target for the first raid. It was a city that had suffered two minor attacks during 1944 as well as one heavier one in which 300 tons of bombs had been dropped by US Army Air Force B-24s on 16 January 1945.

Bad weather over Europe on 13 February prevented the daylight raid by American bombers with which it had been intended that the assault on Dresden should begin, and Bomber Command thus opened the attack. Two waves of bombers were dispatched to the target — 244 Lancasters in the first wave dropping over 800 tons of bombs in a moderately successful first attack, followed by 529 Lancasters dropping more than 1,800

tons of bombs in a second wave. A firestorm similar to that seen in Hamburg in July 1943 was caused, resulting in enormous damage in the centre of the city, much of which was totally destroyed. It was never possible to calculate the number of casualties caused because there was no record of the number of refugees in the city, but the death toll may well have been around 50,000. It is a comment on the shattered state of German air defences as the air campaign neared its end that, despite the very long route from Britain to Dresden and back, some 1,200 miles even without tactical routeing, only six Lancasters were lost in the air. Three others crashed at the end of their mission.

The third of these three significant attacks in the late stages of the war — and a demonstration of the enormous destructive potential of concentrated bombing against a small target — was made against the island of Heligoland on 18 April 1945. A force of 969 aircraft bombed the naval base, the airfield and the town on the island, turning much of it into a moonlike landscape and completely destroying all the many military facilities.

With these raids and the very large effort that was mounted in preparation for the crossing of the Rhine towards the end of March, the air war in Europe was virtually over. The last bombing operation was launched against Kiel on 2/3 May, where, it was believed, German ships were assembling to transfer troops to the garrison in Norway so as to continue the war from that country. Sixteen Mosquito bombers were launched to attack airfields near Kiel, while another 126, supported by 89 radio countermeasures Mosquitos and two Halifaxes in the same role, attacked Kiel itself. The last operational losses in Bomber Command were sustained in this raid, when the two Halifaxes collided during their bombing run with the loss of both crews. On 4 May the German forces in North-West Europe surrendered, and on 7 May a German representative signed a document of unconditional surrender, to be effective two days later. The campaign in North-West Europe from D-Day to the end of the war had cost Bomber Command 2,128 aircraft and approximately 10,000 air crew killed.

During the whole war the total losses were of course very much higher. To put them into proper perspective, it should be remembered that Bomber Command had operated on 71.4 per cent of all nights and 52.5 per cent of all days since 3 September 1939. A total of 8,953 aircraft had been lost by the Command, and out of approximately 125,000 air crew who served in squadrons or in training or conversion units during the war, there were 55,500 casualties (including those lost in accidents), while another 18,700 were wounded, injured

De Havilland Mosquito

The bomber versions of this aircraft marked a return to Trenchard's belief that it would be possible for a bomber to circumvent opposing defences by sheer performance rather than have it fight its way through to the target. With its service ceiling of 40,000ft and its twin 1,250hp Rolls-Royce Merlin XXIs giving it a top speed of 415mph, the Mk XVI version of the Mosquito, which first flew in late 1943, could indeed overfly all anti-aircraft fire and outrun the enemy fighters of the day. Defensive armament was therefore not needed, and all the weapons payload could thus be devoted to bombs, of which up to 4,000lb could be carried. The Mosquito turned out to be so successful that as time went by it was also employed in the roles of rocket-firing ground attack, maritime strike, intruder and night fighter. The marks of aircraft engaged in these other roles variously carried four 20mm cannon and four .303 machine guns, a 6pdr gun or eight 60lb rockets as well as 250lb or 500lb bombs. Total Mosquito production, including those built in Canada and Australia, amounted to 7,781 machines.

the German Minister for Armaments and War Production for most of the conflict, the raid on Hamburg in August of that year raised for the first time the prospect that Germany might be defeated by the rapid destruction of other such large cities. But such a sustained effort on that scale was beyond the capability of Bomber Command at the time and, as Speer pointed out, thereafter the German population became accustomed to the gradual increase in the intensity and frequency of the air attacks. German morale never cracked. It certainly fell; but in the tightly controlled police state that Germany had become this was not enough to make any real impact on the determination of the workforce to maintain industrial output, as the German records show.

What the bomber offensive did do, apart from imposing severe shortages of many key commodities (particularly oil), was cause a massive diversion of war resources to air defence in efforts to counter it. In 1944, for example, 30 per cent of all German guns produced were anti-aircraft weapons and 20 per cent of all heavy shells manufactured were for the same purpose. Over 50 per cent of the military capacity of the electro-technical industry was devoted to the production of radar, or of signals-related equipment for use in defence against bombers, and 33 per cent of the optical industry was engaged on anti-aircraft devices of one kind or another.

The best judgement that can be offered about the whole of the effort by Bomber Command is that it was a campaign fought with extraordinary devotion to duty by men who were asked to go out in cold blood night after night against daunting odds, and that ultimately these efforts played a major part in the collapse of German resistance on all fronts after six long years of war.

or made prisoner. It is interesting to note the nationalities of the casualties. To deal with fatalities only, 38,462 were British, 9,919 Canadian, 5,720 Australian and New Zealand, 929 Polish and 534 others (including Allies such as the Czechs and the French as well as air crew from elsewhere in the Commonwealth).

To what extent the Combined Bombing Offensive contributed to the defeat of Germany is still a matter of debate. It is clear, however, that at the strategic level it had the effect of opening a 'second front' in the skies over Europe, certainly from early 1942 onwards. In that year, according to the post-war interrogation of Albert Speer,

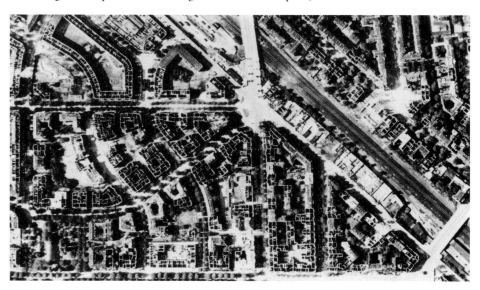

Left: Typical bomb damage in Berlin: part of the Steglitz district, 9 September 1943. (AHB)

CHAPTER 8

TOWARDS VICTORY

In the war against U-boats in the Atlantic, November 1942 had seen a rise to crisis levels in terms of Allied merchant ships lost as the Allies struggled to build and to deploy their warships and maritime aircraft to meet the threat. Coastal Command was under particularly heavy pressure. Extra air effort had been thrown into convoy protection work to shepherd across the Atlantic the American forces building up for Operation 'Torch', the landings in North-West Africa on 8 November 1942. Maritime air squadrons had taken part in the build-up at Gibraltar in support of the invasion itself, while nine of the eighteen very long-range Liberator aircraft in the Command were based in Iceland to help shrink the air gap in the North Atlantic. Finally, the Command had been obliged to dispatch aircraft and crews not only to Freetown in West Africa to close the gap there in air cover for convoys making their way along the Cape route, but also to the Far East in efforts to plug some of the more glaring deficiencies in maritime air power in that theatre of war.

As the commanders at the operational level struggled with the gross overstretch of resources that all this entailed, solid foundations were being laid for an eventual recovery from these low points in the war at sea. Among the technical improvements in train as far as the Royal Air Force was concerned was an enhanced version of ASV, the Mk III model with a wavelength of only 10cm instead of the 150cm of the Mk II. This had passed its trials in May 1942, and after a familiar dispute over priorities in resources between Coastal and Bomber Commands, by January 1943 the first Liberator was carrying ASV Mk III on daylight patrols. To complement ASV Mk III at night, the Leigh Light was by now becoming more widely available. This was a 24in searchlight carried initially by Wellington aircraft, and, following the detection of a surfaced submarine by ASV, it was now possible to illuminate the target before it could submerge. At the same time, depth charges filled with Torpex rather than with Amatol were being introduced, a modification that produced a roughly 30 per cent increase in explosive power; and, finally, a better

fuse for the charges had also by now been developed. Taken together, these enhancements to maritime air power would prove to be a crucial advantage.

SUCCESS AGAINST THE U-BOATS

During the winter of 1942–43 these improvements had still to work their way to the operational squadrons, and meanwhile the sinkings of Allied merchant ships continued at an alarming rate. March 1943 was a particularly bad month, with 120 Allied and neutral ships lost, 82 of them in the North Atlantic. By this time there were around 400 U-boats in service altogether. About half of them were operational, and around 100 were active in the central North Atlantic. Not only was this a formidable force, and one with healthy reserves, but, although fifteen U-boats were destroyed during this same month, German submarine construction was by now almost keeping pace with the losses.

But behind this operational picture there was another important factor at work — the hidden war of operational intelligence, based largely on the penetration of enemy ciphers. On the German side, the B-Dienst (B Service) had been breaking into British merchant and some Admiralty traffic with various degrees of success since before the war. On the British side, the most critical German ciphers, such as 'Hydra', were penetrated in June 1941, a success which, with interruptions caused by changing cipher procedures, continued for the remainder of the conflict. These attacks on the communications of the opponent help to explain many of the swings of fortune that so characterized the Atlantic campaign against the threat from German submarines. In mid-march, for example, Dönitz was able to assemble a U-boat wolfpack of 38 submarines to attack three Allied convoys then at sea in the North Atlantic, largely because U-boat Headquarters was able to read crucial signals concerning the intended track of the convoys but also because just at this time the Allied radio interception services were having difficulty breaking into German communications. The result was the sinking of 22

Left: Beaufighters of Coastal Command attack enemy shipping off La Rochelle, 13 August 1944. (AHB)

merchant ships from these convoys alone, an important share of the 97 ships lost to all causes during the first twenty days of March. The sinkings might well have been much heavier but for the efforts of the first of the Liberators operating out of Iceland and Northern Ireland, whose efforts succeeded on many occasions in

Left: Liberator GR.III of Coastal Command in November 1943, The Mk III was the Very Long Range version that did so much to close the Atlantic gap. (AHB)

Right: Air Marshal Sir John Slessor, photographed when C-in-C Coastal Command at the height of the Battle of the Atlantic. Slessor was one of the great air strategists as well as a very able operational commander. He was Chief of the Air Staff from 1950 until the end of 1952. (IWM)

driving U-boats down and thus away from their intended targets.

Although the sinkings of Allied vessels continued after March, they began to show a decreasing trend. At the same time U-boat losses began to rise; fifteen U-boats were sunk in March and another fifteen in April, but 41 during May, seventeen in June and 37 in July. One reason for this increase was the inexperience of the new crews, who often found themselves up against the by now very seasoned and skilful Allied escorts. Another reason was the resumption by the Allies of German signals traffic penetration, and thus the availability of a renewed flow of accurate and timely intelligence. But a third reason, and one of growing importance, was the increasing overall effectiveness of Coastal Command.

During the spring of 1943 the improvements in tactical capability that have been mentioned were gradually being matched by some important increases in overall strength. When Air Marshal Sir John Slessor became Commander-in-Chief of Coastal Command in February 1943 he inherited a force that had expanded to around 800 aircraft deployed in 60 squadrons, including three United States squadrons under command. Most of the units, involving a total of 430 aircraft, were equipped

for the anti-submarine role. This key element of the Command included eight Sunderland squadrons, four of Catalinas, and, of great importance for future operations, two of Liberators with their effective radius of action of 850 miles.

Together with a reorganized system of convoy escorting and routeing, agreed in Washington by the Americans, the Canadians and the British in March 1943, the growing effectiveness of maritime air power now began to drive down shipping losses and to increase the number of U-boats destroyed. During May no fewer than 41 German submarines were sunk, for the loss of 58 merchant ships, only 31 of the latter in the North Atlantic. In the middle of that month 33 U-boats gathered to attack one particular convoy, SC.130, but lost five of their number without managing to sink a single merchantman. Dönitz wrongly attributed the sudden failure of the U-boats to the Allies' use of radar, and particularly to radar location by aircraft, robbing the submarines of their ability to operate on the surface. But, whatever the cause, he could not tolerate losses on this scale, and on 24 May he ordered his U-boats to leave the North Atlantic and to deploy to the area south-west of the Azores.

Coastal Command had also been involved during all this time in airborne strikes on enemy surface shipping, a role already mentioned in Chapter 6. The earlier disappointments, and to some extent the high loss rate, had been overcome by the end of 1943, and during 1944 the Strike Wings went from strength to strength. No 455 Squadron RAAF, together with No 489 RNZAF, had received Torbeaus by the start of the year and were deployed at Leuchars, while No 333 (Norwegian) Squadron operating Catalinas was engaged in maritime surveillance off the coast of Norway. These and other units would steadily increase the pressure on enemy surface movements along the coast of Europe, until by the closing months of the war it had been virtually halted. At the same time a halt was forced in the very occasional transit of German blockade-runners trying to escape the vigilance of Coastal Command patrol and strike squadrons operating in the South-Western Approaches. During the whole war 437 enemy surface vessels would be sunk by aircraft under RAF control, 343 of them by Coastal Command, 25 by Bomber Command and 69 by Fighter Command.

With their withdrawal from the North Atlantic in May 1943, the U-boats had lost the battle in those waters, and they were never again to pose so lethal a threat to transatlantic lines of communication. Nevertheless, and after a very quiet month during June, as the submarines redeployed, July saw a sharp increase in shipping losses in the South Atlantic, the Mediterranean and the Indian Ocean. But to reach those operating areas five out of six submarines had to transit the Bay of Biscay, an area perhaps 300 miles by 120, and when the U-boats shifted their activities southwards the patrols by Coastal Command both from the United Kingdom and from Gibraltar were concentrated over these same waters. The tactics adopted by the U-boats were to cross the Bay of Biscay in groups, submerged at night but prepared to fight it out with aircraft on the surface during the hours of daylight. In order to do this their anti-aircraft armament was increased, and some submarines were equipped as flak boats. This led to some heavy engagements not only between aircraft and submarines but also between Beaufighters of Coastal Command and Mosquitos of Fighter Command on the one hand and Luftwaffe Ju 88s and even FW 190s on the other. At one time during the summer of 1943 Coastal Command was losing an average of one aircraft each day over the Bay of Biscay.

At this point in the campaign a surface hunting group of the Royal Navy was dispatched to the Bay and a period of very successful joint anti-U-boat operations followed, reaching a climax during July when a total of 86 submarines crossed these waters. Fifty-five of the boats were sighted, six were forced to return to harbour and seventeen were sunk — all but one of them by aircraft. Fourteen Allied maritime aircraft were also lost, but again the U-boat losses were more than could be sustained and another German change of tactics was seen. The idea of fighting on the surface was abandoned by Dönitz when it became clear that the advantage lay with attacking aircraft, the more so if, as was now becoming increasingly common, co-ordinated attacks by several aircraft could be made.

Instead the U-boats began to make the crossing by hugging the coast of Spain and travelling submerged. This also had the effect of moving the scene of operations closer to the Luftwaffe's bases in France, a factor that contributed to the loss of one of the surface hunters and severe damage to another. The Royal Navy's surface units were therefore obliged to move out further to the west, and when there were signs that the U-boats might be returning to operations in the North Atlantic the surface forces shifted most of their effort back to that area.

By now, German submarine losses had included several of their 'Milch Cows', or resupply boats, and in another swing in fortunes this caused U-boat operations in more distant waters to be severely constrained.

Altogether the number of submarines sunk during the three months from June to August 1943 amounted to a total of 79 boats, while in the same period only 82 ships had been lost to submarines in all theatres. Nevertheless there were enough U-boats available at sea for Dönitz to make yet another attempt against the main Atlantic trade routes, and starting on 20 September a force of 21 submarines launched what turned out to be the last successful assault on North Atlantic convoys.

Heavy air cover both from shore bases and from escort carriers was available for the two convoys involved, a mass of shipping that totalled 79 merchantmen and fourteen escort vessels; but bad weather reduced the effectiveness of the air patrols and the resulting convoy losses were comparatively severe for this stage of the campaign when the defences were gaining the upper hand across so wide an area. Six merchantmen were sunk and three escorting warships were lost and a further two seriously damaged. One reason for this reverse was the use by the U-boats for the first time of a new acoustic torpedo, a weapon with which it was hoped to 'decimate the escort', as Dönitz put it. In this it failed, and a highly effective countermeasure to the new torpedo in the form of a towed noise-generator was soon produced and made available.

A further technological advance was seen at this time when the German High Command stopped production of the existing types of U-boats and switched construction to two new types, the XXI and XXIII. The first was a boat that could travel at a maximum speed of 16kts under water, though only for about 25 miles. The second was a much smaller craft, but this could make up to 10kts under water for a distance of around 40 miles. Until these much improved submarines could be brought into service, some of the older boats were hastily fitted with another invention that was to become very familiar in the future — the Schnorchel (Snorkel) tube. This device enabled submarines to run submerged on their diesel engines instead of on the batteries with their limited endurance, and the small size of the exhaust pipe that appeared above the water made it extremely difficult to detect either visually or by radar.

None of this was, however, enough to stave off this second defeat for the U-boats in the North Atlantic, and in the early autumn of 1943 Dönitz again withdrew his boats from the main routes to Europe. By now it was clear that the Allied invasion of the Continent would not be long delayed, and the U-boat force prepared to throw its weight against the fleet of Allied ships that would be bound to take part. In fact on D-Day, 6 June 1944, Dönitz was able to muster only 34 U-boats to oppose the

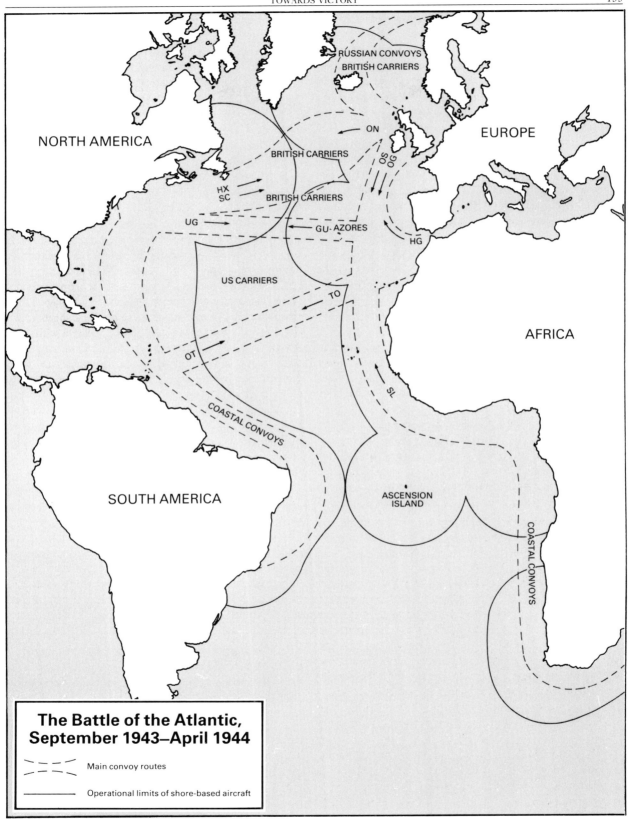

RUSSIAN CONVOYS
BRITISH CARRIERS

NORTH AMERICA

EUROPE

ON

BRITISH CARRIERS

OS
OG

HX
SC

BRITISH CARRIERS

UG

GU-AZORES

HG

US CARRIERS

TO

AFRICA

OT

SL

COASTAL CONVOYS

SOUTH AMERICA

ASCENSION
ISLAND

COASTAL CONVOYS

**The Battle of the Atlantic,
September 1943–April 1944**

- - - - - Main convoy routes

————— Operational limits of shore-based aircraft

passage of the invasion fleet, and only nine of these were equipped with the new Snorkels. The vast Allied flotilla of 6,939 vessels presented a remarkably fruitful target; but it included 1,213 warships, among them over 200 escort ships, including a number of escort carriers.

A major part in shepherding this armada safely across the Channel was played by maritime aircraft which successfully blocked the South-Western Approaches, the main direction from which any hostile submarines were bound to appear. The scale of this effort shows clearly the striking rise in capability that had been taking place in Allied air power at sea. Under Air Chief Marshal Sir Sholto Douglas, who had succeeded Slessor as Commander-in-Chief of Coastal Command in January 1945, 29 squadrons from No 19 Group alone, with 350 Beaufighters, Halifaxes, Mosquitos, Sunderlands and Wellingtons, covered the whole area to such effect that any surfaced submarine was certain to be detected on radar at least every thirty minutes. The outcome was a disaster for the U-boats. The nine Snorkel craft made for mid-Channel south of the Isle of Wight, while seven unmodified boats headed for the waters off Devon. The remaining eighteen craft formed a stop-line in the Bay of Biscay in the hope of intercepting any invasion force heading for those more southerly shores.

Of the seven non-Snorkel boats in the Channel, four were sunk and the other three so badly damaged that they had to return to harbour within four days without achieving any successes. The Snorkel craft meanwhile were joined by some of the 21 U-boats that had been awaiting a possible invasion in Norway, and two Allied frigates were sunk by submarines on 15 June. Apart from the loss of four Liberty ships to a single U-boat on 29 June, these were the only successes achieved by an arm that had only recently posed such a mortal threat. All told, 25 U-boats were destroyed during the month of June, twelve of them in the Channel or the Bay of Biscay. Of those, seven were claimed by aircraft which also claimed a half share in two other sinkings. It was a devastating loss rate, and one that led to the recall of all non-Snorkel boats to their bases, explicitly because of the pressure of attack upon them from the air.

During September, as the Allied advance through France went ahead, all the U-boats in the Atlantic ports of that country that could get to sea were ordered to do so and to make for Norway. From there the U-boats operated almost entirely off the British Isles, though with no more success than had rewarded them during the summer months. During October no merchant ships at all were lost in the Atlantic, but thirteen U-boats were destroyed. During November the score was three ships

and seven submarines and in December one merchantmen for fourteen U-boats. Despite the very unfavourable weather, Coastal Command was playing a full part in keeping up the pressure on the submarines, flying 9,126 anti-submarine sorties between the end of August and the end of the year, during which operations 62 U-boats were sighted, seven were sunk by aircraft and two more were sunk by surface ships that had responded to submarine detection by Coastal Command.

By the end of 1944, however, the new submarine types were coming out of German shipyards in respectable numbers. Sixty Type XXIs and 35 of the Type XXIII were working up or fitting out, and others had been launched. Fitted with Snorkels of an advanced model, these boats were recognized to be a serious potential threat, and two measures were adopted by Coastal Command to counter it. The first was the obvious one of improving the skills of airborne radar operators against the very small target 'blip' represented by the Snorkel tube, and then designing appropriate tactics to heighten effectiveness in attack. The other change was one of technology. Sonobuoys had been under development for some time, and although these devices were still at the experimental stage, by the turn of the year no fewer than ten of the Liberator squadrons were equipped with them. They were basically short-range radios dropped by aircraft to transmit from the surface of the sea the cavitation noise made by the propellers of submarines, and two U-boats were sunk during March using location by this means. The war was over before the full potential of the buoys could be realized, though it was a technology that would develop a very high degree of sophistication in the post-war years.

But these measures were not enough to prevent some German successes when the new classes of submarines went to sea, as they did during these same early months of 1945. Seven of the Type XXIII arrived in the waters off Britain, and they sank seven ships between them without loss, and without even being detected. By the end of April one of the Type XXIs had also become operational and no fewer than 111 more had been launched and were working up or fitting out. Had these boats reached operational status before the end of hostilities, they would have posed a threat as serious as any that the war at sea had seen.

As it was, the old Type VIIs were still operating in or near British home waters, though with the same lack of overall success that they had met the previous year. During February there were 51 of them at sea, but they managed to sink only eleven ships for the loss of 22 of their own number from all causes, including three to

Right: A Beaufighter TF.X anti-shipping strike aircraft - the last major production mark of this aircraft. It could carry a torpedo, rockets or bombs, or a combination of these weapons. The aircraft shown is carrying the distinctive black and white recognition bands introduced for the invasion of Normandy. (AHB)

mines and one in an accident. In March the score was ten ships for fifteen U-boats. The total of U-boats destroyed for the month was, however, much higher. Thirty-two were written off, thirteen of them being wrecked in heavy bombing attacks on German bases. Altogether in the first five months of 1945 the Type VIIs sank 46 ships, including eight small warships, for the loss of 56 of their own number.

During the last five weeks of the war the pressure on the U-boat fleet was of an unremitting intensity. Fifty submarines were sunk in the Baltic or its approaches and 33 elsewhere. Bombing raids on the German bases claimed many others while Beaufighters and Mosquitos destroyed even more of the submarines as they attempted to escape from the Baltic to ports in Norway. The last U-boat kill of the whole war was made, appropriately enough, by a Catalina of Coastal Command which so badly damaged *U320* that she sank two days later, on 9 May 1945.

It is perhaps surprising that, after the experiences of the First World War, when U-boats posed a very serious threat to Allied shipping, the menace was so little considered in the years running up to the Second World War. As we have seen, far too much faith had been put before the war in the effectiveness of asdic, a system that was of little use against submarines on the surface. Yet, because the enemy boats were actually submersibles rather than true submarines, their endurance under water was very limited and not only were they compelled to spend much of their time on the surface but this operational mode was in fact their most efficient. It was only when ASV radar was reasonably well developed that

the balance began to swing against the U-boat, and a whole series of shifts in advantage then followed as other technologies came into play. Towards the end of the U-boat campaign, sheer weight of effort on the part of the Allies told heavily against the boats; but had the war lasted longer, or had the Kriegsmarine been able to deploy its new classes of U-boat earlier, the latter stages of the conflict might well have seen another and highly destructive phase of the assault on Allied shipping.

As we have also seen, Coastal Command was an important element in the huge expansion that took place in British maritime strength during the war, both in terms of anti-submarine warfare and in terms of the twenty or so squadrons of maritime strike aircraft. By the end of the conflict there were seven Groups in the Command, including No 17 Training Group, No 106 Photographic Reconnaissance Group and No 247 Group in the Azores, in addition to the two independent Headquarters, one in Gibraltar and the other in Iceland. It had been a costly war: no fewer than 1,777 aircraft of Coastal Command had been lost to all operational causes. The success rate had, however, also been very high, particularly against the difficult targets that submarines represented. Out of 785 German submarines that had been lost to all causes (including accidents), the RAF unaided had destroyed 188. In the European theatre as a whole, Allied shore-based aircraft had sunk 326 German and Italian boats, and in both cases many more had been sunk as the result of joint action. It should also be recorded that Allied air attacks on Germany during these same years had written off another 154 U-boats, either sunk in their harbour or destroyed in the course of

Left: A strike by Mosquitos of Nos 404 and 114 Squadrons on shipping off the coast of Norway, 19 September 1944. (IWM)

Below right: Loading a jeep into a Dakota, Burma, 1944. Jeeps were much less trouble than the mules that were often transported in this way! (AHB)

construction. Above and beyond the statistics, however, the real achievement of the maritime war, submarine and surface, was that it became possible to transport across the seas the support that was essential to Britain: it imposed a virtually total blockade on Germany; and, even more important, it made feasible the transfer of vast resources from America. In that sense it was not, as is sometimes assumed, a defensive campaign; rather it was an essential part of the great offensive in Europe during 1944 and 1945.

THE BURMA CAMPAIGN

In the Far East, the disasters of 1942 had ended with Australia exposed to attack from the north and the British facing the Japanese on only one front, that along the Indo-Burmese border. At that point the Japanese advance temporarily halted, and by the end of the year Japanese air activities in the Burma theatre were confined almost entirely to sporadic raids by night on the Indian city of Calcutta. In response, a Flight of Beaufighters was dispatched to the region in January 1943, and after the Japanese had suffered the loss of five aircraft their incursions for a time ceased. Meanwhile transport aircraft of No 31 Squadron joined the very extensive American air effort that was being employed to fly supplies into China from India across the difficult terrain, soon christened 'The Hump', that separates the two countries. This hazardous route across mountains up to 17,000ft high, covered in very bad weather particularly during the monsoon period, was probably the most demanding in the world at that time. It was a route that

would see a flow of RAF aircraft to and fro right up until the last day of December 1945. The other task of the RAF units in the theatre at this time was, like that of the ground forces, simply to build up enough strength for an offensive against the Japanese, who were by now considerably stretched by the success of their expansion right across South-East Asia.

By the middle of 1942 a reorganization of the RAF Command in India had led to the formation of six Groups, three of them forming the main fighting strength of the RAF in the theatre: No 221, originally at Rangoon, was re-formed at Calcutta and was responsible for all bombing and reconnaissance work; No 222 was based in Colombo to watch over the Indian Ocean; No 224 was responsible for all fighter operations over the Assam area; No 225 Group looked after the south and west of India; No 226 was a maintenance Group back at Karachi; and No 227 at Lahore was a training Group. As to aircraft, there were by now 26 squadrons in the area, twelve equipped with Hurricane IIB and IIC fighters and fighter-bombers, three with Blenheim IV medium bombers and one with Vultee Vengeance dive bombers. Six Hurricane squadrons and two Vengeance squadrons of the Indian Air Force were also now joining the front line, and there were in addition two transport squadrons on strength, bringing the total force up to 400 serviceable aircraft, about 100 of which were held as reserves.

Supported by this considerable air strength, Wavell, transferred from the Middle East to Far East Command, now launched two offensives between mid-1942 and mid-1943. The first was his advance on Akyab, which, though ultimately unsuccessful, received valuable air force support both in the form of direct air intervention in the land fighting and in the use of Dakotas to resupply troops in forward positions. At the same time the first operations by seven columns of Wingate's Chindits were undertaken to cause disruption well behind the Japanese lines, operations that depended entirely on supply by air — a task carried out with distinction by Nos 31 and 194 Squadrons, despite the many difficulties involved.

More reinforcements for the Command continued to arrive in the meantime, until by the end of the year there were 48 squadrons of the RAF at hand, including more Hurricanes to replace the obsolescent Blenheims in the light/medium bombing role and the first squadrons of Spitfire Mk Vs, aircraft that were to transform the air situation. At the end of 1943 the RAF formations were brought together with the seventeen American squadrons in the theatre to form the air element of South-East Asia Command, a unified organization under Admiral Lord Louis Mountbatten which embraced all the Commonwealth and American forces in the theatre. The commander of the air forces was Air Chief Marshal Sir Richard Peirse, lately of Bomber Command, who now headed not only the RAF in India but also the US Tenth Air Force. In all he had 1,105 aircraft under command, 900 or so of them modern types. In this same region, including Indo-China, Malaya and Sumatra, the Japanese

Douglas Dakota I

The Vernon transport was replaced by the Vickers Victoria in 1927 and another similar biplane, the Valentia, followed the Victoria into service during 1935. Some of these old biplanes were still flying in the Middle East as late as 1944. Before then, however, the pressures of war had led to a massive increase in the air transport capability of the RAF, much of it relying on the Dakota, a military version of the Douglas DC-3 commercial airliner. Although the advent of the Dakota was preceded by a handful of other monoplane transports in the Service, including a few DC-2s, it was the arrival of the Dakota starting in mid-1942 that brought the RAF into a more modern transport age. The Dakota was powered by two Pratt and Whitney R-180-92 Twin Wasp engines, which gave the aircraft a cruising speed of 185mph. It had a crew of three, and in the passenger role it could carry 28 troops.

had a total of something like 750 aircraft, of which perhaps half were modern machines.

A great deal of construction work was needed to put and to keep so large an Allied air force in the field, and because of the many local difficulties it had been possible to make only a slow start on building the 215 airfields that had been planned in March 1942. The pace of work gradually accelerated, however, so that by the

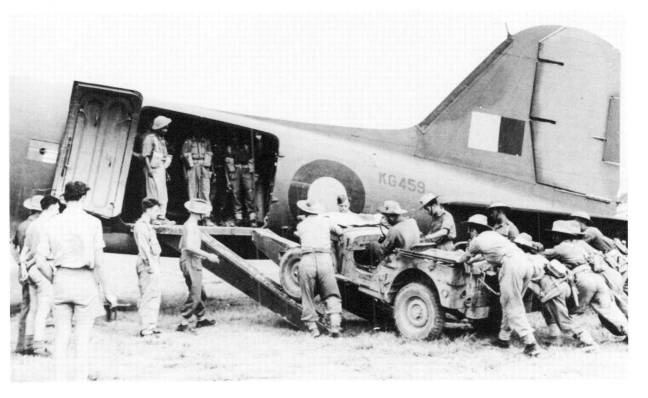

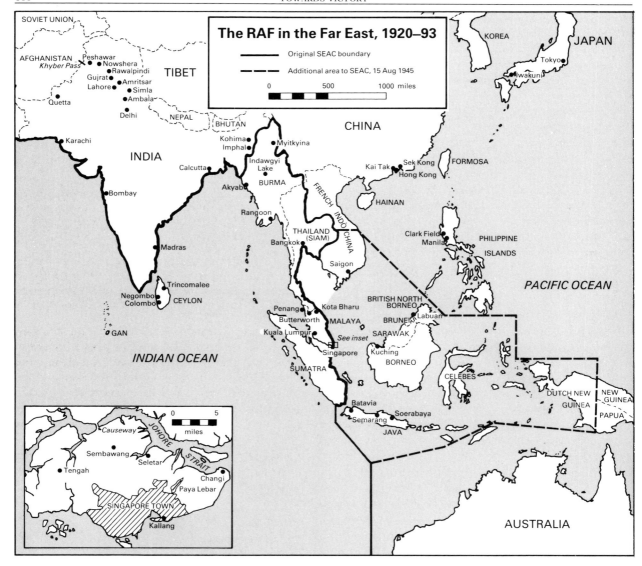

The RAF in the Far East, 1920–93

—— Original SEAC boundary

- - - Additional area to SEAC, 15 Aug 1945

0   500   1000 miles

time SEAC was formed there were 140 airfields each with two runways, another 64 with one and 71 airstrips that could be used in dry weather. Arrangements for efficient maintenance, salvage and repair work soon followed, and a further feature essential to successful air operations in the region, that of a radar and observer screen, was put out along the Indo-Burmese border, so that by early 1943 the growing Allied capability in the air was matched by a much enhanced resilience on the ground.

As Wavell prepared his second offensive into Arakan, Japanese air activity over the Bay of Bengal increased and further air raids on Calcutta were made. But by now the Allied air cover had been greatly improved, particularly since the arrival of the new

Spitfire Mk VIII, a version with a speed advantage of around 50mph over contemporary Japanese fighters such as the Nakajima Ki-44-II of early 1943, with its maximum performance of 375mph. Japanese losses were heavy in these raids: for example, when a Japanese formation of 60 bombers with fighter escorts attacked shipping in the Bay of Bengal on 31 December 1943, twelve of them were shot down.

After a successful initial drive down the Burmese coast by Wavell's forces, supported by heavy Allied air activity, the Japanese managed to cut off the 7th Indian Division, despite a further Allied division being landed to strengthen the position. The substantial airlift that had accompanied the advance had now to be supplemented by bringing air transport in from over 'The Hump', but

Right: A bombing attack by Hurricanes near the Tiddim River, Burma, 2 October 1944. (AHB)

after a critical month of very heavy fighting in the area during February the Japanese launched a major new offensive of their own from northern Burma towards India, relieving the pressure in the coastal sector as they did so. By early March four Indian divisions in the north faced three advancing divisions of Japanese, who managed to cut the road behind the 17th Indian Division.

Once more aircraft had to be diverted from 'The Hump' operation, but this time to fly in a large part of the 5th Indian Division, amounting to 3,056 men — a massive task and one in which No 194 Squadron played a full part. This force of troops, together with Nos 17 and 20 Indian Divisions, was thus holding the area around Imphal, while the 33rd Indian Division, which had moved forward to Kohima, quickly found itself

surrounded there. These dispositions meant that there were by now some 150,000 Commonwealth troops deployed 138 miles in front of the nearest railhead, and a massive effort amounting to about 400 tons of air-dropped supplies each day was needed to sustain them. It was the first really major air supply operation ever mounted by the Royal Air Force. At the same time four squadrons of Hurricanes provided air cover and close air support for the isolated troops and flew interdiction missions against Japanese supply dumps and camps further inland.

A lesser but equally effective air bridge operation was mounted in early March, this time to set down four brigades of Chindits at three previously prepared strips behind the Japanese lines, with the aim of cutting the

Right: An attack by a Beaufighter on a Japanese train in Burma, 10 July 1944. (AHB)

supply routes of Japanese forces facing American and
Chinese defenders in the far north. During a unique six-
day airlift in which just over 9,000 troops, 1,360 pack
animals and more than half a million pounds of stores

were flown in to the three landing strips, two other
features are worth noting. The operation saw Sunderland
flying boats landing in the middle of Burma to fly out
casualties from Indawgyi Lake, and it also saw one of the
earliest uses of helicopters in a combat zone when
American-operated Sikorsky Hoverflys were engaged in
the same work of casualty evacuation.

Fighting continued both behind the Japanese lines
and in the north-west from March to June 1944, and by
that time the aircraft available to the Allied command had
increased to 64 Commonwealth squadrons and 26 from
the USAAF. There were no fewer than 34 fighter and
fighter-bomber squadrons equipped with Hurricanes,
while other units held such types as Spitfires, Mustangs
and Thunderbolts. Among the 23 bomber units there
were holdings of Wellingtons, Liberators, and Mitchells,
while twelve transport squadrons flew Dakotas and
Hudsons. Five photo-reconnaissance squadrons were
equipped with Spitfires, Mosquitos, P-38 Lightnings and
other recent types, and there were two torpedo bomber
squadrons as well as two squadrons on special duties and
another engaged in air/sea rescue. During the second
half of 1944 the capability of the force was further
improved with the arrival of Thunderbolts to replace
nine squadrons of the Hurricanes, Mosquitos to take over
from Vengeance aircraft and more Liberators in place of
some of the Wellingtons. A change of command also took
place, with Air Chief Marshal Sir Keith Park, who had
led No 11 Group during the Battle of Britain and then

the air forces on Malta during the worst days of the siege, replacing Peirse.

Although the Japanese still had about 120 aircraft in Burma, half of them fighters, Allied air forces were now so powerful that enemy activity was limited to occasional forays and to very minor successes. Park's aircraft meanwhile were ranging over the whole theatre of operations, interdicting the railway lines by which the Japanese were receiving about half their supplies in Burma, attacking enemy shipping down as far as Singapore, destroying targets on or close to the battlefields when requested to by the Army, and making fighter sweeps to targets as far away as Bangkok.

The air forces had come a very long way in just over two years, and the ground had now been prepared for the re-conquest of Burma. This operation began in October with Allied drives on three fronts, one in the north by General Stilwell's troops, one down the coast by XV Corps and a thrust down through the centre of Burma by the Fourteenth Army. October 1944 had seen the creation of the Combat Cargo Task Force with responsibility for all air movement of troops and freight in the campaign. The RAF component of this key formation was No 232 Group, equipped with up to nine squadrons of transports, and together with eight squadrons of the USAAF detached to the theatre until 1

June, by which time they were due to be withdrawn for operations elsewhere, these squadrons of Dakotas sustained an army in the field amounting to almost 300,000 men. Despite an increasing strain on the whole supply system, largely caused by the longer flights to the advancing Allied forces, the air bridge was maintained right through the early months of 1945, eventually carrying not only reinforcements, casualties and supplies but also such items as heavy engineering plant with which to repair airfields and eventually even including eighteen dismantled railway locomotives for use on the partly restored rail system.

Rangoon fell to XV Corps in a combined parachute and sea assault on 3 May, while the Fourteenth Army, by now assisted by 'cab ranks' of close air support aircraft operating from strips only a few miles behind the advancing troops, fought its way south. There was one final and heavy battle at the mouth of the Sittang River in early July, again with squadrons of the RAF operating in close support, and apart from the many smaller actions necessary to clear out the last remaining pockets of Japanese resistance, the campaign in Burma was over. It had been a campaign in which extraordinary demands had been made on the air forces involved, and without the successful efforts of the Royal Air Force both in its combat roles and in the role of air transport, the

Above left: Hurricanes on a forward airstrip in Burma, 1 December 1944. (AHB)

Below left: A Beaufighter attack on a camouflaged Japanese ferry near Moalo, Burma, 5 November 1943. (AHB)

Right: After the Japanese surrendered in Singapore, some of their pilots flew their aircraft under RAF supervision so as to allow the Allies to determine the characteristics of these machines. The two versions of the Mitsubishi A6M2 Zero shown here are carrying the RAF roundel and letters standing for 'Allied Tactical Air Intelligence Unit – South-East Asia'.

reconquest of Burma could not have been contemplated in 1944 and 1945.

When the war in the Far East ended on 14 August, plans for the invasion of Malaya in the September became redundant; but there was a final task for the RAF in flying help in to the many camps holding Allied prisoners of war in the Far East, and then in flying the prisoners themselves out. It was work that went on for many weeks, and by the end of September 53,700 prisoners and internees had been evacuated from South-East Asia by sea and air. This left the question of bringing home the many personnel in the Far East who would not be needed for occupation or post-war garrison duties, particularly those 90 per cent of the whole who were not regulars but 'hostilities only' servicemen and women. The fact was that the transport capacity to move them all home quickly did not exist, and there were outbreaks of disaffection. Airmen at Mauripur, Karachi, held a protest demonstration early in 1946, and there was discontent in Ceylon, Singapore and Burma before repatriation got fully under way and the trouble subsided over the following months. It was understandable that servicemen were so anxious to come home, and that firm leadership at junior levels was lacking in so large a force of hastily trained 'hostilities only' personnel; but it was nevertheless an unhappy episode in a Service that had performed so well during the war in the Far East.

Meanwhile the years from 1942 to 1945 that had seen so complete a reversal of fortunes in the Far East had also witnessed three victorious campaigns closer to home, those in North Africa, in Italy and finally in Western Europe itself.

VICTORY IN NORTH AFRICA

Chapter 6 has described how the Eighth Army had been driven back in 1942 to the borders of Egypt, halting between El Alamein and the Qattara Depression on a geographical feature that favoured the defence. Meanwhile, in the central Mediterranean, a two-month pause in the air offensive against Malta had been broken on 1 July when the elements of the Luftwaffe still based in Sicily began another attempt to neutralize the island. A force of 567 German and Italian aircraft was now available in that area to the German air commander in the Mediterranean, Kesselring, against an RAF force on the island of less than 200 machines. But, of these, more than half were now Spitfires and for the first time the defence was able to put up a substantial resistance in the air. By 14 August Malta had lost 39 fighters, though 26 pilots survived to fight again. Against that, however, the

losses to the enemy amounted to 44 aircraft including all the crews, and the raids began to tail off after mid-July.

In that same month Air Vice-Marshal Keith Park had taken over as the air commander in Malta, just before a desperately needed convoy to resupply the island was about to sail from the United Kingdom. In order to see this essential convoy safely through, over 100 extra aircraft were deployed to Malta, increasing the air strength on the island to about 250 machines. Fourteen merchant ships with an escort of three aircraft carriers, two battleships, seven cruisers and 24 destroyers passed through the Strait of Gibraltar on 11 August heading for Malta, only to be attacked over the next few days by around 150 bombers and 80 torpedo bombers. Claims of enemy aircraft totalled 41, but the convoy had paid a heavy price by the time its surviving ships reached Grand Harbour. The carrier HMS *Eagle* had been sunk, two cruisers had been lost as well as a destroyer, and eighteen aircraft had been shot down. Only five of the fourteen supply ships eventually arrived in Grand Harbour, but the relief they brought was enough to enable the island to play its full part in the battles to come in North Africa.

In North Africa during August and September, as both sides consolidated their positions, there was an opportunity for Tedder and his staff to correct some of the weaknesses that had become apparent in tactical air support for the Army, as already also mentioned in Chapter 6. The implementation of the improvements that were made was greatly facilitated by the arrival of Lieutenant-General B. L. Montgomery to command the Eighth Army, and by the fact that Montgomery was not, as his predecessor Auchinleck had been for his last two months in North Africa, simultaneously acting as Commander-in-Chief. That was an arrangement that had caused the Eighth Army Headquarters to be sited separately from that of the Western Desert Air Force, but now they were again brought together. Co-ordination between the two commanders became very close indeed, and co-operation down the chain of command of both the Services was immensely strengthened under the insistent attention of both Tedder and Montgomery. It was the start of an approach to land/air operations that would bear invaluable fruit later on, first in Italy and then even more effectively during the campaign in Western Europe.

Very welcome air reinforcements had meanwhile arrived during July and August when American Army Air Force units began to arrive in the Middle East. Nine B-17 Flying Fortresses arrived from the Tenth Air Force in India, followed by three squadrons of P-40 Warhawks,

Right: A Hurricane IID carrying two 40mm Vickers 'S' guns. This type played an important part in the North African campaign from June 1942 onwards. (AHB)

Below: Air Marshal Sir Arthur Coningham in 1944 when AOC Tactical Air Force, Mediterranean. He was soon to become AOC No 2 Tactical Air Force of the RAF, based in Britain ready for the invasion of Normandy. (IWM)

which came along the Takoradi route, and six squadrons of bombers, half of them Liberators and the other half Mitchells that flew direct to the Middle East from the United States. These aircraft were the foundation for what later became the Ninth Air Force, but in the meantime they worked very closely with Tedder's units, some of them coming under Coningham's operational control. This build-up was accompanied by an increasing flow of Army reinforcements and supplies of every kind,

so that when at the end of August Rommel attacked the British position at Alam-el-Halfa he met strong resistance on the ground as well as massive Allied air superiority.

At the same time Rommel's supply lines across the Mediterranean came under heavy attack by the Royal Navy and by Allied air, and among the many ships sunk were several tankers, thus starving Rommel of the one commodity that was vital to any success that he had hoped to achieve — fuel. An important part of this maritime interdiction effort had been mounted from Malta, and in an attempt to ease the crisis the Luftwaffe launched yet another air offensive against the island. For nine days in mid-October well over 200 enemy aircraft attacked the island each day and up to twenty aircraft made harassing raids each night. On 18 October the air assault began to tail off as Kesselring withdrew his Ju 88s so as to reduce his losses, relying instead on fighter sweeps to maintain the pressure. But this was to be the last really heavy throw against much-bombed Malta, and it was one that had cost the German and Italian Air Forces almost 100 aircraft for the loss of 30 Spitfires.

Some 900 miles further to the east, meanwhile, all was now ready for the start of the British offensive in North Africa. On the ground the Eighth Army numbered 165,000 men, with 600 tanks and over 2,200 guns, against an enemy force of around 93,000 men, 470 tanks and almost 1,500 guns. By this stage of the campaign the Allied air forces in the Middle East totalled over 1,500 first-line aircraft, about 1,200 of them in Egypt and Palestine. Of the Allies' 96 operational squadrons in the whole Middle East theatre, 60 were British, including

Fleet Air Arm units, the rest a remarkable international mix of American, South African, Australian, Rhodesian, Greek and French squadrons, and even one Yugoslav. Facing them were about 690 Axis aircraft in North Africa, but only around half of them serviceable, and about another 2,300 spread across the rest of the Mediterranean. Three weeks before the Battle of El Alamein was due to start, Tedder seized a fleeting opportunity to dispatch almost 500 of his aircraft to attack two enemy airfield complexes, greatly weakening the opposing air forces in preparation for his main offensive on 19 October, itself timed to start four days ahead of Montgomery's assault.

Allied air superiority had prevented any attempt by the enemy to conduct reconnaissance flights over the preparations for the assault being made by the Eighth Army, and the assault went in on the night of 23 October. The same weight of allied air capability also meant that, while bombers made constant attacks on enemy positions, fighter-bombers went in against enemy armour and fighters checked any attempt by opposing aircraft to intervene. Under this massive air effort heavy fighting continued on the ground until, on 4 November, the 1st Armoured Division broke through and Rommel's forces began to retreat.

Four days later, at the far end of the Mediterranean, and preceded by a massive build-up of air resources at Gibraltar, Operation 'Torch' began, the Anglo-American landings in French North Africa designed to cut off the enemy's line of retreat. Despite difficult conditions, and severely handicapped both by poor logistic and maintenance facilities and by a lack of suitable airfields, squadrons of RAF Spitfires and Bisley bombers struggled to support the Allied forces as they fought their way through Tunisia. In the air the Luftwaffe was still putting up a determined fight, while on the ground the onset of torrential rain during December added to the problems facing the Allied forces, and the advance bogged down.

At the Command level there were other difficulties, particularly the fact that the Royal Air Force units, holding around 450 aircraft, formed Middle East, Malta and Eastern Air Commands, while the American units, with a combat strength of about 1,250 machines, were under the US Twelfth Air Force. Each answered directly to Eisenhower. At Tedder's suggestion, and as approved by the Casablanca Conference of January 1943, the whole air effort was unified and Eisenhower appointed Tedder to command all the air units in the region. Headquarters North-West Africa Air Forces was created, bringing together four subordinate Commands: the North-West

Above: From left to right: Coningham, commander of the North-West Africa Tactical Air Force; General Spaatz, Chief of Staff to Tedder; and Tedder, Air Commander-in-Chief, Mediterranean Air Command. The photograph was taken in early 1943. (AHB)

Africa Tactical Air Force under Coningham, with the Desert Air Force, the US XII Air Support Command and the Tactical Bomber Force; the North-West Africa Strategic Air Force under General Doolittle, made up of No 205 Group of the RAF together with three Wings of US bombers and escort fighters; the North-West Africa Coastal Air Force, commanded by Air Vice-Marshal Lloyd and consisting of 37 squadrons of RAF, Fleet Air Arm, RAAF, American and French squadrons; and North-West Africa Troop Carrier Command, with mostly American transport squadrons but including two from the Royal Air Force. Royal Air Force Malta and Royal Air Force Middle East remained as they were for the time being and were also under Tedder's overall command, but for these two areas he remained responsible directly to the British Chiefs of Staff.

These new arrangements were put in place during the third week of February 1943, with fully integrated British and American staffs at all levels. The new arrangement was an improvement of sorts, but the sheer number of Headquarters scattered over the region — twenty-four of them if the RAF Groups are included but not counting the many USAAF subordinate commands — was clearly very cumbersome, and further rationalization would be essential as the Mediterranean campaign continued.

With the onset of good weather in March the Allied advance on Tunisia from east and west resumed, until the retreating German forces facing the Eighth Army dug in at Mareth. After bitter fighting, and under the cover of almost total air superiority, the enemy line was turned and his retreat continued. Particularly effective in breaking up enemy efforts to concentrate his armour for action were the 'tank-busting' Hurricane IIDs, each armed with two 40mm cannon. All this time medium and heavy bombers of the North-West Africa Air Forces and the Middle East Air Force ranged far and wide over the shrinking enemy perimeter in Tunisia as well as over his supply ports in Sicily, Southern Italy and Sardinia. Together with increasing success against the few enemy convoys attempting to cross the Mediterranean, this activity by the Allied air forces threatened to halt altogether the movements of Axis supplies and support in the region.

In efforts to overcome the interdiction of their surface lines of communication, the German and Italian Air Forces now attempted to supply their forces by air using large formations of Ju 52s and Me 323s. This latter was a huge and slow six-engine heavy lift aircraft, many of which were employed to carry much-needed fuel into the shrinking enemy perimeter. Their losses to the numerous Allied fighters in the area were, however, heavy and, because of the highly inflammable nature of their cargo, often spectacular. Over a period of about four weeks the enemy was estimated to have lost 432 transport aircraft, while the Allies had lost only 35 machines to German escort fighters. The handful of enemy aircraft still in North Africa now began to pull out to airfields in Sicily and southern Italy, and the final moves in the campaign opened on 20 April with an attack by the Eighth Army followed by an assault by the US First Army two days later. More than a week of heavy fighting ensued, during which carpet-bombing and direct air support to the armies on a lavish scale helped to break the final enemy resistance, and on 12 May the Axis forces in North Africa capitulated.

INVASION OF ITALY

Two months later, on 10 July 1943, the first invasion of the European mainland took place when the US Seventh Army and the British Eighth Army landed on the southeast coast of Sicily. By now the air forces available for this enterprise represented a huge armada. No fewer than 260 squadrons had been assembled, 121 of them British. The air forces as a whole were given four tasks in support of the invasion: first, to gain the all-important air superiority, without which other operations would be very costly and perhaps even impossible; second, to give air cover to the convoys at sea; third, to operate over the eight beach-heads so as to provide cover for Allied ships

Below: A Spitfire Mk VIII. This advanced version of the type was fitted with a Merlin Series 61 powerplant and had a four-bladed propeller. All machines of this mark were fully tropicalized (note the filter under the nose) and many served in the desert, in Italy and in Burma from 1943. (AHB)

offshore, and to attack enemy defences on shore; and fourth, to support the subsequent advance of the armies through Sicily.

For six weeks before the landings, the Strategic Air Force attacked enemy ports and other targets in his rear and laid down a heavy bombardment on the islands of Pantelleria and Lampedusa, which quickly surrendered. Enemy airfields on Sicily were then bombarded, to such effect that by the date of the invasion virtually all Luftwaffe activity in Sicily had been paralysed. Ahead of the amphibious landings an airborne assault by night using gliders and paratroops had been planned, but the effort turned into a fiasco. Bad weather and inexperience among the air crews caused most of the paratroops to be scattered over a very wide area and 69 of the 137 gliders that were released landed in the sea. Only twelve of them finally put down on the intended landing zone, all of these having been towed by aircraft of the Royal Air Force. From the sea, eight divisions and a brigade landed successfully with little air opposition from the enemy, and by 13 July the first Spitfires from Malta had landed to operate from hastily repaired Sicilian airstrips. A second airborne assault was put in to capture a key bridge ahead of the Allied advance, and this time over a dozen gliders landed at the assigned zone. The troop-carrying aircraft, however, flew over the invasion fleet just as the Luftwaffe attacked it with Ju 88s, with the result that fourteen RAF aircraft were shot down by the Royal Navy. Other aircraft lost their way and, being unable to find the landing zone, returned to base. The outcome was that, although the bridge was captured, about 80 per cent of the sorties flown were aborted.

By 17 July German resistance on the island had stiffened, and although its capture by the Allies was inevitable, the enemy conducted an orderly withdrawal to rescue what resources he could. So as to weaken the enemy's hold by cutting off his supplies, heavy and frequent bombing raids were now made against targets in southern Italy and as far north as Rome, where, accompanied by a certain amount of international protest, transportation targets came under air bombardment. As the enemy in Sicily fell back towards the Straits of Messina, intensive air attack was also concentrated against the harbours on both sides of that stretch of water and the shipping plying across it. In places the crossing is only three miles wide; this short run, together with the effect of the very heavy anti-aircraft defences deployed by the Germans along both coasts, meant that although the enemy's withdrawal was hampered by Allied air activity he brought most of his forces out of Sicily and redeploy them in southern Italy.

For the Allied air forces, the five-week campaign had cost fewer than 400 aircraft, for the destruction or capture of 1,850 enemy machines. Perhaps more important, however, was the progress that had been made and the lessons that had been learned, some of them very painful, in joint operations. This experience would prove invaluable as the war in Europe continued.

Heavy air attacks were now made on many targets in Italy. Particularly destructive raids were carried out by Bomber Command on Milan, the intention being to hasten Italy's withdrawal from the war. Indeed, by mid-August secret negotiations with the Allies had already begun. The invasion of Italy proper meanwhile went ahead across the Straits of Messina on 3 September, and on 9 September the Allies landed three divisions across the beaches at Salerno, about 30 miles south of Naples. Allied air power was by now in even greater strength as more aircraft and more trained crews arrived in the theatre, so that by the date of this invasion there was the vast total of 3,127 aircraft available for operations. With an air fleet of this size the need for a more simple chain of command became overwhelming, and, although it takes the story ahead by several months, on 10 December 1943 the headquarters of the North-West Africa Air Forces merged with those of Mediterranean Air Command to become Headquarters Mediterranean Allied Air Forces, again with joint Anglo-American staffs at all levels.

On the same day as the Salerno landings, and by prior arrangement, Italy surrendered and Allied airfields in the region were on standby to accept Italian aircraft making their way out of the area still controlled by the Germans. As for the Luftwaffe, heavy attacks on its airfields had prevented all but a very modest reaction to the latest landings. Allied air cover by day was provided by Spitfires based on Sicily and by Seafires from aircraft carriers of the Royal Navy, while Beaufighters from Sicily provided protection at night. The distance from these Sicilian bases meant that the Spitfires were operating at extremes of range, a factor that helps to explain several successes scored against Allied ships by German aircraft employing newly developed guided bombs, the PC 1400X and the Hs 293, weapons that severely damaged HMS *Warspite* and sank the Italian battleship Roma on its way to surrender in Malta. Once the bridgehead at Salerno was firmly established, however, airstrips were rapidly constructed and more effective air cover became possible.

This same period also saw significant improvements in air/land co-ordination. The system for providing air support for ground forces had worked well in the later stages of the campaign in North Africa but in

Right: One of a formation of Marauders of the Desert Air Force over Yugoslavia in support of partisans, 11 June 1944. (AHB)

the broken terrain of central Italy it was not enough. Hitherto the allocation of aircraft to targets selected by the ground forces had been carried out at the level of Headquarters Desert Air Force and Army Area Headquarters. This system was found not to be responsive enough, and mobile observation posts (known as 'tentacles') were now created to be with the forward troops at brigade level. At the same time, with air superiority assured and with no shortage of aircraft, 'cab ranks' of ground attack aircraft were held overflying the battle area, ready to be called down as soon as suitable targets were identified. Using common grids on air photographs or maps, and with much improved radio communications, it now became possible to direct flexible firepower not only on fixed enemy positions but, because of the very short reaction time, even on moving enemy vehicles. It was a system which, with some later improvements, served the Allied forces very well for the campaign in Italy, and indeed during the whole of the rest of the war.

In parallel with the drive up the length of Italy, the Allies made an unsuccessful attempt to capture a number of islands in the Aegean Sea, hoping to use the airfields there as bases from which to launch shorter-range air attacks in the Balkans and threaten the whole southern flank of the German Eastern Front. Far more successful was the use of the captured Italian airfields in the area of Foggia, from where, during April 1944, strategic bombing attacks were started against targets in south-east Europe. These raids, carried out by the nine squadrons of No 205 Group and over 100 bomber and fighter escort squadrons of the United States Fifteenth Air Force, reached as far afield as Budapest, Ploesti and Vienna and would continue for the rest of the war.

Another successful feature of the air war in this theatre of operations was the Allied effort in the Balkans. Supply-dropping to the Yugoslav Partisan Army had begun in a small way during May 1942 with missions flown by Liberators based in Egypt. Fighting in the country extended in the months that followed, until, by February 1944, no fewer than fourteen German and six Bulgarian divisions were being contained by the Partisans. This was a very serious diversion of Axis effort, and a containment that was largely sustained by Allied airlift as well as by direct air intervention against German troop concentrations, coastal shipping, road and rail communications and other worthwhile targets. The Allied effort in Yugoslavia eventually led to the formation in June 1944 of the Balkan Air Force, subordinate to Middle East Command, holding eight squadrons of aircraft.

This will be an appropriate point at which to say something about the wider contribution made by the Special Duties squadrons of the Royal Air Force, some of which were engaged in these activities over Yugoslavia. Special Operations had begun in the Royal Air Force as early as August 1940 when No 419 Flight, equipped with Lysanders, began flying missions in support of the Special Operations Executive, SOE, the organization helping to run subversive operations in occupied Europe. One year later, this unit became No 138 (Special Duties) Squadron, and by February 1942 it was joined by No 161 Squadron. Between them these units held about twelve Whitleys, six Lysanders, three Halifaxes or Wellingtons and a Hudson, all based at Tempsford. Over the following three years thousands of clandestine flights were made by these aircraft to destinations as far apart as Norway and the south of France. Similar operations began in the Balkans during May 1942, with four Liberators of No 108 Squadron based in Egypt dropping supplies to Yugoslav guerrillas. In March 1943, as more aircraft became available, this unit became No 148 Squadron with fourteen Halifaxes added to the inventory. Later on, No 624 Squadron was added to the force and eventually the three squadrons became No 334 Wing and then the Special Operations Air Force which, by the time the Balkan Air Force was formed in June 1944, held eight squadrons and one Flight, drawn from five different nations. By the end of the war 11,600 sorties had been flown into Yugoslavia, thousands of tons of supplies had been delivered and many thousands of passengers flown in and out of the country. During August 1944 the activities of this unusual force even extended as far as Poland, when ultimately unsuccessful efforts were made to supply the beleaguered Polish resistance forces in Warsaw.

To return to the main campaign in the Mediterranean, the Allied advance through Italy continued from June to September 1944 but then slowed down and stopped as winter weather began to grip both land and air operations. The line stabilized across the Italian peninsula between Gaeta, 75 miles south of Rome, and the River Sangro on the East coast. The key to the west-coast route to Rome was Monte Cassino, and on 22 January an attempt to break the deadlock was made by outflanking Cassino with another amphibious landing, this time at Anzio. Preceded by air attacks against Luftwaffe airfields and German supply lines, the landings by 50,000 Anglo-American troops achieved complete surprise, but the German reaction to the assault was more swift than the Allies' attempts to exploit their initial success, with the result that the bridgehead was contained by the enemy until early May. A heavy German counter-attack was held with great difficulty in mid-February, and with the Allied troops exhausted by the winter fighting it was then decided to break the enemy main line by launching a devastating air attack on

Above: The docks at Leghorn, Italy, on 20 July 1944 showing the damage caused by earlier air attacks. (AHB)

Monte Cassino. Though as it turned out, the monastery at Cassino was not fortified by the enemy, after some hesitation the USAAF air bombardment went in on 15 February. The monastery was devastated, over 300 civilians were killed and the nearby German troops were now able to set up strong defensive positions among the ruins. Cassino would not be captured by the Allies until 18 May.

We have seen so far in this Mediterranean campaign the importance of air superiority in opening the way for action by ground and naval forces, and we have seen the first steps taken by the Allies towards closely co-ordinated air and ground action on the battlefield. On 19 March 1943 there began the first of two attempts in Italy to employ air power in another of its roles, that of interdiction. The term implies much more than merely hindering support activity behind the enemy's front by a general air offensive; it means destroying his lines of communication and the resources trying to move along them so as to isolate his forces in the front line.

Operation 'Strangle', as it was called, involved concentrated attacks well behind the German positions by the bombers of the Tactical Air Force on key transportation facilities such as railway bridges while the fighter-bombers took on rail targets closer to the front. Although opposition by the Luftwaffe was only slight, the results of the operation were disappointing. Bad weather, which hampered the continuity of the attacks, was one factor, but a more important one was that there was no concurrent assault by the Allied ground forces.

Since the air resources available to the Allies were never enough to keep out of action all the many routes to the south, the modest logistic support needed by the German forces was able to evade the air attempts to stop it and 'Strangle' thus failed.

A second interdiction attempt, Operation 'Diadem', was made throughout the autumn in an effort to cut the enemy off from his support, but although much damage was done, particularly when the Germans resorted to the use of road convoys in daylight, this attempt too was inconclusive. These disappointments led to the realization that, to be effective, interdiction would call for three things: first, a geographical line such as a river across which all traffic could be halted; second, air attack on such essential transport facilities as railway repair shops; and third, attrition against the opposing ground forces so as to compel them to consume more resources than could reach them through the air blockade.

The lessons learned from these somewhat disappointing interdiction efforts in Italy eventually became the basis of the very successful 'Transportation Plan' which would be employed to such good effect during the Normandy campaign, a campaign whose opening was by now only a few months away. Before moving the narrative to that theatre of operations, however, we need to follow the closing phases of the campaign in Italy. The Allied spring offensive opened on 11 May 1944 and Rome fell to the advancing armies on 4 June. Heavy Allied air action, amounting to an average of 1,000 sorties each day from the Tactical Air Force alone, accompanied the German retreat for 140 or so miles until, in mid-June, the enemy came to a halt on the 'Gothic Line'. Successive defensive positions south of this line caused the Allied advance to slow right down, and although widespread and heavy air activity continued, a redisposition of ground forces by both sides now changed the operational picture.

On the German side, reinforcements amounting to eight divisions arrived in northern Italy, while on the Allied side seven divisions were redeployed ready for the invasion of southern France. It was highly significant that the principal Allied commanders in the Mediterranean, among them Tedder, Leigh-Mallory and Coningham as well as Eisenhower and Montgomery, were now transferred to Britain in preparation for the campaign in Western Europe. Although fighting in Italy, on the ground and in the air, continued right up to May 1945, the days of rapid advance were now over and the centre of gravity of the war in the West would now move to Normandy.

'OVERLORD'

Initial planning for what became Operation 'Overlord', the Allied invasion of Europe, began in January 1943, and, after careful study, the part of the coast chosen for it was Normandy. This was a less obvious area than the Pas de Calais, which would have been much closer to the airfields in Britain from which so much support would be needed, but it was still within the range of air cover. During the early months of 1944 it became clear that there was some uncertainty about the operational aims of the Allied air forces in the massive amphibious assault that was to be undertaken. The directive for the Combined Bombing Offensive, agreed at Casablanca in January 1943, read in part that the aim of that offensive was 'to bring about the progressive destruction of the German military, industrial and economic system and the undermining of the morale of the German people to a point where their capacity for armed resistance is fatally weakened'.

Bomber Command of the Royal Air Force had, as we have seen, opted for night attacks, and Harris put his emphasis on the phrase 'undermining the morale of the German people'. At the same time the two United States Air Forces under General Spaatz, the Eighth in Britain and the Ninth in the Mediterranean, concentrated on point targets and on the phrase 'the destruction and dislocation of the German military, industrial and economic system'. But before the plan was finally adopted by the Combined Chiefs of Staff, a very important sentence was added to the Casablanca Directive, as it became known, which read, 'This is construed as meaning so weakened as to permit initiation of final combined operations on the Continent'.

Thus it was that three interpretations of the Directive existed; one held by Bomber Command, another by the USAAF and a third by the senior soldiers and sailors and, to a large extent by the US President and the British Prime Minister — the interpretation that the Combined Bomber Offensive was intended to prepare the way for the invasion of Europe.

This extraordinary lack of an agreed aim was not rectified until two months before the invasion, when General Eisenhower, the Supreme Allied Commander, was given operational control over all the Allied air forces in the theatre. This had two important consequences. First, Eisenhower, through Tedder, his deputy, was able to set priorities for the whole air offensive against the Continent; and second, he could call upon all those air forces if necessary for the direct support of land operations. This centralized control of all air activity was

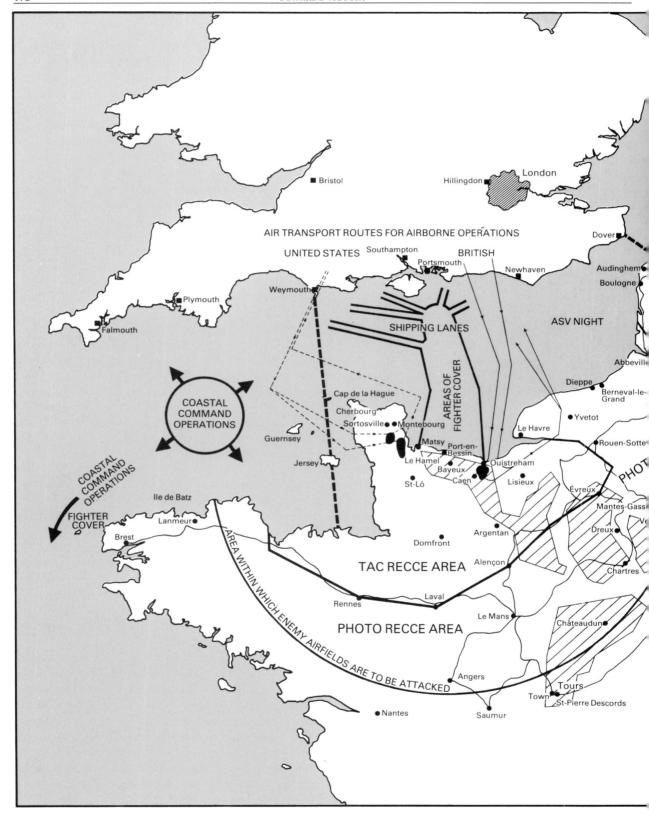

Bristol

Hillingdon   London

Dover

AIR TRANSPORT ROUTES FOR AIRBORNE OPERATIONS

UNITED STATES   Southampton   BRITISH

Audinghem

Portsmouth

Boulogne

Plymouth   Weymouth

ASV NIGHT

SHIPPING LANES

Falmouth

Abbeville

Newhaven

Dieppe

Berneval-le-
Grand

COASTAL
COMMAND
OPERATIONS

Cap de la Hague

Yvetot

Cherbourg

Le Havre

Sortosville   Montebourg

Guernsey

Rouen-Sotte

COASTAL
COMMAND
OPERATIONS

Matsy   Port-en-
Bessin

Jersey

Le Hamel   Ouistreham

PHOT

Bayeux

Évreux

FIGHTER
COVER

St-Lô   Caen

Lisieux

Ile de Batz

Mantes-Gassi

Lanmeur

Dreux

Brest

Argentan

Domfront

Chartres

TAC RECCE AREA   Alençon

Laval

Le Mans

Rennes

Châteaudun

PHOTO RECCE AREA

Angers

Tours

Town   St-Pierre Descords

Nantes

Saumur

AREA WITHIN WHICH ENEMY AIRFIELDS ARE TO BE ATTACKED

AREAS OF
FIGHTER COVER

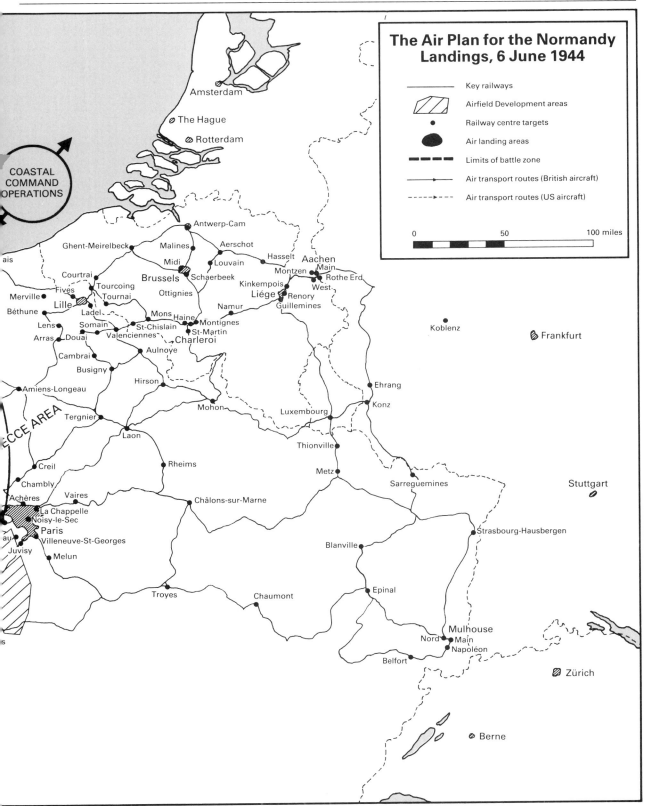

The Air Plan for the Normandy Landings, 6 June 1944

Key railways

Airfield Development areas

Railway centre targets

Air landing areas

Limits of battle zone

Air transport routes (British aircraft)

Air transport routes (US aircraft)

0   50   100 miles

COASTAL
COMMAND
OPERATIONS

Amsterdam

The Hague

Rotterdam

Antwerp-Cam

Ghent-Meirelbeck

Malines

Aerschot

ais

Midi

Louvain

Hasselt

Aachen

Courtrai

Brussels

Schaerbeek

Montzen

Main

Rothe Erd

Fives

Tourcoing

Ottignies

Kinkempois

West

Merville

Tournai

Liége

Renory

Koblenz

Lille

Ladel

Namur

Guillemines

Béthune

Mons

Haine

Montignes

Frankfurt

Lens

Somain

St-Chislain

St-Martin

Arras

Douai

Valenciennes

Charleroi

Cambrai

Aulnoye

Busigny

Hirson

Amiens-Longeau

Mohon

Luxembourg

Ehrang

Konz

ECCE AREA

Tergnier

Thionville

Laon

Rheims

Metz

Creil

Sarreguemines

Stuttgart

Chambly

Vaires

Châlons-sur-Marne

Achères

La Chappelle

Noisy-le-Sec

Paris

Villeneuve-St-Georges

Blanville

Strasbourg-Hausbergen

Juvisy

Melun

Troyes

Chaumont

Epinal

Mulhouse

Nord

Main

Napoléon

Belfort

Zürich

Berne

to be one of the keys to the successes that followed.

Apart from the large and growing bomber forces that were appearing in the United Kingdom during 1943, a start was made in building up a tactical air force for the invasion due to take place in the following year. The Second Tactical Air Force (2TAF) was formed on 1 June 1943, replacing Army Co-operation Command, which disbanded, and absorbing part of Fighter Command. Fighter Command itself was now renamed Air Defence of Great Britain, a title that it kept until 15 October, when it reverted to its former name. In the months that followed, 2TAF would grow to an air armada of three operational Groups, No 2 Group, transferred from Bomber Command, and Nos 83 and 84 (Composite) Groups, holding between them more than 5,000 operational aircraft.

At the same time, the Luftwaffe was by no means a defeated force, and indeed as late in the war as 21 January 1944 London was attacked by a force of some 447 German bombers. It had always been clear to the Allied planners that air superiority would be essential to the success of the invasion, and to this end, starting in February 1944, a massive campaign against the German aircraft industry was launched, primarily by the USAAF in daylight raids. The Luftwaffe came up to fight, with the result that in what became known as the 'Big Week' 210 American heavy bombers were shot down, but only at the catastrophic loss to the Luftwaffe of around 600 fighters. This haemorrhage of German air strength continued over the next three months, so that during February and March alone the Germans force lost about 800 day fighters; but even more serious for the enemy, between January and April 1944 the Luftwaffe lost over 1,000 pilots, including some of its best commanders.

The result of these heavy losses was that even by the fourth day after the invasion, when substantial reinforcements had arrived, the Luftwaffe's order of battle in Western Europe amounted to 1,155 aircraft, of which 679 were serviceable. Of that total, 475 were single-engine fighters with 290 of them serviceable; 464 were bombers of which 267 were serviceable; and the rest were night fighters or twin-engine fighters.

This should be compared with the Allied strength in combat aircraft on 6 June 1944: RAF Bomber Command had 1,408 bombers, the US Eighth Air Force 2,788 bombers and 1,242 fighters and 2TAF 1,520 bombers and 2,840 fighter-bombers. Nor was this great fleet of aircraft a matter of numbers only. Several very successful new aircraft types had joined the front line, including the North American Mustang, a machine built specifically for the Royal Air Force as a fighter but which proved to be more suited to the ground attack role when it entered service with No 2 Squadron in April 1942. A similar transformation had overtaken a second aircraft type that would play an important role in the months to come, the Hawker Typhoon. This machine had been designed as a fighter with its origins in Air Ministry Specification F18 of 1937, and the first version of the aircraft had joined the front line with No 56 Squadron in 1941. It proved, however, to be unsuitable as a fighter but its very good low-level performance had led to its production as a close-support aircraft. By D-Day twenty-six squadrons were flying an improved model of this aircraft, the Typhoon Ib, equipped with four 20mm cannon and capable of carrying two 1,000lb bombs or eight 60lb ballistic rockets, which last proved to be outstandingly successful against a variety of ground targets including enemy armour.

Before the invasion itself the very high degree of Allied air superiority had effectively prevented any German reconnaissance of the south of England during the preparations for the cross-Channel assault and thus made it possible to inflict tactical surprise on the enemy even though an invasion somewhere on the coast of North-West Europe was a strategic certainty. This same massive air strength also made it possible to conceal from the defence the area chosen for the landings: two Allied sorties were flown outside the Normandy region for every one flown within it during the run-up to the landings.

Mention was made earlier of the 'Transportation Plan' for the Normandy invasion, and this was to be a key feature of the air effort. The plan had two parts, a strategic phase, to be implemented ahead of the invasion, directed against the French rail system to put it out of action and force traffic on to the roads, and a tactical phase from D-Day onwards, in which enemy reserve divisions would be destroyed as they tried to move along the road network. Together with the Americans, Bomber Command attacked rail bridges and rail centres from 6 March onwards, and by D-Day over 66,000 tons of bombs had fallen on 80 selected targets. Twenty-one of the twenty-four rail bridges over the River Seine were put out of action, and many railway marshalling yards were devastated.

From D-Day onwards and over the next months, bombers and fighter-bombers attacked enemy columns as they sought to redeploy, and, particularly during the first few critical days of the invasion, they were highly successful. To give only one example, parts of the German 275th Infantry Division, ordered to move to the Front from the south coast of Brittany, took between

Right: A novel way of keeping down the dust at a dispersal in Normandy, 1944. (AHB)

Below right: The remains of an enemy column east of Chambois, Normandy, after an Allied air attack. (AHB)

seven and ten days to make the journey. On the way it suffered many casualties, lost all its vehicles and saw all five railway trains that it was using as transport so badly damaged that the elements of the division that did finally arrive in Normandy did so on foot.

Apart from the Transportation Plan, Allied air forces flew a huge number of other operational missions of all kinds in support of the invasion. For example, many sorties were directed against German gun positions and radars on the coast; No 617 Squadron employed sixteen Lancasters to simulate a large convoy crossing the Channel near the Strait of Dover by laying down a slowly advancing cloud of 'Window'; No 218 Squadron carried out a similar operation off Boulogne; and the Halifaxes and Stirlings of Nos 138, 149 and 161 Squadrons simulated ground combat in yet another diversionary area, using pyrotechnics and dummy parachutists. Meanwhile 406 transport aircraft of the Royal Air Force joined with 1,167 American machines to drop paratroops or to tow gliders across the Channel; and air defence cover was given to the 7,000 and more ships of all types that made up the initial invasion fleet.

All told, Operation 'Overlord', the most ambitious military undertaking in history, saw 11,590 Allied aircraft of all types participating, of which 5,510 were from the Royal Air Force. This contribution included 61 squadrons of Spitfires, 21 of Typhoons, twelve of Mustangs, two each of Tempests, Beaufighters and Hurricanes, 22 of Mosquitos, thirteen medium or heavy bomber squadrons and several other units such as those engaged on air/sea rescue duties. The RAF flew 5,656 of the 14,674 sorties dispatched during the first day, losing only 113 aircraft — a telling comment on the degree of air superiority that had been achieved against the Luftwaffe, who managed to fly only 319 missions.

Supermarine Spitfire XIX

During the Second World War the need for intelligence on targets deep in enemy-held territory led to the use of high-speed aircraft capable of operating at altitudes well above those at which there was a risk of interception by hostile fighters. Stripped of armament, and modified to give the best possible speeds at maximum height, several marks of Spitfire were employed on these duties, the XIX being the most advanced. It proved to be so successful in the role that it remained in front-line service until April 1954, when one of these machines flew the last operational sortie by a Spitfire with No 81 Squadron in Malaya. The Spitfire XIX had a top speed of 460mph, a range of 1,550 miles and an operational ceiling of 43,000ft. It carried no armament.

Right: Members of the RAF Regiment defending an airfield in Holland, 1944. (AHB)

Far right: One of the dropping zones at Arnhem, 18 September 1944. (AHB)

ADVANCE INTO GERMANY

Once the bridgehead was firmly established in Normandy, Allied tactical aircraft were flown into operating strips that had been built by airfield construction units, and by 27 June there were 38 Allied fighter and fighter-bomber squadrons operating from thirteen improvised airfields. This made it possible to maintain an air umbrella over the whole Allied position, and to operate in conditions of air supremacy the 'cab rank' system of close air support that had its origins in the Italian campaign. By using Air Observation Post aircraft not only to spot enemy dispositions but also to report the positions of friendly troops, commanders were kept in the closest possible touch with developments on the ground. At the same time Army air liaison officers and RAF controllers working well forward, often in armoured vehicles and moving with the Allied ground forces, made it possible to call in air strikes with very little delay and, vital once operations became more mobile, these strikes were carried out with great accuracy.

Apart from the intense activity by the tactical squadrons over north-west France, the campaign also saw several interventions by strategic bombers in direct support of the Allied ground forces. Between 7 July and 15 August six carpet-bombing raids were made in front of the Allied positions to assist the break-out from the Normandy bridgehead, laying down a total of over 24,000 tons of high explosive. These air attacks wreaked considerable destruction among the German troops and their equipment, but on two occasions there were also casualties among the Allied forces on the ground. Nor were the longer term effects always to the advantage of

the attacking Allied troops: as at Monte Cassino, it was found that heavy bombing raids such as that on Caen both hindered the Allies' advance and gave cover among the rubble to the enemy defenders.

After heavy fighting during late July and early August, in which the rocket-firing Typhoons played a major role, particularly against enemy armour, the Allied armies broke out of their bridgehead and by mid-August had outmanoeuvred the defence, trapping the remnants of sixteen German divisions near Falaise. For ten days the Allied tactical squadrons bombarded the enemy ground forces, turning their retreat into a major disaster. By now the arrangements under which close air support could be provided had reached a peak of efficiency, with the kind of 'cab rank' system that had evolved in Italy, but in Normandy augmented by 'contact cars' which operated in the forward areas alongside the leading armoured screen of the Allied ground forces.

At the same time a bombing offensive was launched against ports along the Channel coast such as Boulogne, Le Havre and St-Nazaire, where the isolated German garrisons were still holding out in so-called fortresses. Between 5 and 11 September 1944 seven daylight raids were made by Bomber Command against Le Havre, in which a total of more than 9,500 tons of bombs was dropped. Similar treatment against Boulogne followed on 17 September, and against Calais in three heavy attacks on 20, 25 and 27 September. All the ports eventually surrendered, but not before Bomber Command had flown around 6,000 sorties against them, losing only fourteen aircraft in the whole series of raids. Meanwhile, as the German forces fell back on the Seine, 2TAF flew something like 1,200 sorties each day for ten days, joined by the Mosquitos and Mitchells of No 2 Group, which

concentrated much of their considerable effort on the Seine crossings themselves. The Allied advance became a pursuit across northern France and into Belgium, and on 3 September Allied troops were in Brussels. It was an advance so rapid that it caused major logistic and support problems, not least for the tactical air squadrons. Even after the fall of Brussels, in order to keep the aircraft operating well forward some seventeen new airfields had to be built and 37 reconstructed by the Royal Engineers and the airfield construction units of the Royal Air Force, while to secure the bases against possible attack no fewer than 46 squadrons of the Royal Air Force Regiment were deployed, nineteen of them anti-aircraft units, 21 of them rifle squadrons, and six equipped with armoured cars.

While this campaign on the ground was unfolding, the Germans had opened an entirely new one in the air, this time using the V1 flying bombs briefly mentioned in Chapter 5. Starting on 13 June 1944 with ten of the missiles, an offensive against Britain grew in intensity, reaching a total of 800 of the new weapons in the first week of July. Air attacks on the launching sites for the V1s had begun as early as 5 December 1943, and a new urgency now led to heavy air attacks on the sites along the coast of Europe and to a redisposition of air defences in the United Kingdom so as to intercept the missiles that crossed the English coast. As a result, up to half the available bombing effort in Britain was diverted to what were known as 'Crossbow' targets, most of the effort being directed against the launching sites, complemented by attacks on the production and storage facilities. When this weight of air attack failed to halt the bombardment the priorities were reversed, but although, for example, during August 1944 some 118,000 tons of bombs fell on targets associated with V1s and those associated with the emerging ballistic missile, the V2, the bombardment continued. In Britain, meanwhile, all available anti-aircraft guns, 1,180 of them, were moved into a concentrated belt on the south coast, leaving to the 21 squadrons of fighters deployed against the V1s a space of around 45 miles between the gun-line and London in which to operate. With the missiles coming in at a speed of nearly 400mph, there was little room for error in directing fighters to their targets, and some fighter types were unable to engage at all because of the high speed of the V1. But the Spitfire XIV, the Mustang III, the Mosquito and particularly the new Tempest V carried out many successful interceptions, and it was also during this defence against the V1s that the new Meteor jet fighter first saw action after the first examples arrived on No 616 Squadron during July 1944. Despite the difficulties of interception, of 8,892 flying bombs launched from ramps and perhaps 1,600 launched from Heinkel 111s, between then and the end of the war 1,847 were destroyed by fighters over the Channel or over the south of England. Almost exactly the same number, 1,878, fell to anti-aircraft gunfire and 232 were brought down by barrage balloons.

On the Continent, the Allied advance continued until by October 1944 all seemed ready for a final advance into Germany itself. In order to hasten the German collapse in Holland and thus outflank the Siegfried Line, a large operation by Allied airborne forces had been set in train to take place in mid-September. Because of a shortage of transport aircraft, the Royal Air Force planned to lift the 1st Airborne Division in three waves, the first on 17 September and the other two on the following two days. On the first day two squadrons of

Left: Part of the fleet of aircraft taking part in the Rhine crossing, 24 March 1944. (AHB)

Right: Flak over the town of Wesel, seen from the west bank of the Rhine during the raid on the night of 23/24 March 1945 by Bomber Command in preparation for the assault crossing. (AHB)

Halifaxes, two of Albemarles, six of Dakotas and six of Stirlings released 285 Hamilcar and Horsa gliders over Arnhem, another 35 having been lost en route. A force of 1,240 fighters and 1,113 bombers operated in support of the landings, which, because intelligence on local German dispositions had been overlooked or ignored, was made in an area strongly held by German troops.

The vital lift of airborne troops and supplies on the second day was then delayed for six hours by bad weather over Britain, and on the third day the incoming transports, having failed to meet up with their fighter escorts, ran into opposition both from the Luftwaffe and from anti-aircraft fire, suffering heavy losses in the process. This chapter of misfortunes, together with the fact that a great deal of resupply resources fell outside the British perimeter, contributed to the eventual failure of the whole mission, and after six days the survivors fought their way out or surrendered. On top of the serious losses among the 1st Airborne Division, Transport Command had 57 aircraft shot down or destroyed in crashes. The whole operation had been an expensive failure, and the causes of it have been much discussed over the years. But it seems clear that the whole concept of projecting an airborne force so far forward was misconceived. As far as the efforts by the Royal Air Force were concerned, the transport squadrons did all that they could within their finite resources and under difficult conditions. Far worse than the inadequacies in transport support that quickly became apparent, however, was the fact that no provision had been made for the all-important contribution of

tactical air support. Without that compensating factor, lightly armed airborne forces had little chance against the substantial German forces deployed in the area around Arnhem.

There were to be three other operations of note before the campaign in North-West Europe drew to a close. The first was the German offensive in the Ardennes, which began on 16 December and soon developed into a serious penetration of the Allied positions, with German columns advancing at up to 20km a day. Very poor weather prevented any intervention by the Allied air forces until, on 23 December, conditions at last began to improve. On Christmas Eve the tactical air units were able to fly 600 missions in support of the Allied ground forces, and the pressure was kept up on subsequent days until the enemy columns, which by now had in any case begun to lose momentum, were halted and then driven back.

A second operation took the form of a spectacular attack by something in excess of 800 German aircraft on the airfields of 2TAF early on New Year's Day 1945. For this operation the Luftwaffe had scraped together aircraft and crews from all over Europe, some of them with combat experience but others from training units. It was a remarkable success — 224 Allied aircraft were destroyed on the ground, 144 of them in the British area, together with another 84 damaged. Overconfidence had led to expensive complacency, but this was to be the last throw by the Luftwaffe. Not only were 194 German aircraft destroyed in the operation, but around 200 of

be proper air preparation and support. The assault was preceded by a massive attack from the air on bridges, railway centres, airfields, barracks and finally German towns such as Wesel on the east bank and the troops crossed late at night on 23 March. Early the next morning Nos 38 and 46 Groups of Transport Command put 440 aircraft and gliders into the air from bases in Britain, to be joined by another 243 machines provided by the US IX Troop Carrier Command. No 2 Group operated in conditions of air supremacy and thus without the need for escorts, while whole Wings of fighters and fighter-bombers of Nos 83 and 84 Groups were airborne to give their support. In the event, little of this tactical air effort was needed, so crushing had been the air bombardment and so overwhelming the weight of the assault across the river.

After this operation a general collapse in German resistance was not long in coming, and by the final days of April the Allied armies were so close to the Soviet forces advancing from the east that targets for air attacks had often to be cleared with the Soviets in order to avoid casualties to their forces. Though the Luftwaffe in these final stages of the war in Europe still had several hundred serviceable aircraft at its disposal, and although there were new aircraft still pouring off the German production lines to add to the 4,000 or so machines awaiting delivery from the factories, a chronic shortage of fuel (largely caused by strategic air bombardment), together with a lack of trained air crews, kept them out of action. Thus, in the end, the devastating effects of the bomber offensive against Germany converged with the final Allied advance into the heart of that country.

their valuable and by now irreplaceable air crew were also lost.

The third operation to be mentioned from these final stages of the war in Europe was the crossing of the River Rhine by the British 6th Airborne Division on 24 March, as part of a wider Allied assault across that obstacle. By now the lessons of Arnhem had been well absorbed, and for the Rhine crossing the airborne landings would take place in one lift, and only after a successful attack across the river by Commandos and other troops. Most important of all, this time there would

Right: A Tempest V in 'D-Day' markings. The aircraft was armed with four 20mm guns. (AHB)

CHAPTER 9

INTO THE JET AGE

In the early years after the Second World War the size and shape of the Royal Air Force was governed by four main factors. The first was the inevitable run-down from the enormous force that had developed to meet all the demands of what amounted to two very extensive and simultaneous wars, that in Europe and that in the Far East. Second, and coupled with that, there was the need to reduce the huge Defence Budget so as to help rescue a national economy that was close to collapse. One question, therefore, was how the institutions of the Royal Air Force should most effectively be organized to survive what seemed likely to be a lean future. Third, there was the impact of new technology. To a great extent

accelerated rather than inspired by the pressures of the recent war, invention and innovation had produced a rich harvest of capabilities, from radar to jet engines and finally to the atomic bomb. Very many of these new techniques and technologies were particularly relevant to the science of aviation, and the Royal Air Force needed to harness them if it were to retain its position as a viable fighting force. Fourth, and as it turned out even more significant in the long term, there was the post-war international situation. It became clear even as early as

Below: Some of the varied aircraft types at the Empire Test Pilots' School, December 1943. (AHB)

February 1946 that the new world order did not include harmonious relations between East and West. In that month Stalin made his first major post-war speech, in which he gave rearmament absolute priority over consumer needs. A month later Churchill gave his 'Iron Curtain' speech at Fulton, Missouri, and gradually the road to the 'Cold War' was opened. By 1950, as this chapter will discuss, the international situation had deteriorated so much that the run-down of British forces was abandoned, to be replaced by a programme of rearmament far more urgent and comprehensive than that of only sixteen years earlier. And this would be a burden additional to that imposed by numerous national overseas commitments during the post-war years, a topic that will be dealt with separately in Chapter 11.

POST-WAR RUN-DOWN

For more than two years after the war, Western Governments and strategists tried to absorb not only the implications of the post-war situation but also the spectacular manner in which the war had ended over Hiroshima and Nagasaki. In looking at the uncertain future, the Defence White Paper of 1947 talked of a period of transition, and it made several important statements. One of them announced the retention of National Service: Britain would for the foreseeable future have partly conscript Air Force. In another section the White Paper pointed out that 'the main problem [for the Service] is to preserve the structure and continuity of the Royal Air Force'.

This was well said. By May 1945 the Royal Air Force had grown to a strength of 55,469 aircraft, of which 9,200 were in the first line, while personnel strengths had risen to 1,079,835 RAF, Dominion and Allied officers and men, of whom no fewer than 193,313 were air crew. The difficulty was to manage the huge outflow of personnel that now became inevitable. Under the Air Staff Plan E of mid-1947, the Royal Air Force proposed a front-line force for the future of 1,500 aircraft, to be made up of 51 fighter squadrons, 41 bomber squadrons, thirteen of maritime aircraft and 42 of transports, excluding a total of twelve reserve squadrons. These ideals could not, however, survive the harsh economic climate of the time, and the prospect of severe cuts in strength became a reality in 1947 when the Cabinet accepted that deliberate war in the immediate future was unlikely.

There were echoes here of the notorious 'Ten Year Rule' of the 1920s, though it has to be said that the assumptions in 1947 were far less explicit. Nor were they driven only by budgetary considerations. On the basis of intelligence about future Soviet capabilities, together with strategic judgement and the need to cut back on military spending, it was accepted that the likelihood of war in the next five years was slight but that it might increase during the following five. The significance of all this was that it permitted the deferment of expensive re-equipment programmes. In the event, the growing confrontation with the Soviet Union in 1948 weakened the assumptions, and the outbreak of the Korean War in 1950 caused them to be altogether abandoned; but this early post-war policy helps to explain the lack of continuity for three or four years in any progress towards a more modern air force.

The post-war run-down of the Service meanwhile continued, and already by June 1948 the front line had fallen to figures of 25 squadrons in Fighter Command with 207 aircraft, 24 bomber squadrons holding 160 aircraft, twenty squadrons in Transport Command making up a total of 160 aircraft, eleven Coastal squadrons mustering 87 aircraft, and a total of 33 squadrons overseas — in other words, the force was about half what had been suggested by the Air Staff only a year before. A reduction on this scale was difficult to manage, but it was made more complicated by the need to run down manpower. In the financial year 1946–47 the authorized strength of the Service had been 760,000, including 142,000 on pre-release leave. The next year the figure fell to under 375,000, and in the year 1948–49 it was down to 325,000. By April 1950 the actual strength of the Royal Air Force had fallen to 202,000. That would have been bad enough, but the priorities for release from the Service were based on factors other than those of Air Force needs, so that all manner of distortions emerged in manning the various trades and, as a result, by 1948 the RAF was under considerable strain, caused not so much by pure lack of numbers as by lack of appropriate skills. This would continue for at least the next two years, when the weight of two factors led to an important change to the manning pattern of the whole Service.

The first was that, at a time of very high employment levels in the economy, the RAF was depending heavily on conscripts, whose time in the Service was very limited. In order to draw the maximum value from them, it was necessary to keep their training as short as could reasonably be managed. The second factor was that the more complex aircraft and other systems that were coming into service demanded a much wider variety of skills. Until 1951 there had been about one hundred trades for non-commissioned ranks in the Royal Air Force, divided into four bands of skills, A to

D, with pay differentials between them. The problem with this structure was twofold: first, specializations tended to be too broad, and second, advancement often meant remustering to the lower bracket of another trade. To overcome these weaknesses, in January 1951 a New Trade Structure was introduced with 22 Trade Groups. Each of them corresponded to a major trade function, for example radio engineering, aircraft engineering, radar operating and mechanical transport. Within each Group there was a variety of jobs, ranging from totally unskilled to highly skilled, so that under the new scheme a recruit could specialize within a particular Group to gain advancement.

At the same time two promotion 'ladders' were created: one, the technician stream, was for those with good technical skills; the other, the Command stream, was for men and women whose strengths lay in leadership. The old rank titles were retained for the Command careerists, but new ranks were introduced for the technicians — Chief Technician, Senior Technician, Corporal Technician and Junior Technician, with rank badges consisting of inverted chevrons. The new scheme was much modified over the following years, particularly in 1955 and in 1964 when the structure of RAF trades was again updated.

That the basis of it remained was, however, in marked contrast to an attempt in these early post-war years to reorganize the Flying or General Duties Branch, to give it its proper title. In July 1946 new categories of rank for non-commissioned air crew were brought in with titles such as Pilot One and Navigator Two, the numbers in these two particular examples equating to

Flight Sergeant and Sergeant respectively, ranks that were indicated on uniforms by means of a number of stars placed within a laurel leaf emblem. These devices were soon known unofficially as 'star and garter badges'. At the same time an attempt was made to introduce Aircrew Messes that were to be organized and run separately from the customary Officers' and Sergeants' Messes, a remarkably divisive notion in a service that relied on such high levels of co-operation between air and ground branches. Not surprisingly, the whole scheme turned out

Above: A newly qualified pilot wearing one of the short-lived air-crew rank badges in January 1949. He is a Pilot IV, equivalent to a corporal; the aircraft is a Harvard. (AHB)

Left: HM The Queen presents her Colour to No 1 School of Technical Training, Halton, on 25 July 1952. (AHB)

Far right: Hunting Percival Provost T.1s. The piston-engine Provost was the standard basic trainer from 1954 until 1961. (AHB)

De Havilland Tiger Moth

Following on from the Avro 504 and the Avro Tutor, the Tiger Moth became the last of the RAF biplane trainers. It entered service in 1932, and was still in use with Flying Training Command as late as 1947. A few remained even later than that with the RAF flying training scheme in Rhodesia, the last examples being withdrawn in 1951. Before the war Tiger Moths equipped 44 flying training schools, and during the war itself they were in use at a total of 83 schools in the United Kingdom and throughout the Commonwealth. The 130hp Gypsy Major engine gave the aircraft a top speed of 109mph at 1,000ft; endurance was 3 hours.

to be highly unpopular, and it was quickly abandoned. The new badges were abolished in August 1950, and the only relic of these ill-fated schemes is the rank and badge of Master Aircrew, equating to Warrant Officer.

As far as higher organization is concerned, the Service decided after the war to retain the three Commands that had been created in 1936, Fighter, Bomber and Coastal, as well as Transport Command which had been called into being during 1943. These operational Commands were to be supported by Flying Training, Technical Training and Maintenance Commands. A Reserve Command was re-formed in May 1946, and there would be three overseas Commands, Mediterranean/Middle East Command, formed at the end of 1945, Far East Air Force, which took that title in June 1949, and the British Air Forces of Occupation in Germany, which were to be renamed 2nd Tactical Air Force in September 1951.

Several other important decisions on the structure of the Service were also taken in these same five years after the war. One was to re-form the Central Flying School at Little Rissington in May 1946. This promised a firm foundation for a much needed improvement in flying skills, partly so as to reduce the unacceptably high rate of aircraft accidents that the Service was suffering at that time. Statistics in that year were showing that 66 per cent of all RAF aircraft accidents involved some degree of pilot error. New standards of proficiency for the Service were now drawn up, starting with Transport Command, and a system of ratings for instrument flying was instituted to cover all pilots. These improvements were followed in 1948 by a new scheme for training pilots, and although it takes the story well past the early years after the war, it will be convenient to trace the developments here.

By the end of the war the usual pattern of training was a basic course with one instructor on de Havilland Tiger Moths followed by a course with another instructor on the North American Harvard, after which the pilot was awarded his 'wings'. He would then go on to an Advanced Flying School, where he would learn to fly an operational type such as the Wellington or the Spitfire before joining a squadron. The 1948 pattern, however, was to be an 'all-through' course, with the same instructor staying with his student from *ab initio* training right up to his 'wings'. The new course also involved more instrument and all-weather flying, and two new types of aircraft, one specifically designed for basic training and the other for advanced training, were introduced.

The aircraft for the first role emerged as the Percival Prentice, an underpowered and unpopular machine, while that for the second was the Boulton Paul Balliol. But by the time that this last aircraft finally entered service in 1953, after a long series of delays, it had become clear that training could be streamlined by using a jet aircraft for the advanced stage of flying

Left: The de Havilland Chipmunk was the *ab initio* trainer for many National Service pilots. Here five aircraft are seen over the RAF College at Cranwell. (AHB)

Below right: Jet Provosts began to replace the piston-engined version of this trainer in 1955. The T Mk 5, examples of which are seen here over the radar domes at Fylingdales, entered service in 1969. (BAe)

training. The Balliol was therefore replaced within a year by the only suitable machine available, the Vampire T.11. At the same time the sluggish Prentice was replaced by the popular and lively Percival Provost, so that pilots now completed about 60 hours on this piston-engine trainer and around 120 on Vampires before going on to an Operational Training Unit, to fly Hawker Hunters, Gloster Javelins or English Electric Canberras before joining a front-line squadron. In the years that followed, the piston-engine Provost was replaced by an equally popular jet-engine version, so that from the early 1960s onward budding pilots completed all their training on jet machines. Later, a mix of Folland Gnats and Hawker Hunters replaced the Vampires as advanced trainers, until the Hawker Siddeley Hawk was introduced — an aircraft that is still in service.

The general pattern of basic and advanced pilot training was concentrated into about eighteen months, except for cadets at the Royal Air Force College, which had reopened in October 1946 by absorbing No 19 Flying Training School, at that time based at Cranwell. Here, for two decades and more after the war, the student pilots were given a flying course of almost 300 hours, though it was spread over two and a half years and accompanied by a heavy academic syllabus. The result was not entirely satisfactory, with the result that the College entered a period during which a great number of changes, large and small, were inflicted on the syllabus, until finally, in 1970, the old cadet entry scheme was abandoned altogether. The flying syllabus at Cranwell then fell into line with that of the other flying training schools.

Left: Trenchard's Apprentice School at Halton did not close during the war and in the post-war years it continued to train highly skilled men for the Service. Shown here is the Apprentice Pipe Band with its mascot Lewis III (the name standing for London, England, Wales, Ireland, Scotland). The photograph was taken on 29 July 1952. (AHB)

The apprentice schools had kept going throughout the war, and indeed had continued to produce a stream of well-trained technicians. Other institutions, however, had closed or changed their character, and now during these years of the late 1940s a number of Service colleges, schools and other institutions were revived or started up. One of the most important of the new schools was the Royal Air Force Flying College, founded in June 1949 at Manby by amalgamating the Empire Air Armament School already based at that same airfield with the Empire Flying School from Hullavington. Another school that came to have an important influence on Service flying was the Central Fighter Establishment, which had been originally formed in 1944 from several smaller operational training units. Its continuing value was recognized when it was moved to West Raynham in August 1945 and expanded in size so that by the next month it had no fewer than 170 aircraft on strength. Yet a third key establishment was the Royal Air Force

Technical College, formed at Henlow in 1947 from the RAF School of Aeronautical Engineering to train technical cadets as well as to give initial and post-graduate training to the engineer officers so vital to the Service. The College would remain at Henlow until 1966 when, because the facilities there were judged to be inadequate to meet future needs, it moved to new premises at Cranwell and was amalgamated with the Royal Air Force College. There were many other changes in the early post-war years affecting the training infrastructure of the Service, but one more key institution must be mentioned, the RAF Staff College, which had moved from Andover to Bulstrode Park near Gerrards Cross in January 1942. In February 1945 it moved again, this time to Bracknell, leaving a smaller sister staff college at Bulstrode Park for Allied officers and a cadre of RAF students. Bulstrode later moved to Andover, and in January 1970 the college at Andover joined the main institution at Bracknell, which remains the home of the RAF Staff College today.

Not least among the many adjustments in the Service to meet the conditions of peacetime was the re-formation of the Auxiliary Air Force in June 1946, to be made up of thirteen day fighter squadrons, three of night fighters and four equipped with light bombers. The prefix 'Royal' was conferred seven months later. Then in the next month, July 1946, it was announced that the RAF Regiment would continue as a permanent element of the Service, with rifle, armoured and light anti-aircraft (LAA) squadrons. The Regiment was a force that had expanded from its formation in 1942 to a strength by the end of the war amounting to 30 Wings with well over 200 squadrons. The post-war cut-back in the Regiment was particularly severe, and after a rapid run-down and reorganization, by August 1947 there were only 21 RAF

Right: A mixed formation from the Central Fighter Establishment at West Raynham on 12 November 1953. The aircraft are a Meteor NF.11, a Venom NF.2, a Sabre, a Meteor 4, a Venom FB.1, a Meteor 8, an Attacker and a Sea Hawk. (AHB)

North American Mustang

Although the Spitfires and Hurricanes of Fighter Command were proving to be highly successful in the skies over Britain, there was clearly a need even in 1940 for a more advanced fighter that could meet future challenges. This led to the production of the Mustang, specifically designed to meet RAF needs. The Mustang Mk I, however, gave such a disappointing performance at altitude that it was soon relegated to armed reconnaissance duties, in which it proved very effective from April 1942 onwards. But in the Mk III and Mk IV versions of the Mustang the original Allison engine was replaced by a Packard-built Rolls-Royce Merlin powerplant, and the aircraft then became one of the classic fighters of the war. The Mks III and IV not only went on to equip 23 squadrons of the RAF, but the type was adopted by the USAAF and fourteen of the fifteen American fighter Groups ('Wings' in RAF terminology) based in Britain flew them. The last RAF Mustangs were not withdrawn from the front line until November 1946, while in the United States Air Force (as the USAAF became in 1947) Mustangs operated in the early stages of the Korean War during 1950. The Mustang III and IV had a service ceiling of 42,500ft and a top speed of 442mph at 24,500ft, 20–40mph better than the maximum speed of the late marks of Spitfire. Of particular significance was the aircraft's tactical radius of action — about 325 miles on internal fuel but 750 miles with two drop tanks. The Mustang was thus a very important escort fighter. The early marks carried four .50 guns and four of .30 calibre; later marks were fitted with just the four .50s.

Regiment squadrons still in existence.

Another move towards the greater use of reserves was included in the 1947 Defence White Paper, which among other items announced the reintroduction of Auxiliary and Reserve training, the reopening of the Royal Air Force Volunteer Reserve and the re-formation of the University Air Squadron Scheme with units at eleven universities. Two years later the Women's Auxiliary Air Force was renamed the Women's Royal Air Force, giving permanent peacetime status to another element of the Service that had been greatly expanded during the war. In September 1939 there had been about 1,740 women of all ranks in RAF uniform, and by 1943 a peak strength of 181,835 had been reached, with women serving in some 80 or so of the ground trades. In common with the rest of the Service, the WRAF would in future be a very much smaller force, but one that made an invaluable contribution in many specializations, including such operational activities as Fighter and Air Traffic Control.

Alongside these important post-war adjustments, other changes were made that reflected a return to peace-time routine. Ceremonial once more came into its own, exemplified most clearly perhaps by the introduction of Standards and Colours into the Service. In 1943, on the twenty-fifth anniversary of the foundation of the Royal Air Force, King George VI had announced his intention of awarding a ceremonial flag, to be called a Standard, to operational squadrons of the Service, and later he made known his wish that Colours should be introduced as well. Originally there were to have been three King's Colours: one for the RAF at home, one for Royal Air Force Germany and one for No 1 School of Technical Training. After the death of the King, Queen Elizabeth approved the award of a fourth Colour, that for the RAF Regiment. In fact, the first Colour was presented to the RAF College Cranwell by King George VI on 6 July 1948, followed by that for the Royal Air Force at home on 26 May 1951. No 1 SofTT was so honoured on 25 July 1952, and the RAF Regiment on 17 March 1952. Squadron Standards soon followed, the first to No 1 Squadron on 24 April 1953 and that to No 600 Squadron a month later. Many other presentations would be made in succeeding years.

NEW TECHNOLOGIES

One very important post-war challenge for a Service that was essentially in the business of technology was how to equip the front line for the future. During the first two years or so immediately after the war, operational replacements were drawn from the overrun of the more battleworthy wartime aircraft types, such as the Lancaster and the Spitfire. But there were one or two notable exceptions. The first was the development of jet aircraft such as the Meteor and Vampire, though it must be said that the construction and the aerodynamics of these machines was very conventional for the time: they simply had jets instead of piston engines. A far more significant venture was Specification E24/43, issued in the autumn of 1943. This was an extraordinarily bold concept, calling for an aircraft with a speed of 1,000mph and the ability to operate at 36,000ft — capabilities that must have seemed very fanciful at that time. The Miles aircraft company was awarded a contract to design and build a jet-propelled supersonic research aircraft to meet the specification, and work went ahead on the project for three years until, in 1946, and in common with several other advanced ideas, it fell victim to the notorious decision by the British Government in that year not to proceed with any supersonic designs.

It was a decision that is still the subject of controversy; but that it was a disaster for advanced

British aircraft during the first decade or so after the war is shown by a statement in a Government White Paper of February 1955, *The Supply of Military Aircraft*, where we read that 'The decision was also taken in 1946 that, in the light of the limited knowledge then available, the risk of attempting supersonic flight in manned aircraft was unacceptably great and that our research into the problems involved should be conducted in the first place by means of air launched models. It is easy to be wise after the event, but it is clear now that this decision seriously delayed the progress of aeronautical research in the UK'.

The natural overrun of wartime aircraft types meanwhile continued, and indeed the last of the Spitfires, an F Mk 24, came off the production line as late as October 1947, incidentally bringing the total Spitfire production figure for the Royal Air Force to 20,351 machines. The final operational flight by a Royal Air Force Spitfire did not take place until April 1954, during the anti-terrorist campaign in Malaya. The last of the Lancasters left the production line in February 1946 after 7,377 had been built (including those manufactured in Canada), and this sturdy aircraft, too, continued in service with the Royal Air Force until 1954, when in February of that year the last was withdrawn from its role of maritime reconnaissance. The replacement for the Lancaster was the Avro Lincoln, a direct offspring, and indeed it was originally known as the Lancaster Mk IV and V. This aircraft first flew in June 1944 and it entered squadron service just in time to be included in the plan for an air assault on Japan by Tiger Force, which of course was aborted when the war in the Far East ended. Lincolns went on to equip 21 squadrons of Bomber Command as well as three in Signals Command during the early post-war years, and the last of the type was not finally withdrawn until March 1963.

The important point about aircraft such as the Lincoln being produced in Britain just after the war is that they were originally intended only as stop-gaps until more advanced aircraft became available. What these new aircraft would be, once supersonic concepts had been ruled out, was another matter. But it had been clear from the early stages of the war that a new era was opening in aeronautics, and by the end of the conflict a remarkably wide horizon for the future of military aviation had been revealed.

One important change had been seen in aircraft structures. The traditional pre-war form of airframe construction had been one in which the load-bearing framework of an aircraft was made up of bulkheads and stringers covered with canvas, or sometimes with metal sheet. The Hurricane was one of the last types with this construction to see operational service; the front fuselage was skinned in light alloy, but the rear fuselage was a canvas-covered frame of metal tubes. Starting with the Spitfire, stressed-skin principles were increasingly used in British military aircraft. In this type of construction, part of the loading on the airframe is carried by bulkheads and stringers, but much of it can be transferred to the light alloy outer skin of the machine, thus spreading the stresses over a greater area and in turn making possible lighter but very robust structures.

A second technical change during these years was in the long term more revolutionary in character, namely the advent of the jet engine. The pioneer in Britain of this new method of aircraft propulsion was Air Commodore Frank Whittle (later Sir Frank), an ex-aircraft apprentice and a former cadet at the Royal Air Force College. There is no space here to recount the story of his jet engines, but after many set-backs the Gloster Whittle E28/39 first flew on 15 May 1941, and it was from this modest beginning that first the Meteor and then other jet aircraft would eventually emerge. There were many technical problems to be solved along the way, but jet-engine aircraft offered several advantages over propeller-driven machines, and this novel form of propulsion was greeted with great enthusiasm.

Jets have a comparatively simple layout, with only one major moving part, the rotating turbine. Piston engines, on the other hand, rely on a mass of

Below: Group Captain (later Air Commodore Sir Frank) Whittle. (IWM)

Gloster Meteor I

A new era in British aviation began with the arrival of the first Meteor Mk Is on No 616 Squadron in July 1944. This first jet aircraft to enter service with the Royal Air Force was powered by two Rolls-Royce Welland I engines each delivering 1,700lb of thrust, giving the aircraft a maximum speed of 385mph at sea level and an initial rate of climb of 2,155ft/min. This performance would be greatly improved in later marks of the aircraft. Like most of the later models of the Meteor that followed over the next decade and more, the Mk I was armed with four fuselage-mounted 20mm cannon.

reciprocating parts, with all that this implies for stress on components and thus for reliability, particularly at high levels of performance. More important than that, however, is the question of comparative performance. Propellers are more efficient than jet engines at low speeds, reaching a maximum of perhaps 80 per cent efficiency at around 350kts. But above that speed the propeller tips are rotating through the air at supersonic velocity, and the result is a sharp fall in efficiency. In contrast, jet engines show a marked increase in propulsive efficiency as speed increases, giving figures of roughly 40 per cent at 400kts but around 60 per cent at 700kts and actually increasing further above that speed.

Another very important difference between the two forms of propulsion is that when a piston engine operates at high altitude the weight of the fuel mixture being fed into the cylinders decreases because of the fall in air density with altitude, which in turn leads to a fall in power output. This can be partly overcome by fitting one or more superchargers, which increase the pressure of the fuel/air mixture. There is a limit to this process, however, and because power continues to fall off as altitude is increased, a piston-engine aircraft would not normally be expected to operate at altitudes much above 35,000ft. With jet engines, not only is power still available at extreme altitudes, but the amount of fuel used up decreases, so that, for example, around 40,000ft the fuel consumption for a given distance covered over the ground is only about half what it is at sea level.

The high speed potential of the emerging jet aircraft was convincingly demonstrated during the first post-war attempt at the official speed record on 7 September 1946, when a stripped-down Meteor Mk 4 of the Royal Air Force High Speed Flight, a unit that had been re-formed in June 1946, covered a measured 3km course off the coast of Kent at a speed of 616mph, at least 80mph faster than most other fighters in service at that time. In that same year, the first two Wings of jet fighters in the Royal Air Force were formed, both equipped with operational versions of the Meteor F.3: one was at Bentwaters, made up of Nos 56, 74 and 245 Squadrons;

the second followed at Boxted with Nos 222, 234 and 263 Squadrons. The Meteor was a popular aircraft, being relatively easy to handle and pleasant to fly. If not treated with respect, however, it could produce vicious characteristics when flying at low speeds on one engine. There were to be a considerable number of fatal accidents from this cause over the next few years, and not only among inexperienced pilots. Nevertheless, variants of the Meteor would remain in front-line service until August 1961 because at the time there was little else with which to replace it. The early marks into the front line, the F.3 and F.4, were succeeded by the F Mk 8, which formed the backbone of the day fighter force between 1950 and

1955, when the Hawker Hunter began to appear in large numbers. During the same period, the Meteor FR.9 and PR.10 took over most of the reconnaissance commitment from the Spitfire FR.18 and PR.19, while the night fighter versions of the Meteor, the NF Mks 11, 12, 13 and 14, took over the that role until the Gloster Javelin could enter service, which it did in February 1956 with No 46 Squadron. Meanwhile it is worth noting the amount of 'stretch' that was available even in so unadventurous a design as the Meteor. The Mk I version had a total engine thrust of 3,400lb and a maximum loaded weight of 15,175lb; the figures for the NF.11 were 7,200lb and 22,000lb respectively.

Left: The first jet-powered aircraft to enter RAF service was the Meteor in 1945, and by the early 1950s the Mk 8 version had become the most numerous single-seat day interceptor in Fighter Command. On 2 June 1953, 216 of these aircraft took part in the Coronation Review flypast at Odiham. Shown here are eighteen Mk 8s of the Biggin Hill Wing about to take off for that event. (AHB)

Above: The Vampire was the second jet-powered aircraft to enter RAF service. Shown here is an early production Mk I. (BAe)

De Havilland Vampire FB.5

By early 1943 the army co-operation role in the Royal Air Force was being taken over by new aircraft such as the Tomahawk, the Kittyhawk and the Mustang. Then, from early 1944, the term 'close air support' came into more common use, reflecting the new battlefield mission of these tactical aircraft, and at the same time many of the ground attack squadrons were re-equipped with the Hawker Typhoon. By D-Day there were no fewer than twenty-six squadrons of them. In the years just after the war, as jet aircraft arrived in the front line, a version of the Vampire, the FB.5, became the RAF's first jet ground attack aircraft. By January 1952 thirteen of the sixteen squadrons of the RAF in Germany were equipped with these aircraft, and others were deployed in the Middle and Far East. Earlier variants of the Vampire had seen service in the day fighter role, and the FB.5 also retained an air-to-air capability. Carrying 2,000lb of bombs or eight 60lb rockets as well as its four 20mm fuselage-mounted cannon, this aircraft was a formidable weapon against semi-armoured and even armoured targets. The FB.5 had a maximum speed of 540mph at 20,000ft and it had a ferry range of over 700 miles.

The year 1946 also saw the advent of the other principal fighter to enter Royal Air Force service just after the war, the Vampire. No 247 Squadron was the first to receive this aircraft in the first months of that year, followed by Nos 54 and 72 Squadrons during September, when all three units came together to form a Wing at Odiham. This de Havilland design was a small single-engine aircraft with an unusual twin-tailboom layout, but it was a machine of viceless characteristics, though oddly enough it was not on the whole as popular as the Meteor. Like the Meteor, the Vampire would be developed through several marks during the next few years.

The first of these Vampire variants was the two-seat night fighter version originally intended for the Egyptian Air Force but diverted to the RAF as an interim machine when an embargo was placed on arms exports to that country in 1951. This aircraft became the Vampire NF Mk 10. Based on the original Vampire day fighter meanwhile, another twin-boom machine, the Venom, came into service in 1952. It was originally to have been designated Vampire Mk 8, but the differences between the old and the new justified a change of name. This aircraft had a higher-rated engine than the Vampire, and it had a mainplane of reduced thickness/chord ratio as well as a leading edge swept back at just over 17 degrees, design features that increased the performance to a maximum speed of 640mph, or more than 100mph better than that of the Vampire. Like the day fighter Vampire, the day fighter Venom was followed by a two-seat night fighter version, the Venom NF Mk 2, which came into service in 1953.

Towards the end of that year a modified version entered service, the Venom NF Mk 3, with powered ailerons, a frameless cockpit canopy and various other improvements. But it was to be the last of the night fighters adapted from day fighter designs, and the next RAF aircraft in the role would be the Javelin delta-winged all-weather fighter, which, as has already been mentioned, joined the front line in 1956. The Javelin was the first aircraft in RAF service designed from the start as an all-weather fighter, previous machines in the role having all been adaptations of day interceptors. It was also the first twin-jet delta-wing fighter in the world, and it had a good performance in its role of bomber interception at high altitudes and subsonic speeds. All told, 363 of these aircraft would be delivered to the Royal Air Force, the last of them eventually being phased out with No 64 Squadron in Singapore during June 1967, to be replaced there by the Lightnings of No 74 Squadron.

Meteors, Vampires and Venoms remained in the front line for well over a decade, though it has to be said that they were virtually obsolescent from the start. Their straight-wing construction put them firmly into the airframe era of the Second World War, and they were swiftly outclassed by more advanced aircraft in other parts of the world. In the United States, for example, the F-86 Sabre fighter with its 35 degree sweep-back and top speed of Mach 0.9 entered service in 1949, while in the Soviet Union the excellent MiG-15 had first flown at the end of 1947. It was this Soviet aircraft that was to demonstrate the extent of the gap between British fighters and those of the other major aircraft producers when, in the spring of 1951, Meteors of No 77 Squadron Royal Australian Air Force came up against MiG-15s over North Korea. The Meteors fared so disastrously in the air-to-air combats that followed that they were very soon relegated to ground-attack duties. Despite this realization that both the Meteor and the Vampire were outclassed by several other contemporary fighter aircraft, many later marks of each would be produced over the following years, partly because the logic was that these aircraft would be engaging Soviet bombers rather than fighters and partly because little else was available with which to replace them. This last factor stemmed from the absence of any real stimulus for the British aeronautical industry from Government investment. The necessary resources were not forthcoming, and it is clear in retrospect that during the decade or more after the Second World War the British aircraft industry and thus the Royal Air Force lost most of the decisive lead that it had until then shared with the other leading aeronautical powers of the world.

Progress was badly needed because the basically outmoded design both of the Meteor and the Vampire meant that these aircraft were limited by an official maximum handling speed of Mach 0.76, while if their speed was increased towards Mach 0.80 they became virtually uncontrollable. This aspect, too, of early jet age problems deserves some explanation, though it must here be a very simplified one. Already during the war, pilots of high-speed aircraft had been reporting heavy buffeting of the airframe accompanied by control snatching once speeds of around 500mph were reached (which could happen, for example, in a dive), and in some cases aircraft had been known to break up in flight. It was gradually realized that these unwelcome effects were being caused by what is known as 'compressibility effect', a phenomenon that occurs as an aircraft approaches the speed of sound. At the kind of speeds with which airmen had until then been familiar, the air just ahead of the leading surfaces of an aircraft is affected by sound waves which cause the air to part just before it meets and flows over the contours of the structure. As the aircraft flies closer to the speed of sound, the sound waves become compressed and pile up, until a point is reached at which the sound waves are close enough and dense enough to affect the smooth flow of air over the surfaces of the aircraft. Shock waves then form on the surface of the airframe, and unless the aerodynamic surfaces are designed with these problems in mind, severe vibration of the aircraft and its control surfaces, effects known as buffeting, will occur, followed by undemanded changes of aircraft attitude, usually in pitch, leading to a temporary loss of control.

At the level of aircraft procurement in these early post-war years, the Royal Air Force had focused much of its attention on the need for an offensive capability, as it had always done except in the years of the late 1930s and early 1940s. As a result the specifications drawn up in 1944 included a replacement for the Mosquito light bomber as well as the parameters of a larger aircraft that would be capable of carrying the atomic bomb, a topic that will be dealt with separately in Chapter 10. Within British industry at this same time, Hawker, de Havilland, Supermarine and Gloster were starting on the design of jet fighters, leaving Avro, Vickers and Handley Page to draw up ideas for jet bombers.

A fourth company in the competition for bomber orders was English Electric, which had entered the aircraft business as late as 1937 when it built a large aircraft factory at Salmesbury, between Preston and Blackburn, to produce Handley Page Hampdens and later Halifaxes as part of the wartime Nuffield Shadow Factory Scheme. Discussions took place in 1945 between English Electric and Rolls-Royce to harmonize a possible airframe with a suitable model of jet engine, leading to

agreement on a twin axial-flow engine layout with the powerplants mounted on the mainplanes. This configuration would leave the fuselage free to take a substantial load of fuel, as well as up to 10,000lb of operational stores such as bombs.

By this time aerodynamicists were well aware that sweeping back the wings of an aircraft could delay the onset of the compressibility effect; but since the engines being discussed with Rolls-Royce were expected to deliver only 6,500lb of thrust, thus limiting the aircraft to a top speed of something like 500kts and Mach 0.8, this factor did not seem important and it was not pursued. All the same, and to improve control at the anticipated onset of the compressibility effect, a symmetrical aerodynamic section was chosen for the mainplane of the aircraft, a feature that would put the centre of pressure well aft and thus avoid the sudden trim changes that might be expected at high sub-Mach numbers. A further design feature to improve high speed control was an all-moving tailplane, which could give a very strong correcting moment in the pitching plane if indeed there turned out to be unusually high trim changes. Finally, the aircraft was to be fitted with spring tabs so as to lighten the control forces needed in all conditions of flight. This was the design that became the Canberra.

This first jet bomber for the Royal Air Force had been originally intended to carry a radar aiming system for high-altitude attack, but the equipment fell behind schedule and, with international tension by now growing at the start of the Cold War, a new Operational Requirement was set, B5/47, which among other things accepted a visual bombing capability and specified a third crew member, a bomb-aimer, to manage the extra workload involved. Although the prototype had not yet flown, so pressing was the need for this new aircraft that

Right: The Meteor was replaced in service by the Hawker Hunter. Shown here is the prototype, which first flew on 20 July 1951. (BAe)

in March 1949 a production order was placed for 132 aircraft, made up of a mixture of Mk 2 bombers and Mk 3 photographic reconnaissance versions. Many other variants of this robust basic design were to follow in later years, eventually including, for example, the RB-57F for the US Air Force, an aircraft which, by virtue of extended wing span and new powerplants delivering 45,000lb of thrust, was able to carry out reconnaissance flights over the Soviet Union and China at altitudes of more than 80,000ft. The eventual contribution made to the front line of the Royal Air Force by the remarkable Canberra family will be described later.

AIR DEFENCE

Jet-age aircraft were not the only technological challenge facing the Service during these years immediately after the war. Equally important was the whole question of the air defence infrastructure, in other words the radars, communications and other facilities without which the interceptors would be of very limited value. As the Battle of Britain had shown, the key to a successful air defence system was some means of detecting, identifying and only then intercepting incoming air attacks. Since 1940, however, the nature of the threat had changed. Instead of relatively slow-moving intruders, the defence was now faced with the possibility of fast and high-flying jet aircraft, which implied the control of very much larger airspaces from the ground stations as well as much more advanced interceptor aircraft. It was therefore decided to create six air defence sectors to cover the whole of Britain, each with a Sector Controller who would scramble fighters from the airfields allocated to him but then hand over responsibility to radar-equipped Ground Controlled Intercept (GCI) stations for the close control of the actual interception. This system was based on

earlier experience, except that because the sectors now covered a much wider area they had in effect taken over the functions of the Fighter Command Group operations rooms, and the Groups thus no longer controlled the air battle.

The next development in air defence again takes us a few years ahead of the main account, but for the sake of continuity it will be easiest to explain here the subsequent improvements in what became known as the Air Defence Ground Environment, in other words the ground-based features of the whole air defence system. At the end of the 1940s the possibility of air attack against Britain with atomic weapons had to be taken into account and the result was a scheme known as the 'Rotor Plan', drawn up during 1951. At great expense the Sector Operational Centres and the GCI Stations were moved into underground shelters, work that was completed by 1954. At the same time the 16-year-old Chain Home Type 7 radars were replaced at the most important GCI stations with Type 80 radars. These gave a much improved coverage, of sometimes as much as 200 nautical miles against targets at heights of around 40,000ft, and they offered a sharper radar response that made possible a more accurate control of the fighters.

However, exercises showed these improvements to be still inadequate. It was found that in the face of a heavy incoming raid of, say, 30 to 40 aircraft, the system was swamped, so that fighters intercepted other fighters while many of the attacking bombers got through. The problem turned out to be that the high speed of the incoming raids overtook the ability of the ground-based infrastructure to handle the mass of information that was passing through the system. A major step forward came during 1954, when a new American radar, the FPS3, was deployed at certain of the GCI sites. It offered two important advantages. First, it had a range of a good 200 miles, which meant that instead of only the controller at Sector having a grasp of the wider air defence picture, the controller at the GCI station could see the same plot. Second, the new radar plot could be projected on to a screen measuring about seven feet across, thus replacing the old, small manual plotting tables and cutting out another source of administrative delay in updating the air defence picture. Further air defence exercises during 1954 and 1955 then showed that the old filter rooms were no longer necessary, and the previous system of manual plotting tables at Sector Operation Centres was replaced by control at newly designated Master Radar Stations. These changes were very successful in moving the initial reaction point against intruders well out from the coast, thus giving the controllers more time to assess the situation and to decide upon their response.

THE BERLIN AIRLIFT

To return to the wider international scene against which these various measures were being introduced, for two or three years after the Second World War any steps taken to improve the air defence capabilities of Britain were, as we have seen, generally hesitant and constrained. But then, in 1948, an unmistakable indication of Soviet intransigence as well as a pointer to probable future relationships was given by the Soviet blockade of Berlin. On 24 June 1948 the Soviet authorities in East Germany cut all road, rail and canal routes from the Western Zones

of Occupation into West Berlin. There had been indications of impending trouble before this, and both the United States Air Force and the Royal Air Force had each been able to draw up contingency plans to support their own garrisons. Nevertheless, the Western Allies at first thought that the blockade would be only a temporary inconvenience; few people believed that the siege would be sustained for an extended period, and it seems equally unlikely that the Soviets expected the Allies to be able to supply the city purely by air. Yet both things came about. The Allies' reaction was swift. At the strategic level, heavy bombers of the USAF flew the Atlantic and took up station on RAF airfields as a precaution against a possible extension of the crisis, while, in Europe, Transport Command of the Royal Air Force and the United States Air Force had joined together within four days of the start of the blockade to set up the first airlifts. Thirteen Dakota transports flew 44 tons of food from Wunstorf to Gatow on that first day of the operation. The aim was, if the blockade continued, to move 400 tons of supplies each day until 3 July, and 750 tons daily thereafter.

Two large air bases in the American Zone were used by the USAF, while the RAF set up airheads at six airfields in the British Zone as well as a flying boat base at Finkenwerde on the Elbe near Hamburg. There were two available reception airfields in Berlin, Tempelhof in the American Sector and Gatow in the British. Gatow had been a grass airfield, and when the blockade began,

work to lay a 2,000yd runway was still in progress. This effort was now accelerated, and the runway was finished within six weeks.

Rapid handling at all the air bases was essential if the full capacity of the available aircraft were to be used, and this was particularly important at the obvious bottlenecks in Berlin. A pattern at Gatow was soon established in which there was one take-off and one landing every three minutes by day and by night, except that in bad weather the interval would be extended to five minutes. Full use was made of Eureka Beacons and Ground Controlled Approach radars to guide the traffic, and a new runway approach lighting system, named the Calvert System (after its originator at Farnborough), was installed at Gatow. This was the first use of a system in which crossbar sodium lights are positioned at right angles to a continuous line of lights set on the runway heading, thus giving the pilot on his approach a good horizontal reference and a better impression of his position on the glide path. The Calvert System now forms the basis for virtually all modern military and civil approach lighting systems.

At the start of the airlift Transport Command was carrying mainly food and construction plant into the city and bringing out the first of a total of about 50,000 refugees on the return flights. Most of the aircraft engaged were Dakotas and Avro York transports. Sixty-four Dakotas of the RAF eventually took part in the airlift, as well as 56 Yorks, in six squadrons. This last aircraft was from the same stable as the Lancaster bomber. The aircraft had the same mainplanes and power units as the Lancaster but the fuselage had been completely redesigned so as to give twice the capacity of the bomber. It had actually been first flown in 1942, but only a handful had been produced by the end of the war. After the war 257 Yorks were built, mainly for the RAF but a few of them destined for civil operators.

In July civil aircraft on charter were also brought into the airlift, and in October 1948 the Yorks and Sunderlands were joined by Handley Page Hastings C Mk 1s, which had just come into service and which would eventually replace the Yorks in the airlift. The problem was that the York had not been designed with intensive operations in mind, and it was not long before serious problems arose in keeping the aircraft serviceable.

During the next month the airfield at Tegel, in the French Sector, became operational, and then, as winter approached, the Sunderlands were obliged to stop their flights because of ice on their Berlin base, the Havelsee. In order to smooth the pattern of traffic during the winter months, when weather could clearly become a serious limitation, the RAF and the USAF together now formed what was called a Combined Airlift Task Force so as to co-ordinate more fully their operations. The controllers in the Task Force operated what became a well-established pattern of flights. There were three air corridors connecting Berlin with the Western Zones.

Below: York transports at Gatow during the Berlin Airlift, September 1948. (AHB)

The USAF flights were making use of the southern corridor into the city, while the RAF used the northern one. Both air forces used the centre corridor for the return flights, and although there were many problems caused by the differing performances of the several aircraft types engaged, the system was effective.

In September and October, only three months after the air bridge had been established, the daily totals of freight lifted into the city had reached the figure of 4,600 tons and it was an effort that continued with little abatement throughout the winter, though bad weather caused a drop to an average delivery of 3,800 tons during November. Thereafter the figure rose again, culminating in an average daily lift of almost 8,000 tons during April. That winter was one in which West Berlin had to depend on the airlift for, among all the other supplies, coal for heating and lighting, and indeed coal proved to be the main element of the freight delivered in the course of the whole operation. The Soviet authorities did not lift their blockade until 12 May 1949, by which time 1,586,530 tons of coal had been flown in as well as 739,279 tons of other supplies. By the end of the airlift 40 Yorks, 40 Dakotas and fourteen Hastings had been engaged in the operation. The RAF had flown over 18 million miles, carrying over 300,000 tons of freight and almost 70,000 passengers in or out of the city.

THE COMMUNIST THREAT

Even before the blockade of Berlin, the deteriorating international situation had led to proposals for a Western defensive alliance, and in March the Brussels Treaty was signed under which France, the Benelux countries and the United Kingdom pledged mutual military assistance in the event of aggression in Europe. This was followed by the North Atlantic Treaty in April 1949, and in that year the British annual Defence White Paper spoke of 'an increased rate of re-equipment of Fighter squadrons, a gradual replacement of transport and training types, *and the reconditioning of stocks of wartime aircraft*' [author's italics]. It was another indication of the ground that had been lost in British military aviation, but these modest proposals were soon to be pushed aside.

In the autumn, with the blockade of Berlin under way and with the growing realization that the Soviet Union was making remarkable progress in many significant fields of military technology, the Air Staff drafted Operational Requirements for several types of guided weapons and other advanced systems. A further stimulus was applied to a gradually accelerating process of rearmament when, in September 1949, the United States announced that the Soviet Union had in the previous few weeks exploded an atomic weapon. The growing concern that resulted was reflected in the White Paper of March 1950, which, among other measures, referred to some squadrons of Boeing B-29 bombers, known to the RAF as Washingtons, being provided under the US Mutual Defence Assistance Act and announced that a doubling of the strength of Fighter Command 'will be completed'.

Then on 25 June that year, North Korea invaded the South, and although this was a distant and relatively small-scale conflict in its early stages, the invasion was widely thought to be merely a first step by the Communist powers towards a wider bid for domination across the world. The result was a sudden and massive rearmament programme in the Western world, a drive towards adequacy that quickly came to affect Britain and the Royal Air Force. During the following months, certain reservists were called up, others were given training courses to fit them for emergency service, a fourfold increase was announced in the number of combat aircraft to be produced and the annual intake of trainee pilots was increased tenfold. The number of day fighters had meanwhile already been doubled, but now the night fighter force was to be greatly strengthened, a run-down of Transport Command had been halted and an offer by Canada to train RAF pilots and navigators was announced. The impact of this rearmament programme on Bomber Command will be dealt with in Chapter 10, but its influence on the RAF as a whole at home and on what had started out as the British Air Forces of Occupation in Germany was, of course, equally profound. But first, just what was the extent of the military threat against which rearmament was to buttress the West?

At the end of the Second World War the Soviet Union had transported back to that country large numbers of German aeronautical experts as well as many specimens of advanced aircraft on which the German industry had been working. This was to be the foundation for some remarkable progress in Soviet aviation in the years that followed, made easier as far as bombers were concerned by the Soviet retention of three American B-29 Superfortresses that had made forced landings in the Soviet Union after raiding Japan in November 1944. The Soviets had thus acquired one of the most advanced bombers of the day, together with its powerful engines, modern avionics and ancillary systems, and the result was a production run of a modified Soviet version, the Tu-4, of something like 1,500 aircraft before the line ended in 1954.

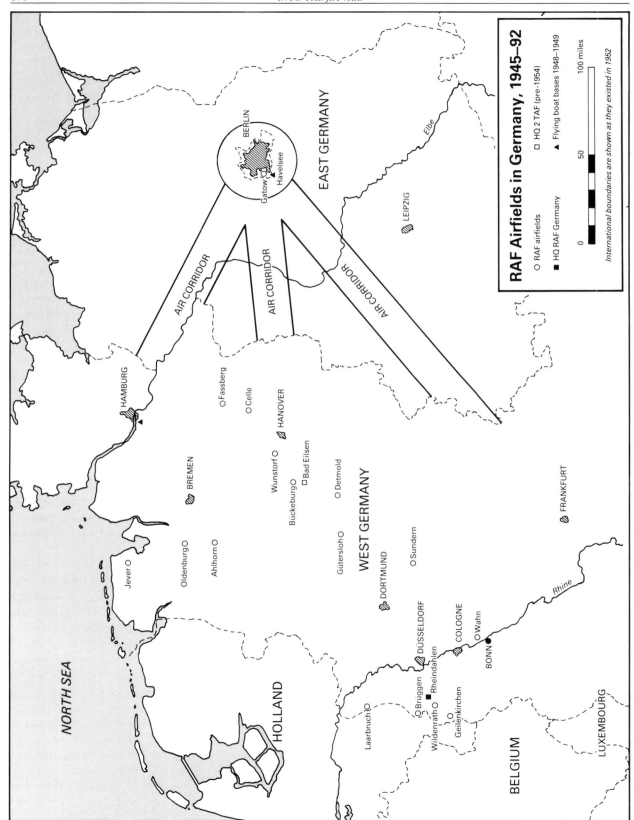

RAF Airfields in Germany, 1945–92

○ RAF airfields   □ HQ 2 TAF (pre-1954)
■ HQ RAF Germany   ▲ Flying boat bases 1948–1949

0   50   100 miles

International boundaries are shown as they existed in 1952

NORTH SEA

HOLLAND

BELGIUM

LUXEMBOURG

WEST GERMANY

EAST GERMANY

BERLIN

Gatow ○ Havelsee

LEIPZIG

AIR CORRIDOR

AIR CORRIDOR

AIR CORRIDOR

Elbe

HAMBURG ▲

Fassberg ○

Celle ○

HANOVER

Wunstorf ○   □ Bad Eilsen

Detmold ○

Bückeburg ○

Bremen

Jever ○

Oldenburg ○   Ahlhorn ○

Gütersloh ○

Sundern ○

DORTMUND

DUSSELDORF

COLOGNE   Wahn ○

Rheindahlen ■

Brüggen ○

Wildenrath ○   Geilenkirchen ○

Laarbruch ○

BONN ●

Rhine

FRANKFURT

The aviation expertise available to the Soviet Union was given a further boost in 1947 when a Labour Government in Britain allowed the export to the Soviet Union of 25 Rolls-Royce Nene 2 engines and thirty Derwent 5s. Copies were soon produced by Soviet industry, and one local version, the RD-45, powered the prototype MiG-15 fighter during its tests in 1948. All told, between 15,000 and 16,000 MiG-15s then flowed off the production lines between 1948 and 1956. This aircraft type was first encountered in combat by the West over Korea during November 1950, when opposing F-51 Mustangs of the USAF were at once found to be outclassed. Although it was generally vulnerable to the F-86 Sabre, the MiG had a better rate of climb, a higher operational ceiling and a better rate of turn at altitude. With this impressive post-war start to Soviet fighter strength, other and improved aircraft soon followed — the MiG-17 in 1951 and the MiG-19, a supersonic aircraft, entering service from 1955 onwards.

The Tu-4 bomber was followed in 1955 by the Tu-20, an aircraft with the range to reach key targets in the United States from bases in the Soviet Union and return. Although the aircraft had a top speed of only around 500mph, which would have made it highly vulnerable to US defences, the fact that the Soviets had exploded an atomic bomb in 1949 and then a thermonuclear weapon in 1953 gave a new impetus to Western air defence preparations. As it turned out, the Soviets never put the kind of emphasis on long-range strategic bombers that was so prominent a feature both of USAF thinking and of doctrine in the Royal Air Force. The result was that while the Royal Air Force was building up its force of V-bombers the Soviet Union was coming to put more faith in strategic missiles. One significant pointer to Soviet thinking in this field of policy was the creation, as a separate arm, of the Soviet Rocket Forces in May 1960.

The Soviet Union's emphasis on missiles was not, however, allowed to weaken the case for manned aircraft in her forces, particularly in the growing military confrontation in Europe. In a much-quoted book *Military Strategy* by Sokolovsky, published in 1962, it was made clear that although nuclear weapons were of prime importance, a nuclear war would also require conventional forces; in any case, as the author pointed out, not all wars would necessarily be nuclear. In retrospect, we can see that aircraft such as the Yak-25 two-seat interceptor, the MiG-21 'Fishbed' and the Su-7 'Fitter', which all came into service during the late 1950s, were a second generation of Soviet machines. Ten years later, a third generation of aircraft was deployed, and a much increased emphasis was placed on tactical aviation,

known to the Soviets as Frontal Aviation. Indeed, not only did expenditure on the Soviet Air Force as a whole rise more than that on the other Services between 1967 and 1977, but Frontal Aviation increased its inventory of aircraft by over 50 per cent in that same period. Among the aircraft of this third generation were the MiG-23/27 'Flogger' family, the MiG-25 'Foxbat' and the Tu-26 'Backfire' swing-wing bomber.

During the 1980s a fourth generation of aircraft made its appearance in the shape of, for example, the variable-geometry Su-24 'Fencer', an aircraft not unlike the American F-111 bomber; the Su-27 'Flanker', an aircraft with some similarities to the US F-15 Eagle fighter; the MiG-29 'Fulcrum', a machine about the size of the US F/A-18 Hornet and not unlike it in general layout; and, finally, the Su-25 'Frogfoot' ground attack aircraft. In addition to these increasingly advanced conventional combat aircraft, the Soviet Union from about 1967 onwards put a great deal of emphasis on military helicopters, some of which were intended as assault aircraft carrying infantry into tactical situations while others, notably the Mi-24 'Hind', were developed as tank-killers. There is no space here to give more than that sketch of an increasingly powerful Soviet Air Force as it developed over the years, but it is perhaps enough to indicate the imperative that there was in the West and therefore in the Royal Air Force to maintain a front line equipped with advanced aircraft.

One threat resulting from so effective a Soviet force was that posed by the intensive concentration of Soviet Frontal Aviation, along with the other air forces of the Warsaw Pact, in Eastern Europe. A second threat was that represented by Soviet bomber aircraft, many of which had the range to reach targets in the British Isles either on a direct route over the North Sea or from bases in the far north of the Soviet Union and down through the Norwegian Sea. To deal with Central Europe first, numbers of aircraft as well as types were of course an essential feature of the armed confrontation. Yet, in looking at numbers, it has to be remembered that combat aircraft were only one element in the overall balance of air power. The other elements included the presence of very large numbers of anti-aircraft guns and surface-to-air missiles, the efficiency of the opposing command and control systems and, not least, the asymmetric roles of the opposing air forces. Warsaw Pact air forces planned to neutralise NATO's theatre nuclear weapons, to give direct support to their ground forces and to prepare the way for a massive advance through Germany. The air forces of NATO on the other hand were designed to offset the numerical imbalance of Soviet forces on the ground by concentrating decisive firepower against the main enemy thrusts. Finally, in looking at the balance of forces in the Central Region, it must be remembered that the Royal Air Force squadrons represented only one of seven national air force contributions, and by no means the largest one. To deal here with the numbers of Soviet and other Warsaw Pact aircraft in that balance of forces would therefore be less than helpful in a history that must confine itself to the Royal Air Force, but perhaps it will be enough to say that the Warsaw Pact air forces were always very substantial in numbers, and that (for example) in November 1988 the overall numbers of combat aircraft ranged against each other between the Atlantic and the Urals in this confrontation was 8,250 in the Warsaw Pact and 3,977 aircraft on the inventory of the NATO Alliance.

This RAF commitment on the continent of Europe had its beginnings in 1945, and at the end of that year there were 36 operational squadrons based in Germany in the British Air Forces of Occupation, as the wartime Second Tactical Air Force had been renamed. It was a force made up of four Groups: No 2 Group held light bombers, mainly Mosquitos; Nos 83 and 84 Groups were fighter and fighter-reconnaissance Groups holding mainly the new Vampire Mk Is and Tempest Mk IIs, the latter specializing in the ground attack role; and No 85 Group was concerned mainly with technical and other support. During 1946 Nos 83 and 85 Groups were disbanded and in 1947 the other two Groups followed, leaving a Command headquarters directly controlling a

force that had by then been reduced to ten squadrons.

The RAF squadrons in Germany had settled into old Luftwaffe airfields as they were repaired after the war, and over a period of two years BAFO occupied Bückeburg, Fassberg, Jever, Celle, Gütersloh, Wunstorf Ahlhorn and Detmold, from where they could maintain a watch on the long frontier with the increasingly intransigent Soviets with their substantial forces based in the Eastern Zone. This deployment had to change during the Berlin Airlift in order to make room for the massive air transport operation that was using the bases of Wunstorf and Fassberg, so that for most of the Airlift period there were five squadrons at Gütersloh and four at

Above: The developing Cold War meant conscription for many thousands of young men. These somewhat stunned looking recruits are being kitted out. (AHB)

Left: Meteor night-fighters of No 256 Squadron, Ahlhorn, Germany, May 1953. (AHB)

Wahn. The following year saw the start of a modest expansion of the force as the international situation grew more grave, until at the beginning of 1952 the Command held sixteen squadrons on five bases, thirteen of them equipped with Vampires and the other three with Meteors, the Mosquitos having been phased out in the meantime. At the same time the Command arrangements were adjusted to manage the increased force, and No 2 Group was re-formed.

Once the NATO command structure was set up, taking effect on 1 April 1951 with headquarters in Paris, all sixteen squadrons were 'assigned' to the Supreme Allied Commander Europe (SACEUR), a post filled by General Dwight D. Eisenhower. 'Assignment' is a NATO term indicating that the forces concerned 'chop' (as the expression is) automatically from national to NATO control at a specified stage of alert. At this same time, the outdated title BAFO was dropped in favour of the earlier one that now accurately reflected the role of the Command, and the RAF units in Germany became the Second Tactical Air Force.

Soviet hostility did not end with the raising of the Berlin blockade, and as has already been mentioned the outbreak of the war in Korea led to alarm in the Alliance lest Communist forces attempt a similar aggression in Europe. This possibility led to a re-examination of the forward deployment that had been adopted by the British forces in northern Germany, and it was decided to move the RAF squadrons to new airfields that would now be constructed west of the Rhine. In 1951 SACEUR produced what was known as his Medium Term Plan, detailing the forces that he considered essential if he were to carry out his defensive tasks. For the Royal Air Force this led to plans for a rapid expansion of 2TAF from the existing sixteen squadrons to 31 by the end of 1952, 50 squadrons by 1953 and a final total of 56 by the following year. Within this much enlarged force the balance of roles was to shift so that there would be only sixteen fighter/ground attack units but 39 squadrons of light bombers which, in the event of hostilities, would carry the air war into enemy territory using both conventional weapons and the tactical nuclear weapons that would shortly become available.

THE CANBERRA

Like many other plans over the years, this one was never completed. When the Canberras joined Bomber Command in 1952 the type proved to be so versatile that it was decided to retain most of the aircraft in the United Kingdom and, instead of assigning them to SACEUR, to 'earmark' them for assignment, a NATO term meaning that the units could be assigned in a crisis, but only at the discretion of the Government concerned. In the event, the Canberra turned out to be the longest-serving aircraft that ever entered the inventory of the Royal Air Force, and it will be as well at this point to give an outline of its service over the following decades.

Binbrook was the base for the first Canberra Wing, and five squadrons were operational there by autumn

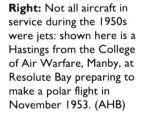

Right: Not all aircraft in service during the 1950s were jets: shown here is a Hastings from the College of Air Warfare, Manby, at Resolute Bay preparing to make a polar flight in November 1953. (AHB)

1952, Nos 9, 12, 50, 101, and 617. A second bomber Wing soon followed at Hemswell, and the build-up then continued with Nos 82 and 540 Squadrons forming at Wyton in the reconnaissance role with Canberra PR.3s. A bomber Wing of five squadrons at Coningsby came next, and then another of four squadrons at Scampton. Wittering became the home of one of the squadrons, Marham took another, Hemswell became the home for two, and two more went to Watton. The build-up of the force in the United Kingdom to its ceiling of 35 squadrons was completed in 1954, when the last five squadrons deployed to Marham, Wittering or Honington.

The Royal Air Force in Germany received its first Canberras in that same year, 1954, as part of the expansion of that Command. Because most of the Canberra strike force was to be retained in the United Kingdom, the first Canberra squadrons to move to Germany were some of the reconnaissance units. Thus No 69 Squadron formed with PR.3s at Laarbruch, followed into the Command by Nos 58 and 542

Squadrons with PR.7s. The build-up continued with a Wing of B.2s at Gütersloh and was completed in 1955 when Nos 31 and 80 Squadrons deployed to Laarbruch with PR.3s and PR.7s respectively.

In the mid-1950s it became clear that the developing threat to high-flying aircraft that would before long be posed by the emerging Soviet surface-to-air missiles would call for a dedicated penetration capability at very low level, and an interdiction version of the Canberra, the B(I) Mk 8, was the result. This aircraft could carry conventional bombs and rockets, as well as a gun pack of four 20mm Hispano cannon in the bomb bay. Though this was not publicized at the time, the B(I).8 was also fitted to carry American theatre nuclear weapons. To accommodate the new aircraft in the Command, the three Canberra B.2 squadrons in Germany disbanded, to be replaced by No 213 Squadron at Ahlhorn with the B(I).6, an interim version of the Mk 8, and No 88 Squadron (later renumbered No 14 Squadron) at Wildenrath with B(I).8s. This latter unit would remain at that base for the next fourteen years, and it would be joined there by No 17 Squadron which had meanwhile formed at Wahn with Canberra PR.3s.

In 1957, with the arrival of the V-Bombers in Royal Air Force squadrons, the whole Canberra Force began to be run down. In that year ten squadrons disbanded, seven of them to re-form later as V-bomber units. At the same time four B.2 squadrons formed in the Middle East, joining No 13 Squadron which had been flying PR.7s from Akrotiri, Cyprus, in Middle East Command since May the previous year. Finally, No 45 Squadron, which had been flying Venoms in the Far East, re-equipped with Canberra B.2s at the end of 1957. Further disbandments took place in the Canberra Force as more V-bomber squadrons formed so that by the end of 1959 there were only 21 squadrons operating Canberras and by the end of 1961 only 18, seven in Germany, six in the

---

English Electric Canberra PR.9

The Canberra was the first jet bomber to enter RAF service, but apart from that original role several other versions of the aircraft were later produced, including one to replace the Mosquito PR.34s and 35s, which had remained in service for six years after the war. The PR.3 variant of the Canberra appeared in 1953 and the PR.7 two years later. In 1960 a much improved variant, the PR.9 high-level reconnaissance variant, joined the front line with No 58 Squadron. This aircraft is still in service. It has an increased wing span, and a thinner wing, compared with earlier marks of Canberra; it also has half as much power again from its Avon RA 24 engines as was delivered by the Mk 109 Avons of the PR.7.

Middle East and two in the Far East. The last three Canberra squadrons in the United Kingdom stood down at the end of 1961, No 35 being the last to operate the bomber version from a home base.

It was expected at this time that the Canberra would be phased out altogether, but in April 1965 an incoming Labour Government cancelled the intended replacement for the aircraft, the TSR.2. This set-back was then followed by the collapse of the Anglo-French Variable-Geometry bomber project and later by the cancellation of an order for American F-111 aircraft. There was thus no choice but to retain the Canberra as the main tactical strike aircraft until the early 1970s when, despite RAF protests that they were entirely unsuitable for the role, ex-naval Buccaneers were brought into the front line. These aircraft were later joined by F-4 Phantoms, purchased from the United States and modified at very great expense to include the substitution of Rolls-Royce engines for the original American powerplants. Thus it was that even as late as the end of 1968 there were still twenty Canberra squadrons in the front line, fifteen of them overseas, and indeed there were more Canberras in service at that time than there were of any other single type. But now the force was again reduced. Nos 6, 32, 73 and 249 Squadrons disbanded in Cyprus during early 1969, followed by Nos 17, 80 and 213 in Germany that same year and by No 45 Squadron in Singapore in late 1970. By 1971 there were still nine Canberra units, five of them in the United Kingdom, in addition to Nos 13 and 39 in Malta and Nos 3 and 16 in Germany. No 7 Squadron had formed at St Mawgan with Canberra TT.18s in early 1970, and right up to the time of writing, 1992, there are still six small squadrons operating in the target facility, calibration or electronic warfare roles; these are Nos 51, 85, 98, 100 and 360 Squadrons, this last a joint Royal Navy/Royal Air Force unit. One operational squadron remains, No 39 which carries out photographic and survey tasks.

Although it had seen action only at Suez and in the Far East, and despite its limitations, the Canberra had been a very successful aircraft in all its roles, from high-level conventional bombing to interdiction at very low levels, in photographic reconnaissance both at high and at low level, and in the role of nuclear deterrence. Not only that, but it had not been an overly expensive aircraft: the total cost of research, development and production for all the 823 Canberras built for the Royal Air Force is estimated to have been £134 million, or very roughly £1.4 billion at 1992 prices.

CHANGES IN THE 1950s

To return to the expansion of 2TAF in 1952 under SACEUR's Medium Term Plan, by the end of 1952, although the Command held no light bombers, it could boast 25 squadrons of Meteors, Vampires and Venoms. The Venom began to replace the Vampire in August 1952 when the first of them arrived on No 11 Squadron. It was a lively and popular aircraft, and although, like the Meteor, it was still outclassed by the MiG-15, it was at least some improvement over the Vampire. By now it was clear that the force in Germany was large enough to justify the re-creation of No 83 Group, which duly formed and moved into RAF Wahn. To house the extra units the airfields at Jever and Oldenburg were brought under command, and a new base was built at Wildenrath, the first of what became known as the 'Clutch' stations west of the Rhine and in the heavily wooded area up against the Dutch border. At the same time, to help rectify the glaring inadequacy both of the Vampire and the Meteor when compared to the contemporary Soviet MiG-15, some 430 North American F-86 Sabre aircraft, provided under the Mutual Defence Assistance

Programme and built under licence in Canada, were acquired from the United States to equip RAF fighter squadrons in Fighter Command and in Germany. The Sabre had a top speed of around 700mph, or Mach 0.95 in level flight and was supersonic in a shallow dive — a performance that enabled it to hold its own, and more, against the MiG-15 in Korea. These aircraft began to arrive at Wildenrath in March 1953, where they joined Nos 3, 67 and 71 Squadrons. Within a few months, the Sabre was in the front line with ten of the Germany squadrons.

A whole combination of wider considerations had meanwhile entered the defence picture. A Conservative Government came into power in October 1951, inheriting a defence programme that would cost £4,700 (£70 billion at 1992 values) million over a three-year period. This was proving to be far more than the country could afford, and in any case it implied a programme greater than the capacity of British industry could absorb. Some retrenchment was essential. Only two months before that, the Soviet Union had exploded her first atomic device, a development that now called into question the whole concept of conventional force expansion. This then led in January 1952 to the acceptance by the Cabinet of the Global Strategy Paper produced by the Chiefs of Staff, which explicitly substituted strategic nuclear deterrence for expensive conventional forces. The plans for 2TAF were therefore changed once more, though, partly because their implementation took time and partly because there would otherwise have been a gap in capabilities until the V-Force began to join the front line, the Command continued its modest expansion from 1953 to 1955, reaching a peak strength of 35 squadrons by the end of that period.

In the April of that same year, 1955, the first Hawker Hunter F Mk 4s had arrived on No 98 Squadron in Germany to replace the Venoms, and by 1956 thirteen of the Germany squadrons would be similarly equipped in the day fighter/ground attack role. In the middle of the year, two squadrons of Supermarine Swift FR.5s began to arrive, the fighter reconnaissance version of an aircraft that had been ordered in November 1950 as an insurance against any possible failure in the Hawker Hunter programme. In the event, although the Swift remained in service in Germany until mid-1961, it was never a very satisfactory machine and its demise was unlamented.

By June 1956 all the Sabres in Germany had been replaced by Hunters, and a few months later, in a modest retrenchment, two of the 35 squadrons in the Command

were withdrawn. In 1954 it became possible to move more of the operational units of the Command to sites behind the Rhine when the airfields of Brüggen, Geilenkirchen and Laarbruch were completed. At the same time the HQ staffs of RAF Germany and the British Army of the Rhine moved into the new Joint Headquarters at Rheindahlen, joined later by the NATO HQs of the Second Allied Tactical Air Force and Northern Army Group. The RAF Hospital facilities at nearby Wegberg, together with all the support facilities and married quarters for all the 'Clutch' complexes, were soon completed, having been designed and supervised by sappers of the British Army, while the revenue for this huge programme was found from Occupation Costs and paid for by German funds in advance of the ratification of the Bonn Convention.

A more sweeping change then hit the Command in 1957, when the Defence White Paper of that year, to be described in more detail later, introduced a policy of replacing conventional forces with nuclear weapons. In a move that was immensely unpopular with the Royal Air Force, and perhaps particularly with those elements of the Service stationed in Germany, sixteen of the 33 squadrons were withdrawn, most of them to be almost immediately disbanded and the aircraft scrapped. No 83 Group was disbanded in June 1958 and No 2 Group followed five months later. With the exception of Gütersloh, the forward airfields were given up and the remaining squadrons concentrated on that airfield and on the four 'Clutch' bases. This represented a complete change in the fortunes of the Command, and it will be a convenient point at which to turn to developments that had meanwhile been taking place in the other principal areas of concern to the Royal Air Force in the European theatre — the Air Defence of the United Kingdom and Coastal Command.

Fighter Command had ended the war with a mixture of late-mark Spitfires such as the 21, powered by a Griffon 61 or 85 engine, early Meteor jets and Mosquitos. At the end of the decade the Spitfires at home were all withdrawn, leaving the fighter role to later marks of Meteor, Vampire and, for night work until the Javelin arrived in service, two-seat versions of the Meteor, the NF.11 and the NF.14. Another stop-gap aircraft of this period, as has been mentioned, was the Venom NF.2 and NF.3, which joined the front line during 1953 and went on to equip seven night-fighter squadrons until Javelins came along in several marks between late 1956 and November 1959. The Javelin in turn then remained in Fighter Command until October 1964, when No 23 Squadron, the last unit in the United

Above: By 1958 all RAF day fighter squadrons in Europe were equipped with Hunter Mk 6s. At the 1958 Farnborough Air Show, No 111 Squadron created a sensation by flying a formation loop with twenty-two of them. The formation is shown here at rehearsal, the mixed colour schemes caused by the squadron's strength being increased from the usual sixteen aircraft to twenty-two by means of 'loans' from No 56 Squadron. (AHB)

Kingdom to fly them, converted to Lightnings.

In the day fighter role, Meteor Mk 8s became the standard aircraft: starting in July 1950, over 1,000 of them being delivered to replace the Meteor Mk 4s and the Vampires in home-based units. Nineteen regular squadrons would eventually fly this version, and it also equipped ten squadrons of the Royal Auxiliary Air Force. An interesting indication of the importance of the Meteor F.8 at this stage in the fortunes of Fighter Command was given at the Coronation Review in July 1953, when no fewer than 216 of them flew in a mass formation past HM The Queen, who took the salute at RAF Odiham.

From 1955 onwards large numbers of Hawker Hunters began to reach the squadrons, and over 1,000 were eventually delivered, seeing service in five variants between that year and 1959. Eighteen squadrons of Fighter Command were equipped with Hunters at various times during the late 1950s, most of them flying the Mk 6. It was a popular and an impressive aircraft, being capable of 715mph at sea level and Mach 0.95 at 36,000ft in its later marks and of achieving a service ceiling of 51,500ft. Its armament was made up of four 30mm Aden cannons mounted in a removable pack under the forward fuselage so as to give a rapid turn-

round, and it could carry two 1,000lb bombs on wing stations, or 2in or 3in rockets for ground attack work, or drop tanks. The powerful controls and the 10,000lb thrust Avon 203 engine of the F.6 made it an ideal aircraft for aerobatics, and the formation displays by No 111 Squadron ('The Black Arrows') and then by No 92 Squadron ('The Blue Diamonds') made these teams the most impressive in the world. A peak of performance was perhaps reached at the 1958 Farnborough Air Show, when No 111 Squadron flew a 22-aircraft formation loop.

Fighter Command reached its highest post-war strength at around the end of 1956, when it was made up of about 600 front-line aircraft in 35 squadrons. Sixteen of the latter were equipped with the Hunter, two still had Meteor 8s, there were eight Venom and eight Meteor night-fighter squadrons and the first Javelin squadron had just received its first aircraft. But, as we have seen when discussing 2 TAF, fundamental changes in British defence policy were on the way. In April 1957 the White Paper *Defence – Outline of Future Policy* was issued under Defence Minister Duncan Sandys. At the heart of this ten-page document lay three decisions crucial to the future of the Royal Air Force. First, the importance of a national nuclear deterrent provided by the V-Force was stressed. Second, it was announced that the V-bombers would be supplemented by ballistic rockets. And third, the White Paper said this: 'The defence of the bomber airfields is an essential part of the deterrent and it is a feasible task. A manned fighter force, smaller than at present but adequate for this limited purpose, will be maintained and will progressively be equipped with air-to-air guided missiles. Fighter aircraft will in due course be replaced by a ground-to-air guided missile system.' This was a reference to what was intended to be a family of surface-to-air missiles, the first of which, the Bloodhound, entered service in June the following year. It was an important change of direction for the Service, and although the new policy proved not in the event to be very long-lived, its effects remained with the Royal Air Force for more than two decades.

Bloodhound was designed to engage targets flying at between 10,000 and 60,000ft and at ranges up to 20 miles. Its main propulsive power came from two Thor ramjets, but it also had four short-burning rocket motors which accelerated the missile up to its cruising speed of Mach 2.0. During the three years 1958 to 1961, a surprising total of 352 of these weapons was deployed, forming four Wings: No 2 Wing at Lindholme covering the more northerly V-bomber bases; No 148 at North Coates giving protection to the V-bomber airfields of Coningsby, Scampton and Waddington; No 151 Wing at

North Luffenham defending the more southerly V-bomber bases; and No 24 Wing at Watton covering the bases in East Anglia. The missiles of each Wing were controlled by a Tactical Control Centre.

In operation, the air defence Control and Reporting system would detect and identify an incoming target, and the appropriate Master Radar station would decide whether to scramble fighters or rely upon a Bloodhound engagement. In this latter case, the position, height, heading and speed of the target would be passed to the appropriate TCC by the Master Radar Station and the controller there would allocate the target to one of his launching sites. Once fired, the missile homed on to the radar reflection at the target produced by a target illuminating radar at the same site, and when within lethal range the high explosive warhead was detonated by a proximity fuse.

But after only three years in service, most of the Bloodhound units fell victim to another round of defence cuts, a demolition accelerated by difficulties with the TCCs, which proved to be susceptible to electronic jamming. An improved and air-transportable version of the Bloodhound, the Mk 2, then entered service with No 25(SAM) Squadron in 1964, with the main role of overseas reinforcement. After six years, however, the unit redeployed to the 'Clutch' airfields in Germany, its place in the United Kingdom being taken by a re-formed No 85(SAM) Squadron at West Raynham.

This less than successful transfer of air defence responsibility from fighters to missiles still lay in the future as the massive cuts in aircraft strength flowing from the 1957 White Paper began. In 1958, Fighter Command was reduced from its 1956 strength of around 600 aircraft in 35 squadrons, first to 320 aircraft, then to 272 in 1960 and then down to only 140 fighters in eleven squadrons by 1962. Not only that, but in 1957 all the fighter squadrons of the Royal Auxiliary Air Force were disbanded, a further serious loss of strength and ability to deal with the unexpected.

COASTAL COMMAND RESTRUCTURED

One other important change in the Royal Air Force at home during these first twelve years or so after the war was the restructuring of Coastal Command. In common with the rest of the Service, the Command had run down rapidly after 1945, so that already by October 1946 there were only two Groups, No 18 at Pitreavie Castle near Edinburgh and No 19 at Plymouth, controlling between them eight squadrons and all of them on a cadre basis. Two of the squadrons held a maximum of five Sunderland flying boats each, there were two medium range strike squadrons, one with up to eight Mosquito FB Mk VIs and another with a maximum of eight Beaufighter TF Mk Xs, and four squadrons, each with up to six aircraft, of Lancaster GR.IIIs, a variant brought into service during 1946 for general maritime reconnaissance. The Command also controlled a mixed bag of Spitfires, Mosquitos and Lancasters in two photographic reconnaissance squadrons, and one squadron of Handley Page Halifax Mk VIs for meteorological work. This last role was particularly important in forecasting weather not only over the British Isles but also over the North Atlantic air routes, in an era when commercial aircraft did not have the performance to fly above the weather.

The return to the United States of the Very Long Range Liberators and Catalinas at the end of the war that had left the surveillance and anti-submarine roles in the hands of the Lancasters and Sunderlands with their much shorter ranges, though the Lancaster had an operating radius of 950 miles when carrying a full warload and the Sunderland could by now manage 625 miles. Both types carried ASV radar, a load of 250lb depth charges, and sonobuoys. At first these last were the relatively simple wartime non-directional versions, but in 1950 an uprated variant was brought into service capable of giving a bearing on the propeller cavitation noise made by submarines.

By 1950 it was clear that Soviet rearmament plans included a Navy of greatly increased size with a very substantial force of submarines, and it was recognized that there was as much urgency about the need to re-equip Coastal Command as there was about the rest of the front line. A specification, R5/46, had been issued in 1946 for a long-range maritime aircraft and the result was the Shackleton. This aircraft was based on the Lincoln Mk III, a projected maritime version of the Lancaster's replacement, and it retained many of the features of the Lincoln. The fuselage was slightly shorter and the 2,450hp' Rolls-Royce Griffon 57a replaced the 1,680hp Merlin of the Lincoln, but the wings of the Lincoln were retained. With a warload of 4,000lb, the Shackleton produced an operating radius of 1,500 miles, a very useful improvement over that of the Lancaster.

The difficulty with the Shackleton in 1950 was that it could not be delivered in numbers for at least eighteen months. An interim aircraft was therefore sought, and the result was the introduction of the US P2V-5

Neptune, of which 52 were procured, again under the Mutual Defence Assistance Programme, to equip four squadrons. It was an aircraft with a 1,275-mile radius of action, but this somewhat modest performance was offset by other attributes, including an APS-20 search radar, an APS-31 attack radar and a powerful wing-mounted searchlight. By mid-1954 the front line of the Command had expanded to nine Shackleton squadrons, two of Sunderlands and the four of Neptunes as well as the meteorological unit, by now flying Hastings. The total strength was 119 aircraft, including one of the Shackleton units based in Gibraltar. This welcome increase in strength was not all: it was at this time that the operational effectiveness of the Command received a boost in the shape of the Mk 30 homing torpedo to complement the advantages of the directional sonobuoys.

In February 1955, a new dimension was brought to a long-standing role of the Command when the first search and rescue helicopters, Whirlwind HAR.2s, arrived at RAF Thorney Island to equip No 22 Squadron. A little later the Squadron would deploy detachments at various points around the British Isles, giving another boost to the Royal Air Force organization for Search and Rescue. In the years that followed, this modest beginning would grow to a helicopter coverage that extended well beyond maritime activities, to include mountain rescue, carrying emergency civilian medical cases, transporting urgently needed drugs and vaccines to hospitals, and a host of other and varied tasks.

Coastal Command was not as badly hit as the rest of the Service in the cuts of 1957, mainly because it was clear that NATO faced a serious and growing maritime threat, but nevertheless four of the Neptune squadrons were disbanded between August 1957 and the following March as the full force of Shackletons joined the front line, and the last two squadrons of Sunderlands were withdrawn. With these measures, by the end of the 1957 run-down of the Service, Coastal Command had been reduced to ten squadrons.

Right: A Neptune from Kinloss practising asymmetric flight (that is, using only one of its two engines) in May 1953. (AHB)

CHAPTER 10
Nuclear Deterrence

For twelve years, from mid-1957 until mid-1969, a force of British-built bombers armed with nuclear weapons not only formed the core of the Royal Air Force but also represented the foundation on which national defence as a whole rested. There is no room here to relate the events leading to the development of British atomic weapons, which were of course central to the whole concept of this force, save to say that at the close of the Second World War it was seen to be a decision appropriate to Britain's status at that time. There was little hesitation in either of the main political parties in the United Kingdom about the development of a national programme, and since British scientists had played an important part in the American programme Britain had access to the technologies involved.

Two American atomic weapons had of course been dropped by B-29 strategic bombers over Japan, and in the immediate post-war years aircraft remained the obvious weapon platform for atomic bombs. Ballistic missiles were in their infancy, and although the wartime German V2 rocket had pointed the way ahead, this had been a relatively primitive system. Its range was only 290km, its accuracy could wander as much as one mile in

thirty and its warload was only 990kg. An atomic bomb of this era on the other hand weighed over 10,000lb, and if, as was quietly assumed by the air staff planners of the Royal Air Force, the most likely target for any future use of these weapons was the Soviet Union, then a range of something like 1,500km would be needed, even if the missiles were launched from bases in Allied-occupied Germany. Attention therefore focused on strategic bombers as the carrier for atomic bombs; and meanwhile, particularly in the United States, research was begun into what was then firmly expected to be the natural successor to the manned bombers — the cruise missile.

GENESIS OF THE V-FORCE

During the later years of the war it had been obvious to the Air Staff that bombers of the Halifax and Lancaster type were not going to meet the demands of the future. These aircraft had a cruising speed of only some 180–210kts and their normal operating height was around 20,000ft. The Lincoln was very little better than its forerunner the Lancaster, and clearly something much more advanced than this was called for. Of the possible

Right: Two aircraft of different generations, but each designed with the same concept in mind, that of evading rather than confronting enemy defences: a Mosquito and a Vulcan. (RAFM)

operational profiles for bombers armed with atomic weapons, low flying was not seriously considered. For one thing, it was difficult to see how the aircraft could escape the effects of its own weapon and, for another, the fuel consumption of a jet engine at low level is about twice what it is at very high altitude and the operational range of the aircraft is thus halved. The very high level option indicated by the experience of the Mosquito force during the war, however, was much more attractive. The Mosquito had proved to be remarkably successful at very-high-altitude penetration to distant targets with very little risk of loss or damage, and the planners were particularly impressed by the minimal losses suffered by Mosquitos over Germany. For example, from 18 November 1943 up to the end of January 1944 there were fourteen night bombing raids against Berlin with between 370 and 750 aircraft taking part each night. The heavy bombers suffered losses of 385 aircraft out of 7,275 operational sorties, a rate of 5.3 per cent, but the Mosquitos had lost only one aircraft out of the 122 missions flown, a rate of 0.8 per cent. During the whole Bomber Command offensive in Europe, Lancasters lost 2.28 per cent of all aircraft dispatched while Mosquitos showed a loss rate of only 0.65 per cent.

As to the more advanced air defences that might be encountered in the future, although rudimentary air-to-air missiles were under development by this time, it was thought that the use of very high and very fast bombers would make it virtually impossible for an interceptor to manoeuvre into a missile-firing position in the first place. Another possible threat to the high-level bomber, it was realized, might eventually be posed by surface-to-air missiles. In the late stages of the war the Germans had developed and test-fired weapons of this category such as the Wasserfall, but that had been a rather crude and unsatisfactory system and it was believed in the West that really effective high-level SAMs were a long way off. High level was thus the preferred way ahead, and if the bomber flew high enough and fast enough it would be able to evade or outrun any anti-aircraft defences that were likely to be encountered.

During 1946 this concept was translated into Operational Requirement 229, which sought to replace the Lincoln with a four-jet bomber capable of carrying the 10,000lb atomic bomb of the day at heights up to 45,000ft and with a speed of 500kts. This eventually became Specification B35/46, which called for the ability to carry a 10,000lb bomb over a range of 3,350 miles by day or night at a cruising altitude of 45,000ft, rising to above 50,000ft after 2½ hours (as fuel was burned and the all-up weight of the aircraft was reduced). The specification also spelled out the need for radio countermeasures, and it included provision for armament in the tail if that should prove necessary. The aircraft would carry a crew of two pilots, two navigator/bomb-aimers and a radio countermeasures operator.

In January 1947 the Ministry of Supply invited all six of the major British aircraft manufacturers at that time to submit tenders to this specification. The submission from English Electric resembled a modified Canberra, a proposal that was judged not to be sufficiently advanced; and that from Vickers was similarly disappointing. Shorts and Armstrong-Whitworth made submissions based on designs that resembled flying wings, a concept that was thought to err in the other direction by being too adventurous a leap into the unknowns of aerodynamics. This left two contenders, the Handley Page 80, and the Avro 698. The first was based on a crescent-wing design and the second relied on a delta-wing configuration.

Even these designs were quite unlike anything that had gone before, and they were clearly not without risk. The Advanced Bomber Group, a committee of experts that had been set up specifically to advise on the way ahead in this field, therefore recommended that the risk involved in what was bound to be a bold venture should be spread by adopting more than one design. Two main options were suggested: first, an aircraft with a conventional layout whose mainplanes would have an aspect ratio of 5 or 6 and a sweepback of 45 degrees (this was very close to the basic features of the HP 80); and second, an aircraft of tailless delta configuration with an aspect ratio of 3 (this was very close to the concept for the Avro 698). The group also recommended that, so as to spread the risks still further, an intermediate design between these two be produced.

Also concerned about the risk involved in these forward-looking proposals, the Air Staff in August 1947 issued Specification 14/46. This eventually resulted in the Shorts SA4, known as the Sperrin, an aircraft of conventional layout though with its four jet engines mounted in two vertical pairs on the mainplanes. The Sperrin performed well enough on its trials but meanwhile the firm of Vickers had drawn up a design, the Type 660, for an intermediate jet bomber to meet Air Ministry Specification B9/48, and it was this aircraft that later became the Valiant. On 18 May 1951 the Type 660 made its first flight, three months before that of the Sperrin; and when it proved to have a better performance than the Sperrin, the Shorts aircraft was cancelled after only two prototypes had been built.

Meanwhile, on 20 April 1951 (and thus even before

Vickers Valiant B(PR)K.1

Fourteen aircraft to this mark of the Valiant V-bomber were built for the RAF, not only to operate in that role but also as strategic reconnaissance machines or flight-refuelling tankers. An earlier model of the Valiant had been used in air-to-air refuelling trials during 1959, and this led the way for a whole generation of tankers, which have included the Handley Page Victor K.1 and K.2, the later VC10 conversions, the more recent TriStar K.1 and KC.1 versions of the Lockheed commercial airliner and finally the four Royal Air Force Hercules that have been modified for the same task.

the prototype had flown), the Ministry of Supply on behalf of the Royal Air Force ordered 25 of the Vickers Valiant aircraft, a machine that proved to be capable of Mach 0.86 with a maximum operating height of 46,000ft and a range of 3,000 miles when underwing fuel tanks were fitted. For an aircraft that represented an intermediate stage on the way to the future strategic bombers, this was a very satisfactory performance, and the production order was extended. The first Valiants came into service with No 232 Operational Conversion Unit at Gaydon, and shortly afterwards with No 138 Squadron on the same airfield, starting in early 1955. Valiant bombers would eventually be followed into service by three other versions of the basic type: the Valiant B(PR).1, a long-range strategic reconnaissance aircraft operated by No 543 Squadron, of which eleven were built; the B(PR)K.1 bomber/tanker/refueller, of which fourteen were constructed; and the BK.1

bomber/tanker, which had a production run of forty-five aircraft. The last Valiant was delivered in September 1957 after a total of 104 production aircraft had been built. Apart from the units at Gaydon, the Valiant went on to equip Nos 49 and 18 Squadrons at Wittering, Nos 148, 207 and 214 Squadrons at Marham and Nos 7, 90 and 199 Squadrons at Honington, as well as No 543(PR) Squadron at Wyton.

The replacement for the increasingly dated Lincoln was the English Electric Canberra but the capacity of its bomb bay restricted the internal warload to 10,000lb, which meant that it was never in the running to carry the atomic weapons of the early 1950s, and until the new V-bombers could be brought into service there was bound to be a gap in the front line of the Royal Air Force. Contemporary estimates suggested that this hiatus in vital capability might last as long as five years. This might not have been so serious but for a continuing deterioration in the international situation, including the grave concerns aroused by the Berlin blockade which began in June 1948. Continuing Soviet intransigence over the following eighteen months then led to a decision in January 1950 that the Royal Air Force would equip its bomber force with seventy B-29s from the United States, provided on loan as part of that country's Military Defence Assistance Programmes.

These aircraft were taken out of cocooned storage in the United States and modernized before being flown across the Atlantic to be issued to RAF squadrons, starting with No 149 at Marham in March 1950. They were given the name 'Washington' in July 1950 and the number eventually delivered reached 88, making it possible to equip another seven squadrons with

Left: The interim Washington bomber. (AHB)

reasonably capable aircraft — Nos 15, 35, 44, 57, 90, 115 and 207. Although the Washingtons were still piston-engine aircraft at a time when the trend was towards jets, their four 18-cylinder Wright Cyclone air-cooled radials delivered 2,231hp, giving the aircraft a top speed of 350mph and a cruising speed of 300mph. The service ceiling was more than 35,000ft and a bomb load of 6,000lb could be carried over a distance of 3,000 miles. A crew of ten was carried in some comfort in this all-pressurized aircraft, including gunners to operate the defensive armament at all five twin .50-calibre machine gun stations. During the early 1950s, as more Canberras left the production lines and arrived on squadrons, the Washingtons were gradually phased out, until by the end of 1954 most of them had been returned to the United States. A small number, however, remained with No 90 (Signals) Group until as late as 1959. Their service with the Royal Air Force had been very brief, but these aircraft had filled an important gap in the front line at a difficult time.

In mid-1950, the international climate changed from one of crisis to one of alarm when, on 25 June, the Korean War broke out. In Britain plans were at once announced for a £3,600 million defence programme (£58 billion at 1992 prices), to be spread over three years, and in January the next year this was revised upwards to £4,700 million (£70 billion) over three years. In the event these programmes were to prove incapable of fulfilment.

At the end of 1951, because of growing concern about the state the British economy still exhausted by the exertions of the Second World War, the whole question of future defence effort came under review. The Chiefs of Staff held two weeks of high-level discussions at Greenwich, the outcome of which was a formative document with the title *Global Strategic Paper*. It was a paper that bore the clear imprint of the then Chief of the Air Staff, Air Chief Marshal Sir John Slessor. Taken by the Cabinet in January 1952, this paper proposed the creation of a British bomber force able to complement that of the USAF by attacking targets that were vital to the Soviet Union yet which posed no direct threat to the United States. This was the start of the nuclear deterrent role of the Royal Air Force, which was to play so large a part in the size and shape of the Service over the following seventeen years, until the role was taken over by the Polaris submarine fleet. Once the *Global Strategy Paper* had been accepted by the Government, the 'super-priority' that had been give to the production of fighter aircraft early in 1952 was extended during that year to the Canberra, to the Valiant and then to the production

of the future bomber force, to be made up of the Avro 698 (christened the Vulcan in October 1952) and the HP 80 (given the name Victor in early 1953). The estimated cost of the proposed production run, amounting to 220 of these new V-bombers, was £275 million (£3.62 billion at 1992 values), an investment that was intended to make huge savings in the cost of the earlier rearmament programme with its emphasis on large conventional forces.

In the case of the Vulcan, what began as a pure delta design with wing-tip fins changed to a layout with a conventional nose and a single dorsal fin and rudder, while the original elevons became separate elevators and ailerons. A wing of constant aerofoil section had been intended, but wind-tunnel tests showed that the increase in drag caused by the compressibility effect would occur at a lower airspeed than had been thought. The chosen solution was to vary the aerofoil section inboard along the span, so that towards the wing root its maximum depth was close to the leading edge. This accounts for the massive thickness of the front section of the wing, a feature that not only provided a huge storage space but also made it possible to fit the larger engines which fortuitously soon became available. The Vulcan first flew on 30 August 1952, just two years after the first contract for an initial order of 25 production models had been awarded, and the first production aircraft was airborne on 4 February 1955.

One of the Air Staff requirements of the V-bombers was that they should have good manoeuvrability at altitude, and with the original Avon powerplants this requirement seemed to be satisfied. Early in 1955, however, high altitude trials began with the more powerful Olympus series engine. These engines delivered almost 50 per cent more thrust, but the trials with the new powerplants showed that at high angles of attack and high subsonic Mach numbers the airflow over the outer section of the wing separated, causing high-frequency buffeting. This was a characteristic that could easily lead to structural damage, and the cure adopted was to change the entire planform of the wing. Instead of the leading edge sweeping back at a constant angle of 52 degrees, the angle was decreased to 42 degrees between the mid-span point and 78 per cent of span, and the original angle resumed outboard of that point. This increased the chord of the outer mainplane, and thus its lift, making it possible for the pilot to apply a useful *g* loading at high speed and high altitude without unwelcome side effects.

This first model of the Vulcan, the Mk 1, entered service with No 230 OCU at Waddington in February

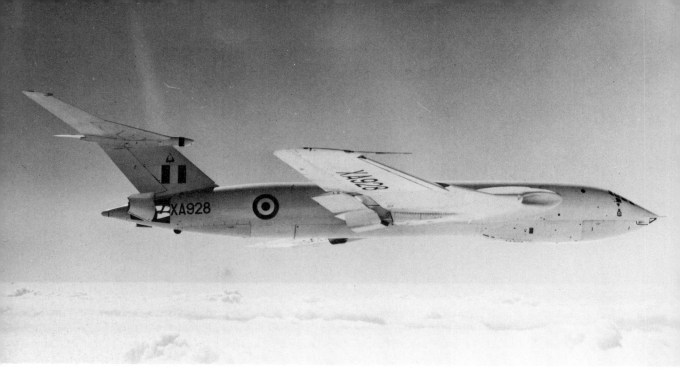

1957 and joined the front line with No 83 Squadron in July of that year, also at Waddington. It then went on to equip Nos 27, 44, 50, 101 and 617 Squadrons, the last of the forty-five Vulcan B.1s produced being delivered in April 1959.

During this same period the Victor bomber was also making good progress. Its layout was far removed from that of the Vulcan aircraft, being designed from the start with its characteristic crescent-shaped mainplane. In order to meet the demanding requirements of Air Staff Specification 35/46, which had included a range of over 3,350 miles and a speed of Mach 0.875 at 50,000ft, the design team opted for a wing of high aspect ratio and high angle of sweep. The difficulty here was that swept wings tend to stall first at the tips, so that the centre of pressure moves forward, giving the aircraft a nose-up pitch. These conditions are also likely to generate a strong twisting moment along the span of the mainplane, leading to severe stress and to structural problems. These potential disadvantages were countered by tapering the wing and by carrying the structure forward at its tips. The resulting profile ingeniously combined the advantages of a swept wing with those of an unswept wing, and, by varying the thickness of the aerofoil along the span, a constant critical Mach number along the whole wing was achieved. This avoided trim problems that would otherwise have been encountered with the onset of compressibility. The only remaining handling problem was that wings of high aspect ratios give much reduced lift at low airspeeds, for example in the landing

configuration. To cure this problem automatic leading edge flaps were fitted, and in order to counter the strong trim changes as these flaps ran out an all-moving tailplane was fitted, swept at an angle of 45 degrees. These somewhat technical factors accounted for the unusually untidy-looking appearance of the Victor as it came in to land.

A further characteristic of the Victor was the enormous capacity of its bomb bay. Because of the high angle of sweep, the torque box for the mainplane was well forward of the centre of gravity. This meant that a large space was available aft of the spars for the payload.

Avro Vulcan B.I

This was the first large bomber in the world to have a delta-wing layout, and although it bore no physical resemblance to the de Havilland Mosquito of the Second World War its operational concept was exactly the same, that is, to avoid and outrun enemy air defences rather than fight a way to the target. To achieve this, a specification was drawn up in 1946 calling for a design that would give a speed of Mach 0.875 at 50,000ft and a range of 3,350 miles and the Vulcan was one of three types produced to meet it; in fact, the later Mk 2 version of the aircraft exceeded this performance. It had a top speed of Mach 0.98 at 55,000ft and a service ceiling above 60,000ft. Like the Mosquito, no defensive armament was carried, but the Vulcan could take a maximum load of twenty-one 1,000lb bombs or a nuclear weapon. The Vulcan was in service from 1957 until 1982.

Thus, although the Victor was only about 5ft longer than the Vulcan, it had twice the bomb bay capacity and it could carry up to forty-eight 1,000lb bombs, though the load was normally limited to thirty-two of these weapons.

In June 1952, six months before the prototype first flew, Handley Page were given an order for 25 production models of the Victor and the first one flew on 1 February 1956. At the end of November 1957, the first aircraft into service arrived at No 232 Operational Conversion Unit at Gaydon, and as more Victors came off the production line they went on to equip Nos 10, 15, 55 and 57 Squadrons. All three types of V-bomber were now in service together. It is of some interest to note here that particular qualifications were required of the air crews in the V-Force. At this period, SNCO air crew members were not uncommon in the Royal Air Force, but none were accepted for the V-Force; furthermore, no one at all could actually apply to join the force — appointment was by selection only. The selection process itself was rigorous. First, pilots had to have at least 1,750 hours in command, with both jet and four-piston-engine experience behind them, and they had to be rated 'above the average' in flying ability. All navigators had to have completed at least one flying tour on Canberras, and no first-tour signallers were accepted. Clearly the intention was to create an élite force; but these requirements were carrying things too far, and gradually the various restrictions were reduced or altogether abandoned.

Among the technical improvements in prospect as the V-Force formed up were those offered by the more powerful engines that were becoming available. With the Vulcan B Mk 1 in production, attention turned to the possibilities offered by the Olympus 200 series powerplant, which could deliver 26 per cent more thrust than the original 100 series. This degree of extra power would give a higher operating ceiling for the Vulcan and it would make possible a greater payload. The new engine was incorporated into an aircraft with a redesigned wing, which included an increase of 12ft to the span as well as increased chord in the outer mainplane sections so as to reduce the thickness/chord ratio, while modifications to the control surfaces included a reversion to the earlier elevons. This aircraft was the Vulcan B Mk 2. A variety of other changes from the original design included an electronic warfare suite, a revamped tail, a strengthened undercarriage and enlarged air intakes. At the same time, and in common with the rest of the V-Force, all Vulcans were given a dazzling white anti-flash finish, a feature that led the humorists in the RAF to refer to the aircraft as the 'Great White Detergent'! After some delays the first of the new mark of Vulcan entered the front line with No 83 Squadron at Scampton, and then equipped Nos 27 and 617 Squadrons. During 1962 Mk 2s went on to join Nos 9, 12 and 35 Squadrons at Coningsby, completing the force. Twenty-nine of the Vulcan B.1s were at the same time withdrawn from squadrons to be modified up to Mk 1A standard, which involved fitting the electronic warfare suite but little else, and these machines, together with the other remaining B.1s, had, by August 1961, equipped

Nos 40, 50 and 101 Squadrons, all at Waddington.

A similar pattern of improvements was introduced for the Handley Page Victor. The B.2 version of this machine was given Rolls-Royce Conway Co.17 series powerplants delivering 17,250lb of thrust, a remarkable jump from the original Armstrong Siddeley Sapphires which produced only 11,000lb. To take advantage of these powerful new engines the wing span was increased by 10ft and, like the Vulcan B.2, the aircraft was now fitted with an electronic countermeasures suite. Two bomber squadrons were equipped with this version of the Victor, Nos 100 and 139, while No 543 Squadron took delivery of the B/SR.2 strategic reconnaissance variant. Deliveries of the 34 Victor Mk 2 models that were produced were completed in May 1963.

In all a total of 325 production-model V-bombers were built, some replacing others in service, so that at the maximum strength the Force was to reach, in June 1964, there were 159 aircraft operational: 50 of them were Valiants, 70 were Vulcans and 39 were Victors. This gave a margin above the strength of 144 aircraft that had been planned in August 1957, but it tends to exaggerate the size of the force in its steady state. A more accurate picture of the Force is given by the following list of deployments, derived from November 1962:

Station	Squadrons	Aircraft
Marham	49, 148, 207	Valiant
Waddington	44, 50, 101	Vulcan B.1
Cottesmore	10, 15	Victor B.1
Honington	55, 57	Victor B.1
Scampton	27, 83, 617	Vulcan B.2
Wittering	100, 139	Victor B.2
Coningsby	9, 12, 35	Vulcan B.2

BLUE STEEL

Some years before all this, and before the V-Force was even deployed, it had been recognized that Soviet air defences for key targets were being developed that would, perhaps by the 1960s, make necessary a more advanced form of delivery for nuclear weapons than that provided by the V-bombers with their free-fall weapons. One solution was set out in Specification R156T, which called for a very long range supersonic reconnaissance aircraft and bomber, capable of cruising at Mach 2.5 or better, able to fly at 60,000ft and possessing a range of at least 5,000 miles. Out of the four submissions for this aircraft, the Avro 730 was selected. If successful, this aircraft would have been the first Mach 2+ bomber in the world. The other solution was an intermediate range

ballistic missile, which became the Blue Streak programme.

In the event, neither system was developed. In the 1957 Defence White Paper the Avro 730 was cancelled, the intention being that the funds released would be diverted into the Blue Streak venture, reflecting the overall preference in that White Paper for missiles rather than for manned aircraft. But then only two years later, in 1959, it was assessed by intelligence that the Soviets had the capability to strike the intended Blue Streak sites in East Anglia with their own ballistic missiles. And since the liquid-fuel system of the Blue Streak required some 20 minutes' preparation time, and on top of that could not for long be held in a fuelled-up state, it was clear that this weapon could be taken out by a Soviet pre-emptive strike. This project, too, was therefore cancelled.

The only other systems that might now be available to deliver British nuclear weapons in the future were the American Skybolt air-to-ground missile and the Polaris submarine with its complement of ballistic missiles. It was therefore to these systems that attention now turned. Negotiations took place, and in March 1960 the United States agreed to sell Skybolt missiles to the United Kingdom, the arrangement being that these weapons would carry British nuclear warheads. In return the Americans were to be given facilities in Scotland for their nuclear submarines. Feasibility studies then showed that in fact Skybolt could not be fitted under the mainplanes of the Victor aircraft, but fortunately there was no such difficulty with the Vulcan and it was planned that 72 B.2s would be modified to carry two Skybolts each on attachment points outboard of the undercarriage. Some of these attachments were actually fitted — and, as it happened, they turned out to be very useful during the Falklands Campaign over twenty years later, when they carried first Martel air-to-surface and then Shrike anti-radiation missiles.

But all the plans for Skybolt came to nothing in November 1962, when, partly because there had been serious and recurring problems with the missile in tests and partly because the Minuteman ballistic missile was in any case more suitable for the Americans as a first-strike weapon, the project was cancelled. The eventual outcome of the diplomatic moves that now followed was that the American Government agreed to sell Polaris missiles to Britain to equip submarines that would eventually take over the British nuclear deterrent role. Meanwhile the responsibility still rested with the V-Force.

During the six years before this set-back, however, development had been proceeding with a British airborne stand-off missile, the Avro Blue Steel. This was a nuclear-tipped weapon that was designed to be released from a height of 50,000ft, there to climb under the power of a 20,000lb thrust motor to a height of 70,000ft and then travel towards its target at a speed of Mach 2.5. An inertial navigation system then guided the weapon until it reached a predetermined angle of inclination from the target, where it would begin a descent at around Mach 1.5 to hit the target with an accuracy of a few hundred yards. After successful trials this new weapon was accepted into service in December 1962, and it went on to equip the Wittering Wing with Nos 100 and 139 Squadrons flying Victor B.2Rs (the R standing for 'Retrofit') and Nos 617, 27, and 83 Squadrons with their Vulcan B.2As at Scampton.

The advantages of Blue Steel were that it needed no external guidance and it therefore could not be jammed. Its variable parameters were also useful for tactical route planning. It was, however, severely limited by its range of only 200 miles, and from a technical point of view it was never an easy weapon to handle. The fuel used in its Stentor engines was high test peroxide and kerosene, and HTP is potentially a very dangerous chemical. The greatest care had to be taken with the missiles and their fuel at all times and special buildings had to be constructed at Scampton and Wittering for storage, preparation and so on. There were also many complications in loading and checking the missile (this was particularly true with the Victor because of the very limited ground clearance). In all cases, loading took over two hours, and only when loading was complete could full compatibility checks between aircraft and missile be carried out. If any faults were then found, the missile had to be laboriously downloaded, with all the checks and procedures that this involved, made necessary both by the nature of the warhead and by the highly volatile fuel. Rectification would then be carried out, and the whole laborious uploading procedure repeated.

Meanwhile, in May 1962 the American U-2 aircraft flown by Gary Powers had been shot down over Sverdlovsk — a clear indication of growing Soviet capability in surface-to-air missiles. The development of Soviet SAMs over the preceding few years was reasonably well known to Western intelligence, and although the incident was an unmistakable indication of the quality of Soviet SAM technology, the fact that the U-2 had been able to penetrate so deeply into the Soviet Union before being shot down was an indication that the Soviet air defences did not yet cover the whole country. It had to be assumed, however, that such an extension of the Soviet air defences would not be long delayed, and by 1963 it was assessed that Soviet high-level SAMs and

interceptors were reaching such a state of effectiveness that the viability of the V-bombers, even carrying the Blue Steel stand-off weapon, was being brought into serious doubt. But it was essential to keep the V-Force going for perhaps five or six years until the fleet of Polaris boats was in service with the Royal Navy, and the only practicable alternative to the existing high-level attack profile was to operate the bombers at very low level. In this profile, and by careful tactical routeing, the V-bombers would be able to make their way to their targets between or beneath the lobes of opposing air defence radars. And thus it was that despite all the design, development and modification work that had gone into pushing the V-bombers to ever-greater operating altitudes, the efforts of the V-Force were now directed to the quite different challenges of low flying in a hi-lo-hi sortie profile. In 1964, the white paint scheme of the V-Force was exchanged for a more familiar camouflage finish, and training for the new low-level role began.

In fact the first of the V-bombers to go into the low level role were Valiants. These aircraft had replaced some of the Canberra force assigned to SACEUR, starting with No 207 Squadron at Marham in January 1960. No 148 Squadron followed, and in June 1962 No 49 Squadron was similarly assigned, bringing the whole Marham Wing under SACEUR's direction in the conventional role by August 1962. While they had been assigned to SACEUR, under standard NATO procedures an element of the Canberra Force had always been kept at fifteen minutes' readiness, and this posture was now taken on by the Valiant force. Each of the three squadrons kept one crew at readiness, obliged to live in trailers at the squadron sites until NATO funding became available for special-to-type accommodation. From February 1962 the Vulcans and Victors also adopted this system of readiness, known throughout NATO as Quick Reaction Alert, or QRA. In the case of the V-Force, one crew on each squadron was always at fifteen minutes' readiness, though in fact it usually took under four minutes for the aircraft to get airborne.

TANKERS, ALERT DUTIES AND EXERCISES

During the early 1960s air-to-air refuelling, which had been the subject of desultory experiments since before the war, was introduced into the V-Force. Originally this capability had been was introduced in order to extend the range of contemporary fighters, which had a very limited range, but for the V-Force this air-to-air refuelling not only extended the range of the bombers between staging posts en route (for example to the Far East) but it meant that pre-positioned tankers could make it possible to do away with some of the intermediate stops altogether, thus saving the very considerable time that would otherwise have been taken up in turning the aircraft round. Later on, as we shall see, the tankers would come to have the additional role of supporting transport aircraft and air defence interceptors operating distant CAPs (combat air patrols) out over the Norwegian Sea.

The Valiant was chosen as the tanker aircraft for the Royal Air Force and two new marks were produced to meet the task: the Valiant B(PR)K Mk 1, an aircraft that had a capability in the bombing and reconnaissance as well as in the tanking role, of which fourteen were built; and the Valiant BK Mk1, equipped for bombing or tanking duties, of which 45 were delivered. Once Valiant-to-Valiant proving trials had taken place, the next step was to extend air-to-air refuelling to the V-Force as a whole, and modifications to provide a fixed refuelling probe to the Vulcan B.1A were authorized during the summer of 1959. This system was then used in a non-stop flight from Scampton to Australia by Squadron Leader (later Air Chief Marshal Sir) Michael Beavis in June the following year, a transit that took 20 hours 3 minutes. In August 1961 the Valiants of No 90 Squadron at Honington converted to the tanker/receiver role, followed by No 214 Squadron, and on 1 April 1962 both these squadrons relinquished their residual bomber commitment to become the first units in the Royal Air Force dedicated to the air tanker role. This change was followed by the conversion to the receiver role of No 50 Squadron (Vulcan) and No 57 Squadron (Victor), and when the Mk 2 Vulcans and Victors came off the production lines they were already fitted with refuelling probes. Although crews were at first trained in the refuelling receiver role, the value of this capability was not very high and it was exercised less frequently as the years went on. Like the Skybolt attachments, however, it all turned out to have a utility during the final operational days of the Vulcan in the South Atlantic in 1982.

Once the Soviet Union deployed ballistic missiles capable of a strike on the United Kingdom from bases in Russia, the question of the vulnerability of V-Force aircraft on the ground at their bases arose. Strategic Air Command of the USAF solved this problem by assigning a squadron of twelve refuelling aircraft to each Wing of B-52 strategic bombers and keeping a proportion of the force airborne at all times. This concept was, however, beyond the capabilities of the V-Force. The cramped cockpits of the V-bombers excluded the American

solution of carrying a second crew, and although an experiment was tried in which Vulcans from Waddington maintained an airborne alert by rotating aircraft every six hours, the results showed that this posture could not be sustained beyond about two weeks. The next best thing was to hold a proportion of the aircraft on high ground alert, and thus QRA was adopted by the whole of the V-Force.

Both QRA duties and constant-alert exercises became a pervasive feature of life in the V-Force, as did dispersal exercises, these last being probably the most operationally oriented of all the exercises in which the force took part. Dispersal exercises depended on a network of 26 bases in the United Kingdom, each furnished with permanent accommodation for the ground and air crews, and all but a handful provided with Operation Readiness Platforms from which the aircraft could move straight on to the runway for rapid take-off. Dedicated communication links connected each ORP with the Bomber Controller at HQ Strike Command. Including the ten main V-Force bases there were thus 36 sites on which to disperse the force of 144 aircraft in groups of four, which was the usual practice.

Sometimes an exercise would involve individual squadrons refamiliarizing ground and air crews with their dispersal base, for which the codeword was 'Finnigan'; or it might be a 'Mick', which usually involved a whole station or two. On a much larger scale, there were also 'Mickey Finns', which were held only rarely because of the high risk that all aircraft might converge on preset mission profiles from their dispersal bases, despite the application of timing delays (known as 'tromboning'). Scrambles were controlled by Group Headquarters, and the flight profiles consisted of a high-level transit, a let-down to low level, simulated ingress to enemy territory, a bombing run and finally a recovery to base. These exercises later developed to include practice interceptions by fighters and the release of 'Window' (by now known as chaff), all conducted whilst maintaining HF radio contact with the Bomber Controller. Bombing results were usually judged by flying through a Radar Bomb Scoring Unit, with tone activation to assess the accuracy of the simulated weapon drop, a procedure which was often backed up by the use of an on-board F95 camera.

Detachment overseas of more than two V-bombers at a time was unusual except for operations, or to exercise a particular operational role. 'Sunspots' fell into this latter category. Using Cyprus as a base, aircraft practised their role with CENTO, the Central Treaty Organization of 1959–79, by detaching forward to airfields in Iran. Since Blue Steel aircraft could not be used for the

Right: Valiants also served as refuelling tankers. One is seen here tanking a Lightning. (RAFM)

CENTO commitment, these desirable detachments led to a certain amount of jealousy between the 'free-fall' and the Blue Steel crews and between the various V-Force bases. Another complication caused by the arrival of the Blue Steel missile was that the aircraft modified to carry them, by having concave bomb-bay doors to accept the semi-recessed weapon, were not interchangeable with the free-fall aircraft. The result was that only a very limited number of Blue Steel V-bombers were allowed out of Britain at any one time, often barring the crews concerned from taking part in the more exotic detachments. Among the more distant of these detachments were those to Tengah, Singapore, codenamed 'Moonflower' and 'Sunflower'. V-bomber facilities had been built at that base, and Victors from Cottesmore made frequent visits to Singapore and to the airfield at Butterworth.

These exercises were 'team' events; the solo aircraft detachments were known as 'Rangers' and they covered a range of taskings, some of them training flights, while others were concerned with 'showing the flag'. 'Goose Rangers' for example involved a deployment to Goose Bay airfield in Labrador, Canada, where crews could practise their low-flying skills over unfamiliar terrain and in conditions where ice-lakes could produce interesting radar picture reversals. These exercises were often enlivened by interception training with USAF F-105 and F-106 fighters, while periods on the ground were spent in improving winter survival skills. 'Western Rangers' were based at Offutt Air Base, Omaha, Nebraska, where a small permanent RAF detachment supported sorties that were flown in all directions and included experience in operating at high and low level over mountains, desert, flat plains and open countryside. The routes flown here,

following those set by the host USAF, were known as 'Oil-Burners', though once the oil crisis of 1973 erupted it was thought tactful to rename them 'Olive Branches'!

'Lone Rangers' were single-aircraft detachments to other destinations all over the Western world, extending, for example, from Gardermoen in south Norway to New Zealand and including events such as the Independence celebrations in Barbados in 1966. Many Lone Rangers involved participation in a local flying display, and even those that did not were much sought after because of the break from routine that they offered. Once a V-bomber did reach its distant destination on any of these overseas exercises it was not unknown for the aircraft to be struck by unserviceabilities unrelated to any known engineering fault. Far less exciting for all concerned were the exercises in which the crews never expected to get off the ground. These were alerts that were fed into the QRA system to test the reaction of crews and the efficiency of the communications. Crews would be called out, usually at night, to 'generate' their aircraft either to a readiness to start engines or a readiness to take off.

But although it seemed to be so to those in the V-Force at the time, life was not only about QRA, alert exercises and Rangers. In the very earliest days of the Force, for example, a vital part in the development of the British deterrent was played by Valiants of No 49 Squadron. In the trials of the British atomic weapon at Maralinga, Australia, in September 1956, two aircraft of 'C' Flight of No 138 Squadron took part in Operation 'Buffalo'. After nine postponements because of unfavourable weather, on 11 October a 'Blue Danube' atomic weapon was successfully dropped within about 110yds of the aiming point in what turned out to be a dress rehearsal for the British nuclear weapon tests that

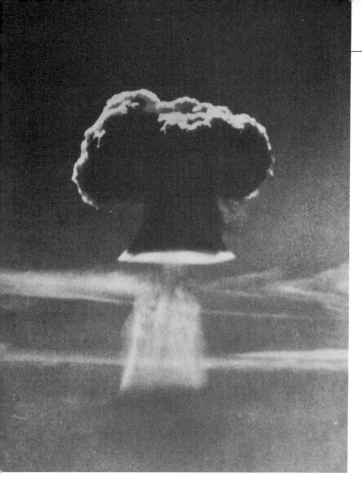

Above: The detonation of the first British atomic weapon over Maralinga, 11 October 1956. (IWM)

and sensitive instruments were taken on board so as to measure the atmospheric results. Quite apart from the eight Valiants which took part, Shackletons from Nos 206 and 240 Squadrons were tasked to carry out surveys of the ocean and to monitor the region before and after the tests. No 76 Squadron Canberras had the role of sampling the air after the explosions, while No 100 Squadron, equipped with Canberra PR.7s, carried out high-level meteorological surveys. Not least, the force deployed included a flight of Dakotas for communications and No 22 Squadron with Whirlwind helicopters to provide air/sea rescue and other local facilities.

On 15 May 1957 the first weapon, a device weighing 10,000lb in its 'Blue Danube' casing, was released from a height of 45,000ft to detonate at 10,000ft over Malden Island and some 245yds from the aiming point. At 45,000ft and with a carefully designed escape manoeuvre including an airspeed of around 600mph, the Valiant had a safe margin in which to avoid the massive explosion and its atmospheric aftermath. Other tests followed with a total of seven nuclear bombs and two smaller devices detonated from balloons, the whole operation lasting until September 1958. Operation 'Grapple' had been the largest joint-service operation since the Second World War, and it successfully proved the effectiveness of the British nuclear deterrent which was to figure so prominently in defence policy during the following decades.

DEMISE OF THE V-FORCE

As we have seen, the V-Force reached its full strength in 1962; but only two years later there was a major set-back when, on 6 August 1964, a Valiant tanker suffered the failure of a main spar in flight. The crew were very fortunate in being able to land the aircraft, but worse was to follow when a detailed technical examination of the Valiant fleet showed that the problem lay in the type of light zinc-bearing forged alloys that had been used for the massive main spars of the wings. These alloys had been chosen because they combined great strength with relatively low weight, but this had been before the effects of metal fatigue was fully understood. It might have been possible to re-spar the whole Valiant fleet, albeit at exorbitant cost, but the decision was made to scrap all the aircraft. It was therefore fortunate that a programme was already under way to convert some of the Victors to the tanking role, and this venture was now accelerated. Six interim Victor tankers were delivered to No 55 Squadron in mid-1965, and by June 1967 six two-point Victor

were carried out in the South Pacific during the following year. This operation, codenamed 'Grapple', was based on Christmas Island, the largest coral reef in the Pacific and about 35 miles by 24 in size. By November 1956 a naval task force had transported sappers of the Royal Engineers as well as many other technical specialists, who had constructed a small township as well as a runway 2,150yds long. When everything was complete, around 20,000 tons of stores had been landed and the military population of the island had reached about 3,000 men.

The target for the test was on Malden Island, some 400 miles to the south, and in March 1957 Valiants from 'C' Flight, No 138 Squadron, now expanded to become No 49 Squadron, arrived to carry out the bombing mission. These aircraft had been heavily modified. They had been given a coat of special protective paint, the crew were issued with a range of protective equipment and various shields and filters were fitted to the aircraft, while tail cameras were carried to record the explosion tankers and 24 three-point tankers were operational with Nos 55, 57 and 214 Squadrons at Marham.

In the meantime concern had been growing during the early 1960s over the extended activities of the Soviet blue-water fleet, and in those days before surveillance by satellite a clear need was identified for long-range airborne reconnaissance. When it was found that a suitably modified Victor Mk 2 could offer an improvement in range over the Valiant B(PR).1s of around 40 per cent, the last nine aircraft off the production line were modified to become Victor B/SR Mk 1s and replaced the Valiants of No 543 Squadron. The Victor strategic reconnaissance aircraft was very successful, its high capabilities being illustrated by the fact that it could map by radar an area of 750,000 square miles in six hours and could plot the position of every ship in the Mediterranean in the course of a single sortie. Victor B/SR.2s remained in service with No 543 Squadron until May 1974, when the unit disbanded and five Vulcan SR.2s of No 27 Squadron at Scampton took over the role.

It had been intended to withdraw all the strategic bombers of the Royal Air Force once the Polaris missile-firing submarines of the Royal Navy became operational, which they were expected to do in about 1972. But two new factors now intervened. First, the TSR.2 aircraft, intended to replace the ageing Canberra in the tactical strike role, was cancelled by an incoming Labour Government in April 1966. As a stop-gap, until a projected Anglo-French variable-geometry aircraft became available, the Government decided to buy 45 F-111 aircraft from the United States and, as the White Paper of that year announced, 'to supplement them in the strike role by the V-bombers, which will cease to form part of our contribution to the strategic forces of the Alliance when the Polaris submarines come into service'. In June 1967, however, the French withdrew from the variable-geometry project and in January 1968 the F-111 purchase was in turn cancelled by the Labour Government on the grounds that, since Britain intended to withdraw from her commitments in the Far East and the Persian Gulf by the end of 1971, the aircraft was no longer needed. There was thus nothing for the V-Force to 'supplement' and the Victors and Vulcans continued in their vital nuclear role.

The second unexpected factor in the fortunes of the V-Force at this late stage in its existence was the intervention by SACEUR. Because of the overwhelming preponderance of Warsaw Pact ground forces in the Central Region of Europe, SACEUR's defence plans depended to a very great extent on the ability of tactical air to bring concentrated firepower to bear to threatened sectors and thus offset the enemy's superior numerical strength. Pressure was therefore exerted through NATO to retain the V-bombers in the Order of Battle until aircraft more suited to the role could be procured.

In the case of the Victor, low-level operations soon revealed structural weaknesses that made the aircraft unsuited to prolonged service in that role, and by the end of 1968 the type was withdrawn from the bomber role. Twenty-seven B.2s and SR.2s were, however, later converted to the tanker role as K.2s, to replace the Victor K.1s at Marham. As to the Vulcan, some mainplanes had already been strengthened to take the ill-fated Skybolt, and with further modifications the aircraft was well able to accept the stresses of an extended life in the low-level role that was now demanded of it. The aircraft were fitted with a terrain following radar, SAM radar jammers and an ECM suite to enhance their survivability, and not only did the Vulcans of Nos 9 and 35 Squadrons replace the Canberra strike force in Cyprus, but the remaining home-based squadrons, Nos 27, 83 and 617 at Scampton and Nos 44, 50 and 101 at Waddington, remained as a strike element in SACEUR's Order of Battle even after the Polaris boats became operational in June 1969.

During the crisis in Cyprus in 1974, the two Vulcan squadrons that had been based at Akrotiri, Nos 9 and 35, were withdrawn to Lincolnshire and remained there until the whole of the remaining V-Force began to disband during 1981. No 83 Squadron went first, followed by No 617 Squadron which was withdrawn at the end of December 1981, and then Nos 35 and 27 Squadrons. It had been planned that the final stages of this process of dismantling the V-Force would take place with the withdrawal of Nos 9, 44, 50 and 101 Squadrons in the first half of 1982, when their strike role would be taken over by the newly formed squadrons of Tornado aircraft. But then, after all the years of readiness in the nuclear role, the Vulcan was destined to operate in the conventional role and in a totally unexpected part of the world, when Argentina invaded the Falkland Islands in early 1982.

THOR

While this story of manned strategic bombers over the years had been unfolding, a quite different field of military technology had been developing. On 4 October 1957 the Soviet Union caused considerable alarm in the West when she launched her Sputnik satellite, an event that then contributed to an American initiative to deploy the Thor intermediate range ballistic missile throughout

NATO. Britain had already reached a bilateral agreement with the United States to station a number of these 1,500-mile-range weapons with their megaton-range warheads in the United Kingdom, though in the event only Italy and Turkey joined Britain in agreeing to accept them.

In Britain the first Thor missiles arrived at Feltwell, Norfolk, with No 77 Squadron on 19 September 1958 and by March 1960 the whole deployment of sixty operational missiles in the United Kingdom was complete, the weapons being allocated to a total of twenty RAF squadrons. Four complexes of Thor sites were constructed, based on Feltwell, North Luffenham, Helmswell and Driffield, with each of those main bases controlling four satellite sites, giving a total of five sites for each complex. Each of the sites consisted of three launching pads laid out in a triangular pattern behind dense barbed wire that was well illuminated at night, giving an other-worldly appearance to the whole deployment from the air during the hours of darkness. It was, however, a deployment that spread the missiles over a fairly wide area up through eastern England, thus giving at least some assurance of survival in the face of a possible Soviet pre-emptive strike — a very real problem since it took some fifteen minutes to fuel, align and then fire a Thor missile.

Although the missiles themselves were British-owned, and indeed carried the familiar RAF roundel, the nuclear warheads were American, which meant that at each site there were American custodial officers who held a second key to free the missiles for launch. Although these missiles were under the operational control and administrative management of HQ Bomber Command, in fact a launch required a positive joint decision by both Governments. Meanwhile the 1,200 men and women in the Thor force evolved a system of round-the-clock rosters on their isolated and heavily protected sites, with launch control officers of the Royal Air Force working in harmony with authentication officers of the United States Air Force. But after only four years the United States decide to rely more heavily on the longer-range inter-continental ballistic missiles that were by then becoming available, and during 1963 all the Thors in Britain were phased out to be returned to the United States.

With the intermediate-range Thors withdrawn, the V-Force continued alone in the role of strategic nuclear deterrence until 30 June 1969. On that date the third Polaris submarine for the Royal Navy, HMS *Renown*, was declared operational, the three boats were now able to maintain between them a constant sea deployment and

Above: The first of the RAF's Thor missiles goes through contractor's checks near Feltwell on 27 November 1958.

the role of nuclear deterrence passed to the Navy. It was no longer necessary to keep aircraft of the V-Force at immediate readiness, and apart from the Vulcans that had replaced the Canberra squadrons in the strike role at Akrotiri in support of CENTO, the bombers would now operate in the theatre strike role under SACEUR's control.

Although, in the earliest days of the V-Force, Valiants had seen action in the conventional bombing role during the Suez campaign, the real value of the Force was that because it was held at high readiness for major war it contributed to a wider global nuclear stability. Not only that, but the fact that the aircraft, their crews and their nuclear weapons were entirely indigenous gave Britain a dimension in international affairs that it would not otherwise have had.

CHAPTER 11
THE RAF OVERSEAS, 1945-82

Any hopes that the end of the Second World War might lead to an era of peace were quickly dissipated, particularly in the Far East where local independence movements took advantage of the sudden collapse of Japan. One of the first indications of trouble came in the Dutch East Indies, where the Japanese had set up an independent Indonesian Republic before they surrendered. The Dutch had no forces with which to re-occupy their territories, and South-East Asia Command had little choice but to send in troops. An army division was dispatched to the main trouble spot, Java, at the end of September 1945, together with an Air Headquarters formed from No 221 Group in Burma, with No 904 Wing under command.

A ground party of 2,600 airmen then followed by sea, landing on 18 October and taking over Kemajoran, the airfield outside the capital, Batavia (now Djakarta), into which two squadrons of Thunderbolts, Nos 60 and 81, were flown. This small force was soon supplemented by No 84 Squadron with Mosquitos, as well as detachments from two other Mosquito squadrons, Nos 47 and 110, the 24 Dakotas of No 31 Squadron, a PR Spitfire for reconnaissance work, a Beaufighter for jungle search and rescue, and elements of No 321 (Dutch) Squadron of the RAF.

A principal task for the Allied forces was to locate and then evacuate the many thousands of prisoners of war and civilian internees scattered all over the Dutch East Indies, particularly those in the main island, Java, a huge land mass some 600 miles long and up to 90 miles wide. There were not enough Allied forces available to occupy the whole island, and instead three bridgeheads were set up, each with an airstrip and a port, into which the evacuees could be moved; one was around Batavia at the western end of the island, one lay around Semarang about three hundred miles to the east, while the third was centred on Soerabaya on the north-east coast.

Many of the prisoners were now flown out from remote camps by the Dakotas, which kept up a daily sortie rate of 28 round trips throughout November and December. In the Batavia sector, evacuation by road was very difficult both because of the poor state of the routes and because of the armed resistance of the Indonesian irregular forces. When road transport was used, the Thunderbolts and Mosquitos provided air cover, often strafing enemy positions along the routes. Fortunately there were few prison camps in the west of Java, for the situation there outside the towns was so bad that not only was movement by road prohibited by the Allied military commanders, but overflying was also forbidden. The wisdom of these precautions was all too clearly demonstrated on 23 November, when a Dakota of No 31 Squadron en route from Kemajoran to Semarang was forced by engine trouble to turn back to base. It made a forced landing only five miles short of Kemajoran, and although the crew and passengers survived the landing they were later murdered in a local village jail. In retaliation, the whole village was later razed to the ground by the Army.

In central Java the situation was even worse. Heavy fighting took place over a period of three weeks at the end of November, during which concentrated bombing attacks were directed against Indonesian positions along the roads being used to extract internees. On one occasion a Gurkha garrison, which found itself cut off,

Below: A Thunderbolt at Batavia, November 1945. (AHB)

had to rely on the Dakotas of No 31 Squadron for resupply. It soon became clear that it would not be possible for the British forces to push through to the more distant prison camps in this central region, and there was no alternative but to come to some accommodation with the Indonesian authorities in Batavia. This was duly arranged, and fighting in the area therefore died down at the end of November.

In the eastern sector, matters were just as threatening. No 49 Brigade had made an unopposed landing from the sea; but when Brigadier Mallaby was murdered whilst conducting negotiations with the local Indonesian forces two more brigades were dispatched to subdue the opposition together with eight Thunderbolts and two Mosquitos of No 904 Wing. An ultimatum to the Indonesians to surrender was rejected and three weeks of severe fighting followed, in which the Dakotas of No 31 Squadron kept up a steady stream of resupply missions while the Thunderbolts and Mosquitos were on call to give air support to the ground forces, including very accurate bombing attacks on specific buildings being held by the irregulars in urban areas.

By the New Year the situation in Java had become much quieter and the opportunity was taken to reorganize the Allied forces in the country. No 904 Wing and its squadrons remained at Kemajoran, while Soerabaya became an RAF station with No 60 Squadron and No 321 (Dutch) Squadron, by now equipped with Catalina flying boats based there, together with a detachment from No 43 Squadron with Mosquitos and No 656 AOP Squadron. With the gradual arrival of the first Dutch troops in Indonesia during early 1946 trouble broke out again, necessitating further air action by the Thunderbolts and Mosquitos in support of British

ground forces. But gradually, and despite strong local resentment that was demonstrated in November when the last British and Indian forces withdrew, control was handed over to the Dutch authorities.

It had been fifteen months of sometimes vicious fighting, and the ground forces had suffered well over 1,000 casualties including several hundred killed. For the Royal Air Force, two Dakotas had been written off in accidents while two Mosquitos and three Thunderbolts had been lost to hostile action. Thirteen officers had been killed, and 23 other ranks; three airmen had died, and another 44 of all ranks had been injured. This had been the penalty paid for rescuing and repatriating the many thousands of POWs and internees who were brought to safety, largely by the efforts of No 31 Squadron, which had flown 24,436 hours and lifted more than 127,000 passengers as well as 26,000 tons of freight during the fifteen months that the whole operation had lasted.

Meanwhile in Burma and Siam units of the Japanese forces in those countries were kept more or less intact, so as to preserve some kind of order, but put under Allied command. In those countries too, the task of repatriating prisoners and rounding up the Japanese now began. On the whole there was little trouble, and even in French Indo-China, which was shortly to witness two decades of war, things went fairly smoothly. On 8 September 1945 an advance party of engineers was flown into Tan Son Nhut airfield, Saigon: the 20th Division arrived by sea and air to be complete on 26 September, while No 273 Squadron equipped with Spitfires and No 684 with Mosquitos in the reconnaissance role, together with No 1307 Wing of the Royal Air Force Regiment, based themselves at that same airfield.

In December Annamite forces had begun to show

Left: Thunderbolts taxying out for a strike against Indonesian guerrillas, Jibardak, 10 January 1946. (AHB)

Right: Spitfires of No 132 (Bombay) Squadron at Kai Tak, Hong Kong, 20 December 1945. (AHB)

Below: Venom FB.4s of No 28 Squadron over Kowloon in 1957. The original runway extension at Kai Tak can be seen on the extreme right of the photograph. (Author)

their hand by attacking some of the newly arrived French garrisons in the country, but by then arrangements for handing over control to the French administration were well advanced, and although No 273 Squadron was engaged in at least one operation in support of French ground forces, enough French troops had arrived by the end of January for the British units to be withdrawn.

The re-occupation of Malaya and Singapore by British forces caused fewer difficulties than was the case in the other countries in South-East Asia Command, and within a few months the airfields that had been so badly neglected during the Japanese occupation were restored to a more usable condition, so that the Service units still in the country began to settle down to garrison life as demobilization and repatriation of the very sizeable British forces in the region took effect.

By the beginning of 1948 FEAF (actually still known until June 1949 by its wartime title of Air Component Far East) held a force of eight RAF squadrons. This was made up of three Dakota squadrons, Nos 48, 52 and 110, No 81 Squadron flying reconnaissance Mosquitos and No 84 Squadron with Beaufighters in the light bomber role. These five units were based at Changi, where, incidentally, Japanese prisoners had been employed to restore the runway that had been deliberately jerry-built by Allied prisoners of war. Tengah held two squadrons of Spitfires, Nos 28 and 60, while a cadre of No 209 Squadron with Sunderlands was at Seletar. Another squadron of Sunderlands, No 88, had by now been deployed to Hong Kong, and a third, No 205, was in Ceylon together with No 45 Squadron flying first of all Beaufighters and then Brigands. Later Nos 28 and 80 Squadrons would be dispatched to Hong Kong, where the latter unit disbanded in 1955; No 28 went on much later to exchange its Spitfires for Vampire FB.9s before moving on to Venoms, Hunters and finally Wessex helicopters.

THE MALAYAN EMERGENCY

This peacetime FEAF strength of around a hundred aircraft, together with the Army garrisons in the region, was intended to help preserve British interests in the Far East, and if necessary to defend them. But any hope that the mere presence of these modest forces might deter or forestall hostilities had to be abandoned in June 1948 when, after a growing number of terrorist incidents including the murder of several British planters, a state of emergency was declared in Malaya. The terrorists were a group of perhaps 2,500, organized in ten regiments each between 200 and 500 strong, with four or five companies of ten or so platoons in each regiment.

Above: Armourers of No 57 Squadron bomb up a Lincoln ready for operations against bandits in Malaya. (AHB)

There were also around another 600 terrorists organized into mobile killer squads that were to lead the first phase of the insurrection. With numbers like this, and with the terrorists' familiarity with the jungle, it was clear that the security forces had a major campaign on their hands.

Essentially the campaign that followed was fought by small units on the ground, but air support of one kind or another became a pervasive feature of almost all operational activity. So as to facilitate the FEAF contribution to the campaign, in July 1948 an air task force was formed in Kuala Lumpur. This was made up of detachments of Spitfire FR.18s from Nos 28 and 60 Squadrons, Beaufighter Mk Xs from No 45 Squadron, Dakotas from No 110 Squadron and a mix of Mosquito PR.34s and Spitfire FR.18s and 19s of No 81 Squadron operating in the photo-reconnaissance role. This last was vital to the success of any operations, since the pre-war maps were both inaccurate and out of date. The necessary air survey and map-making work took four years to complete, but once good maps became available it was possible to locate targets and dropping zones with far greater efficiency.

By 1950 the RAF combat force engaged had grown to a total of seven squadrons. Two of them, Nos 45 and 84, were in the light bomber role flying first the Beaufighter and then the very unreliable Brigand. Two others, No 33 Squadron equipped with Tempests and No 60 flying Spitfire VIIIs, were operating in the day fighter/ground attack role. There were also two Sunderland squadrons, Nos 205 and 209, and No 81

Squadron, still in the reconnaissance role with Spitfires and Mosquitos, these last aircraft remaining on strength until as late as mid-1953.

This force was gradually reduced in size over the following two years, so that in 1953 there was one medium bomber squadron, another of light bombers, three more squadrons flying Vampire FB.9 day fighter/ground attack aircraft and No 81 Squadron by now re-equipped with Meteor PR.10s. In addition, since there were initially no heavy bombers in Malaya, Lincolns were regularly detached from the United Kingdom to take part in operations. But because little of operation value to the crews was derived from these detachments, and because the results of bombing operations were so disappointing, this practice was never popular with HQ Bomber Command and it tailed off once the Lincolns of No 1 RAAF Squadron arrived at Tengah — though Canberras still carried out occasional detachments from 1958 onwards.

By 1951 most of the terrorists were living in remote, well-hidden camps in the jungle. Little in the way of arms or ammunition was able to reach them from external sources, but they had retained a sizeable quantity of Allied military stores that had been delivered to them during the guerrilla war in Malaya against the occupying Japanese forces. For food and other supplies of that kind they often cultivated small plots in the jungle. Apart from that source, however, since almost all the terrorists were of Chinese ethnic origin, they could count on the passive support of some of the Chinese-Malay population. One answer to that was the decision by the security forces to move almost 462,000 Chinese into 509 settlements protected by police and home guardsmen and surrounded by barbed wire. Once the terrorists had been isolated in this way the war against them in the jungle could begin in earnest. The strategy adopted was to use most of the ground forces to dominate as much of the jungle as possible, starting in the south with the province of Johore and working up the peninsula.

The part played then by the Royal Air Force in the campaign had many facets. One of the most important contributions was that of visual and photographic reconnaissance so as to build up the all-important intelligence picture. Just as vital to the ground forces as they operated in that very difficult terrain were the tasks of supply-dropping and troop-lifting, and indeed it was in these roles that the Royal Air Force can be said to have made its most effective and most important contribution to the eventual defeat of the terrorists.

The total of supplies dropped during the campaign

was estimated to have been 25,000 tons, and at the height of the counter-insurgency operations eight sorties a day were flown in this role. It was not at all uncommon for whole battalions to be supported entirely by air for extended periods, often running into several months. Apart from the supply role, troops were constantly being lifted into jungle clearings, from where they could more quickly advance on suspected terrorist positions, and then flown out once an operation was completed.

During the peak month for this activity, October 1958, no fewer than 4,133 fully equipped troops were lifted in and out of jungle clearings in south Johore, over half of them by Sycamore helicopter. Casualty evacuation was another major role for the helicopters, as it was for short take-off and landing fixed-wing aircraft such as the Single and Twin Pioneer. Aerial broadcasting by slow-flying Dakotas in the hope of persuading terrorists to surrender was yet another support activity, as were crop-spraying (to destroy the terrorists' cultivated plots) and leaflet dropping.

Using air power to attack the terrorists directly was, however, never easy. Because of the dense jungle canopy and the problems of reliable radio communications, the 'cab rank' concept so successfully developed in Italy and in North-West Europe during 1943 and 1944 could not be employed. From 1949 until late 1952 air strikes were therefore generally made against areas of the jungle extending to about 1,000yds square, and on line targets sometimes stretching for 6,000yds. The object of this type of carpet bombing was simply to

Below: A Whirlwind of No 155 Squadron with men of the RAF Regiment (Malaya) in Selangor State, April 1957. (AHB)

flush any terrorist band out of concealment, and into ground force ambushes that were waiting for them. When, as often happened, the strikes produced no visible result, the commanders tried to take comfort from the fact that the air strikes at least had the effect of keeping the terrorists awake and on the move. But clearly, little of this could be seen as an effective use of air resources.

By 1954 new aircraft types were arriving in the Far East Air Force. The Bristol Brigand had, as we have seen, been issued to No 84 Squadron in 1950, but this aircraft experienced so many technical failures, and caused such a worrying rate of casualties, that the unit was disbanded in early 1953. Neither had the Mosquitos of No 81 Squadron stood up well to the extreme climatic conditions, and after doing much valuable work in supplementing intelligence they were replaced by four Pembroke C(PR).1s in 1955, a modest enough unit and one that was augmented by Canberra detachments from Bomber Command. The Hornets that had equipped Nos 33 and 45 Squadrons had also fared badly in the humid heat of Malaya, and in March 1955 they too were replaced, this time by Venom FB.1s in No 45 Squadron, which at the same time absorbed No 33 Squadron. No 60 Squadron, which had exchanged its Spitfire FR.18s for Vampires in May 1955, was now also re-equipped with Venoms.

With these new arrivals there was a need for the combat squadrons of the Far East Air Force to concentrate on their primary roles, particularly since those roles had little connection with the somewhat wasteful air attack operations that were still being conducted against the terrorists. Thus it was that from 1955 onwards the use of offensive air attacks against the terrorists diminished until during the last six months of the Emergency the bids for air strikes had fallen to as few as one a week. By August 1959 the air attacks had stopped altogether.

During the campaign a total of around 35,000 tons of bombs, 74,159 air-to-ground rockets and 9.8 million rounds of cannon or machine-gun ammunition had been expended by aircraft against the terrorists. It is still difficult to assess the other side of the balance sheet in terms of the number of terrorists that were killed by air action, though it cannot have been a very impressive score. One indication is given by the number killed by the end of 1950, when it was assessed that out of 1,641 claimed by the security forces as a whole, 126 had been killed by air action and another 141 were claimed but unconfirmed.

If this were all, it would be thought highly unsatisfactory; but the real contribution that FEAF made was in exercising its numerous support roles, without which the tenacious efforts of the troops on the ground would have been far more difficult. The Communist terrorists never surrendered, but by July 1960 nearly 7,000 of them had been killed and another 4,000 had been captured or had surrendered, and it was possible to raise the state of emergency. Malaya had meanwhile gained her independence on 31 August 1957, and AHQ Malaya left Kuala Lumpur to become HQ No 224 Group in Singapore.

At the same time the British Government was anxious to substitute a reinforcement capability for the expensive peacetime garrisons that had for so long been maintained in the Middle and Far East, and one resultant move was the decision to form a Commonwealth Strategic Reserve. The RAF squadrons on their bases in Singapore were to form a part of this force, and it would be a garrison that could be backed up by a rapid reinforcement capability from the United Kingdom. This meant reinforcement by air rather than by the slow-moving troopships of pre-war and wartime days, but the difficulty with the air routes was that the unsettled state of the Middle East and the possibility of instability in the Indian Subcontinent might lead to the suspension of overflying rights on which they depended.

During the first decade and more after the war the main air route ran from the United Kingdom through Malta or Libya, thence through the Canal Zone and Habbaniya in Iraq, down to Mauripur near Karachi, on to Negombo in Ceylon and so to Singapore. The routes were flown mostly by the Handley Page Hastings strategic transport, the first of which entered service in October 1946. This was a workhorse of an aircraft that eventually equipped thirteen squadrons before being phased out from 1959 onwards. Air routes within the Far East, and indeed within the Middle East, were operated by Vickers Valetta transports, military versions of the civil Viking and the replacement for the wartime Dakotas.

By mid-1956, however, the longer-range Comet and Beverley transports were entering service, followed by the Britannia in 1959; these were three aircraft types that added real capability to Government intentions. But if aircraft en route to the Far East circumvented the Middle East and avoided the Indian Subcontinent there was still the very long flight across the Indian Ocean, a particular problem for the 'shorter-legged' combat aircraft that might have to fly the route, and clearly there was a need for an intermediate base. The choice fell on the coral island of Gan in the Maldives, and in January 1957 work began on clearing the site. Two years later the

base was complete and Gan became a vital link on the Far East route, handling a wide variety of operational aircraft as well as strategic transports.

KOREA

This, then, was the pattern into which the Far East Air Force settled once the Malayan Emergency was over, and the Command entered a period of stability. As we shall see, however, it would last for only a very few years until December 1962, when trouble broke out in Borneo.

But that takes us some way ahead, and meanwhile there had been another limited but important war in the Far East, that in Korea starting on 25 June 1950, when the North invaded the South. At that time the United States was still maintaining what amounted to a tactical air force in Japan, and with eventual reinforcement the squadrons of this force bore the brunt of the air fighting that now followed in Korea. The RAF meanwhile was already over-committed across the Far East, not least by the Emergency in Malaya. But at least the Sunderlands of the Far East Flying Boat Wing, made up of Nos 88 Squadron in Hong Kong and Nos 205 and 209 Squadrons based at Seletar, could provide reconnaissance and transport facilities to the United Nations forces operating in and around the Korean peninsula. These aircraft therefore began rotational detachments to Korean waters.

From Iwakuni on the southern tip of the island of Honshu, these aircraft flew 1,100 lengthy missions in the theatre of operations, and although they saw no combat the crews amassed a total of 12,500 flying hours on maritime patrols in conditions that were often both demanding and uncomfortable. One of the Sunderlands was lost during the war, when it crashed between Iwakuni and Hong Kong, killing fourteen crew and passengers.

De Havilland Comet 2

Like most other RAF transport aircraft, the Comet was designed for commercial use, and when it joined No 216 Squadron in June 1956 it became the first pure-jet aircraft in the world to be employed on military transport duties. The Comet 2 was powered by four 7,350lb thrust Rolls-Royce Avon 117/118 engines, giving the aircraft a maximum cruising speed of 480mph at 40,000ft. With a load of 44 passengers the Comet had a maximum stage length of 2,500 miles. The aircraft remained in RAF service until 1975.

Bristol Britannia C.1

Another landmark in the development of RAF transport capability came with the introduction of the Britannia, which replaced the Hastings in 1959. The Britannia was the first turboprop transport in the Service, and it operated on the strategic routes until 1976. Its four Bristol Proteus 255 engines developed 4,445hp each, giving the aircraft a cruising speed of 360mph. With its maximum payload of 113 troops or 37,400lb of freight, the Britannia had a range of 4,268 miles.

Although no other RAF squadrons took part in the Korean War, 21 RAF pilots operated with various fighter squadrons of the US Air Force and another 29 served with No 77 Squadron of the Royal Australian Air Force. This latter unit entered the war with Meteor 8s, at that time the standard aircraft with Fighter Command in the United Kingdom. The Australians had for some time harboured doubts about the combat capability of the Meteor when compared to other jet fighters of this era, and their worst fears were confirmed during September 1951 when No 77 Squadron RAAF came up against the Soviet-built MiG-15s that over Korea. After suffering unacceptable losses No 77 Squadron was withdrawn from high-level fighter duties. In the United Kingdom, meanwhile, the realization that the current fighters on the inventory of the Royal Air Force were so far inferior to those available to the Soviet Union contributed to the decision to take on loan 430 North American Sabres from the United States, as we have seen. Meanwhile, during their attachment to USAF units or to the Australian squadron in Korea, five pilots of the Royal Air Force were credited with one Soviet-built MiG-15 fighter each, one got half credits for two more and seven DFCs were won. But there were losses to be counted as well. Ten RAF air crew were killed in those same fighter squadrons and one more pilot was lost while flying with a squadron of the Fleet Air Arm.

THE INDONESIAN CONFRONTATION

Eight years after the end of the Korean conflict in 1954 there was another crisis in the Far East when trouble broke out in Borneo at the end of 1962. This began with minor rebellions in British-protected Brunei and in the colony of Sarawak, which led to the dispatch by air of British troops from Singapore. Within a few days over 3,000 men and much equipment had been flown into the airfield at Labuan, and shortly after that a joint force

Headquarters was set up. During the first two months of 1963 the rebellion was put down, despite the support it had been receiving from Indonesia. But when in September 1963 the new state of Malaysia was formed, Indonesia sent guerrilla bands across the ill-defined border that runs through the island of Borneo and what became known as the Confrontation began.

It was a campaign not unlike that in Malaya, except that as far as FEAF was concerned much better aircraft were by now to hand, particularly in the all-important role of air transport. This role saw many aircraft types engaged. There was the lumbering but capacious Beverley, with its remarkable short landing and take-off capabilities. The Hastings, Valettas and Twin Pioneers that had all served so well in Malaya only a few years before were again committed. But there were also the Armstrong Whitworth Argosys which had entered service in the spring of 1962 and which now equipped No 215 Squadron. There were the Bristol Freighters of No 41 Squadron RNZAF, as well as the Bristol Belvedere helicopters of No 66 Squadron that had joined FEAF in May 1962, and the Whirlwinds of 103 and 110 Squadrons were available. For the whole of the next four years this fleet of transport aircraft would be fully occupied in ferrying troops to and from the operational zones, in casualty evacuation and in the general support of all the ground forces deployed in often very remote and inhospitable parts of Borneo. Bulk supplies were brought in by sea, but urgent supplies were airlifted to Labuan or to Kuching from Singapore by Hastings, Beverleys, Argosys and Bristol Freighters. These loads were then lifted into the many small forward airstrips by the Pioneers, the helicopters and sometimes even by the Beverleys or Valettas.

At the very start of the Confrontation, beginning on 19 September 1962, three Argosys and a Hastings flew to Djakarta under a guarantee of safety in order to take on board the first of 400 people who were to be evacuated to Singapore; but thereafter Indonesian airspace was closed to RAF traffic. This caused a great deal of inconvenience to RAF aircraft on the route to Australia but it did not prevent Indonesian aircraft from making incursions into Malaysian airspace. To deal with this potential threat, FEAF established an Air Defence Identification Zone (ADIZ) around the borders of Sarawak and Sabah and deployed a force of fighters to secure it. This element of the Command was made up of four Hunters from No 20 Squadron deployed to Labuan and another four at Kuching, together with two Javelins of No 60 Squadron at each of those two bases. At the same time No 81 Squadron, by now equipped with

Canberra PR.7s, carried out invaluable work photographing terrain that had hitherto been virtually unmapped, while Shackletons of No 205 Squadron made regular maritime patrols in order to secure the extensive and broken coastline against any possible Indonesian incursions.

But the whole affair remained from start to finish an undeclared war, and although very considerable combat air power was available, the sanctity of the frontier had to be scrupulously observed and even the 'hot pursuit' of Indonesian infiltrators by the aircraft of FEAF could not be countenanced. Very few targets were therefore available to the squadrons deployed, and they were obliged to content themselves with the deterrent role that they had adopted. A change of pace in the Confrontation took place in August 1964, however, when about a hundred Indonesian regular troops came ashore at three separate points on the west coast of Malaya, followed ten days later by attacks on an oil installation off Singapore and on a Malaysian patrol craft at sea. Even more serious from the point of view of FEAF with its air defence responsibilities was the arrival on 2 September of 96 Indonesian paratroops who had been dropped by a C-130 transport in north central Johore. All strike/attack aircraft in Malaya were called to combat readiness and No 20 Squadron was launched to carry out fourteen ground attack sorties with rocket projectiles and guns against this incursion. Although the familiar difficulties of precisely locating enemy positions in the jungle meant that area bombing had to be employed, this air action and particularly the difficult follow-up operation by ground forces resulted in all but ten of the infiltrators being accounted for.

These incursions were followed by others, and between mid-August 1964 and the end of March 1965 forty-one incidents had been reported. These ranged from seaborne landings, and attempted landings, to acts of sabotage and a variety of other hostile activities. In reaction to one of these incursions, on 23 December 1964 Hunters of No 20 Squadron and Canberras of No 45 Squadron carried out attacks on infiltrators which, together with action by ground forces, resulted in their elimination. By now Air Defence reinforcements were being dispatched from the United Kingdom. These units included Gannets of the Royal Navy disembarked from HMS Victorious, an LAA regiment of the Royal Artillery from Germany and eight more Javelin all-weather fighters of No 64 Squadron to augment those already deployed in No 60 Squadron. In addition to these precautions, a detachment of Victor bombers from No 57 Squadron, which had been in Singapore on a routine

exercise, were retained beyond the intended period of their stay in FEAF.

Indonesian harassment over the next few months included firings by anti-aircraft artillery against aircraft approaching Singapore from the south. Occasional seaborne raids on the west coast of Malaya continued, at least one of which again led to air intervention by No 20 Squadron. Meanwhile, in Borneo which was the scene of the main confrontation, Indonesian activities grew to include small scale raids across the border by regular units of their forces. Launched from camps just inside Indonesia, these incursions were very difficult to counter until political approval was given in January 1965 for the British forces to carry out offensive patrols up to a depth of 10,000yds inside Indonesian territory.

In the air, every reported incursion over Borneo by Indonesian aircraft led to a scramble by Javelins or Hunters from Labuan, while a similar presence over Malaysian territorial waters by Shackletons played a large part in deterring Indonesian infiltrations by sea. All these aircraft detachments, together with a mix of five or six Beverleys, Hastings, Argosys and Valettas, added to the workload at the Labuan satellite of Changi. It was by now an airfield that was already heavily engaged in short-range transport duties employing detachments of Twin Pioneers, Whirlwinds and Belvederes. Activity there grew even more intense, so that by 1965 Labuan was holding up to 30 aircraft of nine different types at any one time. Two thousand aircraft movements each month were being recorded, and well over five hundred tons of supplies each month were being dropped to the ground forces by aircraft from what had been a very modest local airfield.

These air activities, together with a constant shuttling of troops to and from their defensive positions close to the Indonesian border, continued into the second half of 1965, and at first they were scarcely diminished by the repercussions of a coup by the Indonesian

Communist Party in Djakarta on 30 September. By the middle of the next year, however, the Indonesian Government had come to realize that military success was beyond reach and that there was no international sympathy for its claims on Malaysia. Finally, on 11 August 1966, Indonesia signed a peace treaty with Malaysia and the 44-month-long confrontation was over. Seventeen flying squadrons of the RAF had taken part at one time or another in the campaign, most of them resident units in FEAF. Six of them were combat squadrons equipped with Hunters, Javelins or Canberras while one was operating Shackletons. But the other ten were all operating in the transport or supply roles, and, just as in Malaya from 1948 to 1960, it was in these essential activities that the Royal Air Force had made its major contribution to the success of the campaign.

With the end of Confrontation some 10,000 Army and RAF personnel were returned to the United Kingdom, a re-alignment that was followed in 1966 by a review on the part of the British Government of its entire defence policy. The main feature to emerge from this re-examination was a renewed emphasis on mobility and reinforcement, and the implication of reduced garrisons overseas was confirmed in the White Paper of 1967, which announced a reduction by half of the forces deployed in Singapore and Malaysia. By the next year, however, the process had been accelerated and the 1968 White Paper not only talked of a more rapid reduction of forces in the Far East but also announced the intention to make a complete withdrawal of forces from Singapore

and Malaysia by 1971. As a result some of the RAF squadrons were brought home; but other units, such as the Javelin force with its ageing aircraft, were disbanded in Singapore.

With a change of Government in Britain in June 1970, the intended total withdrawal from the Far East was replaced by a number of commitments to a new treaty organization, ANZUK, based on Singapore; but the run-down was by now well under way, and the days of the Far East Air Force were over. On 31 October 1971 the Command was disbanded. Other retrenchment followed, and by 1972 what had been a powerful and long-standing element of the Royal Air force was reduced to the very modest contribution to ANZUS, to the staging post at Gan and to the solitary No 28 Squadron in Hong Kong, where, with one short break caused by a temporary disbandment, that unit has now been stationed for the past 45 years.

THE MIDDLE EAST

Those events have taken us well ahead of what was happening during the early post-war years in other parts of the world, and in particular it has overtaken developments in the Middle East, the `Clapham Junction' of Trenchard's vision of so many years before. At the end of the Second World War, although the RAF presence in the Middle East and Mediterranean was swiftly reduced in strength, it still covered a vast area of responsibility stretching from Malta to Greece, to

Above left: Overseas postings held many attractions during the post-war years. This is the Yacht Club at RAF Changi, Singapore, during the fourth Annual Regatta, January 1950. (AHB)

Right: A Beverley of No 34 Squadron unloading stores at Brunei airport for the Queen's Own Highlanders at the start of the Confrontation with Indonesia in December 1962.

include Cyprus, Palestine, Iraq, the Persian Gulf, Aden, Kenya, the Sudan and the Suez Canal Zone. In those days the defence of Palestine was seen to be essential to the security of Egypt, which in turn was the main base for British forces in the Mediterranean; and it was in Palestine that the first post-war challenges erupted.

Much of the RAF strength in the region was based in Palestine at the time. By 1947 there were in that country four fighter squadrons, equipped either with Hurricanes or Spitfires, two others with Halifaxes in support of Airborne Forces and two more flying Lancasters in the maritime reconnaissance role, as well as photographic reconnaissance and air/sea rescue units and a squadron of AOP Austers. In order to give some of the essential protection on the ground against increasingly bold and effective Jewish terrorists, there were also two Wings of the RAF Regiment and some six Regiment squadrons had been deployed. These units played a major part in RAF efforts to contain the deteriorating internal security situation, though they were not enough to prevent the destruction in February 1946 of the Mount Carmel radar station nor, a few days later, raids by terrorists on three RAF bases which managed to blow up eleven of the Halifax aircraft, seven Spitfires and two Avro Ansons.

Once it became clear that the British Government was no longer prepared to act as a policeman in this intercommunal feud, the role of the RAF units in Palestine became one of offering what protection it could to the Army as it engaged in the delicate task of withdrawal. As time went on the remnants of the Halifax squadrons were evacuated to the Canal Zone, from where they continued to give support and training to the 6th Airborne Division, while the Lancasters were withdrawn to Malta and two of the fighter squadrons redeployed to Nicosia.

The date for the ending of the British mandate had been set for 30 June 1948, and as it drew nearer the British forces gradually evacuated the country in the face of increasing terrorist activity both from Jews and Arabs. In the final stages of the British withdrawal two fighter squadrons were left to give protection to convoys and to facilities such as water and oil pipelines, while the Lancaster squadrons maintained their maritime patrols so as to monitor and if possible prevent the arrival of shiploads of Jewish immigrants. When the final evacuation took place it was covered by four Spitfires that had all by now redeployed to Nicosia; with that, the unhappy finale to the long RAF association with Palestine was over. It had not been a notable campaign in the history of the Royal Air Force, but the contribution

made in these impossible circumstances both by the patrolling maritime reconnaissance aircraft and particularly by the dedicated efforts of the considerable force of RAF Regiment units in protecting convoys, airfields and other facilities should not go unremarked.

In another rearrangement of the dispositions inherited from the war, Britain reluctantly agreed in 1946 to withdraw her forces from Egypt proper, deciding to concentrate them in the Suez Canal Zone. This became a garrison of very considerable size: by late 1947, for example, there were no fewer than 65,151 Army personnel and 14,218 officers and men of the Royal Air Force in camps along the Canal. Deployed on airfields in the Zone were three squadrons of Tempest fighters, making a total of 48 aircraft, five small squadrons of Dakota transports with 40 aircraft between them, one squadron of FR Spitfires, one of Mosquitos in the PR role and one more of Mosquitos in the night fighter role.

Further from the scene of growing crisis between the Arab states and the newly formed Israel, the RAF had at its disposal sixteen Vampires in Malta and 32 Spitfires in Cyprus. As the situation developed, a squadron of these Spitfires was called forward to the Canal Zone in January 1949, in time to take part in several aerial engagements between Israeli forces on the one side and Anglo-Egyptian units on the other. All but one of these combats were minor affairs. But then on 7 January 1949 one Spitfire was lost to AA fire and the other three in the same reconnaissance mission were shot down by Israeli Spitfires. Six more Spitfires set out to locate the missing aircraft, covered by fifteen Tempests, and in the confusion of the ensuing engagement, largely caused by the fact that the Israeli Spitfires were virtually identical in all respects to those of the RAF, a Royal Air Force Tempest was shot down by the Israelis. The affair served to emphasize the difficult position in which the RAF units found themselves, but fortunately the hostilities between Israel and Egypt soon afterwards came to an end and the RAF Command, by now renamed Middle East Air Force, was able to revert to a less warlike posture.

Nevertheless the potential for further trouble remained throughout the area, and the operational capability of the squadrons in the Canal Zone was as a result heightened during the following year. A mix of Lancasters and Mosquitos was deployed for long-range reconnaissance duties and the combat capability of the force was strengthened by re-equipping four fighter squadrons with Vampire FB.5s. By the end of 1951 the RAF force in the Canal Zone had grown to fourteen squadrons, with a front-line strength of 152 aircraft. This

Left: A Beverley on an up-country airstrip during operations in Arabia during 1963. (RAFM)

represented the bulk of the MEAF squadrons. Of the other five squadrons in the theatre as a whole, one was in Aden and four more were based in Malta.

Apart from the squadrons stationed in the Canal Zone and the reinforcements available in theatre, frequent detachments of aircraft from the United Kingdom took place. Many of them were engaged in bombing practice, and in 1953 two Lincolns were diverted from this exercise take part in operations against the Mau Mau in Kenya. A state of emergency had been declared in that colony in October 1952 and Hastings transports, supplemented by charter aircraft, had brought reinforcements in for the small garrison. To give air support to the ground forces now deploying, North American Harvards from the Rhodesian Air Training Group, by this time preparing to disband, were armed with machine guns and 20lb bombs. When this effort turned out to have little effect in the dense bush, and when it was realized that the two Lincoln bombers had made a useful impact against the terrorists, a permanent detachment of six of these aircraft was set up at Eastleigh, Nairobi. Together with a pair of Meteor PR.10s from the Canal Zone, eight Harvards, two Austers, a Pembroke and a Sycamore helicopter, these bombers formed No 1340 Flight, a unit that operated against the Mau Mau until June 1955, when the last Lincoln bombing sorties took place. Although the operation against the Mau Mau had been a very minor campaign from the point of view of the RAF, it had been one of the more successful colonial campaigns; and although the aircraft concerned had been designed and deployed for quite different roles, they had proved to be a very valuable adjunct to the internal security forces on the ground.

Meanwhile the earlier move into the Canal Zone of the British forces in Egypt had done nothing to reduce

the level of tension in that area, and the security situation around the British Canal Zone facilities gradually became even more serious. At the end of 1953 it was therefore decided to move out of the Canal Zone and to make Cyprus the main British base in the Middle East. A certain amount of redeployment had already begun with the move of No 683 Squadron's Lancasters and No 6 Squadron's Vampires to Habbaniya during 1952, and this was followed during 1954 by the redeployment of No 249 Squadron's Vampires to Amman. With the Zone so denuded, it was logical to pull out HQ MEAF itself, and in this same year the headquarters was relocated in Cyprus, leaving No 205 Group as the local headquarters in the Zone.

During the following year No 32 Squadron took its Vampires to Malta, where the night fighter Mosquitos of No 39 Squadron joined them, while the Valettas of No 70 Squadron went to Nicosia. In early 1956 there were more redeployments to Cyprus. No 13 Squadron with PR Mosquitos, No 84 (renumbered from No 204) with Valettas, No 114 with the same aircraft type and finally No 208 Squadron equipped with Meteor FR.9s all relocated on the island. The other three squadrons were disbanded, and the remaining RAF facilities in the Canal Zone were progressively handed over to the Egyptians. By April 1956 No 205 Group had disbanded and the last units had gone.

All this led to predictable overcrowding at Nicosia, and the construction of a major new airfield at Akrotiri had begun. By January 1956 a single runway was ready for use, and work was concentrated on the extensive infrastructure that was to serve the RAF at this very large facility right up to the present time. The provision of this base was a timely development. In the year 1956 there was a succession of crises throughout the Middle East, resulting in the airfields at Nicosia and Akrotiri being used at various times to receive British troops and reinforcement squadrons ready to intervene as trouble broke out at various times during that year in Jordan, Iraq and Cyprus itself.

The permanent redeployments to Cyprus from the Canal Zone that had meanwhile taken place were now matched in the spring of 1956 by a change in the command structure of MEAF. AHQ Levant, which had been at Habbaniya, transferred to Cyprus and was made responsible for the RAF units in the northern tier of countries, i.e. Cyprus, Iraq, Jordan and Libya. At the same time a new type of overseas command, a Unified Command, was established in Aden with responsibility for all units in Aden itself, in the Persian Gulf, on the South Arabian Coast and in East Africa. The air element of this command was Air Forces Arabian Peninsula, a title that was retained until March 1961 when the unified command became Middle East Command, and the air force element was renamed Air Forces Middle East.

SUEZ

Later in the same year, 1956, the generally unsettled state of affairs in the Middle East lurched into serious crisis when, on 26 July, and only six weeks after the last British forces had been withdrawn from the Zone, Nasser abrogated the Canal Agreement and nationalized the waterway. Britain and France, the two countries most closely affected by this move, now began to prepare plans for military intervention in what became Operation

'Musketeer'. The ground forces eventually made available to General Keightley, the Allied commander, included a British contingent of a parachute brigade group, one infantry division, another of armour and a brigade of Royal Marine Commandos. The French contributed one airborne division and a mechanized division.

At the start of the crisis there had been only a very modest RAF presence in Cyprus, the obvious base from which to operate most of the air elements that would be engaged. This force was made up of one squadron of Venoms (No 6) and two of PR Meteors at Akrotiri (Nos 13 and 208), and another squadron of Venoms (No 73) together with three of transport aircraft (No 70 with Hastings and Nos 84 and 114 with Valettas) at Nicosia. At the end of the next three months, as the Allied forces gradually assembled, there would be a total of 426 Allied land-based aircraft in the central and eastern Mediterranean. The Royal Air Force deployment was made up as follows: at Akrotiri, 49 Venoms from Nos 6, 8 and 249 Squadrons; at Nicosia, 62 Canberras from Nos 10, 15, 18, 27, 44, 61, and 139 Squadrons, together with 24 Hunters of Nos 1 and 34 Squadrons, eight Meteor NF.13s of No 13 Squadron (which was in the process of re-equipping with Canberra PR.7s), 31 Valettas and sixteen Hastings transport aircraft; and at Luqa and Hal Far in Malta, 29 Canberras of Nos 9, 12, 101 and 109

Below: Canberras lined up at Hal Far, Malta, ready to take part in the Suez expedition of 1956. (AHB)

Squadrons together with 24 Valiant bombers of Nos 138, 148, 207 and 214 Squadrons.

Neither of the two RAF airfields in Cyprus was suited to an operation of this size: Akrotiri was still under construction and Nicosia was in the process of being modernized. A third airfield, Tymbou, used by some of the French transports, was merely a dilapidated satellite of Nicosia. With so many aircraft crowded into Cyprus, one of the main concerns of the commanders was the possibility of a pre-emptive air attack on them by the Egyptian Air Force. The strength of this air force was reasonably well-known from photographic reconnaissance to comprise 80 MiG-15s, 45 Il-28 bombers, 25 Meteors, 57 Vampires and about 200 assorted training and transport types. On paper at least, this was a force to be reckoned with. Not only did the Egyptian inventory include MiGs of a type that had given such an unpleasant surprise to the UN air forces in Korea only three years earlier, but the Egyptians had gained recent combat experience against the Israelis. As it turned out, the Egyptians had lost a number of their best aircraft in training accidents, few of their air crew had yet reached an operational standard on the Soviet aircraft types and most of their pilots were found to lack aggression in the air.

The Allied air plan for the campaign had three parts. First, it was essential to gain air superiority, and the target for the initial strikes would therefore be the Egyptian Air Force. The second phase would be directed against military and other installations with the aim of disrupting the Egyptian capacity for coordinated resistance — in other words, this was the controversial concept of breaking the Egyptian will to resist by means of an extended air bombardment. Third, the Allied air forces would then concentrate their efforts on direct air support for the amphibious and airborne landings that were to take place on 5 November 1956.

Phase I of the air operations began in the afternoon of 31 October when Canberras and Valiants attacked four of the seven major Egyptian airfields, among them Almaza and Inchas near Cairo and Abu Sueir and Kabrit in the Canal Zone, these last being airfields only recently vacated by some of the units now ranged against them. The raids continued during the next day, with carrier-borne aircraft of the Royal Navy taking part together with Venoms from Akrotiri and French attack aircraft. That night the attacks were followed up by 64 Canberras and Valiants, which between them dropped over four hundred 1,000lb bombs on four Egyptian airfields, including the large one at Cairo West.

This seemed highly satisfactory; but the bombing attacks proved not to have been successful in putting the Egyptian airfields out of action. The bombing had been inaccurate, giving average errors of as much as 1,000yds by the Valiants, aircraft which had not yet received their intended bomb-sights and whose crews had not fully worked up on these new aircraft. Not only that, but the available bombing effort had perforce been spread over too many targets to put any one of them out of commission. As to the enemy aircraft, although some sixty had been destroyed on the ground, most of the rest had fled south to airfields out of range of the Allied attacks and they took no further part in the conflict. It was clear that, had the opposition been more determined, the Egyptians could have continued to fly against the Allied squadrons and might have inflicted many casualties.

Phase II of the air campaign opened on 3 November with attacks on military installations and armed reconnaissance sorties designed to prevent the movement forward of Egyptian troops. Cairo Radio was also attacked, as was the railway marshalling yard at Nfisha; but by now international opinion against the whole operation in Egypt was hardening and the original intention to extend Phase II into a psychological campaign of air attacks was abandoned. Instead, instructions were given that the raids were in future to be confined strictly to military targets. By the third day of the air raids it had become clear that even this limitation would not satisfy the growing international criticism generated by the air attacks, and operations were now restricted to military movements in the Canal Zone itself. After 4 November the use of bombers in any of the air operations was halted.

On 5 November the Allied landings began under conditions of total air superiority, and Allied air action was directed against the modest Egyptian resistance on the ground, using the 'cab rank' techniques developed towards the end of the Second World War. Valetta transports were used to fly signals units into Gamil airfield once it was secured. By the evening of the following day, Allied units had reached a point 23 miles south of Port Said; but at that stage of the operation orders were received from London that a cease-fire was to take effect from midnight on 6 November and informing the Anglo-French commanders that a UN force was being dispatched to take over the Allied positions.

Although the whole venture was disastrously misconceived in the political sense, militarily it had been a very brief but highly successful campaign. Now that it was over, the RAF squadrons dispersed to their various bases. Gamil airfield was kept open as a logistic base during the withdrawal of the Allied force, but when that base was handed over to the UN forces on 20 December it marked the end of the Suez expedition and it was the final act in the long involvement in Egypt by the Royal Air Force.

OMAN AND ADEN

After Suez, the build-up of the RAF base in Cyprus continued, and the timing of this redeployment proved to be fortuitous. There had been serious disturbances in Iraq for some time, and even a re-negotiation in May 1955 of the original treaty of 1930 giving Britain the use of military facilities in the country had not fully resolved matters. With the airfield at Akrotiri now becoming a major base, it was therefore agreed that the RAF stations at Habbaniya and Shaiba should revert to Iraq. The Royal Air Force was to train an Iraqi Air Force, and the RAF would retain certain small facilities, but the two Venom squadrons at Habbaniya, Nos 6 and 73, would be withdrawn by the middle of 1958. Even this compromise was, however, soon overtaken by events. In July 1958 the King of Iraq was assassinated, a revolutionary Government was installed and RAF aircraft were forbidden to use what had by then become only a staging post at Habbaniya. This was too much, and that Royal Air Force station finally closed in May 1959, thus ending a connection with Iraq that had lasted for more than forty years.

At Akrotiri, meanwhile, the completion of the extensive facilities had made it possible to base four Canberra strike squadrons there (Nos 6, 32, 73 and 249), together with No 13 Squadron's four Canberra PR.7s. These units were Britain's contribution to the Baghdad Pact, renamed the Central Treaty Organization in 1959 after the Iraqi Government withdrew, and these squadrons formed the only bomber force at the disposal of the treaty powers, Turkey, Iran and Pakistan. Clearly, it was important that Britain maintain this commitment, and during 1969 the Canberras were replaced by Nos 9 and 35 Squadrons equipped with Vulcan B Mk 2s, aircraft that offered a better night and all-weather capability in the bomber role. Two additional squadrons of Vulcans were declared to CENTO but held back in the United Kingdom to avoid the expense of providing even more facilities at Akrotiri.

In 1965 No 13 Squadron redeployed to Malta, leaving a squadron of transport aircraft, one of fighters and another of helicopters to complete the establishment at Akrotiri. At various times the fighter squadron was a resident unit in what had now become the Near East Air Force, but at others it was provided on a rotational basis by Fighter Command. In January 1975 the international scene in the Middle East had shifted once again and the British Government decided that the time had come to end its CENTO commitment. All the squadrons at Akrotiri except the helicopters were withdrawn, the airfield being retained only as the destination for many armament practice camps or routine overseas detachments and, more significantly, as a mounting base for contingencies in the eastern Mediterranean. In April 1976 NEAF itself was disbanded, to be replaced by AHQ Cyprus, forming a part of RAF Strike Command, and finally, in 1977 and 1978, the two squadrons still in Malta, No 13 with Canberra PR.7s and PR.9s, and No 203 with Nimrods, withdrew in turn. Apart from the modest presence in Cyprus, together with the station at Gibraltar and an RAF detachment at the NATO airfield of Sigonella in Sardinia, the long history of the Royal Air Force in the Mediterranean had, for the time being, come to an end.

Trouble in another Middle East area, this time in Oman on the Persian Gulf, had meanwhile started in a small way during 1952 and it was to continue on and off until 1959. There had long been a border dispute between Oman and Saudi Arabia, and the generally unsettled nature of the area eventually led to a confrontation near the Buraimi oasis in August 1952. Acting together with the ground forces involved, Lincolns, Vampires and Ansons were used in aggressive demonstrations from the air and in reconnaissance work, until the Saudis were compelled to capitulate and agree to being flown home. Minor operations followed against rebels in central Oman during 1957, involving among other things attacks on fortified towers in six villages occupied by natives seeking to overthrow the Sultan of Muscat. Warning leaflets were dropped before the walls of the towers were subjected to rocket attacks by Venoms of Nos 8 and 249 Squadrons in an employment of air power that bore remarkable similarities to the operations by the Royal Air Force in that same region three decades earlier. Sporadic outbreaks of fighting had also taken place further to the west in the Aden Protectorate from 1947 onwards, and air operations on a small scale had been necessary from time to time in that area. During 1954 military incursions from neighbouring Yemen led to a short period of more intense air activity by Lincolns and Vampires, repeated the following year when a punitive expedition had to be launched into the interior, supported again by air action.

In 1956 the Suez Crisis had led to a much more

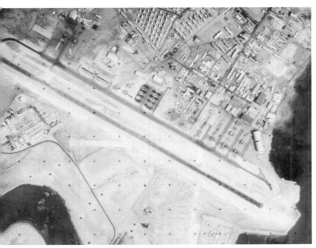

Top: Habbaniya airfield in 1955. (JARIC)

Above: Khormaksar airfield in 1967.(JARIC).

hostile attitude among many Arabs in the Aden area, and at the same time the more widespread anti-British feeling throughout the Middle East meant that it was no longer possible to provide rapid reinforcement for Aden or for the Gulf. The only solution was to have stronger forces stationed in Aden, and the Royal Air Force presence was therefore gradually increased from the 1955 level of a single Venom squadron and a communications unit to a force of six squadrons holding a total of 48 front-line aircraft by the end of 1961. Together with the many other units at Khormaksar at this time, not least the RAF Regiment squadrons, the station soon became one of the busiest and most complex in the whole of the Service.

That same year, 1961, Iraq renewed a long-standing claim to the territory of Kuwait and in June she began to move troops towards her border with that country. Britain was committed to defend the independence of Kuwait, and when the latter asked for

support a contingency plan was put into force. Under this plan four days' notice was assumed, a period that should have allowed the necessary transport aircraft to be positioned ready to lift troops into Kuwait from Cyprus and Kenya. The plan also incorporated the move of two squadrons of Hunters from Aden in the air defence role, a force of Canberras from Cyprus and Germany to undertake interdiction missions and Shackletons from Aden for reconnaissance and bombing tasks. HMS *Bulwark* was fortuitously in the Indian Ocean at this time, and she set sail for Kuwait. She had No 42 Commando embarked, and these seasoned troops were thus available to secure the airfield at Kuwait for the Hunter squadrons, which meanwhile deployed forward to Bahrain as a precaution.

When the contingency plan was activated serious complications at once arose. First, the assumed four days' notice was not given; and second, Turkey and the Sudan refused to give clearance for any overflights. Five Britannias that should have flown to Cyprus to uplift a parachute battalion from that island direct to the Gulf were therefore diverted to Aden via Nairobi, and there took on board No 45 Commando to fly these troops into Kuwait to support No 42 Commando, which had disembarked there on 1 July.

By now the whole transport plan was in disarray, but by 4 July, and as the result of a great deal of improvisation, the maximum number of RAF transport aircraft had been positioned where they were most needed. It was a sizeable force. On the strategic route, and using Bahrain as the main terminal in the Gulf, there were fourteen Britannias, 27 Hastings and twelve Beverleys from Transport Command, augmented by three Canadairs on loan from the Royal Rhodesian Air Force and two Argonauts chartered from East African Airways. From the resources of Middle East Command, twelve Beverleys and six Valettas were engaged mainly in lifting troops forward from Bahrain to Kuwait, where the two Hunter squadrons were by this time taking up a good share of the limited space on the airfield. This same shortage of suitable operating bases caused the twelve Canberras from Germany, four B(I).8s of No 88 Squadron and eight B(I).6s of No 213 Squadron, to deploy to Sharjah, where the lack of a hard-surface runway soon led to considerable operating problems.

Once the airlift was fully under way it was possible to move not only the Commando from Aden but also 24 Brigade from Kenya and 2 Para from Cyprus, as well as further reinforcements from the United Kingdom. By 9 July a total of 5,691 personnel and many hundreds of tons of stores had arrived in Kuwait, and in conditions of extreme heat and discomfort the deployments were completed. By the middle of July the crisis had subsided, and if Iraq had indeed intended to invade, that danger was judged to be over. For the next few months two battalions of infantry together with units of other arms remained in Kuwait while the bulk of the ground forces were withdrawn from 20 July onwards. No 8 Squadron also stayed behind, as did some Twin Pioneers, while twelve Beverleys and detachments of Canberra PR aircraft and Shackletons remained at readiness in Bahrain. Gradually all the British forces were withdrawn from Kuwait, but the British presence in the Gulf was maintained by temporarily building up the scale of the forces deployed in Bahrain.

Not a shot had been fired during the whole Kuwait operation, and the expenditure of so much effort in containing a crisis of dubious severity drew considerable criticism at home. But that was to be wise after the event, and the operation had at least done two things. First, it had shown the effectiveness of a long-range airlift conducted under several unexpected difficulties; and second, it had confirmed the existence of the 'air barrier' across the Middle East, a factor with which the Royal Air Force would henceforth have to deal if the routes to the east were to mean anything at all.

Meanwhile in Aden the internal security position grew steadily worse after a *coup* in Yemen during 1962, and this brought the forces of Arab nationalism right up to the borders of the colony. A state of emergency was declared in December 1963, and operations began in earnest in the Radfan. Two sizeable operations by ground and air forces were launched into the Radfan in January 1964 and in May, with Hunters providing direct fire support and Shackletons dropping bombs and flares while Belvederes, Twin Pioneers, Wessex helicopters of the Royal Navy and aircraft of the Army Air Corps all made their contribution in the field of logistic support. Terrorism in Aden itself was by now becoming a serious threat to military facilities, and particularly to aircraft on the ground at Khormaksar. As many Hunters as reasonably possible were therefore kept on detachment in the Gulf, but in 1966 the British Government announced that Aden would be granted independence in 1968. At this confirmation that the security forces would withdraw, the dissidents increased the level of their activities and fighting continued. Eventually the date for the British withdrawal was brought forward to November 1967. Service families were evacuated from May of that year onwards at a rate of about two hundred women and children each day, until all 6,605 were gradually brought home.

As many facilities in Aden as possible were dismantled and huge quantities of stores were moved out by sea during the middle of the year, while aircraft units that could be spared from the colony were moved out of Khormaksar or earmarked for disbandment. Those moved out included the few Argosys of No 105 Squadron and the Hunters of No 8 Squadron, a unit that had been in Aden for forty years and had flown on active operations somewhere in the Command on virtually every day of its tenure. No 37 Squadron with its four Shackletons was disbanded, but the Hunter FGA.9s of No 43 Squadron and the FR.10s of No 1417 Flight remained for the time being, and indeed continued on operations. No fewer than 142 operational sorties were flown by the Hunters during September alone. Both units later disbanded, No 43 Squadron only temporarily before being re-formed in the United Kingdom, the Hunter aircraft being redistributed to Nos 8 and 208 Squadrons in the Gulf. No 84 Squadron moved its Beverleys to Sharjah, and later exchanged them for Andovers, while No 78 Squadron with its Wessex helicopters also withdrew eventually to Sharjah.

In the final stage of the withdrawal a massive airlift lasting seven days took place. Apart from the locally based transport force of Argosys and Beverleys, this operation was carried out by three RAF VC10s, augmented by three more on charter, fourteen Britannias, two Belfasts and, for the first time in any demanding role, fifteen Hercules — an aircraft that had been in service with the Royal Air Force for only a few weeks. The plan was that all the personnel except the Royal Marine Commandos and a few Royal Navy servicemen remaining for the last and most difficult part of the whole withdrawal operation would leave by air — some 3,700 men.

In each of the seven days that this airlift lasted, four Britannias would fly in to Khormaksar from Muharraq, stay on the ground for only about forty minutes and take off with 110 passengers. Seven Hercules would arrive to take a mixture of passengers and freight, while two flights by the Belfast transports would load up with freight only. After landing at Muharraq, the troops were fed and then transferred to VC10s or Britannias for the onward flight to the United Kingdom. On the penultimate day of the operation about 1,000 servicemen and 350 civilians were flown out of Aden by twenty transport movements, and on the final day, 29 November 1967, 875 men were airlifted out, with about as many again being transferred to ships of the Royal Navy by RN helicopters. Not a shot was fired, nor a life lost.

The withdrawal from Aden by no means marked

Above: A Hunter FGA.9 of No 43 Squadron over the terrain north of Aden in the 1960s. (AHB)

the end of Britain's commitments in other parts of Arabia, and the RAF station at Bahrain was now chosen as the main base in the area. After December 1963, and in deference to local sensibilities, this airfield had been renamed RAF Muharraq. From now on Nos 8 and 208 Squadrons of Hunters from Aden were normally based there, while No 84 Squadron with Andovers and No 78 with Wessex helicopters were stationed at Sharjah or at what was then the minor staging post at Masira. These were the final years of the long RAF involvement in the Gulf, and although quiet in the operational sense they were nonetheless active years for the units involved. Muharraq became a very busy staging post, particularly during the Confrontation with Indonesia, and the resident squadrons in the Gulf area were engaged in their usual heavy training schedule. But Britain was anxious to leave the security of the area in the hands of indigenous forces so that the British units could leave by the end of 1971, and the final run-down began early that year. The squadrons were pulled out, and both Muharraq and Sharjah closed in the middle of December of that year. Only the airfield on Masira island and the forward landing strip at Salala were retained. Masira not only acted still as a staging post en route to Gan and the Far

East, but it had also become the rear base both for the minor British base at Salala further west along the coast of Oman and for the small British forces supporting Omani units that were engaged in a low-intensity but long drawn out war along the western borders of that country.

THE FALKLANDS WAR

After the withdrawals from the Far and Middle East, and with the exception of the bases in Cyprus, Malta, Gibraltar, Hong Kong and Belize, the efforts of the Royal Air Force now leaned towards Europe and tended to concentrate on the many exercises connected directly or indirectly with the commitment to NATO. These included such valuable detachments as the 'Red Flag' series, using the USAF weapons ranges at Nellis Air Force Base, and operational exercises in Canada known as 'Maple Flag'.

Some consideration was given to what were known as 'out of area' operations, that is, deployments out of the NATO area, but after the withdrawals from the turbulent Middle East it was widely assumed that the days of British military involvement outside Europe were finally over. It was therefore something of a shock to conventional defence thinking when, on 2 April 1982, Argentine forces seized the Falkland Islands in a sudden *coup de main.* In response, a swiftly assembled South Atlantic Task Force set sail from Portsmouth on 5 April, including HMS *Hermes* with a force of Royal Naval Sea Harrier FRS Mk 1s embarked. Among the Sea Harrier force were seven pilots drawn from the Royal Air Force, who were on exchange duties with their sister Service.

Although the contribution by the Royal Air Force to this essentially maritime and amphibious operation was comparatively modest, it was also highly significant. A great deal of hasty improvisation was undertaken in the United Kingdom by the Service and by industry in order to provide an effective response to the Argentine aggression, the first tangible result of which was a series of four bombing attacks on the airfield at Port Stanley, 8,000 miles from their base in the United Kingdom, by Vulcan bombers. Five Vulcans, aircraft that were only three months away from the date when they were due to be scrapped after 25 years of service, had been hastily modified for operations in the South Atlantic. ECM jammers and missiles were fitted on the mainplane points originally intended for Skybolt, the long neglected nose-probe and airborne refuelling system were refurbished, and five crews were given brief training in refuelling and in conventional bombing. On 29 April two of the Vulcans deployed to Wideawake airfield on Ascension Island, roughly half way to the South Atlantic. Then, just before midnight on 30 April, these two aircraft, carrying twenty-one 1,000lb bombs each and overweight by about 6,000lb, took off from Ascension accompanied by a first wave of Victor K Mk 2 tankers. One Vulcan was obliged to turn back with a pressurization failure but the other headed south and was refuelled along the way six times. When about 300 miles from the Falklands the Vulcan descended to 250ft above the sea so as to be below the cover of Argentine radar on the islands. As it approached Port Stanley airfield the aircraft pulled up to 10,000ft before releasing its stick of bombs. One bomb landed in the middle of the runway, causing moderate damage and bringing a temporary halt to the use of the airfield by the Argentinian aircraft busy ferrying reinforcements and supplies into Stanley. The Vulcan then made its way back to Ascension, refuelling five more times and landing safely after more than sixteen hours in the air.

The raid failed to close the airfield, but it had two important effects. First, it served notice on the invaders that they were not immune from long-range air attack. Second, although not realized at the time, it was also seen by the Argentines as a clear indication that Buenos Aires itself was vulnerable. This caused them to redeploy their leading fighter squadron away from its position on the mainland opposite the Falklands to a base near Buenos

Aires more than 1,000 miles to the north. This redeployment was almost certainly crucial to the success of British efforts to gain vital air superiority over the area of operations. Similar long-range bombing attacks were made on 4 May and 11 June and sorties were also flown by a Vulcan against radar installations using AGM-45A Shrike anti-radar homing missiles.

The refuelling task for these long-range attacks was a mammoth one. At times over 70 per cent of the combined strength of Nos 55 and 57 Squadrons (Victors) was deployed on Wideawake. Fourteen sorties by ten tankers were necessary to put each Vulcan over the Falklands, with tankers refuelling each other as well as the Vulcan bomber, in order to make sure that the refuelling slots could be met. Attempts at reconnaissance over South Georgia and the Falklands by Victors using equipment taken from recently withdrawn Vulcan B Mk 2(MRR) maritime surveillance aircraft were less than wholly successful. But these aircraft came into their own once more when it became necessary to provide air-to-air refuelling for the Nimrods and Hercules taking part in the operations. All told, the Victor tankers flew nearly 600 sorties during the campaign, amassing some 3,000 flying hours in the process.

While the Task Force was making its way south, No 1 Squadron of the Royal Air Force at Wittering, the only operational Harrier unit based in the United Kingdom, had been practising ski-jump take-offs and carrier landings at RNAS Yeovilton. The aircraft were cleared to carry Sidewinder missiles as well as the 2in rocket projectiles used by the Royal Navy, and the pilots were given simulated air combat experience against French Mirages and Super Etendards, aircraft types which were known to be in the Argentine inventory.

Hawker Siddeley Harrier

From 1952 onwards, the Vampire FB.5 was replaced by the Venom, which in turn gave way to the Hawker Hunter FGA.9. Then, in July 1969, the revolutionary Harrier began to take over the role of close air support, though with the drastic reduction in the size of the front line during the late 1950s and 1960s it did so in very much smaller numbers. More advanced versions of the original Harrier GR.1 were introduced during the following years, these culminating in the current GR.5 aircraft with a greatly improved performance. It can carry up to 8,000lb of weapons on its six wing points and single fuselage point; this centre position can alternatively be fitted with two podded Aden cannon.

Once more the services of the Victor tankers were called upon, this time to give air-to-air refuelling to the first wave of nine Harrier GR Mk 3s as they flew the nine-hour leg from the United Kingdom to Wideawake, where six of them embarked on the container ship *Atlantic Conveyor* for the passage south. Five more Harriers followed to Ascension later, four of them remaining there in the air defence role. The six Harriers on board *Atlantic Conveyer* transferred to HMS *Hermes* on 18 and 19 May and on the 20th they launched their first attack mission, on a fuel dump at Fox Bay. The difficulties of operating from the overcrowded carrier were eased from early June when an 800ft landing strip was prepared within the perimeter of the initial disembarkation area at San Carlos. This move meant that more substantial air support was available for the 10,000 or so troops who were now consolidating their position on shore and preparing to advance across the main island.

Out of the 1,500 or so Harrier sorties flown during the whole campaign, about 125 were carried out by the RAF aircraft in attacks on key ground targets. This small contribution was, however vital, since it made it possible for the Sea Harriers to concentrate virtually all their efforts on the one role of overriding importance to the success of the whole expedition —air superiority. In this role, the Harriers claimed over twenty 'kills' against Argentinian aircraft, losing eight of their own number during the conflict, five of them to ground fire but none of them in air-to-air combat. Three of these losses were GR Mk 3s of the RAF contingent.

Wideawake airfield became a very busy air-head from the day after the Argentinian invasion, when eight Hercules, the first of a constant flow of air movements, arrived with stores for the southward-bound Task Force to collect as it reached that half-way point. The Hercules of Nos 24, 30, 47, and 70 Squadrons from Lyneham were soon joined by the VC10s of No 10 Squadron and by civilian Boeing 707s on charter. Under the same arrangements the ex-RAF Short Belfasts of the private company HeavyLift were also engaged in the airlift. During the course of the campaign this comprehensive airlift was responsible for bringing to Ascension Island 5,500 passengers, 7,000 tons of supplies, almost 100 vehicles and more than twenty helicopters in operations that absorbed some 17,000 flying hours.

In another innovation during Operation 'Corporate', the range of the Hercules aircraft was extended by fitting air-to-air refuelling probes, making possible long-range drops of vital items to the ships of the Task Force as it sailed the 4,000 miles south from Ascension. Because of the speed difference between the

BAe Nimrod MR.I

From 1951 the role of maritime patrol was taken over by the Avro Shackleton, a derivative of the Lincoln bomber and itself a successor to the Lancaster. But in October 1969 a very significant step forward in the maritime role was taken when the first Nimrods were delivered to the Service. The first two prototypes were conversions from the de Havilland Comet airliner, and all the production models that followed clearly show the same design origin. Powered by four Rolls-Royce Spey turbofans each delivering 12,160lb of static thrust, the Nimrod Mk I could, typically, transit about 1,000 miles to its patrol area at a maximum speed of 575mph and remain on station for four hours. Its warload was made up of homing torpedoes, depth charges and sonobouys and it could also carry air-to-surface missiles on wing pylons. The Mk 2 currently in service has an even better performance.

Victor tankers and the Hercules, in-flight refuelling was not an easy manoeuvre. The only way in which it could be carried out was to put the Hercules into a steep descent to gain speed and then refuel on the way down. This rather alarming drill could be abandoned once some of the Hercules, designated C Mk 1Ks, emerged in early August from a rapid modification programme. This work had given the aircraft four long-range fuel tanks in the hold, refuelling hoses leading out through sealed rear doors and a nose probe mounted above the flight deck. Sixteen cargo-carrying Hercules, known as C Mk 1Ps, were modified into the 'receiver only' mode, and of these some were further modified to take an extra fuel tank in the hold which added up to 900 miles to the range of the basic aircraft. It was one of these aircraft that set up what was then an endurance record for the Hercules, with a total continuous flight time during an operational mission of 28 hours. Throughout the whole operation for the reconquest of the Falklands, the transport force was vital to its success. Great ingenuity had been shown by air crews, by ground crews and by many civilian contractors to make sure that this unexpected task was carried out efficiently.

An important but little-heralded part was played in the campaign by Nimrod aircraft flying anti-submarine patrols and maritime reconnaissance missions. In the early stages these tasks were carried out by No 42 Squadron, but urgent modifications were meanwhile being carried out on the aircraft of No 206 Squadron to fit them with a nose refuelling probe, a version then designated Nimrod MR Mk 2P. This gave the aircraft an endurance of up to nineteen hours, a performance that

Left: A Chinook
medium-lift helicopter.
(DPR/RAF)

later made it possible for the Nimrod to fly surveillance missions over waters near the Falklands. These were intended to give a surface plot of shipping in the area, though there were times when an inability actually to identify the ships caused confusion. During the campaign the Nimrods were fitted with Sidewinder air-to-air missiles for self defence and they were also given an attack capability in addition to their anti-submarine equipment, a role for which Stingray torpedoes were carried. Later the Nimrods were again modified, this time to take the AGM-84A Harpoon anti-ship missile. As it turned out, none of these weapons saw action; but it was vital that the otherwise unarmed Nimrods were prepared for the worst in the uncertain conditions of the campaign.

Helicopters of the Royal Navy were prominent during all phases of the operation, and five Chinooks of No 18 Squadron were also dispatched with the Task Force in order to provide a heavy lift capability. One of them remained at Ascension for duties there, but three of the four sent south were lost when *Atlantic Conveyor* was sunk on 25 May by an Exocet missile. The surviving machine went on to perform remarkable feats in the Falklands, lifting a total of 1,530 troops, 600 tons of cargo and 650 Argentine prisoners during a single month.

Many other detachments drawn from the Royal Air Force took part in this brief campaign, not least No 63 Squadron of the RAF Regiment which deployed from Gütersloh to the San Carlos beach-head to provide a measure of anti-aircraft protection with its Rapier missiles. Tactical supply personnel were included in the Task Force, as were medical staff and bomb disposal experts. These latter were particularly in demand once the Argentinian forces had surrendered on 15 June. Over the months and years that followed, the British forces on the Islands were gradually reduced in strength until, by 1991, there was a garrison of about 2,000 men and women of all ranks. A new airfield was built at Mount Pleasant, into which reinforcements could be swiftly flown in the event of a future crisis; and meanwhile the British forces stationed on the islands include various units of the Royal Air Force, much of the whole military presence being sustained by regular transport flights from the United Kingdom.

CHAPTER 12

UNEASY PEACE

As we have seen, during the decade after the Second World War the destinies of the Royal Air Force had been shaped first by a massive contraction to peacetime strength and then by economic pressures on the national budget, by new technologies and by the gradual onset of the Cold War. These last three had combined by 1957 to produce an emphasis in British strategy on the nuclear deterrent, represented by the V-bombers of the Royal Air Force; and while nuclear and aeronautical technologies had together made the V-Force possible, the need to conserve national resources, including manpower, had helped to make its introduction necessary. The transfer of responsibility for nuclear

Below: HRH Prince Charles receives his 'wings' from Air Chief Marshal Sir Denis Spotswood, the Chief of Air Staff, at Cranwell, 20 August 1971. (Commandant, RAF College, Cranwell)

deterrence from the V-Force to the Royal Navy in mid-1969 was a major change in British defence policy, and by coincidence it was followed by a fundamental shift in the defence posture of the NATO alliance in November of that same year.

COMMAND RESTRUCTURING

Ever since the first Soviet deployments of nuclear weapons, there had been doubts about a NATO strategy that relied upon the early use of such weapons in the event of a conventional attack by the forces of the Warsaw Pact. This unease grew over the years, particularly in the mid-1960s when the Soviet Union began to field much larger numbers of inter-continental ballistic missiles; and, from that time on, what had been a clear preponderance of US nuclear strength gradually became something closer to a strategic nuclear balance. Far more attention than before was therefore given to the possibility that, if a major war broke out, it might be fought, at least in its early stages, with conventional weapons. The result was the adoption by NATO in late 1967 of the doctrine of Flexibility in Response, and for the Royal Air Force this meant a new emphasis on conventional capabilities while retaining the theatre nuclear option. For the V-Force in particular, it meant that the Vulcans of Strike Command, hitherto committed to NATO only in the nuclear role, were now also put at the disposal of SACEUR in the conventional role.

Other profound changes were also by this time in train for the higher organization of the Royal Air Force. In 1963 Air Vice-Marshal Spotswood, later to become Chief of the Air Staff, had been appointed to carry out a study into the long-term future of the Royal Air Force. One important result was that all the aircraft of the RAF in the United Kingdom, as well as a number of Headquarters, were brought together in two new Commands, Strike Command and Air Support Command. The old Bomber and Fighter Commands were stood down on 30 April 1968, and merged to form Strike Command; in November of the following year

Coastal Command and Signals Command were similarly absorbed, and by the end of the year Strike Command, with its Headquarters at High Wycombe, was made up of six Groups. These were No 1 Group, with the V-Force, maritime strike force and the air-to-air refuelling force; No 11 Group, responsible for the Lightning and Phantom interceptors as well as the Bloodhound SAMs, the Ballistic Missile Early Warning station at Fylingdales and all the associated air defence radars, communications and other related infrastructure; No 18 Group, responsible for anti-submarine air warfare, maritime reconnaissance and Search and Rescue; No 90 Signals Group; the Central Reconnaissance Establishment, which controlled the UK-based strategic reconnaissance force; and finally the Military Air Traffic Organization (MATO).

Air Support Command replaced the old Transport Command in August 1967, but it was itself then absorbed into Strike Command during September 1972 in the form of two Groups, No 38 Group, which contained the UK-based offensive support squadrons and helicopters, and No 46 Group, controlling the twelve squadrons of strategic and tactical transport aircraft of the Royal Air Force. By 1975 these two Groups between them held a force of 227 aircraft — 60 offensive support fighter/ground attack aircraft, 50 strategic transports, 65 tactical transports and 52 helicopters. Maintenance Command was renamed Support Command in September 1973; and then, to complete what turned out after all the upheavals of the previous decades to be a more permanent command structure between Ministry of Defence level and the stations of the Royal Air Force, on 12 June 1977 a new RAF Support Command was formed at Brampton, combining Support (formerly Maintenance) Command and Training Command.

Those changes in the higher command structure of the Royal Air Force had begun at a time when the whole of Britain's defence needs were under review. In October 1964 a Labour Government had come to office with the very reasonable conviction that military strength had little justification if it were achieved at the cost of economic strength, and a far-reaching examination of national defence commitments was therefore undertaken. The outcome was the publication of a Defence White Paper in February 1966 which, apart from the cancellation of very important several aircraft projects at that time and two months later, reduced the British presence in the Mediterranean and unexpectedly announced the intention to withdraw from South Arabia and Aden in 1968, a date subsequently brought forward to late November 1967. Then in the face of financial pressures, in July 1967 a Supplementary Statement on Defence Policy was issued laying out (among other decisions) a Government intention to withdraw all British forces from Singapore and Malaya within the next few years, a decision that also of course called into question the value of the staging posts on the route to the Far East. In January the following year this pattern of retrenchment was further continued with a Government announcement of sweeping defence cuts, including not only the cancellation of the fifty F-111 aircraft ordered from the United States but also stating a firm intention to withdraw British forces from the Far East and the Gulf by December 1971.

In parallel with these reduced national commitments outside Europe and the inevitable consequential reduction in the strength of the armed forces as a whole, other and more subtle changes had meanwhile been taking place in the ethos of service in the Royal Air Force. The RAF had inherited from its origins in the Navy and particularly from its roots in the Army, a number of domestic features that were increasingly out of tune with contemporary civilian life, a fact that became of great importance once it was announced in 1957 that there would be no call-up for National Service (i.e. no conscription) after 1960. In a now little-remembered venture, what was known as the Benson Experiment was therefore launched at that station in 1954 to examine what improvements might be introduced to do away with some of the more time-wasting and irritating barnacles that had for so long clung to peacetime life in the Royal Air Force. The outcome of this experiment and other initiatives at the time was that by 1957 there had been a great improvement in the day-to-day routine of all ranks. Working Parades, which had customarily been held at the start of each weekday, were done away with. Pay Parades, in which all junior ranks paraded in strict alphabetical order once a fortnight to receive their pay in cash from their section or flight commander, were similarly done away with. Fire Piquets were abolished, as were the time-honoured practice of booking in and out of camp for junior ranks and several other time-wasting customs.

NEW TRANSPORT AIRCRAFT

The major changes during the 1950s and 1960s in the higher organization of the Service, in its size, in its commitments and in the daily life on its stations, were accompanied from the mid-1960s by a far-reaching programme of aircraft re-equipment. To deal with the transport force first, this element of the RAF had, in response to strategic imperatives, begun a significant expansion in March 1956 with the introduction into service of the Comet and the Beverley aircraft, which in that month began to re-equip Nos 216 and 47 Squadrons respectively. Until that time both the strategic and the tactical transport functions had been carried out by the Handley Page Hastings, a long-range transport capable of lifting 50 troops and a machine that had first appeared on No 47 Squadron at Dishforth in late 1948. The RAF Comets were modified versions of the civilian Series 2 machines, ten of which were delivered to No 216 Squadron while another three each went to Nos 51 and 192 Squadrons for special duties. They represented a remarkable improvement in the capabilities of Transport Command. Forty-four passengers could be carried in each, and, for example, the 10,500 miles from their base at Lyneham to Adelaide in South Australia could be covered in just over 38 hours' elapsed time, including less than 28 hours of airborne time, while the round trip to the testing ground for the atomic bomb on Christmas Island could be flown in under four days. A further valuable improvement in this Force came with the arrival in February 1962 of the first Comet C.4, a stretched version with more powerful engines and the ability to carry 94 passengers. This aircraft remained in service until the end of June 1975.

In somewhat stark contrast to the sleek lines and high speed of the Comet, the box-like Blackburn Beverley first appeared on an operational flight line with No 47 Squadron at Abingdon in March 1957. Though possessing a cruising speed of only 173mph at 8,000ft and a radius of action limited to 230 miles with full load, the Beverley proved to be a very useful tactical transport. It could take a payload of almost 22 tons in its cavernous hold, or it could lift 94 troops, and it could drop heavy loads through the rear fuselage, the huge doors being dismountable for this purpose. Even more valuable was the aircraft's short-field performance: it could take-off in 810yds and land in 350, attributes which proved to be invaluable in operations such as those in the deserts of the Aden Protectorate during the early 1960s. Forty-seven Beverleys were delivered to the Royal Air Force, and the type remained in service until December 1968.

Once the Comets entered service the Hastings were relegated to the tactical role alongside the Beverleys, thus bringing a new emphasis to the different requirements of the two types of military transport capabilities, tactical and strategic. It was a division that was reinforced in 1959 when the first of the Bristol Britannias arrived in No 99 Squadron during April of that year. This machine, like the Comet, was also a military version of a civil

aircraft designed for passenger-carrying, and its ability to lift up to 113 troops or 53 stretcher cases made it a very important aircraft on the strategic routes. A total of 23 Britannias eventually entered service, so that by the end of 1960 these aircraft, together with the Comet force, gave the RAF a total of 33 long-range transports. Meanwhile the tactical force consisted of sixteen Beverleys and 28 Hastings.

A considerable boost to the strategic transport force was given by the arrival of the first of the new Belfasts and VC10s, which began to equip Nos 53 and 10 Squadrons respectively in January and July 1966. The Belfast was to survive in service for just over ten years before the entire force of ten machines fell victim to yet another round of defence cuts in 1976; but in the meantime the Belfast brought to the Royal Air Force a very valuable heavy lift capability. Its vast hold, with a capacity of 10,000 cubic feet, could accommodate 150 troops, or a Chieftain tank, or two Wessex helicopters or ten Land-Rovers and trailers. It is a neat irony that the Service has been obliged on several occasions since 1976 to hire back these aircraft from the civilian contractor who purchased them.

Fourteen VC10s were taken into service altogether, the RAF version of this civil airliner design being modified to include uprated Conway powerplants, a side-loading freight door, strengthened floors and a flight-refuelling probe, along with several other less important changes. One hundred and fifty passengers or 76 stretcher cases together with six medical attendants can be carried by the aircraft, and, with transit stops at Muharraq and Gan, VC10s were soon operating a service to Singapore that took just under 20 hours — 12 hours faster than that provided by the Britannias.

In 1960, and looking to the next generation of aircraft, a new Operational Requirement for an advanced tactical transport was issued under OR381, which specified a medium-range, short take-off and landing freighter able to lift a 35,000lb payload. A long ferry range was also demanded, the intention being that the aircraft would be able to deploy over strategic ranges and then give tactical support to Harriers in the field. The most promising of several proposals to meet this requirement was the Hawker Siddeley 681, a four-engine aircraft but also, in one of the projected versions, fitted with auxiliary engines so as to give a vertical take-off capability. Difficulties arose over the choice of engines, leading to considerable delays in the project, so that by the time a new Labour Government came into office in October 1964 this very ambitious Hawker Siddeley (confusingly renamed Whitworth-Gloster, and then

Avro-Whitworth!) 621 project was still in limbo and thus a prime candidate for cancellation, a fate that duly befell it in February the following year. At the same time it was announced that the Royal Air Force would receive the Lockheed Hercules C-130 transport aircraft in its place, a well-proven and robust machine that had entered service with the US Air Force eight years earlier, in late 1956.

There were two other tactical transports in the pipeline for the Royal Air Force by this stage, the Hawker Siddeley Andover to replace the Beverley and the Argosy from the same stable to take over from the Hastings. Entirely new demands were, however, placed upon the transport force with the start of the Indonesian Confrontation in late 1962, almost coinciding with the arrival of the first Argosys in service, so that instead of replacing the Hastings as intended, the Argosys operated alongside them; indeed, the Hastings were still operating in the transport role as late as 1967.

Like the other main transport types, the Argosy was developed from a civil aircraft, and it proved to be a valuable machine in service. A wide range of military equipment could be carried, facilitated by 'crocodile-jaw' rear doors and the high twin-boom fuselage, which gave easy access. As an alternative load, 69 fully equipped troops could be accommodated in the Argosy, and the aircraft's tactical capabilities included a good rough-field and a valuable short-field performance. It was an aircraft that gave very useful service for some nine years until, again as the result of pressures on the defence budget, it was gradually withdrawn in the early 1970s. The other new tactical transport, the Andover C Mk 1, was a military version of the Avro 748 civil aircraft, and this machine entered service with the RAF in July 1966 with No 46 Squadron at Abingdon. At the end of that same year the Andover was issued to No 52 Squadron at Seletar and in August the following year it also replaced the Beverleys of No 84 Squadron at Khormaksar. Altogether, 31 of the type were taken on inventory. Its service was, however, cut short by the defence retrenchments of 1975, when a decision was made in favour of retaining the more capacious Lockheed Hercules, and the Andover was withdrawn. A second version of the Andover, the CC Mk 2, was introduced and retained for the purely passenger-carrying role in communication flights, and in particular with the Queen's Flight, where three of these aircraft gave reliable service until they were replaced by three BAe 146 CC Mk 2 Statesman, four-engine turbofan-powered machines, during 1989.

Starting with No 36 Squadron, the first Hercules aircraft, known to the RAF as the Hercules C Mk 1, had

Lockheed Hercules C.I/C.3

Although intended primarily for tactical transport operations, the Hercules is noteworthy for its versatility, which includes extensive employment on strategic routes. In both roles, as in many others including air-to-air tanking, the Hercules has proved to be a remarkably successful aircraft. It can carry a payload of about 44,000lb and it has a maximum cruising speed of 325kts.

joined the transport fleet on 1 August 1967. This was followed by further deliveries until 66 of these excellent machines had been accepted, four squadrons of them based in the UK and one at Changi, Singapore. Thirteen Hercules were later withdrawn from the front line as part of the defence cuts of 1975, and another squadron was removed the following year, leaving a force of 48 aircraft on strength. The Hercules was conceived as long ago as 1951, when the USAF decided to re-equip its transport force with turboprop machines. It was designed as a medium-range tactical transport with a capacity for 92 troops or 64 paratroops, or 75 stretcher casualties together with two medical personnel. Starting in 1978, the capacity of the RAF Hercules force was considerably enhanced when thirty of the machines were modified by Marshalls of Cambridge by inserting two 'plugs' into the fuselage. One was placed forward of the mainplane and one aft, extending the length of the aircraft by 13ft 4in and thus giving these C Mk 3s, as they are known, a

capacity for longer loads and greater weight and a 40 per cent increase in total payload — a truly remarkable example of versatile adaptability in an original aircraft design.

Constant demands were placed upon the transport assets of the Royal Air Force in the years following the Second World War. These fell into four broad categories: first, regular services along the strategic routes to distant stations such as those in the Far East, a task that took on a much greater importance once the traditional movement of service personnel and their families by troopship was abandoned in December 1962; second, the deployment of substantial British forces on exercise, one example of which was seen in Exercise 'Bersatu Pardu' during April 1970 when 2,265 passengers, over 750 tons of cargo, 350 vehicles and twenty helicopters were deployed from the United Kingdom to Malaysia; third, what are best described as 'surge' operations, such as the Berlin Airlift and the evacuation from Aden, when all available resources are brought in for a period of very intensive activity; and fourth, the very many humanitarian operations over the years, as well as the implementation of many emergency evacuation and other plans and countless disaster relief operations in virtually all corners of the world.

In this brief account, it will perhaps serve as an indication of the extent of these relief missions to say that they have ranged from supply-dropping to famine-stricken natives in Kenya and Somalia during 1961, through Pakistan flood relief flights during 1970, supply dropping in Mali during 1973 and the hazardous

Westland Dragonfly

Although there had been a number of RAF experiments with rotary-wing aircraft, the Dragonfly was the first machine of this type to enter operational service, which it did in 1950 during the Malayan Emergency. The aircraft had only a very modest performance. Flying in its common role of casualty evacuation, the Dragonfly could take only one stretcher patient in a vertical take-off, and then fly for thirty minutes at 60kts. Nevertheless it broke new ground and showed the value of the concept of rotary-wing flight for the Royal Air Force.

evacuation of nearly 1,500 British and friendly nationals during the Indo-Pakistan war of 1971, to the 'Khana Cascade' supply drops to villagers in Nepal during 1973 (incidentally the largest airlift operation at that time since the Berlin Airlift) and similar operations in Colombia, Ethiopia and Yugoslavia, among very many other laudable efforts great and small by the RAF transport force.

HELICOPTER PROCUREMENT

Alongside the story of these fixed-wing transport aircraft of the Royal Air Force must be put the achievements of the helicopter force. The first really effective transport helicopter for the Royal Air Force was the Westland Wessex HC Mk 2, a twin-engine version of the naval machine and one that entered RAF service in February 1964 with No 18 Squadron. Seventy-five of these aircraft were eventually delivered to equip the helicopter support squadrons in the field. A specially finished and internally equipped version of the Wessex was introduced for the Royal Flight at Benson, two of these aircraft being delivered to that unit in April 1969.

RAF helicopters have also for many years provided an invaluable and highly effective search and rescue force around the British Isles. A Westland-built version of the Sikorsky S-55, the Whirlwind HAR.2, was delivered to the RAF for communications and search and rescue duties from 1955 onwards, some 60 being taken on inventory up until 1957. Another thirty of the Mk 4 version, modified for high-temperature and high-altitude operations, were delivered between 1954 and 1956. No 22 Squadron based at Thorney Island became the first search and rescue unit in February 1955, and it added to its Whirlwinds with Wessex helicopters in 1976. No 202 Squadron formed at Leconfield in 1964, also with Whirlwinds, and this unit then added Westland Sea

Left: The workhorse of the RAF Transport Force is the Lockheed C-130 Hercules, known informally to the Royal Air Force as 'Fat Albert'. (DPR/RAF)

Kings to its inventory in 1978. This was a much more advanced machine, and sixteen of them were purchased to replace the obsolescent Whirlwinds which were finally withdrawn in 1981 after giving valuable service for 26 years.

Gradually the helicopter SAR flights took over altogether from the marine craft which had for so long served the Royal Air Force in these duties. There had been seaplane tenders, pinnaces and bomb scows on the inventory of the Service ever since the earliest days of flying boats. Later they were joined by high-speed launches, and eventually during the Battle of Britain the comprehensive search and rescue organization mentioned in an earlier chapter was set up under the control of Coastal Command. Together with the RNLI, the coastguards and Post Office Radio Stations, the marine craft of the RAF and the specialist flying units, usually operating Supermarine Walruses, were responsible for saving many lives both in home waters and abroad. In January 1986 the remaining air/sea rescue craft were handed over to civilian contractors, the Marine Craft Branch was disbanded and the Service responsibility for SAR was left with eight RAF/RN Sea King and four RAF Wessex helicopter Flights.

One of the gaps in the Royal Air Force's capabilities during the 1960s and 1970s, particularly when considering the needs of the British Army in the field, was that of a heavy lift helicopter. All that was available was the Wessex, which could carry a 4,000lb slung load. Some improvement had been offered after September 1961 with the advent of the Westland Belvedere, a machine that could lift 5,250lb of slung load or 6,000lb of freight internally. This capability in the Belvedere was found to be of considerable tactical use during operations in the Radfan as well as throughout the Brunei Campaign of 1962–66, where among other duties the aircraft proved adept at rapidly redeploying underslung 105mm howitzers for the hard-pressed British artillery units. The Belvedere saw service with three squadrons, No 26 in Aden, No 72 in Transport Command and No 66 Squadron initially at Odiham, where it was the first squadron to receive the Belvedere in 1961, and subsequently in the Far East, where this unit took part in the Indonesian Confrontation. For reasons that were never fully determined (though poor engineering support certainly played a part), the success of the Belvederes in Arabia was not matched by a similar performance in the Far East. After carrying out useful work during 1964, the helicopters of No 26 Squadron developed a reputation for unreliability, and after three of the seven Belvederes had suffered catastrophic crashes

the remaining four were transferred to FEAF. No 26 Squadron was disbanded in November 1965, and after serving for another four years in the Far East all the remaining Belvederes were withdrawn when No 66 Squadron disbanded at Seletar in March 1969.

But the fact was that, compared with the capacity of other helicopters that had by this time been developed by the aviation industry in, for example, the United States and the Soviet Union, the load-carrying capacity both of the Wessex and of the Belvedere was very modest. On several occasions during the 1960s and 1970s proposals had been put forward in the Ministry of Defence to procure a heavy-lift helicopter, but these ambitions had fallen victim to the constant pressures for economies in defence spending programmes, with the RAF not unnaturally tending to give a higher priority to its front-line fixed-wing combat aircraft. This picture changed in early 1978 when a decision was at last made to order 30 (later increased to 33 and then to a total of 41) of the Boeing-Vertol CH-47 Chinook. This was a helicopter

Boeing-Vertol Chinook

The need in the Royal Air Force for a medium-lift helicopter had long been recognized but the type originally chosen, the Westland Belvedere, was less than wholly successful and it served only from 1961 until 1969. Other priorities and several defence cuts then intervened, and it was not until ten years later that a firm order was placed for another machine to take on the medium-lift role, the Chinook. This tandem-rotor twin-engine helicopter can carry up to 45 fully equipped troops or a variety of other loads up to a maximum of ten tonnes. Fitted with internal fuel tanks for long-range ferry deployments, the Chinook has a range of 1,000nm.

that had first flown as long ago as September 1961, but since that time it had given sterling service to the US Army as well as to the forces of several other countries. In the version procured for the Royal Air Force, the Chinook HC Mk 1, the helicopter can carry up to 55 troops or 24 stretchers. A rear loading ramp can be left open in flight or removed altogether to permit the carriage of extra long loads or to allow the free-fall delivery of cargo and equipment. Alternatively, and using under-fuselage hooks, the aircraft is capable of lifting up to 28,000lb, or more than five times as much as the earlier support helicopters in service. In 1989 a mid-life update programme was started by Boeing for the RAF which raises the 35 machines on the inventory to HC Mk 1B standard, with modifications that include a new automatic flight control system and a reinforced airframe. The first Chinooks for the Royal Air Force joined the front line with No 18 Squadron at Odiham in February 1982, and the squadron redeployed to Gütersloh in support of No 1(BR) Corps in NATO's Northern Army Group during May the following year.

These same years also saw the arrival of new equipment in the combat squadrons of the Service. The changes in the strategic and tactical bomber forces have already been discussed, and there was a parallel move forward in No 18 (Maritime) Group of Strike Command in October 1969 when the first Nimrod MR Mk 1 arrived on No 236 Operational Training Unit at St Mawgan. Between 1965 and early 1971 the maritime force had been reduced from eight to four squadrons, each with six Avro Shackleton aircraft, machines that owed much of their design to the era of the Second World War, retaining several features of the Lincoln and thus of the Lancaster. The Shackleton was the last piston-engine aircraft to see front-line service with the Royal Air Force.

The Nimrod represented a new generation of maritime capability. It is a much modified version of the de Havilland Comet airliner and an aircraft well able to meet the specification for a Shackleton replacement, requiring principally a fast transit speed to an operating area 1,000 miles from base, an ability to remain on station at low level for at least four hours while carrying a substantial weapons load and a performance consistent with the existing maritime airfields of Strike Command. These parameters were exceeded by a handsome margin: the Nimrod offered a time on station of more than six hours at a range of 1,150 miles. The first Nimrod MR.1 to join the front line arrived with No 201 Squadron at Kinloss in the summer of 1970 and a total of forty-six aircraft was eventually delivered, including three examples designated Nimrod R.1 which replaced Comets of No 51 Squadron, engaged on special electronic warfare and reconnaissance duties. In its main role, that of maritime reconnaissance and anti-submarine warfare, the Nimrod is a remarkably successful machine.

THE TSR.2 FIASCO

Brief mention has already been made of the aircraft projects that were cancelled in 1966, and these will now be dealt with in more detail. The most important of these cancellations was the demise announced in the Budget Speech of April that year of the intended Canberra replacement, the TSR.2. This decision caused a hiatus in the Tactical Strike and Reconnaissance capability of the Royal Air Force and helps to explain the direction that the procurement of RAF combat aircraft, tactical and interceptor, took for many years that followed. TSR.2 was designed to meet Operational Requirement OR343 of 1958. This was an exceptionally complex and

Above left: For more than four decades after the war, air/sea rescue launches of the RAF maintained their readiness. Here such a boat is seen off Newhaven on 24 September 1958. (AHB)

Right: The ill-fated TSR.2. (BAe)

demanding requirement that called for speeds of up to Mach 1.1 at very low level and more than Mach 2 at medium height, as well as a radius of action of 1,000 nautical miles on internal fuel and a ground roll of not more than 550m when taking off from rough airstrips. The aircraft was to incorporate a fully automatic navigation system capable of giving an accuracy of 0.3 per cent of distance flown, it would carry a sideways looking radar that would automatically update the system computer and it would be fitted with an automatic terrain following radar. In addition, the aircraft was to have a low gust response so as to minimize crew fatigue, a long structural life and a high thrust to weight ratio. It was, in other words, to be an aircraft able to carry out all roles from long-range nuclear strike, through all types of reconnaissance to close air support, and it was to combine all that with a performance better than that of the very advanced Lightning, whose first experimental prototype had carried out its maiden flight only four years earlier. Development contracts were issued during the second half of 1959 to the British Aircraft Corporation for the aircraft itself, and to Bristol Siddeley for the engines.

As design work went on, it became clear that the extreme demands of the Operational Requirement were making the TSR.2 a very expensive weapons system, and in mid-1962 the design was 'frozen', with the future performance of the aircraft estimated at that stage to be Mach 1.1 at sea level and Mach 2.05 at altitude, with a radius of action of 1,000 miles and a rough field capability requiring a take-off roll of between 915 and 1,370m. To facilitate operations from tactical airstrips of the kind intended, three special-to-type wheeled vehicles were designed for TSR.2, all of which helped to add further to the rising costs. Those increases were compounded by a heavy and complex management structure for the whole project, and the efforts of this bureaucracy had the inevitable effect of slowing down overall progress. By January 1963 the cost of research and development alone had risen to an estimated £175–200 million (£1.7 to £1.9 billion at 1992 prices) and the in-service date had slipped back to 1968.

In December 1963 one of the new Olympus engines intended for the TSR.2, fitted to a Vulcan for air tests, exploded at Filton while the aircraft was taxying, and despite a great deal of remedial effort two more engines exploded in May and July of the following year. (Much later it was found that the cause was a condition in the powerplant known as 'bell-mode', in which at a certain speed of rotation the engine shaft resonates like a bell and eventually disintegrates under the stresses so induced.) These incidents caused further delays. By this time

TSR.2 had become a target for the Labour opposition in Parliament, and more pressure was put on to the project when a strong Australian interest in TSR.2 was deflected by the Chief of Defence Staff, Lord Mountbatten, who, it seems, told the Australians that he doubted whether TSR.2 would ever enter service. He favoured the Buccaneer as the replacement for the Canberra.

The development of the aircraft continued, however, and the first TSR.2 flew on 27 September 1964. There was then a delay of three months before the second flight, partly because of problems with the undercarriage and partly because the engines were found to deliver less than their specified power. The construction of twenty pre-production TSR.2s had meanwhile continued, and long-lead items were still being purchased; but the growing expense of the project together with the costs of two other aircraft in the pipeline at the time, the HS 681 transport and the P.1154 vertical take-off fighter, were too much for the Labour Government that took office at the end of 1964 and the cancellation of all three projects followed in early 1965.

When the proposed purchase of US General Dynamics F-111 was in turn cancelled, and an Anglo-French variable geometry aircraft project was also abandoned, the Royal Air Force was obliged after all to

---

Blackburn Buccaneer

In the role of maritime attack, Beauforts were followed into service by Mk X Beaufighters, and these aircraft remained in the front line until 1950. In the years just after the Second World War, however, the commitment passed increasingly to the Royal Navy. A very notable naval aircraft that was then specifically designed for these missions was the Blackburn Buccaneer, the first of which joined front-line squadrons of the Royal Navy in mid-1962 with the role of long-range strike/attack at high speed and low level. In 1978 six decades of fixed-wing operations by the Royal Navy were for the time being ended with the decommissioning of the last aircraft carrier, HMS Ark Royal. The naval Phantoms and the Buccaneers were then transferred to the Royal Air Force, the Buccaneers to fill the gap in capability left by the cancellation of the F-111K and by the demise of the Anglo-French Variable Geometry aircraft. Fifty Buccaneers were transferred to the Royal Air Force and another forty-two were built specially for the Service. The Buccaneer has a remarkably rugged construction — the mainplane, for example, is machined out of solid castings — and the aircraft was thus ideally suited for the roles of very low level strike/attack or target-marking with lasers, in which the Royal Air Force employed it. The maximum speed of the aircraft is 645mph at 250ft and its radius of action in a hi-lo-hi mission profile is almost 600 miles.

Right: The Mach 2 Lightning entered service in 1960. The aircraft shown here is an F.6, introduced in 1965. (BAe)

accept the Hawker Siddeley Buccaneer. Forty-two of these aircraft were built for the Service, and about another sixty were taken over from the Royal Navy once HMS *Ark Royal* paid off in December 1978. In October 1969 the first Buccaneers arrived on No 12 Squadron at Honington, and exactly a year later No XV Squadron re-equipped with them before deploying to Laarbruch in January 1971. No 16 Squadron then followed with Buccaneers at Laarbruch, and Nos 208 and 216 formed at Honington in July 1974. Nos 12 and 216 Squadrons moved to Lossiemouth in July 1980 so as to be able better to carry out their maritime strike role, but in that same year serious fatigue problems were found on many of the aircraft, as a result of which the force had to shed a number of the aircraft, leading in turn to the disbandment of No 216 Squadron.

AIR DEFENCE EQUIPMENT

Five years before the TSR.2 fiasco, more steady progress had started in another Royal Air Force operational role with the arrival of the first Lightning F.1 interceptor in No 74 Squadron at Coltishall in July 1960. As has already been explained, in one of its many grave misjudgments, the Defence White Paper of April 1957 had intended that the future manned fighter force in the United Kingdom would not only be a small one, limited in role to the defence of the V-bomber airfields, but that fighter aircraft would in due course be entirely replaced by a ground-to-air guided missile system. Fortunately for the continuity of the United Kingdom's air defences, the Lightning was such an advance on previous interceptors that it was able to discharge the fighter role until it was joined in service by the McDonnell Phantom in

September 1969. Thereafter the Lightning remained in service for another nineteen years, by which time the air defence variant of the Tornado was well established in the front line.

Tests with the prototypes of the English Electric P.1A (it was named 'Lightning' only in October 1958), had begun on 4 August 1954, to be followed soon afterwards by the P.1B on which the first production models were based. Powered by its twin Rolls-Royce Avon 200 series engines, mounted unusually as a superimposed pair, one of the P.1B prototypes became on 25 November 1958 the first British aircraft to fly at twice the speed of sound. An initial batch of fifty of these aircraft was ordered by the RAF in November 1956 to meet Air Ministry Specification F23/49, and the Central Fighter Establishment at Coltishall took delivery of the very first Lightning F.1 in the Service during December 1959.

Quite apart from its very high speed, (more than twice that of the Hunter) and a ceiling of 60,000ft, the Lightning offered a performance that brought Fighter Command into a new era. It was the first RAF single-seat fighter to be designed as an integrated weapons system rather than as a gun platform, and it was fitted with a Ferranti AI (Air Interception) radar, allowing the pilot to search above and below the horizon for his target. An automatic `lock on' gear then tracked the target while corrections were given from processed radar information, enabling the pilot to close to missile firing range. At that stage missile homing heads automatically locked on to the target and the pilot was given a signal when the firing parameters had been met.

Other variants of the original F.1 followed in succeeding years. The F.1A, which joined No 56

Squadron in December 1960, had a number of minor internal changes, and it was also fitted with a probe for in-flight refuelling. More than sixty F.2s then followed, joining Nos 19 and 92 Squadrons at Leconfield in 1963 before redeploying to Germany in late 1966. This was an interim version of the Lightning, and it brought more minor internal modifications but also a fully variable re-heat and more advanced all-weather flying aids. Thirty models of the Mk 2 were later modified to accept either the much larger ventral fuel tank that had been designed for the Mk 6, or a ventral pack that incorporated both a fuel tank and twin Aden 30mm cannon. This variant was designated the Mk 2A.

In 1962 the Mk 3 Lightning appeared, a version powered by Avon 301 series turbojets, each developing 16,360lb of thrust with re-heat as opposed to the 14,430lb re-heat performance of the earlier Avon engines. There was provision in this aircraft for Red Top missiles as an alternative to Firestreaks, the two Aden cannon fitted to earlier models were deleted and two overwing long-range fuel tanks could be fitted to give the Lightning for the first time a useful ferrying capability. Externally the Mk 3 also differed from its predecessors in having a larger, square-tipped tail fin. Three squadrons received the Mk 3, No 74 at Leuchars in April 1964, followed by No 23 at the same airfield and No 111 at Wattisham.

Two years after the Lightning Mk 3 entered service it was followed by a development known first as the Mk 3A and finally as the Mk 6. This variant first entered service with No 5 Squadron at Binbrook in November 1956 and went on to equip four other units of Fighter Command, Nos 11, 23, 56 and 74 Squadrons, this last squadron also serving from June 1967 in the air defence

role at Tengah before disbanding there in August 1971. The Mk 6 had double the fuel capacity of the early models and a modified mainplane that incorporated an extended chord outboard so as to give better manoeuvrability at high altitudes. All home-based Mk 3 aircraft were retrofitted to this new standard. Finally, the two-seat trainer version, the Lightning T.4 must be mentioned, an aircraft with the attributes of the F.1A but with the forward fuselage widened to take two pilots side by side, though in very cramped conditions. This variant, equipped with duplicated attack sights and radar scopes for operational training, arrived on squadrons from 1961 onwards. The T.5 was the two-seat equivalent of the F.3.

When the Hawker P.1154 was cancelled in 1964 another gap had been opened in the future capabilities of the Royal Air Force, and to fill it a decision was made to purchase the McDonnell Phantom, a fighter that had entered service in its original version with the US Navy in 1960. Complications arose when it was decided at the political level in Whitehall to fit Rolls-Royce Spey engines to this American aircraft, and the cost escalated to over £3 million (£27 million at 1992 values) for each aircraft, a level well above and beyond the original estimates. Nevertheless the RAF/RN Phantom proved to be a very effective aircraft, and two versions entered service. Forty-eight FG.1 interceptors were delivered, 28 of them to the Royal Navy, as well as 118 of the FGR.2 ground attack and reconnaissance model. The first FGR.2s reached No 6 Squadron in May 1969, and the FG.1s began to equip No 43 Squadron in September of the same year. Five years later, with the Phantoms well settled in, the Lightning began to be phased out, until by the end of the 1970s only two squadrons, Nos 5 and 11 of

Left: A Phantom of No 92 Squadron fires its cannon in a simulated attack. (RAF Staff College)

the Binbrook Wing, remained. These last examples of the popular and highly effective Lightning were finally withdrawn in June 1988, thus ending the operational history of the only purely British supersonic combat aircraft. From July 1970 Phantom FGR.2s also began to replace the Canberras at Bruggen, until there were four squadrons of them at that base, Nos 2, 14, 17 and 31. Four years later, once the SEPECAT Jaguar entered service in the ground attack and reconnaissance role from March 1974 with the re-formation of No 54 Squadron at Lossiemouth, the Phantom FGR.2s began to be transferred to the pure interceptor role, starting with No 111 Squadron at Coningsby in July 1974.

One of the principal concerns of No 11 Group of Strike Command during these years, apart from the possibility of heavy air attack across Denmark and the North Sea in the event of a major war in Europe, was the Soviet use of long-range reconnaissance aircraft to probe the northern reaches of United Kingdom airspace. By the mid 1960s these incursions by Tu-95 'Bear' aircraft had brought a new urgency to air defence capabilities, in particular the importance of RAF interceptors being able to turn away these intruders at ranges that would inhibit their intelligence-gathering activities. Another and even more serious potential air threat emerging at this time was that posed by Soviet bombers based in the area of the Kola peninsula. These aircraft had the capability to fire air-to-ground cruise missiles against targets in the United Kingdom from launching areas hundreds of miles to the north and north-west of the British Isles. One of the main Soviet types concerned was the Tu-26 'Backfire', a swing-wing medium bomber normally armed with two AS-4 'Kitchen' supersonic air-to-surface missiles with a range of about 300km. Another was the late version of the Tu-25 'Bear' bomber, the 'Bear-H'. This aircraft could carry as many as ten cruise missiles, including the AS-15 'Kent' and the AS-X19. In 1988 the Soviet Union added to its inventory the Tu-160 'Blackjack' aircraft, a long-range supersonic strategic bomber designed to carry twelve AS-16 'Kickback' short-range cruise missiles or six AS-15s or AS-X19s. These were very serious potential threats indeed.

Since it was virtually impossible to intercept missiles of the kind carried by the Soviet bombers, particularly since these aircraft had a multiple launch capability, it was essential to intercept the bombers rather than attempt to shoot down the cruise missiles. This too, argued for an interception capability at long range. In the face of these potential threats, the front-line fighter strength of the Royal Air Force was increased to 70 aircraft in 1969, and again to 76 in 1975. Meanwhile

twelve of the long-serving Shackleton Mk 2s were modified for the airborne early warning role in order to support the interceptor force, these old piston-engined aircraft being fitted with surplus radars taken from Royal Navy Gannets that had been withdrawn from service. These Shackleton AEW.2s, as they were designated, were issued to No 8 Squadron at Lossiemouth starting in January 1972. It was a reflection of the age of the original design of these machines, as well as a minor classic of resigned Service humour, that the Shackleton became referred to by Air Force wags as 'ten thousand rivets flying in formation'; while individual aircraft of No 8 Squadron were given names taken from a contemporary children's television programme, among them such gems as P.C. Knapweed, Mr MacHenery and Ermintrude.

As part of the improvement to the whole air defence infrastructure over these years, the 'Rotor Plan' of the early 1950s had been succeeded by a plan known as 'Razor', the second and final stage of which was completed in 1961. Before it was operational, however, it was overtaken by new requirements that led to a more sophisticated system altogether, known this time as 'Plan Ahead', intended to deal not only with supersonic intruders but also to detect incoming ballistic missiles. This system also fell away in turn, to be replaced by the 'Linesman/Mediator' project. This was a plan to integrate civil and military air traffic control, but it proved to be too ambitious, particularly since during the development of the system NATO was moving away from the strategy of massive nuclear retaliation towards the concept of flexible response. This change called into question some of the assumptions on which Linesman/Mediator was to have been based. Eventually, Linesman covered the military requirements and Mediator was left to deal with the civilian ones. Meanwhile the eleven radar sites that had been set up around the British Isles continued in use much as before, until the Defence White Paper of February 1979 announced that work was under way on an improved UKADGE (Air Defence Ground Environment) network. This system incorporates the eleven radar sites that already existed, plus an additional one in south-west England, organized into three key sectors based on the major radar units at Boulmer, Buchan and Neatishead. All twelve stations are equipped with three-dimensional L- and S-band radars and they are linked together with modern communication equipment. The network also includes provision for a number of mobile radar sets to cover gaps in the radar screen, and the nerve centre of the whole air defence network was moved, together with the other operational functions of Strike Command, to a massive underground bunker at High Wycombe.

Finally in the field of air defence, there are the air-to-air refuelling tankers to consider, and although they have a vital role in support of long-range transit flights, they are also the means of maintaining air defence interceptors on station at long range, and it will therefore be convenient to deal with them here. The conversion of Valiants and Victors to the tanker role was mentioned in Chapter 10, and in May 1984 the original force was augmented by the arrival in service, with the re-formed No 101 Squadron at Brize Norton, of four VC10 K Mk 2s. These were originally Super VC10 civilian airliners operated by Gulf Air. Five more VC10s were then purchased from East African Airways, similarly converted and added to the squadron during 1985 and 1986 as VC10 K Mk 3s. Another fourteen surplus Super VC10s were bought from British Airways during 1981, as well as a Gulf Air VC10 in 1982, most of them to be stripped for spares but six to be available for possible later conversion to tankers.

Discussions had taken place between the Service and civilian airlines during 1980 about the possibility of modifying certain airliners to take an air-to-air refuelling fit in the event of a national emergency. Nothing came of the initiative, but the need for an extra capability in this field was convincingly confirmed during the Falklands Conflict of 1982, and partly as a result of that it was decided to acquire six surplus Lockheed TriStars from British Airways, four for conversion to the dual tanker/passenger role (TriStar K Mk 1s), and two for modification to the tanker/freighter role (KC Mk 1s). Three more TriStars were later acquired from Pan Am for conversion and the whole fleet was allocated to No 216 Squadron at Brize Norton. The tanker force had meanwhile been further augmented during 1982 by the modification earlier described of six Hercules C Mk 1s to C Mk 1K standard.

THE TACTICAL ARM

When Air Support Command had been set up in August 1967 it inherited not only the strategic transport assets controlled by No 46 Group but also the tactical transport and ground attack aircraft of No 38 Group, which had originally been formed in 1960 at Odiham. At its start this ground attack force was made up of two squadrons of Hunter FGA Mk 9s, Nos 1 and 54, which were also equipped to provide fighter reconnaissance. This capability was upgraded by three changes beginning in May 1969 when No 6 Squadron joined the force equipped with Phantoms, followed by No 1 Squadron re-

Lockheed TriStar KC.1

This version of the Lockheed L-1011-500 TriStar commercial airliner is notable for its dual role of tanker/freight transport. It can take up to twenty cargo pallets or 196 passengers, and it is equipped for use as an air-to-air refueller. The aircraft cruises at 525mph and, carrying a payload of 50,000lb, it has a range of over 6,000 miles. TriStars entered service with No 216 Squadron in November 1984.

equipping with Harriers two months later and finally No 54 Squadron which exchanged its Hunters for Phantoms in September of that same year. For a time Hunters stayed on as a small detachment at Wittering. But then the new NATO emphasis on conventional warfare meant that ground attack capabilities gained fresh importance, and to build up the necessary expertise two new Hunter squadrons, Nos 45 and 58, formed at Wittering in 1972 and 1973.

A further expansion of the tactical force then took place in March 1974 when Nos 6 and 54 and later No 41 Squadrons re-equipped with Jaguars and deployed at Coltishall. One hundred and sixty-five single-seat and 35 two-seat versions of this aircraft were eventually delivered to the Royal Air Force. Apart from the three squadrons in the United Kingdom, Jaguars also joined the front line in RAF Germany. No 14 Squadron at Bruggen took delivery of the first of these aircraft in the Command, followed by Nos 17, 20 and 31 Squadrons all in the strike/attack role, and by No 2 Squadron at Laarbruch in the role of tactical reconnaissance. In service the Jaguar has proved to be a very useful aircraft, particularly at low level. In the strike/attack fit it is armed with two 30mm cannon and can carry tactical nuclear weapons or up to 10,500lb of ordnance on five external hardpoints, including Martel missiles and 1,000lb bombs. Although a supersonic aircraft, the Jaguar was not designed for high manoeuvrability. When it is fitted with Matra Magic air-to-air missiles on overwing pylons, these are for limited self defence rather than for the fighter or interceptor role.

To return to the higher organization of the Royal Air Force during these years, yet more changes were in train. Air Support Command was absorbed into Strike Command in September 1972; No 46 Group was re-formed to control the 115 aircraft of the tactical and strategic transport fleet; while No 38 Group retained the 52 helicopters and the 60 offensive support aircraft. This arrangement lasted for eleven years, the Hunter

Above: Jaguars took over the ground attack role from the Phantom starting in 1974. These are Jaguars from No 6 Squadron on a low-level training sortie. (BAe)

Above right: Harriers joined the front line over twenty years ago, equipping four squadrons. The GR.3 version, shown here in arctic camouflage refuelling from a VC10, entered service in 1980. (BAe)

squadrons in the interim disbanding and the tactical training responsibility being taken over by Hunters at Lossiemouth and by a mix of Hunters and Hawks at Brawdy, both from July 1978 onwards. In November 1983 No 38 Group was disbanded, its offensive support assets, the three Jaguar squadrons and No 1 Squadron with its Harriers, being transferred to No 1 Group of Strike Command.

The arrival in service of the Harrier on No 1 Squadron in July 1969 had marked the start of a new era in RAF support operations. In its original version the Harrier carried twin 30mm Aden cannon in underbelly pods, together with a variety of external loads on five pylons, giving it a maximum warload of up to 5,000lb. In practice, however, the size of the warload had to be traded off against the demands of range and of short take-offs, often resulting in an operational profile that was less than ideal. The aircraft were therefore modified in service with an uprated Pegasus engine to give a GR.1A standard, later replaced by the Harrier GR.3. This improved version had an even more powerful variant of the Pegasus engine, the 102 turbofan, and the aircraft was also fitted with Ferranti Laser Ranging and Marker Target Seeker equipment. At a later stage, the Harrier squadrons would receive a variant originally developed for the US Marines, known in its operational

version to that corps as the AV-8B and to the RAF as the Harrier GR.5. This aircraft has almost twice the performance of the original Harrier in terms of warload or range, the two characteristics again being traded off one against the other.

With the transfer of the United Kingdom offensive support force of four squadrons to No 1 Group, that formation retained the dual responsibilities that it had assumed from April 1975 onwards when the force was earmarked for assignment to SACEUR but at the same time retained purely national roles. In the former guise, the squadrons were to operate alongside elements of the United States Third Air Force based in the United Kingdom, as part of SACEUR's Strategic Reserve (Air). But the Harrier squadron had an additional NATO task on the flanks of the Alliance with the Allied Command Europe Mobile Force (AMF). At the same time, and in a separate commitment, one of the Jaguar squadrons was allocated to the United Kingdom Mobile Force to operate together with Puma and Chinook helicopters in support of a readiness force of the British Army.

RAF GERMANY

For RAF Germany, the years immediately after the 1957 Defence White Paper brought several changes. In order to help offset the very considerable cost of setting up the V-Force at the end of the 1950s, economies were sought elsewhere, and one consequence was the withdrawal in 1961 of six more front-line squadrons from Royal Air Force Germany, as 2TAF had been re-named in 1959. The airfield at Jever was handed over to the re-formed Luftwaffe and the remaining twelve squadrons were now spread among Gütersloh and the four 'Clutch' airfields. At the same time, the summer of 1961, the very disappointing Supermarine Swifts of Nos 2 and 79 Squadrons were replaced by Hunters.

Meanwhile the first helicopter squadron in RAF Germany, No 230, arrived at Gütersloh in January 1963 equipped with Whirlwinds to offer greater mobility to some of the forward units of the British Army of the Rhine. Two years later this squadron would redeploy to the Far East, to be replaced by No 18 Squadron flying the much more effective Wessex. Then in 1966 the obsolescent Javelins at Geilenkirchen were replaced by the Lightnings of Nos 19 and 92 Squadrons, and later No 92 Squadron moved forward to Gütersloh so as to give this relatively short-range fighter a better endurance when reacting to air incursions from the east over the inner-German border. The Command was thus now made up of twelve squadrons: four of Canberras in the nuclear role and three more for reconnaissance; two of Lightning interceptors; two of Hunter FR.10s; one of Wessex helicopters; and, not included in the total but a very active component of the whole Command, the Communication squadron of seven Pembrokes and the Commander-in-Chief's Valetta, based at Wildenrath.

During 1967 severe pressures on the Defence Budget forced the unwelcome decision to give up one of the five operational airfields in the Command, and in March the following year the substantial base at Geilenkirchen was handed over to the Luftwaffe. This led to the move of the second Lightning squadron, No 19, to Gütersloh and to the redeployment of No 3 Squadron with its Canberra B(I).8s to Laarbruch.

With those changes RAF Germany entered a period of stability, but meanwhile new aircraft types were entering service with the Royal Air Force and preparations were begun to modernize the force in Germany. In 1970 the two Canberra units at Brüggen, Nos 80 and 213 Squadrons, were withdrawn and replaced by Nos 14 and. 17 Squadrons, which had given up their Canberras at Wildenrath and received Phantoms. Nos 15 and 16 Squadrons with Buccaneers deployed to Laarbruch in the nuclear role, replacing the Canberras at that airfield. And, finally, Wildenrath received Nos 4 and 20 Squadrons, equipped with the Harrier GR.1. For RAF Germany as a whole, the arrival of the Harriers in 1970, together with all the other redeployments and reorganization, meant that by the end of 1972 all the squadrons of the Command, with the exception of No 18, had been re-equipped. The force was now made up of four Phantom squadrons, three of Harriers, two of Buccaneers, two of Lightnings and one of Wessexes.

This extensive re-equipment programme in Germany was matched by other measures designed to improve the active and passive defence of the airfields and other facilities in the Command. A squadron of Bloodhound surface-to-air missiles, No 25(SAM), was deployed by Flights to cover Wildenrath, Brüggen and Laarbruch, while in the mid-1970s each of the four airfields in Germany received a squadron of the RAF Regiment equipped with Rapier missiles for close air defence. No 16 (Regiment) Squadron took up station at Wildenrath, No 26 at Laarbruch, No 37 at Brüggen and No 63 at Gütersloh.

Further to improve the survivability of the operational assets of the Command, from 1974 to 1976 a construction programme of Hardened Aircraft Shelters was undertaken at the three 'Clutch' stations, each of these substantial structures being designed to take one and sometimes two aircraft and give protection against all but a direct hit by incoming weapons. At the same time the conspicuously light-coloured buildings which had been such a prominent feature of all the airfields in the Command were painted in drab greens, a process known as 'tone-down' and one that for pilots made an interesting challenge out of visual approaches to the bases in periods of poor visibility.

These changes in RAF Germany were followed during 1975 and 1976 by yet another re-equipment programme, when Nos 14, 17 and 31 Squadrons at Brüggen exchanged their Phantoms for strike/attack Jaguars, to be joined at that base by No 20 Squadron, which gave up its Harriers and also re-equipped with Jaguars. A fifth Phantom squadron, No 2, re-equipped with the reconnaissance version of the Jaguar and took up station at Laarbruch. The Lightnings at Gütersloh were now replaced by Phantom interceptors, and because these aircraft had a far better range and endurance than the Lightning they were deployed back at Wildenrath. This in turn made it possible to deploy the Harriers of Nos 3 and 4 Squadrons to where they should have been all along, on the forward base at Gütersloh alongside the Wessex helicopters of No 18 Squadron.

These Wessex aircraft were to be the subject of the next re-equipment programme in RAF Germany when, in December 1980, No 18 Squadron moved back to Odiham, to be replaced at Gütersloh by No 230 Squadron flying the larger Puma HC Mk1s. Early in 1983, having by then re-equipped with American-built Chinook HC Mk 1s, No 18 Squadron returned to its base at Gütersloh to complete the support force for No 1 BR Corps. The Puma is a helicopter that can lift twenty troops at a time, it cruises at 163mph and it has a range of about 390 miles. The combination of the Puma and the

Right: After the failure of the Anglo-French Variable Geometry aircraft project, an international consortium, Panavia, was formed in 1969 to develop an aircraft for the 1980s and beyond. The result was the Tornado. Two F.3 (Air Defence Version) machines of No 5 Squadron are shown here. (BAe)

Chinook (with its shorter range but higher speed) constituted a significant improvement over the capability of the original single Wessex helicopter unit.

An even greater improvement in the operational capability of the Command was set in train in September 1983 when the first of the Tornado GR.1s for RAF Germany arrived on No XV Squadron at Laarbruch (the genesis of this aircraft will be described later). In February the following year No 16 Squadron re-equipped with Tornados at the same base, followed by Nos 20, 31, 17, and 14 Squadrons at Brüggen between June 1984 and November 1985. The seventh RAF Germany Tornado squadron was No 9, which redeployed from Honington to Brüggen in October 1986; and the last Tornado unit to join the Command was No 2 Squadron, which brought into the front line the GR Mk 1A all-weather tactical reconnaissance version at Laarbruch in August 1989. These arrivals progressively replaced the Jaguars in Germany, until by the end of 1985 the whole Jaguar force had been withdrawn, leaving a Command that would be little changed until the impact of the defence cuts of 1991 was felt (a subject that will be discussed in Chapter 13).

These Tornados in Germany were not, however, the first of the type to enter service with the Royal Air Force. At the end of January 1981 a Tri-national Tornado Training Establishment had been opened at Cottesmore in the presence of the Chiefs of Air Staff of the RAF, of the Luftwaffe, and of the Italian Air Force and the Commander-in Chief of the German Navy. This was then followed by the opening during January 1982 of the first all-RAF unit to fly the aircraft, the Tornado

Weapons Conversion Unit at Honington. No 9 Squadron became the first operational unit to take delivery of the Tornado GR.1 strike/attack version in June that same year, and by the end of 1982 both United Kingdom strike squadrons, Nos 9 and 617, were working up to full operational status. When No 9 Squadron moved to Germany, No 27 replaced it in the UK strike force, and finally a UK reconnaissance squadron, No 13, accepted Tornados at Honington in January 1990.

The first Air Defence Variants of the RAF Tornado, the interim Mk 2, were delivered to No 229 OCU in November 1984, later followed by twelve of the definitive F Mk 3s. In November 1987 No 29 Squadron became the first front-line air defence unit to re-equip with the Tornado F.3 and was declared to NATO that same month. Six more squadrons in the United Kingdom, Nos 5, 11, 23, 25, 43 and 111 also re-equipped with the ADV between May 1988 and early 1991. Designed to combat the bomber threat in an intense ECM environment, in all weathers and over a vast area of sky, the Tornado enjoys a much better endurance than the Phantom and it carries a powerful look-down/shoot-down weapons system. The aircraft shares some of the outstanding navigation equipment carried by its GR.1 strike counterpart, but although capable in the long-range interceptor role for which it was developed, it lacks the agility of an air superiority fighter.

It had been intended that this Tornado air defence force, together with the two UK Phantom squadrons remaining in service, Nos 56 and 74, would be supported in their mission by Nimrod airborne early warning aircraft, a planned development of the highly successful maritime aircraft. In September 1978 work began on the British AEW project with the dismantling of a Nimrod MR Mk 1 fuselage. This was the first step towards the conversion to the Nimrod AEW.3 standard, an ugly duckling of an aircraft fitted with bulbous excrescences at the nose and tail to house the radar scanners. As the project continued over the next few years, however, it proved impossible to meet the performance specification for the radar facilities, which were of course the whole point of the programme.

Eventually, by September 1986, the delays and the disappointments had accumulated to a point where the Government was obliged to reopen the whole competition for an AEW aircraft. There were several contestants, but the main rival to the Nimrod had always been the Boeing E-3, an option that had been favoured by the Air Staff of the Royal Air Force from an early stage. This American aircraft was a development of the Boeing Model 707-320B airliner, and even as early as June of that year no fewer than 35 of these highly successful AWACS (Airborne Warning and Control Systems) aircraft were already in service with the United States Air Force.

In December 1986 the result of the British competition was announced. The E-3 had won, the eleven Nimrod airframes already modified to AEW standard would be disposed of, £900 million had been wasted and another politically motivated procurement programme had collapsed in fiasco, but the result was that the Royal Air Force would now purchase an effective

AEW system. The first of the seven E-3D Sentrys to be procured arrived in No 8 Squadron at Waddington in mid-1991, and a system that was fully compatible with the eighteen NATO E-3s coming into service at the former RAF Germany base of Geilenkirchen joined the front line of UK air defence.

The advent of the Tornado aircraft had been a far happier endeavour, though one that was not without its set-backs. It was a story that had begun in 1965 with the demise of the TSR.2. That decision meant that there was no RAF programme for an all-weather strike/attack aircraft, and the interim aircraft that were procured, the Buccaneer and the Phantom, were both designs from the 1950s. Their lives were thus limited, and in any case they could not carry the navigation and attack systems that would be needed to meet future operational demands. At the same time there was no obvious replacement for the Phantom air defence aircraft and these machines, too, would clearly have a limited life in RAF service. In 1971 Air Staff Target 395 was therefore issued to cover this particular requirement. Studies showed that, with acceptable variations, the strike/attack and interceptor roles could be filled by the same basic aircraft.

This dual RAF requirement in the second half of the 1960s for a modern strike/attack aircraft and for a more advanced interceptor happened to coincide with forecast gaps on the inventories of the German Air Force and Navy, and in the Italian Air Force. An international consortium, Panavia, was therefore formed in March 1969 to design, develop and produce an aircraft that

would satisfy all five operational requirements. As the international programme developed, the aircraft came to fill no fewer than six major requirements among the partners in the project: these were close air support/battlefield interdiction; deep interdiction strike; air superiority; interception; naval strike; and reconnaissance. This project, originally called the MRCA or Multi-Role Combat Aircraft, and unkindly referred to by cynical Air Force wags as 'Must Refurbish the Canberra Again', was to become one of the largest European industrial programmes ever undertaken. In July 1976 the three Governments concerned signed an agreement to produce a total of 809 MRCAs, a figure later increased to 925. Of this number, 229 of the IDS Interdictor/Strike (GR Mk 1) version would be procured for the Royal Air Force, together with 165 of the Air Defence Variant Tornados.

Tornado GR Mk 1s began to arrive in the front line of the Royal Air Force six years later, in early 1982, and came to equip most of the combat squadrons of the Service in the following years. Two years later a programme was started to modify the Tornado GR Mk 1s to carry nuclear weapons. This was consistent with the NATO concept of flexible response, which, as we saw earlier, had been promulgated in late 1967 and which retained theatre nuclear weapons for use if conventional defence failed. It was a concept of operations that had already removed much of the rigidity from earlier planning assumptions for an air war in the Central Region, plans that had led not only to fixed roles for the

tactical air forces but to pre-determined missions and even to pre-designated individual targets. Such a doctrine had not made full use of the flexibility of air power, or of its ability to deal with the unexpected.

ORGANIZATION OF TRAINING

So much for the front line during the past three decades and more; but none of the varied and demanding roles of the Royal Air Force would have been possible without a sound flying training organization to support them. A step change in the equipment of that training organization began in 1959 when the very successful piston-engine Provost *ab initio* trainer was replaced by the equally popular and robust Jet Provost Mk 3. This was soon followed by the Mk 4, with an uprated engine, and then the Jet Provost was extensively re-designed during the 1960s to produce the pressurized and much modernized Jet Provost Mk 5. This was a trainer that remained in use at No 7 FTS at Church Fenton until late 1989, at the RAF College, Cranwell, until late 1990 and at No 1 FTS Linton-on-Ouse until 1991. It will be finally phased out during 1993.

It was on the Jet Provost that Flight Lieutenant The Prince of Wales gained his RAF pilot's 'wings'. HRH Prince Charles had received his Private Pilot's Licence on Chipmunks in 1969, and from October of that year until February 1971 he flew the Basset CC.1, in which he went solo and gained his instrument rating. At Cranwell between 8 March and 30 July 1971 Prince

Left: An E-3 Sentry AWACS aircraft. (MOD)

Right: By 1972 almost all the Canberras had been withdrawn from the front line. However, seven of the PR.9s, like the one shown here, remain in service today. (DPR[A] MOD)

Charles underwent a jet flying course. He trained with No 1 Graduate Course, but a special training flight of three Jet Provost Mk 5s, named Golden Eagle Flight, was established so as to afford appropriate facilities for the heir to the throne. HRH Prince Charles received his flying badge on 20 August 1971 at a Cranwell ceremony from the then Chief of the Air Staff, Air Chief Marshal Sir Denis Spotswood, in the presence of HRH Prince Philip, the Duke of Edinburgh.

The Cranwell syllabus itself was by now changing. The last of the old Flight Cadet entries, No 101, was replaced from late September by a new scheme under which all entrants would be university graduates. These were young men who had accumulated perhaps 70 hours of flying time in University Air Squadrons on Scottish Aviation Bulldogs, an aircraft that had been procured in the 1960s to replace the Chipmunk in UASs. When the new graduate entries reached Cranwell they were given a basic 75 hours on Jet Provost Mk 5As during a 28-week course, at the end of which they were awarded their pilot's brevet. After that they remained under training on the same aircraft at Cranwell, so that their total stay at the College was about twelve months before they moved on to their advanced and operational training.

By this time the flying training syllabus for direct-entry pilots in the Royal Air Force started with 15 hours on the venerable Chipmunk, followed by 100 hours on the Jet Provost Mk 3 at No 1 FTS at Linton-on-Ouse or Cranwell and another 60 hours on the Jet Provost Mk 5. They too then progressed into the more advanced stages of their flying training. Some went on to complete 70 hours on Hawks at No 4 FTS at Valley, followed by another 50 hours' applied flying at one of the Tactical Weapons Units. Pilots destined for multi-engine roles meanwhile went on to the Handley Page/Scottish Aviation Jetstream, which had in 1973 started to replace the ageing Varsity trainers at No 5 FTS at Oakington, a unit that later moved to Leeming and then to Finningley. Future pilots for the helicopter force had yet another route forward: they went to No 2 FTS at Shawbury, where they converted on to Westland Whirlwinds before joining their operational squadrons.

Navigators and Air Electronic Officers were trained at No 6 FTS Finningley on the Dominie T Mk 1, the first aircraft procured specifically as a jet-powered navigation trainer for the Royal Air Force. This machine was taken into service at No 1 Air Navigation School, Stradishall, during December 1965, where trainee navigators were given 45 hours of training in the aircraft to consolidate their basic navigation course on slower aircraft such as the Varsity.

If the RAF's Jet Provost trainer had a fault, it was that it was actually too easy to fly. This meant that any lack of aptitude in a pupil pilot sometimes appeared only once the more advanced aerial exercises were reached, by which time considerable time, effort and money had been invested in the student and thus wasted. Its replacement, after thirty-two years of excellent service, was a quite different machine, the Shorts Tucano T Mk 1. This aircraft is a much modified version of the Brazilian Embraer trainer. The many changes embodied in the RAF version include a Garrett turboprop engine to give it a higher rate of climb and a higher airspeed than the Embraer, particularly at low altitude; a ventral airbrake; structural strengthening to withstand high manoeuvre loadings; a new cockpit layout which conforms to RAF standards and which incorporates British equipment; and very many minor items. Further modifications were introduced during the production of the aircraft to give it strengthened flying controls and an extended fatigue life, so that in its final version the Tucano basic trainer has only about 25 per cent commonality with the original Brazilian aircraft.

With the failure of the Balliol advanced trainer and

Right: The Tucano trainer, one of the latest RAF acquisitions. (MOD)

the recognition that in a future all-jet Air Force there seemed little point in teaching the quite different techniques of jet-flying, advanced flying training had switched to the Vampire during the mid-1950s. Over 530 of this T.11 version of the Vampire were eventually delivered to the Service. They filled the role of jet conversion training, training from basic standards up to 'wings' standard, dual check flights on operational squadrons and many other similar and associated tasks. Over 3,000 pilots gained their pilot's brevet on this machine.

From February 1962, when the first of the Folland Gnats arrived at the Central Flying School at Little Rissington, this aircraft became the principal advanced trainer for the Royal Air Force. It had been designed in the early 1950s as a private-venture light fighter, and although six Gnats were purchased by the Ministry of Aviation for evaluation the fighter was not adopted by the Service. By the end of 1957, however, its potential as a two-seat advanced jet trainer had been recognized, and from November 1962 until it was succeeded by the Hawk it served with No 4 FTS at Valley.

The Gnat also formed the initial type used by 'The Red Arrows' aerobatic team. The team had its origins in the arrival of the Lightning in service, when it was decided that advanced fighters of this kind were no longer appropriate for air displays, as the Hunter certainly had been, and the task was transferred from Fighter Command to Flying Training Command. A team was formed in 1964 by No 4 FTS flying Gnats, known as 'The Yellowjacks'. The aircraft of this fine team were transferred to CFS the following year, repainted overall in a vivid red scheme and renamed 'The Red Arrows'. They quickly established a reputation second to none in the world of aerobatic display, and continued to fly their Gnats until 1979, when they received Hawk T.1s, with which they still continue to give their immaculate displays.

At about the same time that the Flying Training Schools were receiving more modern aircraft during the 1960s, the various Operational Training Units were being re-equipped with aircraft little different from those on front-line squadrons. Hunters, including the side-by-side two-seat T Mk 7 version, Canberras, Lightnings, Valiants and other types contemporary to the front line at the time all served in OCUs. Others, including Harriers, Buccaneers and Jaguars not only equipped the relevant OCU but the OCUs also took on a secondary operational squadron designation so as to form a reserve for the front line. This concept perhaps reached its highest form when some of the Hawk advanced trainers, including those of 'The Red Arrows', were modified so as to be able to accept a weapons fit including two AIM-9L Sidewiders for the air defence role. The Hawks which had replaced the Hunters at Nos 1 and 2 Tactical Weapons Units, at Brawdy and Chivenor respectively, already had a weapon-carrying fit, and now they were given 'shadow' designations as second-line operational squadrons.

CHAPTER 13

NEW HORIZONS

By early 1990 the Royal Air Force was reaching the final stages of a comprehensive re-equipment programme. The Buccaneer and the Phantom, each of them worthy types but both designed over 30 years before, were reaching the end of their useful lives; the Lightnings had gone; that remarkable survivor from the age of four-engine piston-driven bombers, the Shackleton, was at last being retired; and, not least, the Jet Provost trainer, after 30 years of sterling service, was also being phased out. The modern front line that was being completed brought the Royal Air Force into a new era. In terms of aircraft designed for active combat roles, the front line was made up of nine squadrons flying Tornado GR.1 strike/attack aircraft; three squadrons in the offensive support role equipped with Harriers, and two more with Jaguars; and five reconnaissance squadrons, two with Tornado GR.1As, one with Jaguars, another with Canberra PR.9s and one with Nimrod R.1s. Of the eleven combat air defence squadrons, seven were equipped with Tornado F.3s and four were still operating Phantom FGR.2s. The AEW unit operating in support of this air defence force, No 8 Squadron, was about to exchange its Shackleton AEWs for Boeing E-3 Sentrys.

In the transport role there were six fixed-wing squadrons, one with VC10s, four operating Hercules and one equipped with dual-role tanker/transport TriStar K.1s, KC.1s and C.2s. There were also two dedicated tanker squadrons, one operating Victor K.2s and the other equipped with a mix of VC10 K.2s and K.3s. Five squadrons were committed to the helicopter transport role, two with Chinooks, two with Pumas and one with Wessexes. There were also two squadrons operating in the Search and Rescue role, one equipped with Sea Kings and the other with Wessexes. Two communication squadrons, with a mix of small fixed-wing transports as well as light helicopters, completed the quite sizeable transport assets of the Service.

Air defence missiles had by the 1990s been in the Order of Battle of the Royal Air Force for many years, starting with the Bloodhounds of 1958, but over the years

the Service had come to rely for missile defence almost exclusively on the short-range and highly effective Rapier system. By 1990 there was still one squadron of the ageing Bloodhound SAMs, but there were six squadrons of Rapiers operated by front-line squadrons of the Royal Air Force Regiment and two other air defence squadrons, this time part of the Royal Auxiliary Air Force. These units were equipped with Skyguard anti-aircraft guns, also very effective weapons, numbers of which had been captured from the Argentine forces

Right: As the Cold War continued, more advanced aircraft were brought into the front line so as to maintain an edge over the potential threat. One important new type was the Nimrod maritime patrol aircraft, introduced to squadron service in 1970. A Nimrod is seen here keeping a rendezvous at the North Pole. (DPR[A] MOD)

Far right: Sea Kings have replaced most of the launches that were once such a prominent feature of the air/sea rescue organization around the coasts of Britain. (MOD)

during the Falklands Campaign. Five other squadrons of the regular RAF Regiment and six squadrons of the RAuxAF were either equipped as light armour units or deployed in the light infantry role for the defence of airfields.

Though there was still no ground attack/air superiority aircraft on the inventory, that list of equipment represented a more effective front line than the Service had seen for several decades. But it was a satisfactory state of affairs that had not been reached without considerable sacrifices over the preceding years in other aspects of the Royal Air Force as a whole. Most of these sacrifices had involved unit disbandments, amalgamations, the rationalization of functions and the closure of stations — and sometimes all four. In many cases the retrenchments had represented a sensible management of resources. For example, once the voracious training requirements of National Service intakes fell away, the closure of many large and temporary stations was not only inevitable but welcome.

The large hutted camps of Compton Bassett, Yatesbury and many others fell into this category. Most of these facilities were simply effaced from the landscape.

A whole range of other stations, mainly wartime airfields, had been reopened during the early 1950s to support the sudden expansion of the front line during the Korean War, among them Merryfield, Weston Zoyland, Full Sutton and Worksop. Within a few years, training activity on them ceased again and these stations too could at last be given up as surplus property. Another set of closures followed after the severe cuts in the front line that flowed from the 1957 Defence White Paper. In this case the disbandment of whole Wings of fighters, for instance, had meant that historic airfields such as Duxford, Tangmere and Horsham St Faith were eventually abandoned, though at the same time a number of other airfields were reactivated or renovated in order to take the emerging bombers of the V-Force.

During the following two decades or more many other facilities were reluctantly given up when the Service was forced to make difficult choices in the face of repeated demands for economies in defence spending. Into this category fell the loss of such well-found and popular airfields as Little Rissington, whose Central Flying School moved first to Cranwell and then to Scampton; Leconfield, where the Central Gunnery School closed down; West Raynham, whose Central Fighter Establishment with its Day Fighter Leaders' School moved into the fighter base at Binbrook (though

in an emasculated form); and, not least, Manby, which had for many years been the home of the College of Air Warfare. This was a college with a fine pioneering record in military aviation, particularly in the fields of advanced navigation and polar flights. The aircraft belonging to the Air Warfare College were withdrawn and the institution itself moved into Cranwell, as did the RAF Technical College which had been situated at Henlow. What was left after all the rationalizations of some four decades was, however, a Service with a proper focus on the front line together with taut and efficient support for it.

These same years also saw very many closures overseas, particularly after the announcements during 1968 of forthcoming British military withdrawals from the Far East and Middle East. From that time on, the Service was increasingly to focus almost all its efforts on to NATO commitments. Although the Falklands Campaign was seen as an aberration in this process of withdrawal into Europe, a modest out-of-area capability was still retained. This was several times rehearsed in exercises, among them 'Saif Sareea' ('Sharp Sword') in early 1987 when Tornados, TriStars and other aircraft together with units of the other Services practised a deployment to the Gulf.

It turned out to have been a valuable exercise. Just over three years later, in August 1990, a deployment to the Gulf began in earnest in response to the Iraqi invasion of Kuwait. The campaign that followed is not only the latest in which the Royal Air Force has taken part, though the instability in many parts of the world suggests that it may not be the last, but it also well illustrates the peak of capability that the Service had reached after 75 years of evolution.

THE GULF WAR

Iraq had long entertained claims on parts of Kuwait, in particular on the Rumalia oilfields and on two of the offshore islands. A slump in the price of oil during 1990, and a resulting over-production by some of the Gulf states, put severe economic pressure on Iraq, which was supporting a huge defence expenditure. This situation was made the pretext by the leader of Iraq, Saddam Hussein, for an attack on Kuwait. In preparation for the assault, Iraq began to build up her forces on the Kuwait border during the third week of July 1990, and in the early hours of 2 August the invasion began. Within about four hours Iraqi troops had covered the 60 or so miles to Kuwait City and occupied it.

On 6 August, and despite international condemnation of her aggression, Iraq began to mass armoured formations along her border with Saudi Arabia, leading to grave concern that the Iraqi forces would invade. Such an invasion would have been very difficult for the Saudis to withstand. The forces of Iraq included over a million men, 5,000 tanks and more than 500 aircraft; those of Saudi Arabia comprised only 45,000 soldiers, 700 tanks and around 250 combat aircraft. The Iraqi invasion of Kuwait was formally condemned by the United Nations on 2 August and a military response was put in train in which ultimately seventeen nations participated, including the United Kingdom.

Under new command arrangements that had been outlined as a result of the Falklands Campaign, a joint Headquarters at High Wycombe under the Commander-in-Chief RAF Strike Command, Air Chief Marshal Sir Patrick Hine, was set up to command the British forces

Left: A TriStar tops up a VC10 tanker. (MOD)

Right: A Tornado GR1 over Bahrain. (Wg Cdr Broad-bent)

Below: A deployed Rapier missile detachment of the RAF Regiment at Muharraq. (Wg Cdr Broadbent)

that would be committed in response to the Gulf Crisis. The first elements of the international reaction took the form of an increase in British and United States naval forces in the area. This was followed by the dispatch to northern Saudi Arabia of the 82nd US Airborne Division at light scales in a defensive role, while the first RAF aircraft to go to the theatre were twelve Tornados F.3s which deployed to Dhahran on 11 August. Within two hours of their arrival, a pair of Tornados were airborne again, this time on operational patrol.

Throughout the massive build-up of Coalition forces that now began, there was concern at the possibility that the Iraqi Air Force might launch pre-emptive attacks upon the concentrations of high-value equipment being unloaded at ports and airfields, or against the troops concentrated in their assembly areas. It was a very real possibility, given the strength, at least on paper, of the Iraqi Air Force. In an air force that had been equipped and to some extent trained by the Soviet Union, there was a ground attack force estimated to include some 70 MiG-23 'Floggers', 30 Su-7 'Fitters', 50

Su-20 'Fitter-Cs', 30 Su-25 'Frogfoots', 64 French-supplied Mirage F1EQs and perhaps 40 Chinese-built J-6s, equivalent to the Soviet MiG-19 'Farmer'. There was also a small force of bombers made up of about sixteen Tu-6 'Badgers' and perhaps ten Su-24 'Fencers'. For the air superiority role the Iraqi inventory held about 70 MiG-21 'Fishbeds', eighteen or so Mig-29 'Fulcrums', an estimated 80 Chinese J-7s (equivalent to the MiG-21), an additional 30 French-supplied Mirage F1EQs in the air defence role and 25 of the very modern MiG-25 'Foxbat' interceptors.

What could not be so easily assessed was the effectiveness of this substantial force. On the one hand, a number of the air crew had gained combat experience during the eight years of the Iran-Iraq War; on the other hand, during that war the Iraqi Air Force had shown a distinct lack of aggression, and its aircraft had managed to achieve very little even against the relatively weak Iranian Air Force. Although the Coalition air forces contained some of the finest air combat units in the world, no chances could be taken. All squadrons were on full alert, and the Tornado F.3s were soon flying up to twenty combat air patrols in each 24-hour period, supported by a constant AWACS presence and by a stream of refuelling tankers.

Quite apart from the unknown capabilities of the Iraqi Air Force, the enemy ground-based anti-aircraft defences had to be considered before any attempt could be made to re-take Kuwait. These defences could only be described as massive. In Iraq there were something like 9,000–10,000 anti-aircraft guns and about 17,000 surface-to-air missiles. Almost all of these weapons were highly effective Soviet types, and they were supported by

equally modern and battleworthy radars and communication systems. Even if, as indeed became the case, the Iraqi Air Force proved to be ineffectual, this array of defences could pose a very real threat to Coalition aircraft. Meanwhile, as the build-up of Coalition forces accelerated, the first RAF Jaguars arrived at Thumrait air base in the Sultanate of Oman on 13 August, followed during the next two days by the deployment into Seeb, Oman, of three Nimrod MR Mk 2s from Kinloss. These maritime aircraft flew two sorties each day from now on, passing information on the surface picture to the US Navy carriers in the region. Like many other aircraft deployed to the Gulf, the Nimrods were soon modified for their particular role in

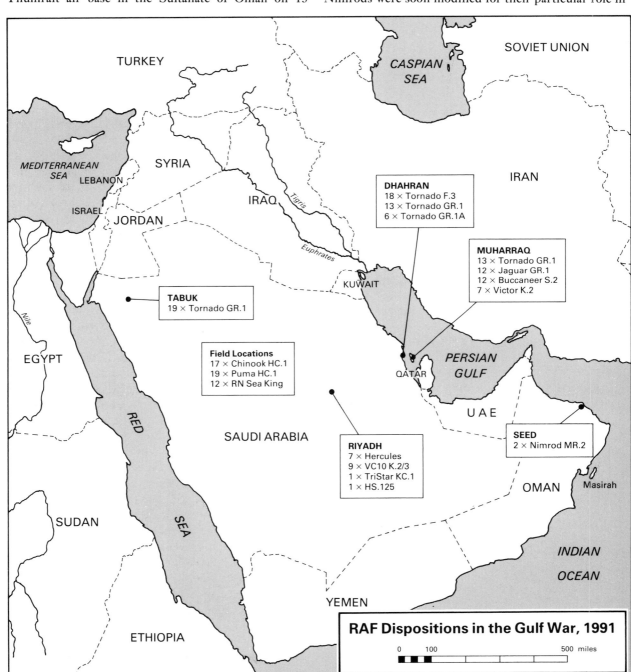

DHAHRAN
18 × Tornado F.3
13 × Tornado GR.1
6 × Tornado GR.1A

MUHARRAQ
13 × Tornado GR.1
12 × Jaguar GR.1
12 × Buccaneer S.2
7 × Victor K.2

TABUK
19 × Tornado GR.1

Field Locations
17 × Chinook HC.1
19 × Puma HC.1
12 × RN Sea King

SEED
2 × Nimrod MR.2

RIYADH
7 × Hercules
9 × VC10 K.2/3
1 × TriStar KC.1
1 × HS.125

RAF Dispositions in the Gulf War, 1991

0   100   500 miles

the theatre, being equipped with a self-defence suite of systems, modified electronics and a turret-mounted infra-red system with which to identify surface vessels by night.

From 10 September onwards, the activities of the Nimrod force extended into the Gulf itself, where the aircraft carried out three tasks: first, they contributed to the 24-hour defensive surveillance of the Coalition Task Force in the north of the Gulf; second, they gave tactical direction to the Sea Skua anti-ship missiles of the Royal Navy; and third, they maintained a search and rescue cover both over the sea and over the nearby desert areas. Though given little publicity, these were vital roles and even before hostilities began the Nimrods had intercepted and challenged over 6,500 ships in support of the United Nations embargo on shipments of certain goods to Iraq, while during the conflict itself they flew 86 combat sorties.

Tankers were to play an essential part in most of the air deployments, air patrols and combat missions that developed during the following six months. A total of seven Victor tankers were eventually deployed to the Gulf, together with ten VC10s or TriStars. It was a small force in comparison with the two hundred or more USAF KC-135 and KC-10 tankers operating in the area, but the Royal Air Force machines flew at something like four times the normal peacetime rate, refuelling not only aircraft of the Royal Air Force but also those from virtually all the other air forces of the Coalition. These

tankers flew 299 missions during the 42 days of actual fighting, and during the whole period of their detachment they offloaded about 13,000 tonnes of fuel.

Meanwhile the air transport element of the Royal Air Force had begun a massive airlift that would become one of the keys to the success of the deployment, and later to the success of the RAF combat operations. From the very early stages of the campaign a small force of Hercules was based at King Khalid International Airport in order to provide in-theatre resupply and communications. At the same time Pumas and Chinooks joined the force operating out of Jubail to give tactical transport support, including troop insertion, resupply, special forces operations, casualty evacuation and many other tasks calling for rapid response and high mobility. Nineteen Pumas were involved altogether, operated by Nos 33 and 230 Squadrons, while Nos 7 and 18 Squadrons flew the seventeen Chinook helicopters that were deployed by the Royal Air Force. These machines would fly some 900 sorties in-theatre during their deployment.

Strategic transport support by the RAF was provided by TriStars, VC10s and Hercules, an effort that was augmented by transports from other nations. To complete the fleet, civilian aircraft on charter including Boeing 747s and 707s, DC-8s were employed and, once again, the ubiquitous ex-RAF Belfast heavy-lift aircraft were on the scene. During the whole operation, and up to 8 March 1991, 46,000 passengers were airlifted to the Gulf from Germany and the United Kingdom, 25,000 of them by RAF military machines, and a total of 46,000 tonnes of freight were similarly moved into the theatre of operations. All told, and including the essential contribution made by the tanker force, seven strategic transport squadrons were involved — Nos 24, 30, 47, and 70 operating Hercules, No 101 flying VC10s, No 216 operating TriStars and No 55 with its Victors.

During the weeks after the initial deployments, one of the main elements of the RAF contribution was made up of 45 Tornado attack aircraft. This was a mixed force of composite squadrons, with GR.1 aircraft and crews drawn at various times from Nos 9, 14, 15, 16, 17, 20, 27, 31 and 617 Squadrons. Six Tornado GR.1A reconnaissance aircraft from Nos 2 and 13 Squadrons were also deployed, giving invaluable tactical intelligence which was beyond the capacity of strategic reconnaissance satellites. Not least in this RAF combat force, twelve Jaguar GR.1A attack/reconnaissance aircraft were dispatched to the Gulf drawn from Nos 6, 41, and 54 Squadrons as well as from No 226 OCU; and finally twelve Buccaneers were deployed from

Tornado GR.1A

This aircraft is the reconnaissance version of the Tornado GR.1 strike/attack/recce machine, the G standing for ground attack and the R for reconnaissance. The first GR.1 Tornados joined the front line during 1980 but the all-weather reconnaissance variant was a later addition to the original force, involving the modification of sixteen machines to the Mk 1A standard. After delays in development, these aircraft came into service some eight years late, and they were given a much updated refit of equipment just in time for the Gulf War of 1991. With its sideways-looking infra-red sensors and a Vinten horizon-to-horizon infra-red linescan system, the GR.1A proved able in operations to produce up to one hour's worth of recorded data for analysis. Video tapes rather than the traditional film for recording are used, and the space for the reconnaissance fit is found by dispensing with the two 27mm cannon of the GR.1 version. Powered by twin Rolls-Royce RB.199 engines, the Tornado has a maximum speed at low level of over 800kts, and at high level it can transit at above Mach 2.

Lossiemouth. The fact that mixed units were sent to the Gulf rather than complete squadrons caused considerable dismay. Originally, this unusual measure was adopted to bring together the most experienced crews; but it very quickly became clear that the aircrew:aircraft ratio was quite inadequate for prolonged operations, and mixed squadrons were perforce employed throughout the war.

One of the principal concerns of the Coalition commanders in the Gulf was that the considerable force of Iraqi aircraft might attack the air bases on which so much depended. Even an airborne assault on some of them was a potential threat that could not be ignored. Ground-based air defences and airfield defence were therefore deployed, including Nos 20, 26 and 66 (Rapier) Squadrons of the Royal Air Force Regiment as well as Nos 1, 34, 51 and 58 Light Armoured Squadrons of that Corps.

This Royal Air Force contribution to the Coalition forces represented only one element of the total air assets of 2,430 ground-based and carrier launched combat and support aircraft that had arrived in the region by the time the air offensive against Iraq was opened in the early hours of 17 January. The aim of the air/land campaign, in accordance with United Nations resolutions, was to compel an Iraqi withdrawal from Kuwait, and to use force to gain 'peace and security in the region' (Resolution 678). This phrase was interpreted by the Coalition to justify operations well beyond the immediate area of Kuwait.

The overall plan for the air campaign was made up of four phases. Phase I would last for one week. Air superiority would be seized while air attacks were also made on Iraqi strategic capabilities including her nuclear

potential, her chemical warfare capability and her 'Scud' surface-to-surface missiles. Phase II would be a one-day assault against Iraqi air defences in the Kuwait theatre of operations. Phase III was planned to include continued attacks on earlier targets together with, for two to three weeks, an assault on the enemy field army in the Kuwait area. Phase IV would involve air support to the ground forces of the Coalition, which at this point would start the offensive on land.

For the Royal Air Force, the tasks allotted within this plan depended a great deal on the capabilities that its squadrons could offer. Almost all of these, as we have seen, had been developed with only the Central Region of NATO in mind, and the result was that the RAF activity fell into three phases. First, there was an initial phase in which night low-level offensive counter-air missions would be flown against Iraqi air bases. Some of these attacks would employ 1,000lb conventional bombs delivered in a stand-off 'toss' manoeuvre so as to avoid the worst of the Iraqi point defences, but, above all, the Tornados would use the JP233 anti-airfield weapons. These weapons had been developed specifically for use against Warsaw Pact airfields in Eastern Europe. Each of them contains 30 runway-cratering submunitions and 215 area-denial submunitions. The two types of munition are dispensed simultaneously from two side-by-side containers slung under the fuselage of the Tornado, their combined effect being to destroy airfield operating surfaces such as runways and to make it extremely hazardous for the enemy to move into the affected area to carry out repairs.

Intelligence showed, however, that the Iraqis had over thirty major airfields up and down the country, each

Right: Loading JP233 weapons. It was these weapons that were used during the early stages of the Gulf campaign to disrupt Iraqi airfields. (Wg Cdr Broadbent)

of which, with no restriction on space in the desert areas, covered a very large area indeed and each of which, furthermore, was provided with a redundancy of operating surfaces including runways up to 10,000ft in length. To give but one example, Talill air base, which lies about 150 miles north-west of Kuwait City, had two very long parallel runways and covered a total area of about 9,000 acres, or twice the spread of Heathrow. In order to protect their aircraft on these huge airfields from air attack the Iraqis had built very modern and well-protected Hardened Aircraft Shelters. Only a direct hit with a powerful weapon would be likely to put these shelters and their contents out of action, and it was naturally impossible to tell which shelters held aircraft and were thus worthwhile targets and which ones were empty.

A ground infrastructure made up of airfields and shelters like this across the whole of Iraq was simply beyond the capacity of the Coalition air forces to put completely and permanently out of action. Nevertheless it was vital to seize and to hold the initiative in the air. Of all the offensive counter-air assets available to the Coalition commanders, only the Tornado GR.1s were capable of delivering any effective airfield attack weapons in the very low-level mode that would be necessary in order to stay below the lethal, and in the very early stages intact, Iraqi air defence systems. These aircraft were therefore tasked to harass over a dozen of the most important Iraqi bases rather than attempt to close completely any smaller number. When their attacks went in they would be supported by F-15 fighters, by USAF F-4G 'Wild Weasels' and by EF-111A 'Raven' electronic countermeasures aircraft. Coalition fighters would fly escort missions, and conduct fighter sweeps. At the same time, and in very closely co-ordinated missions, the F-4Gs, with their HARM anti-radiation missiles, would close down Iraqi weapon-laying radars, while the EF-111s would be busy suppressing the Iraqi early warning radars.

Behind these aircraft, operating in 'attack packages' that gave immediate support to the aircraft carrying out the direct offensive missions, there were others playing an equally important part in the orchestrated assault. In a highly complex air plan involving all the numerous and different air missions that were being flown simultaneously throughout almost all of the conflict, not only were the tankers airborne to refuel outgoing and incoming combat aircraft, but AWACS machines of the United States Air Force were monitoring air movements and electronic emissions, while E-8A Joint-STARS (Joint Surveillance and Target Attack Radar System) aircraft and Rivet Joint RC-135 signals intelligence aircraft from the same air force were monitoring, by means of radar, developments on the ground while maintaining a guard on all signals transmissions.

The second phase of operations for the RAF squadrons would follow the offensive counter-air campaign after about one week, and it would consist of two or three weeks of interdiction missions together with a few continuing attacks on airfields. Then, in the final three weeks that was planned for the purely air offensive, there would be a concentration on targets within the Kuwait area, and another counter-air assault, this time against the airfields in southern Iraq from which it was still possible that enemy aircraft might appear over the battlefield.

Left: A VC10 tanker with Jaguars over Muarraq, December 1990. (Wg Cdr Broadbent)

The start of the war came in the early hours of 17 January when the first wave of attack aircraft crossed the Iraqi border from bases in Saudi Arabia, Bahrain and southern Turkey and from carriers of the US Navy. In this initial attack were USAF F-117A stealth bombers, which attacked key command and control centres in Baghdad, helicopters that took out important Iraqi early warning radars in the southern sector and a first salvo of 62 Tomahawk cruise missiles fired from ships of the US Navy in the Red Sea. In the wake of these missions, a force totalling about 700 conventional aircraft attacked targets across the whole of Iraq.

It was in this complex environment that the Tornados began to make their night attacks, missions that were pressed home with great skill and gallantry, not only in the face of exceptionally strong surface-to-air missile fire but also against heavy fire from the numerous anti-aircraft guns deployed on and around the Iraqi airfields. After the first few missions it was found that attacks with toss-launched 1,000lb bombs against those anti-aircraft artillery sites, timed to coincide precisely with Tornado attacks using JP233, noticeably reduced the effectiveness of the enemy defences. This tactic was therefore adopted, and it contributed to the comparative low rate of loss suffered by RAF aircraft in these raids.

Using these and other measures, within four days of the start of the air offensive the Coalition air forces together had effectively destroyed the Iraqi Air Force and driven its remnants into hiding. Eight enemy airfields had been rendered inoperative and several others had been damaged. Perhaps even more important, a combination of direct attack and the use of electronic countermeasures had so disrupted or destroyed the comprehensive Iraqi SAM coverage that the middle and upper airspace over the whole country was virtually freed for Coalition air activity.

After the success of the initial counter-air phase, most Tornado sorties were switched from 23 January onwards to operations in daylight, and they were now flown at heights above about 12,000ft so as to be beyond the reach of Iraqi anti-aircraft guns. In this phase of the air war the Tornados at first used free-fall bombs, directing them against large area targets such as fuel dumps and the Iraqi airfields. It was very important that these air bases be kept under continuing attack, because it was thought still possible that some elements of the Iraqi Air Force might be able to emerge from their shelters and harass the Coalition ground forces assembling for their later advance.

One of the target systems that came under Coalition air attack from an early stage had been the 'Scud' surface-to-surface missiles on the Iraqi inventory. There was an unknown number of these weapons in Iraq, estimates ranging from about 400 to around 1,000, deployed at over 30 fixed sites and on over 36 mobile launchers. The threat posed by these missiles became very serious when, on 18 January, Iraq began firing them against Israel. From that day on 'Scuds' figured more often in the target lists for the RAF recce aircraft. The six Tornado GR.1A reconnaissance aircraft, carrying infra-red linescan equipment which had only very recently arrived in the front line of the Royal Air Force, proved from the date of their first operational sorties on the night of 18/19 January, to be invaluable in helping to pin-point 'Scud' sites.

At the same time, however, the switch to attacks from medium level created a problem for aircraft such as the Tornado, which had not yet been equipped with its planned laser-designating system, a modification that would have made it possible to employ so-called 'smart' bombs. Toss-bombing without laser designation was far from accurate, and Buccaneers from Nos 12 and 208 Squadrons and from the OCU at Lossiemouth carrying Pave Spike laser systems were therefore dispatched from the UK, the first of them arriving ten days into the war. Most attacks by the RAF units thereafter were made using laser-guided bombs, which gave remarkable precision against point targets. On 10 February there was another improvement in attack capability when the first of two pre-production TIALD (Thermal Imaging Airborne Laser Designation) pods for use by the Tornados arrived. Unlike Pave Spike, TIALD is effective by night as well as in daylight, and by 14 February Tornados from all three of their bases in the Gulf region were carrying out precision-guided bombing missions.

From 3 February priority tasking for the Tornados had been switched to interdiction against the supply lines of the Iraqi forces in the Kuwait area, and the first of the RAF laser-guided bombs were dropped on bridges along the Iraqi supply routes leading to Kuwait on that day. These supply lines ran down the twin valleys of the Tigris and the Euphrates from Baghdad to the Kuwait area, a distance of about 350 miles, and many attacks by Coalition aircraft were made throughout the brief campaign on these vital routes as part of the declared aim of isolating the Iraqi forces in the Kuwait region.

From the start of hostilities the Jaguar aircraft were also fully engaged. On land they flew against Iraqi SAM positions, ammunition dumps, supply depots, barracks, armoured concentrations, artillery positions and coastal defence sites. A variety of weapons were employed, including 1,000lb bombs, cluster bombs and CRV7s, these last powerful high-velocity air-to-ground rockets. The Jaguar force was very active against a whole variety of targets in Iraq, while other missions saw the aircraft operating with great success in the maritime attack role against Iraqi naval vessels in the northern waters of the Gulf.

After 38 days of intensive air attacks, many of them in the later stages of the air campaign directed against Iraqi army formations deployed in desert positions, the land campaign began. There is no space here to deal with the brief conflict that followed, save to say that it was a highly imaginative and skilfully executed affair, and a classic of land/air manoeuvre warfare. The Iraqis, no doubt partly because of the positional style of warfare to which they had become accustomed during their conflict with Iran, were quite unprepared for this. A massive retreat began from Kuwait, but in order to prevent any Iraqi regrouping with the Republican Guard north of Kuwait, air attacks were continued. So complete was the Iraqi defeat that after only a hundred hours of ground fighting the Coalition Governments called a halt. In retrospect, it would have been militarily advisable to have continued the advance for at least another 24 hours so

Left: Eight squadron commanders meet for a conference at Muharraq. From left to right: Wing Commanders Al Threadgould (OC Tornado GR.1As, Dhahran), Gerry Witts (OC Tornados, Dahran), Bill Cope (OC Buccaneers, Muharraq), Bob Iverson (OC TIALD Ops, Tabuk), John Broadbent (OC Tornado Detachment, Muharraq), Mike Heath (OC ALARM Ops, Tabuk), Ivor Evans (Dhahran) and Ian Travers Smith (OC Tornados, Tabuk). Their original squadron appointments were, respectively, Nos. 2, 27, 208, 617, XV, 20, 9 and 16. (Wg Cdr Broadbent)

that all the Iraqi forces in the Kuwait theatre of operations could have been disarmed. But this would have been outside the UN remit, and the cease-fire meant that many Iraqi troops escaped, often taking their equipment with them.

It had been an extraordinary conflict. First, it had been war by appointment. The United Nations had laid down a deadline by which Iraq was to comply with various Resolutions, including one that demanded an Iraqi withdrawal from Kuwait by 15 January. When that withdrawal had not taken place, the fighting began. There was little surprise as far as timing was concerned; but there was undoubtedly a qualitative as well as a quantitative surprise awaiting the Iraqis once the Coalition offensive began. Second, and in contrast to all the major air campaigns that had been waged between 1945 and 1990, this one saw air power applied without restriction against almost any legitimate military targets. There were no sanctuary zones in the country, as there had been in Vietnam; there were no enemy sanctuary air bases outside the area as there had been in Manchuria during the Korean War; there was none of the international outrage over the use of the air weapon as there had been during the Suez Campaign of October 1956. For the first time in over forty years air power had demonstrated its full potential. The result was that, even before the start of the ground offensive, Iraqi army losses were estimated to include 1,560 tanks, 1,508 artillery pieces and 1,210 armoured personnel carriers, figures that represented 37 per cent, 49 per cent and 42 per cent respectively of these assets held by the Iraqis in the Kuwait theatre of operations.

For the Royal Air Force it had been a campaign that involved just over 150 aircraft contributed by eighteen attack/reconnaissance squadrons and OCUs, eight air defence flying units, nine transport and tanker units, four support helicopter support squadrons and three maritime patrol squadrons. Nor should the invaluable efforts of many other units be overlooked, including those of seven squadrons of the RAF Regiment, two squadrons (Nos 4624 and 4626) of the Royal Auxiliary Air Force and two Flights (Nos 7006 and 7644) of the RAF Volunteer Reserve. Other support came from No 1 Aeromed Evacuation Squadron, No 2 Parachute Squadron of the RAF Regiment, a mobile meteorological unit, the RAF War Hospital and, as well as numerous smaller detachments attached to the main force from all over the Royal Air Force, a variety of lesser units representing the huge variety of skills needed to operate in conditions of modern warfare. Finally, there were several unheralded men who served alongside their colleagues from the other Services in Special Forces units.

Of the 110,000 or so sorties flown by the Coalition air forces, over 6,100 were carried out by the Royal Air Force. Tornado GR.1s accounted for around 1,500 of them, and the GR.1As for over 140. The Jaguars flew more than 600 missions and the Buccaneers above 200. All told, the Coalition air forces delivered 88,500 tons of bombs, 7,400 tons of which were precision-guided. The RAF share of the ordnance used included over 3,000 tonnes of weapons, among them over 100 JP233 airfield denial weapons, six thousand 1,000lb bombs (of which over 1,000 were laser-guided), over 100 anti-radar missiles and nearly 700 air-to-ground rockets.

One of the remarkable features of the air campaign was the very low loss rate among the Coalition air forces.

Below: A Victor K Mk 2 returns to Muharraq after a war mission. (Wg Cdr Broadbent)

In all, 42 aircraft were lost and another 33 written off in accidents, a combat loss rate of about one-thirteenth of one per cent. The Tornado losses, six aircraft with five crew members being killed, were the highest among the Coalition forces because of the high-risk profiles being flown, but this was still a rate of only one-third of one per cent. This should be compared with Bomber Command operations throughout the Second World War, which resulted in an overall loss rate of 2.3 per cent, with those of the UN Forces in Korea (2 per cent), the United States in Vietnam (0.4), the Israelis during the Yom Kippur War (1) and the British Forces during the Falklands Conflict (just under 0.5).

Although the Royal Air Force played a relatively small role in the Gulf War, it was a part that covered many roles, and these were carried out with commendable skill. What was not so clear at the time was whether the experience could teach anything about the future requirements of the Service. It had, after all, been a unique campaign in almost every way. First, there was the extraordinary fact of the Coalition itself, in which several unlikely partners took part. No one could have foreseen, even a few months before, that an armed conflict would find, for example, United States forces fighting alongside those of Syria. Next, and partly because of that mixed Coalition, Iraq found herself alone and surrounded by hostile countries from which heavy air attacks could be launched against her. At the same time, the whole of Iraq was within range of those air attacks, while many of the Coalition bases from which they were launched were beyond the reach of the Iraqi Air Force, even had it come out to fight. Third, there was the availability to the Coalition of the most advanced weapons and support systems in the world, an array that was opposed by somewhat less effective Soviet-supplied equipment. Fourth, there was the superior training and readiness of the Western powers in the Coalition. These forces had been for years at high readiness to confront the very substantial and highly capable forces of the Soviet Union. The Iraqis, on the other hand, had the very limited and misleading experience of the Iran-Iraq War behind them. Fifth, and crucial to the success of the whole operation, there was the fact that the United States was prepared to devote her massive resources to the campaign. With resources on that scale, backed by a clear determination by the United States to employ force in support of the United Nations' Resolutions, there was never any chance that Iraq could maintain her occupation of Kuwait.

For the Royal Air Force, the main lesson was the need for flexibility to deal with the unexpected. It was as well that the Gulf War was 'war by appointment', and that there were several months in which to prepare for it. For very understandable reasons, the RAF had for years focused virtually all of its efforts on the Central Region of NATO, circumstances very different from those that had to be confronted in the Gulf. With the end of the Cold War and the consequent changes in Europe, there would now be an opportunity to dismantle many of the features of the Royal Air Force that had been developed for the European theatre and to return to some of the more flexible capabilities that should form the basis of a modern air force.

'OPTIONS FOR CHANGE'

Even before the crisis in the Gulf, a much more significant change had begun to take place on the wider world stage, and one that would come to have a profound effect on the armed Services of the Western powers, including the Royal Air Force. Gorbachev had come to power in the Soviet Union in 1985, with the intention of revitalizing the Communist system in that country. One of the steps he took in an effort to ease the insupportable strain of military expenditure on the Soviet budget was to end the 38-year-long confrontation with the West.

The resulting Soviet intention to reduce all arms of their massive forces, and eventually to withdraw virtually all of their formations from Eastern Europe, was taken as a justification for widespread defence reductions in the West. In the United Kingdom, a study was begun to decide on the future size and shape of the British armed forces. The outcome was a document entitled *Options for Change*, which was presented to Parliament on 25 July 1990, ironically just one week before the sudden demands of the Gulf Crisis emerged. Its findings represented proposals for very substantial cuts in all three Services, and for the Royal Air Force it set out proposals for a cut in the front-line strength, accompanied by reduced numbers of personnel from a level of 89,000 to around 75,000 — a reduction of almost 16 per cent, and to a figure that was the lowest by far since 1938.

It is true that the very extensive overseas commitments that the Royal Air Force has undertaken during the last 72 years are now no more; but it is also the case that the technical, infrastructure and support facilities generally for the Service, and in particular for the front line, have, aircraft for aircraft, increased enormously. Such severe cuts in personnel strength may well cause future problems, though there is some mitigation from the effects of the *Options for Change* reductions in the fact that the Service was already in 1991

McDonnell Phantom

The McDonnell Phantom was one of the most successful post-war combat aircraft. A total of 118 of the FGR.2 ground-attack version were delivered to the RAF, and between 1972 and 1992 that mark served with seventeen units in the United Kingdom, Germany and in the Falklands. Twenty-three of the FG.1 interceptor variant were also delivered to the Service, and more of them were transferred from the Royal Navy. A further fifteen Phantoms, this time refurbished ex-US Navy F-4Js, were also brought on to the inventory. As an interceptor, the aircraft had a top speed of Mach 2.1 at 40,000ft and an initial rate of climb of 32,000ft per minute. In the ground-attack role and with a warload of bombs and rockets, it had a range of 1,750 miles and a tactical radius of action of about 150 miles.

about 6,000 airmen and airwomen below its authorized strength. Redundancies were therefore modest in size, though cuts in the officer corps of around 14 per cent, became inevitable.

Those manpower reductions in *Options for Change* were only one part of the more general retrenchment. During the following eighteen months details of the formations and units that would go were announced, and it became clear that the whole shape of the Service would be affected by the changes themselves and by their consequences. RAF Germany was reduced in strength by almost a half and would revert to the status of a Group under Strike Command. The old No 2 Group from 2TAF days was appropriately resurrected for this formation. The bases of Wildenrath and Gütersloh closed, and the two Phantom air defence squadrons in the Command, Nos 19 and 92, disbanded. Three Tornado GR.1 units also disbanded, Nos 15, 16 and 20 Squadrons from Laarbruch, while No 2 Squadron, with its Tornado GR.1A reconnaissance aircraft at the same base, redeployed to Marham to be joined there by the other Tornado reconnaissance unit, No 13 Squadron.

The two remaining Phantom squadrons in the United Kingdom, Nos 56 and 74 were disbanded, and the Buccaneer units, Nos 12 and 208 Squadrons together with the OCU, were withdrawn. The anti-surface warfare role that they had up until that time filled was taken over by Nos 27 and 617 Tornado squadrons, which moved up from Marham to Lossiemouth. Seven Nimrod MPA aircraft were withdrawn, which entailed the disbandment of No 42 Squadron. One of the two Nimrod maritime airfields, St Mawgan, became a Forward Operating Base for the Nimrod force, all of

which then moved into Kinloss together with No 236 OCU. No 55 Squadron was withdrawn from the tanker force, together with the long-serving Victor aircraft of that unit. Responsibility for the refuelling role would henceforth rest with VC10 and TriStar aircraft.

For the front line, this added up to a reduction in Tornado GR.1 squadrons from nine to six, as well as the loss of four Phantom squadrons, two of Buccaneers and one of Nimrods. The RAF Regiment lost Nos 16, 58, 63 and 51 Squadrons and the Bloodhound SAMs were stood down. In a move that was warmly welcomed in the Service, Royal Approval was given to transfer some of the 'number plates' from the squadrons leaving the front line to training units, which then became reserve squadrons. No 226 Jaguar OCU took over No 16 Squadron's number plate as No 16 Reserve Squadron, No 15 Squadron's number plate was allocated to the Tornado Tactical Weapons Conversion Unit and that of No 20 Squadron went to No 233 Harrier OCU. The number plate of No 42 Squadron went to No 236 Nimrod OCU, that of No 27 Squadron was taken over by No 240 Puma OCU as a reserve squadron, and that of No 55 Squadron went to No 241 VC10 OCU.

The withdrawn Buccaneer squadrons, Nos 12 and 208, were replaced by two Tornado GR.1B Squadrons, No 617, which retained its number plate in the new role, and No 27, which renumbered to No 12. The Tornado F.3 Operational Conversion Unit, No 229, took the number plate of No 56 Squadron, while the Hercules OCU, No 242, took the additional title of No 57 Reserve Squadron.

The Flying Training Schools were also included in the scheme, No 4 FTS taking the number plates of Nos 74 and 208 Reserve Squadrons and No 7 FTS taking those of Nos 19 and 92 Squadrons, while the Multi-Engine Training Unit received the number plate of No 45 Squadron. Finally, the RAF Regiment Rapier Training Unit took the number plate of No 16 RAF Regiment Squadron.

For the training organization itself, Linton-on-Ouse and Cranwell became the only two Basic Flying Training Schools, each also operating a Relief Landing Ground, that for Linton at Church Fenton and the RLG for Cranwell being at Barkston Heath. The Elementary Flying Training School, a unit that gives an introduction to flying for student pilots with no previous experience, moved from Swinderby to Topcliffe, where it joined the Elementary Flying Training School of the Royal Navy already in residence there. The entire flying training programme on the Hawk aircraft, that is the Advanced

Flying Training School and the Tactical Weapons Unit, was combined and deployed on two 'mirror image' bases, Valley and Chivenor. Both airfields, together with the responsibility for all the training, were taken over by Support Command, the TWUs having until autumn 1992 been in Strike Command. Finally, the summer of 1992 saw the introduction of a new course for navigators at Finningley, in which training is carried out on Bulldogs, Dominies, Tucanos and Hawks, making it possible to concentrate training for all navigator streams in one unit. Among the United Kingdom station closures that followed from all these reductions and amalgamations were Abingdon, Brawdy, Hullavington, Church Fenton and Catterick, the RAF Hospital at Ely, the Relief Landing Ground at Elvington, and the RAF sites at Swanton Morley and Harrogate.

These changes in the size and shape of RAF deployments were accompanied by another reorganization at the highest levels of the Service. In the late 1980s there had been a move to shift many of the responsibilities formerly discharged by the single Service Boards away from them and on to the Central Staffs of the Ministry of Defence; at the same time there was a great deal of pressure to rationalize the top structure of all the Services so as to improve efficiency and control. For the Royal Air Force, one result was another fundamental change at Command level. Strike Command remained as it was, though now absorbing No 2 Group (formerly RAF Germany). Support Command, however, was replaced by two new Commands: Logistic Command; and Personnel and Training Command. The first of these two absorbs the supply and maintenance functions of the old Support Command, together with most of the responsibilities of the Air Member for Supply and Organization, a post that is being abolished. At the same time, Personnel and Training Command takes over the ground and air training function that had been under Support Command, together with the responsibilities of the Air Member for Personnel, whose post would also disappear.

In general, the reductions in the strength of the Royal Air Force were seen within the senior echelons of the Service to be in line both with the reduction in the Soviet threat and with the cuts being sustained by the other British Services. Over the next few years it would become a leaner Air Force, but it would still cover a spectrum of vital defence roles including those of AWACS, interception and air combat, strike/attack, air transport, maritime surveillance, air-to-air refuelling and support helicopters. For the longer-term future, developments in the Royal Air Force will be determined in part by the future of air power itself, as has been the case since the Service was founded.

In looking back, we can see that 80 years of progress in aeronautics has brought about four ages in the story of air power. First, there was a decade or more during which much of the operational effect of the air weapon had almost as much to do with its novelty as with its physical impact. This was particularly true during the First World War, and during the colonial campaigns that followed. A second age, starting in the mid-1930s, was about the pursuit of high performance in speed, altitude, payload and sometimes the range of aircraft. This era lasted right through the war and up until the late 1960s, by which time not only was massive propulsive power available and the race for performance virtually over, but it was found that high performance alone was not a

SARDINIA
Detachments by Tornados, Harriers, Jaguars, Hawks

DENMARK
Detachments by Jaguars

NORWAY
Detachments by Harriers, Jaguars, Pumas, Chinooks, Nimrods, E-3D Sentrys, Canberras, Hawks

GERMANY
Tornados, Harriers, Chinooks, Pumas, RAF Regt

TURKEY
Jaguars; detachment by VC10s

CANADA
Detachments by Tornados

BELIZE
Harriers, Pumas, RAF Regt Rapiers

GIBRALTAR
Airbase detachment

FALKLAND ISLANDS
Tornado F.3s, Hercules, Chinooks, Sea Kings, RAF Regt Rapiers

ASCENSION ISLAND
RAF Staging post for air route to Falklands

CYPRUS
Wessexes; detachments by Tornados, Hawks, Nimrods

HONG KONG
Wessexes

THE GULF
Detachments by Nimrods

Pattern of RAF Activity outside the United Kingdom, 1993

panacea for survival in the missile era. Other qualities, including agility in the air, became important.

Those same decades from the 1930s to the 1960s had overlapped a third age in the application of air power, an age in which the often gross inaccuracies in delivering conventional air weapons on to even large targets had led to a substitution of mass attack for precision. There were exceptions, as there are bound to be in these generalizations; but it was this lack of accuracy that made necessary the dispatch of huge air fleets against, for example, Germany during the Second World War. Key features in enemy cities could usually be destroyed only if the city itself was taken under attack. In the case of nuclear weapons, on the other hand, the destructive effects were such that high precision became irrelevant.

A fourth age can be seen to have begun during the 1960s, when really effective precision guided weapons started to emerge. It was just at this time, when the resource cost of the high-performance aircraft then entering inventories was increasing sharply, that the need for very substantial numbers of these aircraft decreased.

High accuracy could offset the earlier need for mass, and, as the conflict in the Falklands showed, a handful of aircraft could now exert a powerful leverage.

More recent developments have shown the consolidation of a fifth age, the age of electronic warfare. Developments in this field also began during the Second World War, with radar and other systems playing a vital role by the end of that conflict. But in many ways the electronic warfare capabilities of those early days were ancillary; they merely improved the combat capabilities of what already existed. Over the past three decades, however, electronic warfare has virtually become an arm in its own right. Earth satellites, and aircraft with no role other than electronic surveillance or the electronic suppression of enemy defences, have entered the equation. In short, electronic systems have themselves become weapons.

Meanwhile many second- or even third-rank nations in the world have acquired reasonably modern systems of air warfare, some of which are virtually automatic in their destructive power and therefore call for no great operational skill; while other systems that are in widespread use throughout the world offer effective capabilities in the electronics field just mentioned. The implication of all this is that even a future conflict on a modest scale might call for the deployment of a wide spectrum of capabilities by air forces taking part, including the Royal Air Force.

It is a striking thought that the size and the shape of the Royal Air Force had been mainly governed for 42 of its 75 years by the potential threat from the Soviet Union. When that threat dissolved, a new age was entered, and it is one in which uncertainties abound. Yet it seems possible to suggest at least two sets of circumstances that might lead to British forces, including the Royal Air Force, once more finding themselves in a combat zone.

The first is a direct consequence of the collapse of the Soviet Union and of the dissolution of the Warsaw Pact. In several of the countries in Eastern Europe there is the prospect of a vacuum, and the possibility that some of the uncommitted space might be filled by serious instability, leading in turn to chaos on the one hand of a kind that overtook Yugoslavia, or to repressive Government on the other. Neither prospect is a comfortable one, and each would suggest that the principal task of the NATO alliance for the future will no longer be that of deterrence and forward defence but the crisis management.

That the alliance itself will be necessary to the stability of Europe seems inescapable. The alternative would be a Europe in which many of the nations, particularly the smaller ones, would seek other and regional security alliances, a development that would take the continent back to the disputes and perhaps even to the kind of wars that have so disfigured it in the past. Nor can the possibility of repressive government together with renewed military ambition in Eastern Europe or the countries of the former Soviet Union be ignored.

In military terms, any potential threat is made up not just of the two components usually discussed, capability and intention: the factor of immediacy needs to be considered. Until four years ago there was a very immediate threat in the Central Region of Europe. It was this that led to a forward deployment by the NATO alliance in order to meet a possible short-notice Blitzkrieg-style assault by Soviet forces. For the Royal Air Force, together with the other allied air forces, this in turn led to a fivefold task: reconaissance; offensive counter-air, air defence, interdiction and close air support to the ground forces. All five elements of the task were more or less simultaneous, with aircraft dedicated to each role for what was expected to be a very short

conventional conflict. The overall aim was to gain time for decisions on the release of nuclear weapons. All that has now changed. The future requirements of the Royal Air Force in Europe are likely to be for far more flexibility in role and in targeting, including the ability to make rapid short-term deployments away from Europe in response to the second possible future contingency, that of crises outside Europe.

It is sometimes said that, in the changed strategic picture we now face, crises outside Europe are becoming relatively more important but that in absolute terms they are no more of a problem than they ever were. This view assumes that the strategic picture outside Europe is static. Yet clearly it is not. The collapse of the Soviet Empire seems certain to lead to new instabilities in several parts of the world, precisely because of the ending of the Cold War. For over 40 years almost every regional conflict in the world has seen the two super-powers polarized into something approaching confrontation: Korea, Vietnam and the three Arab-Israeli wars come immediately to mind. At the same time, however, both the super-powers were anxious to see that these regional conflicts did not escalate in a way that might lead to major war, and perhaps even to a nuclear exchange. Both therefore restrained their allies or surrogates.

Now that the former Soviet Union and the United States have withdrawn from several of their forward commitments, the unstable parts of the world are seeing the emergence of old ambitions, old rivalries and old conflicts, while new ones can also be expected to develop, unchecked by previous super-power stabilities. It had seemed likely that, once the old super-power confrontation ceased to affect the workings of the United Nations, that body would become far more effective in one of its principal original roles, that of peacekeeping, and that this would limit the instabilities that arose. In the event two things happened: first, the United Nations found itself responding to crises on such a scale that member nations became reluctant to provide the necessary resources; and second, there was in many cases no peace to be kept, and there were occasions such as the upheavals in Somalia when UN forces actively intervened in the fighting. Many observers now believe that the UN should re-think the role it might play in future crises, and peace-making rather than peace-keeping could become increasingly important.

There are signs of this already, and the trend affects the Royal Air Force. Under Operation 'Jural', for example, a force of Tornado GR.1s remained at Dharan in Saudi Arabia after the end of the Gulf War to help maintain the no-fly zone set up by the United Nations over southern Iraq. To support the Tornado force, VC10 C.1K tankers deployed to Bahrain. A similar deployment of combat assets, this time of Harrier GR.7s, was made to southern Turkey at the end of the Gulf War, this time to patrol northern Iraq after Saddam Hussein had engaged in operations against the Kurdish population in that territory. This deployment, codenamed Operation 'Warden', was also supported by VC10 tankers.

In April 1993 another task for combat units of the RAF arose when the United Nations Security Council ordered the policing of the skies over Bosnia-Herzegovena. This became Operation 'Deny Flight', as part of which Jaguars and Tornado F.3s based in the United Kingdom deployed to the large NATO-style airbase of Gioia Del Colle in Southern Italy. By early 1995 the Jaguars had flown over 3,000 sorties on attack and reconnaissance missions over former Yugoslavia, while at the same time the F.3s had amassed a total of more than 7,000 hors in their task of providing combat air patrols to enforce the UN-declared no-fly zone. To give surveillance and AEW support to this heavy commitment, E-3D Sentry aircraft were sent out to the Italian base at Aviano, and by early 1995 these aircraft had clocked up more than 9,000 hours of flying time. No less important have been the efforts of the TriStar tankers, which deployed to Palermo in Sicily and from which airfield they had flown over 500 refuelling sorties by early 1995. And finally, as part of the International Maritime Operations to support the arms embargo against the former republic of Yugoslavia and the trade embargo against Serbia and Montenegro, Nimrod maritime patrol aircraft were deployed to the region, where they operated mainly over the Adriatic Sea.

The same tragic civil war in former Yugoslavia also saw aircraft of the Royal Air Force operating in a role that had become all too familiar since the Second World War, that of humanitarian relief. A brief mention of this work during the 1960s and 1970s was made on page 243, and in those particular missions the transport aircraft and their crews were always welcome visitors. But it was a very different matter when in April 1993 the UN decided to use military transport aircraft to supply the beleaguered city of Sarajevo. Even without a threat from anti-aircraft fire and rounds from small arms, the approach to the airfield at Sarajevo is a challenging one because of the surrounding hills. Especially in winter, the frequent poor weather in the area adds to the complications. With a confused war raging in and around the city, and with many military elements on the ground apparently acting under less than strict control, the hazards of operating into the airfield became very serious, often leading to a complete ban on flying that could last for days or even weeks.

In spite of all this, an international force of transport aircraft was deployed to carry out what became known as Operation 'Cheshire'. The Royal Air Force sent Hercules aircraft, which made their base at Alcona in northern Italy. Several of the sorties flown into Sarajevo by these machines came under small arms fire on their way in or out of the airport, though some of the otherwise high risk to the aircraft, and particularly to the crews, was reduced by adopting 'Khe Sahn approaches'. This technique takes its name from the US Marine hill-top base of that name during the war in Vietnam, and it involves making the steepest possible approach to touch-down, thus maintaining height over possible small arms fire until the last moment. Up to the end of 1994, the RAF Hercules had flown more than 1,550 sorties into Sarajevo, lifting 23,000 tonnes of relief supplies as well as many passengers both in and out of the airfield.

Another civil war, this time in the central African state of Rwanda, saw Hercules of the Royal Air Force deployed in Operation 'Gabriel' from July to November 1994 to carry relief supplies and UN troops into Kigali airfield. Because of the highly confused conditions on the ground, this operation was not without risk, though it was somewhat closer to the type of relief effort that has become familiar to RAF transport crews.

Meanwhile, the RAF transport force continues its routine support of our overseas deployments, such as those in Cyprus and the Falklands, and from the same home bases its capability to carry troops and supplies rapidly to distant crisis spots is regularly exercised. One such deployment took place in October 1994, when the air transport force moved troops out to Kuwait in Operation 'Driver', an exercise designed to practice our ability to send reinforcements to the Gulf in the event of another emergency. That deployment also involved the dispatch of Tornado GR.1s, and VC10 C.1Ks in their support; both aircraft types took up station on air bases in Saudi Arabia.

The pattern of peacetime activity for the Royal Air Force thus continues to be a very busy one, and indeed for several months during 1994 there were on any given day over a hundred RAF aircraft operating in various parts of the world outside the United Kingdom. At the same time, representatives of every operational type of aircraft on the inventory of the Royal Air Force was either on operations or on standby for operations.

1995 BRINGS MORE CHANGES TO THE SERVICE

Yet in spite of this pressure on the resources of the Service, the cuts imposed on the RAF under the *Options for*

Change exercise of 1990 were not the end of the search for economies. In 1994 another major cost-cutting initiative, the *Defence Costs Study*, also known as *Front Line First*, was launched. For this study, over thirty small teams were formed made up of serving officers, civil servants, outside consultants and representatives from the Treasury. Their task was to seek savings in each and every area of defence spending, except the front line. The result for the Royal Air Force was a number of rationalizations in the support areas and in the estate.

Flying training across the three Services was one area in which a number of changes were decided upon. Chivenor would close, and all fast jet training, RAF and Naval, would be concentrated at Valley; as a result, one of the newly formed reserve squadrons in No 7 FTS at Chivenor, No 92, would disappear. All military helicopter training would be concentrated at a single site, probably Middle Wallop, with the consequent closure of Shawbury. The activities of the Central Flying School would be reduced, and the unit moved to Cranwell with the resulting closure of the wartime home of No 617 Squadron, RAF Scampton. Crew training would finish at Finningley and move, probably to Cranwell. Finningley would close. Many other rationalizations were also announced, for example the hospitals of all three Services in the UK would amalgamate on the Royal Navy facility at Haslar, leading to the closure of the RAF hospitals at Wroughton and Halton. In another decision, all three single-Service Staff Colleges will amalgamate on one site, probably Camberley, and the RAF Staff College site at Bracknell will be lost. Service veterinary facilities will be combined at Melton Mobray, with the closure of the RAF dog unit at Newton and at the same time the very popular RAF Dog Display Team will disband.

In parallel with the *Defence Costs Study*, two other influences were at work on the future size and shape of the Royal Air Force. First, and continuing the effects of the ending of the Cold War was the further draw-down of all forces assigned to NATO and the withdrawal of the garrison in Berlin. The latter led to the closure of RAF Gatow, which was handed back to the Luftwaffe in 1994. RAF Germany had already been reduced to Group status under *Options for Change*, but now it was decided to close

RAF Laarbruch, probably in 1999. The two Harrier squadrons and the support helicopters at Laarbruch would be withdrawn to bases in the United Kingdom. This will eventually leave RAF Bruggen as the only Royal Air Force base in Germany, and this in turn will certainly mean the closure again of No 2 Group, with the Tornado force at Bruggen coming under the control of No 1 Group at High Wycombe. RAF Benson would also be closed, while The Queen's Flight, which had been based there for many years, would move to Northolt and combine with the resident No 32 Squadron to become No 32 (The Royal) Squadron.

The second influence was a study into the future manpower needs of the Royal Air Force, bearing in mind the very considerable upheavals that had taken place or were in prospect, and looking at the particular requirements of such a modern and high-technology Service. Such a study was overdue, and now Air Vice-Marshal Andy Roberts was appointed to lead the Manpower Structure Study Team. The Roberts Report made very many recommendations on training, trade structure and so on; but its main impact when implemented will be to reduce further the number of people in RAF uniform. *Options for Change* had cut total RAF numbers from 89,000 to around 75,000, but this was now set to fall by another 20,000 by April 1997, leaving a uniformed force of only 55,000. This was a very deep cut, but it was made even worse when the Roberts proposals were reviewed following the *Defence Costs Study*. Another tranche of cuts would be made, and the timescale for the overall cuts would be shortened. The result is that by the year 2000, the Royal Air Force will have a uniformed strength of only about 52,200 (plus 4,500 trainees).

The result of all the many changes that have been made in recent years to the size and shape of the Royal Air Force, and other changes that are planned for the future, will be a leaner fighting Service, but it will be one that retains its essential characteristics. It will continue to have a wide variety of roles; it will still be at readiness to meet the unexpected; and it will have the high-technology equipment that it needs. Above all, however, it continues to attract people of the highest quality, who will carry forward the proud traditions launched by Trenchard nearly eight decades ago.

APPENDIXES

Appendix 1: AIR ESTIMATES 1919 – 74

Year	Contemporary Value (£)	Cost at 1992 Prices (£)
1919	59,000,000	1,034,000,000
1922	15,542,000	321,874,000
1929	16,960,000	392,963,000
1934	20,165,600	540,442,000
1939	220,626,800	5,290,611,000
1946	256,000,000	4,728,320,000
1949	236,690,000	3,995,327,000
1954	496,959,650	6,470,415,000
1959	564,680,000	6,273,594,000
1964	503,800,000	4,886,860,000
1969	592,000,000	4,653,120,000

Note: The conversion of costs to 1992 prices uses figures kindly supplied by the Bank of England. After 1974, a year in which no Defence White Paper was produced, the form of the Annual Defence Estimates was changed so that, instead of Single Service Estimates, an Estimate for the cost of defence as a whole was produced. This was then broken down into functional areas, for example the total cost of the British garrisons (Army and Air Force together) in Germany. It is therefore not possible to give reliable figures for the RAF Estimates after 1969. Furthermore, any attempt to extrapolate (say, by carrying forward the historic share of expenditure for each Service) would be confounded by the effect of major equipment programmes such as those for the Tornado aircraft, or for the Trident submarines. Nevertheless, the table does show the effects of the inter-war economies, the start of the 1934 rearmament programme, the Second World War and the Korean crisis of 1950–54.

Appendix 2: ROYAL AIR FORCE AIRCRAFT STRENGTHS, 1919–94

Year	Operational types	Non-operational types	Total
1919[1]	3,300	Not known	Not known
1924	484[1]	506[1]	990[1]
1929	800[1]	Not known	Not known
1934[2]	827	714	1,541
1939	3,253[3]	302[4]	3,555
1944	9,035	Not available	Not available
1949	1,251	3,001	4,252
1954	2,127	3,086	5,213
1959	1,051	1,790	2,841
1964	949	1,377	2,326
1969	723	1,015	1,738
1974	655	750[5]	1,405[5]
1979	627	776	1,403
1984	632	839	1,471
1989	995[6]	622	1,617
1994	660	440	1,100

1. The early records are scanty. The figures given here are taken from the Trenchard Papers at the RAF Museum and the numbers I quote for 1924 are actually Trenchard's estimates for that year, made in 1923.

2. The total figure is accurate but the breakdown between operational and non-operational types is an estimate.

3. This is the number actually on the IE of Squadrons.

4. Defined in the records as 'service trainers' but excluding all elementary trainers for this year.

5. Estimated from the 1975 figure.

6. The number of operational aircraft in 1989 shows another anomaly in the statistics. The large increase in operational aircraft in this year is caused by the very comprehensive re-equipment programme that was under way. While the new aircraft were entering the inventory and the squadrons were working up, aircraft being withdrawn were often held in short-term storage so that they could be quickly recovered in an emergency. In an important sense they were thus still operationally available and were therefore included in operational strength.

All the figures need to be used with care. They are the best that can be extracted from the existing RAF statistical records, the style of which often changed from year to year. Furthermore, the statistics vary in what it is they are describing. I have tried here to give the figures for aircraft on the flight-line and 'ready to go', as at April of each year; but even this definition can be confused by what are known in the Service as 'in-use reserves'. These are reserve aircraft which are brought forward for use by squadrons but for which no manpower or other support is provided. Then there are general reserves, that is to say aircraft held in short-, medium- or long-term storage: some of these could be brought into the front line very quickly, while others could not be recovered for months.

Reserves are an important part of the whole picture. In 1939, for example, as well as the total of 3,555 aircraft in front-line units quoted above, there were no fewer than 3,441 operational types held in reserve as well as 240 unissued training machines. Another complication is that some records give figures for 'aircraft on charge', an expression that can embrace almost anything that is or once was a flying aircraft — not excluding carcasses used for ground training instruction and even 'gate guardians'.

Appendix 3: ROYAL AIR FORCE PERSONNEL STRENGTHS, 1919–89[1]

Year	RAF Offs	RAF ORs	WRAF Offs	WRAF ORs	Total
1919	17,267	108,753	432	22,744	149,196
1924	3,256	28,146	Nil	Nil	31,402
1929	3,286	31,070	Nil	Nil	34,350
1934	3,343	27,050	Nil	Nil	30,393
1939	7,214	93,849	234	1,500	102,797
1944	88,615	922,892	6,199	168,207	1,185,913
1949	19,685	199,918	520	13,937	219,603
1954	27,731	233,315	1,142	7,982	261,046
1959	23,181	151,876	809	4,051	175,057
1964	21,521	116,403	836	5,469	137,924
1969	19,877	92,556	803	4,573	112,433
1974[2]	18.0	76.3	365	3,901	99.2
1979	14.5	66.2	391	4,883	85.5
1984	14.4	73.0	583	4,728	93.2
1989	14.4	72.5	1.0	5.2	93.1

1. In almost all cases, the statistics given refer to the month of April in the years quoted. However, where these figures are unavailable, the figures for the month nearest to April have been used.

2. From 1974 onwards the strengths given in Defence White Papers are quoted only to the nearest thousand.

It should be noted throughout that the figures may not give true comparisons. For example, in some years the total strengths given in the official statistics included locally employed airmen in Malta and other overseas stations; at other times they did not.

Appendix 4: STRENGTH AND DISPOSITION OF THE ROYAL AIR FORCE, 1995

Strike/Attack

IX Squadron	RAF Bruggen	13 Tornado GR.1
14 Squadron*	RAF Bruggen	13 Tornado GR.1
17 Squadron	RAF Bruggen	13 Tornado GR.1
31 Squadron	RAF Bruggen	13 Tornado GR.1
27 Squadron	RAF Marham	13 Tornado GR.1

(*designated the TIALD target-marking Squadron)

Offensive Support

1(F) Squadron	RAF Wittering	13 Harrier GR.7
		1 Harrier T.4A
3 Squadron	RAF Laarbruch*	12 Harrier GR.7
		1 Harrier T.4A
4 Squadron	RAF Laarbruch*	12 Harrier GR.7
		1 Harrier T.4A
20(R) Squadron (OCU)	RAF Wittering	20 Harrier GR.5/ GR.7/T.4/T.4A
XV(R) Squadron (WCU)	RAF Lossiemouth	25 Tornado GR.1

16(R) Squadron (OCU)	RAF Lossiemouth	10 Jaguar GR.1A/T.2A
6 Squadron	RAF Coltishall	14 Jaguar GR.1A/T.2A
54 Squadron	RAF Coltishall	15 Jaguar GR.1A/T.2A

(*Laarbruch to close 1999)

Reconnaissance

II(AC) Squadron	RAF Marham	13 Tornado GR.1A
13 Squadron	RAF Marham	13 Tornado GR.1A
41 Squadron	RAF Coltishall	14 Jaguar GR.1A/T.2A
51 Squadron	RAF Wyton*	3 Nimrod R.1P
39 (1PRU) Squadron	RAF Wyton*	5 EE Canberra PR.9

(*move to Waddington when airfield at Wyton closes)

Maritime Patrol

CXX Squadron	RAF Kinloss	Nimrod MR.2P
201 Squadron	RAF Kinloss	Nimrod MR.2P
206 Squadron	RAF Kinloss	Nimrod MR.2P (Total MR Nimrods 26)

Marine Attack

617 Squadron	RAF Lossiemouth	13 Tornado GR.1B
12 Squadron	RAF Lossiemouth	13 Tornado GR.1B

Air Defence

5 Squadron	RAF Coningsby	13 Tornado F.3
XI Squadron	RAF Leeming	13 Tornado F.3
25 Squadron	RAF Leeming	13 Tornado F.3
29 Squadron	RAF Coningsby	13 Tornado F.3
43 Squadron	RAF Leuchars	16 Tornado F.3
56 (R) Squadron (OCU)	RAF Coningsby	24 Tornado F.3
111(F) Squadron	RAF Leuchars	16 Tornado F.3
15 Squadron RAF Regt	RAF Leeming	Rapier
26 Squadron RAF Regt	RAF Laarbruch	Rapier
27 Squadron RAF Regt	RAF Leuchars	Rapier
37 Squadron RAF Regt	RAF Bruggen	Rapier
48 Squadron RAF Regt	RAF Lossiemouth	Rapier

Airborne Early Warning

8 Squadron	RAF Waddington	Sentry AEW.1

Tankers

101 Squadron	RAF Brize Norton	9 VC10 K.2/K.3

(But see under Transport Squadrons for units with multiple roles, which include air-to-air refuelling tasks)

EEW Training/Radar Calibration

360 Squadron*	RAF Wyton	10 Canberra T.17/T.17A 2 Canberra PR.7 3 Canberra TR.4

Target Towing

100 Squadron*	RAF Wyton	12 Hawk T.1/T.1A

(*Squadrons disbanding; Wyton to close)

Air Transport

7 Squadron	RAF Odiham	18 Chinook HC.1 1 Gazelle HT.2
10 Squadron	RAF Brize Norton	10 VC10 C1/C1.K
18 Squadron	RAF Laarbruch*	5 Chinook HC.1 5 Puma HC.1
24 Squadron	RAF Lyneham	13 Hercules C.1P/C.3P
28 Squadron	RAF Sek Kong**	8 Wessex
30 Squadron	RAF Lyneham	13 Hercules C.1P/C.3P
32 Squadron***	RAF Northolt	8 Andovers (in process of being withdrawn) 12 BAe 125 C.1/C.2/C.3 4 Gazelle HT.3
33 Squadron	RAF Odiham	12 Puma HC.1
47 Squadron	RAF Lyneham	11 Hercules C.1P/C.3P
57(R) Squadron	RAF Lyneham	Hercules C.1P/C.3P (OCU)
60 Squadron	RAF Benson	9 Wessex HC.2
70 Squadron	RAf Lyneham	12 Hercules C.1P/C.3P
72 Squadron	RAF Aldergr.ove	15 Wessex HC.2
78 Squadron****	RAF Mount Pleasant	Chinook HC.1 Sea King HAS.3
84 Squadron****	RAF Akrotiri	Wessex HC.5C
216 Squadron	RAF Brize Norton	8 TriStar K.1/KC.1/C.2
230 Squadron	RAF Aldergr.ove	15 Puma HC1
The Queen's Flight	RAF Benson	3 BAe 146 CC.2 2 Wessex HCC.4

(* Laarbruch closes 1999.   ** Sek Kong closes 1997.
*** Will be combined.   **** Also an SAR unit.)

Search and Rescue

202 Squadron	RAF Boulmer (HQ & A Flt) RAF Brawdy (B Flt)* RAF Manston (C Flt)* RAF Lossiemouth (D Flt) RAF Leconfield (E Flt) Total 15 Sea King HAR.3	
22 Squadron	RAF St Mawgan (HQ & A Flt) RAF Chivenor (A Flt) RAF Valley (C Flt)	
(22 Sqn cont)	RAF Coltishall (E Flt)* Total 11 Wessex HC.2	

(* To be withdrawn; Manston to be replaced by a Flight at Wattisham).

Air to Air Refuelling

101 Squadron	RAF Brize Norton	9 VC10 K.2/K.3

RAuxAF Units

2503 Sqn R AuxAF Regt*	RAF Waddington
2620 Sqn RAuxAF Regt*	RAF Marham
2622 Sqn RAuxAF Regt*	RAF Honington
2624 Sqn RAuxAF Regt*	RAF Brize Norton
2625 Sqn RAuxAF Regt*	RAF St Mawgan
(*under review)	

Flying Training Units

Central Flying School	RAF Scampton*	Tucano T.1 Chipmunk T.10 Bulldog T.1
Red Arrows Team	RAF Scampton*	11 Hawk
Tri-National Tornado Training Establishment	RAF Cottesmore	17 Tornado GR.1
74(R) Sqn	RAF Valley	Hawk T./1/T.1A
234(R) Sqn	RAF Valley	Hawk T.1/T.1A
45(R) Sqn	RAF Finningley	Jetstream T.1
19(R) Sqn	RAF Chivenor*	Hawk T.1/T.1A
92(R) Sqn	RAF Chivenor*	Hawk T.1/T.1A
Joint** Elementary Flying Training Squadron	RAF Topcliffe	Chipmunk T.10

(* to close. ** i.e., Joint with RN.)

No 1 Flying Training School	RAF Linton-on-Ouse	Tucano T.1
No 2 FTS*	RAF Shawbury	Gazelle HT.2/HT.3 Wessex HC.2
No 3 FTS	RAF Cranwell	Tucano T.1
No 4 FTS (see Nos 74 and 234 Reserve Sqns)		
No 6 FTS	RAF Finningley	Tucano T.1 Bulldog Dominie T.1 Hawk T1 Jetstream**

(* To move; Shawbury closes. ** See No 45 Reserve Sqn.)

Operational Flights

1312 Flight	Mount Pleasant	2 Hercules C.1K
1435 Flight	Mount Pleasant	Tornado F.3

Other Flying Units

Strike/Attack Operational Evaluation Unit (SAOEU)	RAF Boscombe Down	Tornado GR.1 Harrier GR.7/T.4 Jaguar T.2A
Tornado F.3 Operational Evaluation Unit	RAF Coningsby	Tornado F3
Institute of Aviation Medicine	RAF Farnborough*	Hunter T.7 Jaguar T.2A Hawk T.1

(* To close; unit probably moves to Boscombe.)

Ground Combat Units

No 1 Squadron RAF Regt	Laarbruch
No 2 Squadron RAF Regt	Catterick*
No 3 Squadron RAF Regt	Aldergrove
No 34 Squadron RAF Regt	Akrotiri
No 63 Squadron RAF Regt (Queen's Colour Sqn)	Uxbridge

(* to close)

University Air Squadrons*

(All with Bulldog T.1)

Aberdeen, Dundee & St Andrews UAS	RAF Leuchars
Birmingham UAS	RAF Cosford
Bristol UAS	Colerne
Cambridge UAS	Cambridge
East Lowlands UAS	Edinburgh
East Midlands UAS	Newton
Glasgow & Strathclyde UAS	Glasgow
Liverpool UAS	Woodvale
London UAS	Benson
Manchester UAS	Woodvale
Northumbrian UAS	Leeming
Oxford UAS	Benson
Queen's UAS	Sydenham
Southampton UAS	Lee-on-Solent
University of Wales UAS	St Athan
Yorkshire UAS	Finningley

(* Some rationalization likely)

Volunteer Gliding Schools

(These schools offer gliding instruction to Air Cadets of the Air Training Corps and of the RAF Sections of the Combined Cadet Force)

611 VGS	Swanton Morley	Viking T.1
612 VGS	Halton	Vigilant T.1
613 VGS	Halton	Vigilant T.1
614 VGS	Wethersfield	Viking T.1
615 VGS	Kenley	Viking T.1
616 VGS	Henlow	Vigilant T.1
617 VGS	Manston	Viking T.1
618 VGS	West Malling	Viking T.1
621 VGS	Weston-Super-Mare	Viking T.1
622 VGS	Upavon	Viking T.1
624 VGS	Chivenor	Vigilant T.1
625 VGS	Hullavington	Viking T.1
626 VGS	Predanack	Viking T.1
631 VGS	Sealand	Viking T.1
632 VGS	Ternhill	Vigilant T.1
633 VGS	Cosford	Vigilant T.1
634 VGS	St Athan	Viking T.1
635 VGS	Salmesbury	Vigilant T.1
636 VGS	Swansea	Viking T.1
637 VGS	Little Rissington	Vigilant T.1
642 VGS	Linton-on-Ouse	Vigilant T.1
643 VGS	Syerston	Vigilant T.1
644 VGS	Syerston	Vigilant T1
645 VGS	Catterick	Viking T.1
661 VGS	Kirknewton	Viking T.1
662 VGS	Arbroath	Viking T.1
663 VGS	Kinloss	Vigilant T.1
Air Cadet Central Gliding School	Syerston	Vigilant T.1 Viking T.1 Janus C

(Note that several VGSs are on former RAF airfields at which the landing area itself, or part of it, has been retained.)

Air Experience Flights

(These part-time units give passenger air experience to Air Cadets. All are equipped with the Chipmunk T.10, except No

13 AEF, which also has a single Bulldog T.1. A replacement for the Chipmunk is under discussion)

Major Non-Flying Units

No 1 School of Technical Training Cosford
No 4 SofTT   St Athan

No 1 AEF	Manston	No 7 AEF	Shawbury
No 2 AEF	Hurn	No 9 AEF	Finningley
No 3 AEF	Colerne	No 10 AEF	Woodvale
No 4 AEF	Exeter	No 11 AEF	Leeming
No 5 AEF	Teversham	No 12 AEF	Turnhouse
No 6 AEF	Benson	No 13 AEF	Sydenham

No 1 Radio School	Locking
No 7 Maintenance Unit	Quedgeley*
No 11 MU	Chilmark*
No 14 MU	Carlisle*
No 16 MU	Stafford
No 30 MU	Sealand
No 217 MU	Cardington
No 6 Signals Unit	Rudloe Manor
No 7 SU	Byron Heights, Falklands
No 12 SU	Ayios Nikolaos, Cyprus
No 144 SU	Ty Croes, Gwynedd
No 280 SU	Akrotiri
No 303 SU	Mount Kent, Falklands
No 399 SU	Digby
No 591 SU	Digby
No 751 SU	Mount Alice, Falklands
No 840 SU	Lindholme
No 1001 SU	Oakhangar

RAF Hospitals: Halton (due to close), Nocton Hall (reserve), Wroughton (due to close).

RAF Staff College	Bracknell*
RAF Music Services***	Uxbridge
RAF Comms Centre	Rudloe Manor
RAF Mountain Rescue Service:	Kinloss, Leuchars, Leeming, St Athan, Stafford, Valley
RAF Police School	Newton
RAF School of Education	Newton
RAF School of Management Tg	Newton
RAF Signals Engineering Establishment	Henlow
Supply control Centre	Stanbridge
UK Mobile Air Movements Squadron	Lyneham
Central Servicing Development Establishment	Swanton Morley
Gr.ound Radio Servicing Centre*	North Luffenham
Guided Weapons School	Newton
Joint Services Air Trooping Centre	Stanbridge
HQ Provost & Security Service (UK)	Rudloe Manor
No 1 Aeromedical Exacuation Squadron	Brize Norton
4624 Movements Squadron RAuxAF	Brize Norton
4626 Aeromed Evacuation Squadron RAuxAF**	Hullavington

(*Bracknell to close. **Due to move. *** May combine with other Service music schools.)

(Note that as a result of the 1994 *Defence Costs Study*, many changes in the form both of disbandments and relocations are to take place over the next few years. Not all of these are reflected in the main text, and the above list may quickly become dated.)

Appendix 5: ROYAL AIR FORCE RANK INSIGNIA

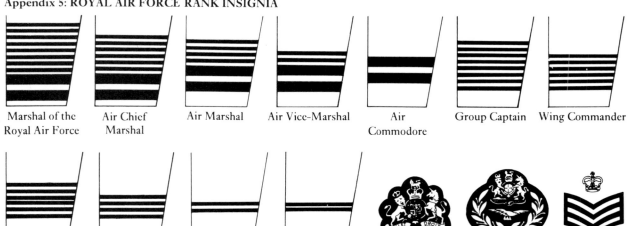

Marshal of the Royal Air Force | Air Chief Marshal | Air Marshal | Air Vice-Marshal | Air Commodore | Group Captain | Wing Commander

Squadron Leader | Flight Lieutenant | Flying Officer | Pilot Officer | Warrant Officer | Master Aircrew | Flight Sergeant

Flight Sergeant Aircrew

Chief Technician

Sergeant

Sergeant Aircrew

Corporal

Junior Technician

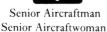

Senior Aircraftman Senior Aircraftwoman

Leading Aircraftman Leading Aircraftwoman

APPENDIX 6: Royal Air Force Command Organization, January 1945

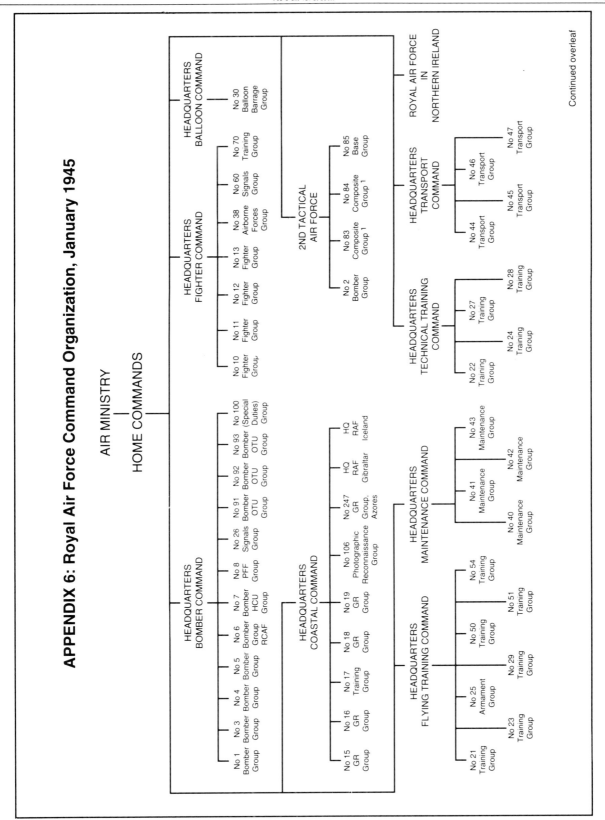

AIR MINISTRY

HOME COMMANDS

HEADQUARTERS BOMBER COMMAND
- No 1 Bomber Group
- No 3 Bomber Group
- No 4 Bomber Group
- No 5 Bomber Group
- No 6 Bomber Group RCAF
- No 7 Bomber HCU Group
- No 8 PFF Group
- No 26 Signals Group
- No 91 Bomber OTU Group
- No 92 Bomber OTU Group
- No 93 Bomber OTU Group
- No 100 (Special Duties) Group

HEADQUARTERS FIGHTER COMMAND
- No 10 Fighter Group
- No 11 Fighter Group
- No 12 Fighter Group
- No 13 Fighter Group
- No 38 Airborne Forces Group
- No 60 Signals Group
- No 70 Training Group

HEADQUARTERS BALLOON COMMAND
- No 30 Balloon Barrage Group

HEADQUARTERS COASTAL COMMAND
- No 15 GR Group
- No 16 GR Group
- No 17 Training Group
- No 18 GR Group
- No 19 GR Group
- No 106 Photographic Reconnaissance Group
- No 247 GR Group, Azores
- HQ RAF Gibraltar
- HQ RAF Iceland

2ND TACTICAL AIR FORCE
- No 2 Bomber Group
- No 83 Composite Group [1]
- No 84 Composite Group [1]
- No 85 Base Group

HEADQUARTERS TRANSPORT COMMAND
- No 44 Transport Group
- No 45 Transport Group
- No 46 Transport Group
- No 47 Transport Group

ROYAL AIR FORCE IN NORTHERN IRELAND

HEADQUARTERS TECHNICAL TRAINING COMMAND
- No 22 Training Group
- No 24 Training Group
- No 27 Training Group
- No 28 Training Group

HEADQUARTERS MAINTENANCE COMMAND
- No 40 Maintenance Group
- No 41 Maintenance Group
- No 42 Maintenance Group
- No 43 Maintenance Group

HEADQUARTERS FLYING TRAINING COMMAND
- No 21 Training Group
- No 23 Training Group
- No 25 Armament Group
- No 29 Training Group
- No 50 Training Group
- No 51 Training Group
- No 54 Training Group

Continued overleaf

Royal Air Force Command Organization, January 1945 (continued)

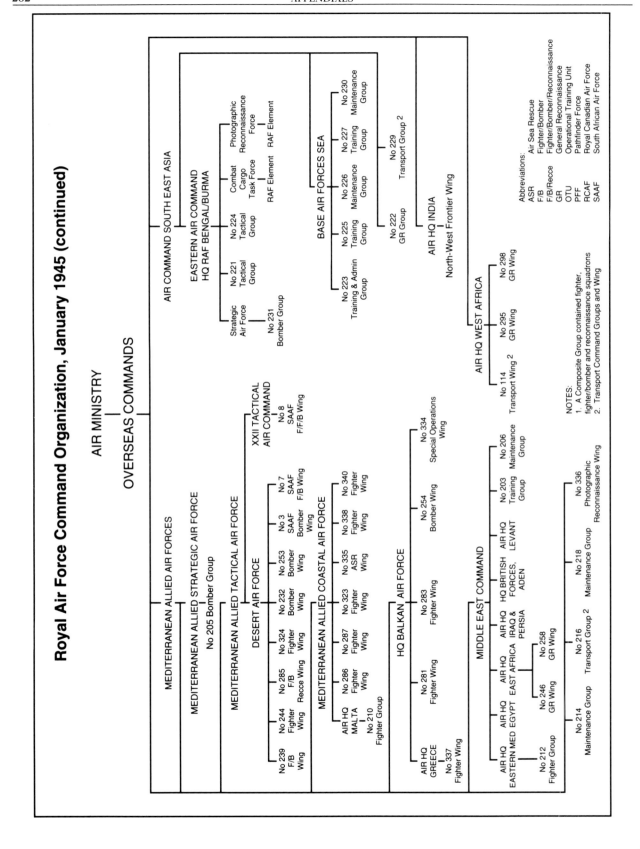

AIR MINISTRY

OVERSEAS COMMANDS

AIR COMMAND SOUTH EAST ASIA

EASTERN AIR COMMAND
HQ RAF BENGAL/BURMA

No 221 Tactical Group
No 224 Tactical Group
Combat Cargo Task Force — RAF Element
Photographic Reconnaissance Force — RAF Element

Strategic Air Force
No 231 Bomber Group

BASE AIR FORCES SEA

No 223 Training & Admin Group
No 225 Training Group
No 226 Maintenance Group
No 227 Training Group
No 230 Maintenance Group

No 222 GR Group
No 229 Transport Group 2

AIR HQ INDIA
North-West Frontier Wing

AIR HQ WEST AFRICA
No 114 Transport Wing 2
No 295 GR Wing
No 298 GR Wing

MEDITERRANEAN ALLIED AIR FORCES

MEDITERRANEAN ALLIED STRATEGIC AIR FORCE
No 205 Bomber Group

MEDITERRANEAN ALLIED TACTICAL AIR FORCE

XXII TACTICAL AIR COMMAND
No 8 SAAF F/B Wing

DESERT AIR FORCE
No 232 Bomber Wing
No 253 Bomber Wing
No 3 SAAF Bomber Wing
No 7 SAAF F/B Wing

No 239 F/B Wing
No 244 Fighter Wing
No 285 F/B Recce Wing
No 324 Fighter Wing

MEDITERRANEAN ALLIED COASTAL AIR FORCE
No 287 Fighter Wing
No 323 Fighter Wing
No 335 ASR Wing
No 338 Fighter Wing
No 340 Fighter Wing

AIR HQ MALTA
No 210 Fighter Group
No 286 Fighter Wing

HQ BALKAN AIR FORCE
No 254 Bomber Wing
No 334 Special Operations Wing

AIR HQ GREECE
No 337 Fighter Wing
No 281 Fighter Wing
No 283 Fighter Wing

MIDDLE EAST COMMAND

HQ BRITISH FORCES, ADEN
AIR HQ LEVANT

No 203 Training Group
No 206 Maintenance Group

AIR HQ EGYPT
AIR HQ EAST AFRICA
AIR HQ IRAQ & PERSIA

No 246 GR Wing
No 258 GR Wing

No 216 Transport Group 2
No 218 Maintenance Group
No 336 Photographic Reconnaissance Wing

AIR HQ EASTERN MED
No 212 Fighter Group
No 214 Maintenance Group

Abbreviations:
ASR   Air Sea Rescue
F/B   Fighter/Bomber
F/B/Recce Fighter/Bomber/Reconnaissance
GR   General Reconnaissance
OTU   Operational Training Unit
PFF   Pathfinder Force
RCAF   Royal Canadian Air Force
SAAF   South African Air Force

NOTES:
1. A Composite Group contained fighter, fighter/bomber and reconnaissance squadrons
2. Transport Command Groups and Wing

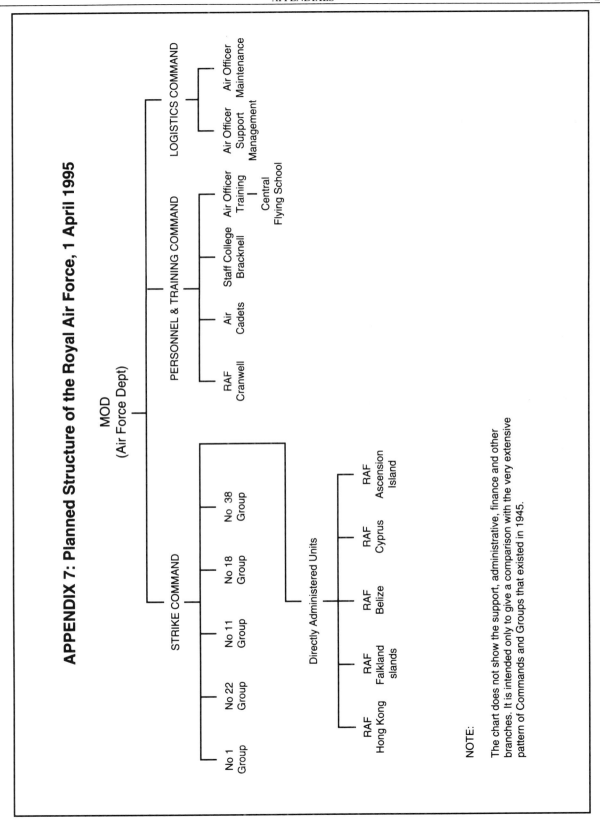

APPENDIX 7: Planned Structure of the Royal Air Force, 1 April 1995

MOD
(Air Force Dept)

STRIKE COMMAND

No 1 Group | No 22 Group | No 11 Group | No 18 Group | No 38 Group

Directly Administered Units

RAF Hong Kong | RAF Falkland Islands | RAF Belize | RAF Cyprus | RAF Ascension Island

PERSONNEL & TRAINING COMMAND

RAF Cranwell | Air Cadets | Staff College Bracknell | Air Officer Training — Central Flying School

LOGISTICS COMMAND

Air Officer Support Management | Air Officer Maintenance

NOTE:

The chart does not show the support, administrative, finance and other branches. It is intended only to give a comparison with the very extensive pattern of Commands and Groups that existed in 1945.

Index